To Laverne,

To my new fr[iend]
from Raider Rome[o]
please come back for
a visit at Casa del Sol!

May the land of Arabia
enchant you!

Meredith Kirk

2

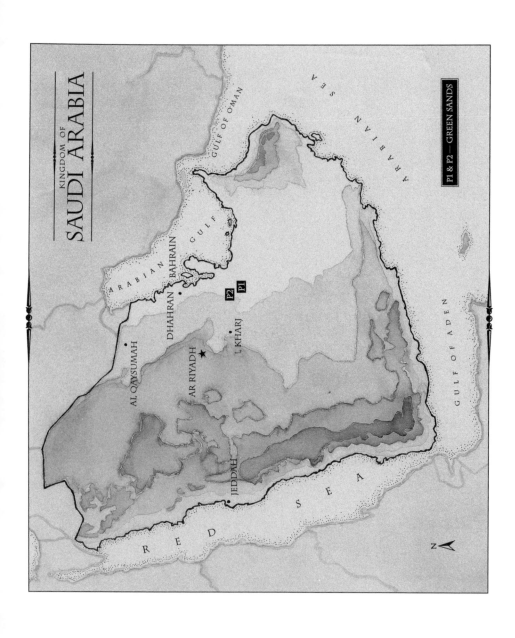

Green Sands

Green Sands

My Five Years
in the Saudi Desert

Martha Kirk

Texas Tech University Press

This book was set in Caslon and printed on acid-free paper that meets the
guidelines for permanence and durability of the Committee on Production
Guidelines for Book Longevity of the Council on Library Resources. ∞

Jacket design by Richard Hendel

Printed in the United States of America

Library of Congress Cataloging-in-Publication Data

Kirk, Martha.
    Green sands : my five years in the Saudi desert / Martha Kirk.
        p.   cm.
    ISBN 0-89672-337-2 (alk. paper)
    1. Saudi Arabia—Description and travel. 2. Kirk, Martha—
Journeys—Saudi Arabia. I. Title.
DS208.K57 1994
953.805′3—dc20
                                                        94-11583
                                                            CIP

94 95 96 97 98 99 00 01 02 / 9 8 7 6 5 4 3 2 1

Texas Tech University Press
Lubbock, Texas 79409-1037 USA
1-800-832-4042

To the women of Saudi Arabia,
who opened my eyes to a world larger than my own.

Acknowledgments

I am grateful to everyone who made this book possible for a woman from a small West Texas town. The Bedouin women who befriended me in the desert inspired me with their grace, fierce pride, and unending hospitality in the harshest of circumstances. The city women who took me into their homes, schools, and shopping centers shared their hearts as much as their cultures. Sheikh Latif, the owner of Green Sands, provided the opportunity of a lifetime and continues to be a wonderful friend. Other friends that I made in Saudi Arabia were instrumental in completing the work. Dick and Kim Cates, Meredith McLeod, Rick Tolmie, Harold Provance, Jennifer King, Barry Bigland, Larry Hottman, Dick Frain, Genia Roberts, Dave and Deanna Koeler, and Evelyn Cash responded to my requests for stories and pictures. My hometown friend Pam Wheeless was the first person to read and edit my rough manuscript, which profited greatly from her ideas and suggestions. When I was discouraged in finding a publisher, Barbara Jenkins, co-author of *The Walk West,* wrote me a letter of encouragement. Tony Privett brought my manuscript to the attention of the Texas Tech University Press.

I am grateful also to Zuhair Shihab, M.D., for reading the manuscript and making suggestions; his faith and knowledge were an invaluable resource. Cathy Buesseler's encouragement, support, and editing were equally invaluable. Pat Gavin, whose husband, Chris, was the second member of Operation Desert Storm to set foot on Saudi soil, shared a sharp proofing eye and marketing advice. Ayman Abdelgawad generously took time from his studies at Texas Tech University to assist in standardizing my spelling of Arabic words. Richard Murphy, former U.S. Ambassador to Saudi Arabia, is as gracious a foreword author as he is a diplomat. Judith Keeling, my editor, listened, helped, and supported.

Most of all, I must acknowledge my family: my husband, Terry, who took a chance on a job eight thousand miles away from home; my parents,

Robert and Mary Work, who wrote to me in Saudi Arabia faithfully each week; and, finally, my children, who grew from infancy during the writing of *Green Sands* and who have my undying gratitude for playing so nicely for so many hours by my computer.

Foreword

Martha Kirk has written a memorable account of the five years she and her husband, a young Texas couple, spent in the formidable Saudi Arabian desert. She arrived there in 1983 to join her husband who the previous year had begun to develop one of the first wheat farms in Saudi Arabia, an extraordinary project sponsored by the Saudi government to attain national self sufficiency.

Drawing on her experience living on an isolated farm ninety miles from the capital, Riyadh, Mrs. Kirk provides incisive sketches of the difficulties of life in one of the world's harshest environments, together with rewarding glimpses into the lives of the many Saudi and third country personalities she befriended. In the process, she shows herself able to appreciate the strengths and idiosyncrasies of her Saudi friends. She couples those insights with a humorous self awareness as she readily acknowledges how odd some of her own habits appeared to them.

Mrs. Kirk writes with particular sensitivity about the Bedouin family with whom she and her husband developed a close friendship. With great empathy, she describes how this family, inheritors of one of the world's oldest surviving cultures, is coming to terms with its rapidly changing environment.

Richard W. Murphy
Senior Fellow for the Middle East,
Council on Foreign Relations
American Ambassador
to Saudi Arabia, 1981-83

Green Sands

Chapter One

As I shifted in the economy seat of the Boeing 747 for the hundredth time, my knees pushed up to my chest, my feet perched on top of a forty-pound carry-on bag, I glanced again at my watch. Instead of reading books and magazines or stitching the embroidery that I brought to occupy myself on the long flight, I simply stared into space, contemplating my future with a mixture of terror, apprehension, and exhilaration.

I comforted myself with the knowledge that the overstuffed bag contained a year's supply of cosmetics and toiletries and a long dress that met the public dress standard for a foreign woman in Saudi Arabia. If my luggage became lost forever in this far-away place, at least I had the clothes on my back, a dress of legal length, and my makeup from America. When I arrived in New York, a six-hour layover loomed ahead of me. To direct my thoughts from the tearful farewells I had exchanged with my parents at the Lubbock, Texas, airport earlier in the day, I contemplated what lay ahead in Saudi Arabia, so foreign to a West Texas girl.

My husband Terry and I had lived our entire lives on the High Plains of West Texas, near the caprock of the beautiful Blanco Canyon, about thirty-five miles east of Lubbock in the small town of Crosbyton. We met while we were in high school, when Terry came to my home to visit my brother. He was a senior, and I was a freshman; our friendship was not allowed to extend to dating until I was sixteen years old. The two of us ended up at Texas Tech University, in Lubbock, where we ignored logic and married young; I was twenty, and he was twenty-two. I graduated with a B.S. in Home Economics Education and Terry completed his Master's degree in Crop Science. We worked, went to school, and ate lots of pasta and other economical meals.

Before college, the world beyond Crosbyton, population 2000, was something we'd experienced only through the evening news and occasional travel books. Even at Texas Tech, we met no one of Middle Eastern origin. We knew nothing about Islam, nor even that the practice of other religious faiths is prohibited within Saudi Arabia. What we learned came from our naive inquiries of real-life Moslems once we arrived in the country. Because of our interest, coupled with our genuine curiosity, Moslem friends revealed intimate religious details of their lives. Fortunately, in our ignorance of the Middle East, we never confused the radical anti-American Shiite Moslems of Iran, whom we had seen on television, with the peaceful Sunnis we would encounter in Saudi Arabia. Thus, we were to develop deep friendships among a people whose existence we knew almost nothing about before our arrival in their country.

We imagined ourselves spending our days in Saudi Arabia much as Lawrence of Arabia would have done. We did little more than read the Saudi Arabia section in an outdated encyclopedia to prepare ourselves for five years in another world.

I did search for Saudi Arabian cookbooks, finding only generic Middle Eastern cookbooks that mentioned recipes from such countries as Egypt, Lebanon, Morocco, and Israel, but nothing specific to Saudi Arabia, nor its neighbors such as Yemen, United Arab Emirates, or Qatar. The cooking practices described in the Middle Eastern recipes astounded me, and I concluded that none of these would be practiced in modern day Saudi Arabia. Little did I realize that the recipe that I found for curdling and drying fresh goat and camel milk would be used by the Bedouin women who camped on our farm. Later I was fascinated to watch the women preserve their milk products as they had done for generations. As they prepared the yogurt-like cakes and explained the procedure in Arabic with intermittent hand signals, I nodded with understanding; after all, I had read of this procedure in English, in a cookbook, before I left the States.

Our only other introduction to the Saudi way of life came from Ed, the agent who was hired by our Saudi boss to place the advertisements for a farm manager in Texas newspapers. When Terry talked to Ed, who lived in Midland, Ed urged him to be immunized for yellow fever and malaria. Without asking a second opinion, and, after some expense and pain, Terry was immunized against two dreaded diseases that we learned later were not a problem in Saudi Arabia and for which immunizations were not required. Ed also talked of the heat, the snakes, the scorpions, the ever-blowing sand, and the prohibition of pork and alcohol. Because neither of us drank alcohol, and we rarely ate pork, these two prohibitions didn't bother us. We were certain that Ed exaggerated the pests and wind. We learned that instead of exaggerating, Ed was, if anything, understating.

Terry tried to prepare by learning the Arabic language. He ordered language tapes, and wearing headphones, he listened to Arabic continuously, struggling to develop some degree of fluency. Because of his keen memory and talent for languages, Terry soon spoke some Arabic. To his dismay, when he spoke his newly acquired language to some of the locals in Saudi Arabia, he discovered that he had learned an Egyptian dialect of Arabic. Despite the slight differences in the two dialects, he soon spoke Arabic very well. Eventually, I learned enough Arabic to make purchases in the market and to greet others in the language.

Now, as I continued my flight to Saudi Arabia, I began to reflect on the events of the past year that led up to my trip. Terry and I had been leading a comfortable life in Lubbock, Texas. We lived near our parents and were active in our church. He was employed by Texas Tech University, and I worked for the Texas Agricultural Extension Service. The last thing on our minds during the Thanksgiving holidays of 1981 was uprooting ourselves and moving eight thousand miles, halfway around the globe. Yet, when Terry read the classified ad, "Farm Manager Wanted in Saudi Arabia," in the *Lubbock Avalanche-Journal* and asked whether he should check it out, I answered, "Sure, go ahead." This began the long process of interviewing, telephoning, waiting, and more waiting.

In March 1982, at the Hilton Inn in Lubbock, Terry made his first acquaintance with an Arab and our future boss Abdul Latif al-Sheikh or "Sheikh Latif" as we called him. As they talked, Terry learned why Sheikh Latif had come all the way to the United States to hire a farmer. The government of Saudi Arabia was concerned that its only source of income and stability for the Kingdom came from oil revenues. In an effort to diversify the economy and to become more self-sufficient in food production, the government decided to subsidize the domestic production of wheat. Because of the enormity of the subsidies, the Saudis could afford to hire the best farmers in the world, and, in their eyes, the best were found in America. The Saudi government offered to pay thirty dollars per bushel for wheat that was grown domestically, a stark contrast to the world market price, of approximately three dollars per bushel. The Saudis wanted U.S. farmers in Saudi Arabia to do the actual farm labor—not to teach the Saudis how to farm, as many U.S. farmers had speculated. Initially, the Saudis weren't interested in how the wheat was grown, but only in domestic wheat to market in Saudi Arabia.

During the interview, Sheikh Latif impressed Terry with his knowledge of U.S. farming and business acumen that he had acquired partially while he studied business in the U.S., in Washington and California colleges. He not only spoke English but had a good understanding of the American intellect and way of life. After an interesting exchange of farming ideas, Sheikh Latif informed Terry, who was only twenty-five years old at the time, that he was too young for the position of farm manager, a job that encompassed managing fifty to seventy-five workers on Green Sands, an emerging farm operation comprising seven thousand acres of prime Saudi desert land.

Terry returned to Texas Tech, convinced that he would not be hired and encouraged an older associate, Franklin Baggerman, to interview for the job. Yet after Frank visited with Sheikh Latif, Terry received an unexpected telephone call. An Arabic voice said, "Terry, this is Abdul." He offered Terry the job of assistant manager of his existing 3,000 acre farm. Terry accepted the offer. Franklin was given the job as the farm manager.

At their second meeting, Terry and Sheikh Latif discussed specifics about the job, including me and how I would occupy my time if I moved with him, ninety miles out into the Saudi desert. Sheikh Latif explained that women aren't allowed to work in Saudi Arabia unless they are issued specific visas to hold such jobs as nursing or teaching. Terry informed Sheikh Latif that I had a degree in Home Economics, but that I operated a computer on the job that I held all through college. Sheikh Latif responded that he had always wanted his business to be computerized; that could be my job. He agreed to pay Terry my salary of twelve hundred dollars a month from the first day Terry began work, even though I wouldn't be allowed to come for at least three months. In theory, this money would be paid to Terry only for his three-month probation period, at which time I was to receive my visa and join Terry. This payment period, without my working, would prove to be much longer than three months.

As Terry and I planned the move to a strange land, far away from our families, we left one safeguard in the operation. Terry agreed that after he arrived in Saudi Arabia, if conditions weren't comfortable enough for me, that he would return home. In other words, if Saudi Arabia was a place where an American woman could not live with comfort and dignity, then

I would never go, and he would return to Texas. Little did I suspect at the time how his standards of comfort and dignity might differ from mine.

On August 11th, 1982, the time finally arrived for Terry's departure. On a recommendation from Ed, Terry purchased large duffel bags from an army surplus store and packed every square inch with a year's supply of every imaginable necessity. I tearfully and apprehensively bid him farewell. As I watched him walk away, I wanted to race after him and beg, "Don't leave me. Let's just forget this crazy idea," but the words stuck in my throat.

Now, as I flew from New York City to Dhahran, Saudi Arabia, I glanced once again at my watch, remembering that August day almost six months ago when Terry had embarked on this same trip. Terry had taken the job as the assistant farm manager in Saudi Arabia with the idea that we would remain there one or two years at the most, save some money, have opportunity for traveling, and then return home.

Being raised in America, we assumed that timetables, dates, appointments, promises, and contracts were generally honored in a reasonable amount of time. We soon learned the Middle East functions on its own timetable. Our education on time frames in the Middle East began with obtaining my visa and air ticket to join Terry in Saudi Arabia.

After the initial three-month probation period had passed, both Terry and I, on opposite sides of the globe, began thinking our separation was almost over. The office personnel in Sheikh Latif's company, Al Emar, which governed Green Sands, told Terry that the visa would be processed in two weeks, then two more weeks, and on and on the time was extended. It's important to note that entry into Saudi Arabia is limited by strict rules and regulations. Entry visas are granted only to people who have specific business in the country, and in a very few special situations, to visitors. In 1982, it was difficult to obtain a visa in Saudi Arabia for a wife traveling alone. When my visa was finally processed, almost six months after Terry's departure, it was stamped: "Unable to Work, With or Without Being Paid."

The six months I spent apart from Terry had been difficult. I maintained a house and yard alone. I detected homesickness and apprehension by the tremble in Terry's voice, each time he called. I sensed that life in Saudi was not going to be anything like I'd ever experienced, and that Terry was assuming a false sense of bravado to ease my fears.

As my flight continued, I was jarred from my reflections by the plane's final descent into Dhahran, a city on the east coast of Saudi Arabia. I glanced at my watch, attempting to calculate the time in Texas. I had left New York at 9:00 P.M. and, after a thirteen-hour flight and the time difference, I calculated the time to be 6:00 P.M. when we landed. I had gained eight hours. My heart raced as the flight began its descent, and my entire body trembled. I fought to hold back a flood of tears; I didn't want to enter my new homeland crying. I would use the three-hour lay-over in Dhahran, before I flew into Riyadh to see Terry, to calm myself and to get to know this strange country that was to become my home.

Shortly before the landing, I became aware of a distracting commotion. During most of the flight I had studied the Arab people who also were flying into Saudi Arabia. The Saudi people have olive to light brown complexions, dark eyes and hair, and are generally of average height. I observed that most of the men smoked, whether or not they were in the smoking section of the airplane, and most of the women who appeared older than twenty-five seemed to be slightly overweight. The younger girls had slim figures and were dressed in tight blue jeans and high heels. Other than a few families, the passengers on the plane were almost entirely men. Up to the point of our descent, the Saudis visited, women with women and men with men, allowing their children to roam the airplane to the extent that the stewardesses allowed. The younger children and babies seemed to be dressed too warmly. I learned later that Saudis tend to over dress their children in the winter, regardless of the temperature. The women flipped through the latest fashion magazines, including those from Paris, and their attire seemed to reflect these fashions. I also noticed that the women spent a great deal of money buying in-flight gifts, including expensive perfumes, from the duty free shop. As we made our descent, I observed that the men who had been wandering around the plane found their way back to their seats.

I watched with curiosity as the Saudis made a slow migration, that built to a stampede, to the toilets. I couldn't imagine why everyone needed to visit the toilet right before landing, and I wondered if perhaps they knew something I didn't know about the availability of rest rooms in the Dhahran airport. As the first Saudi passengers emerged from the rest rooms to make their way back to their seats, even though the "Fasten Seat Belt" sign had been turned on for several minutes, I realized the reason for the exodus. The women who had once worn tight-fitting jeans and fashionable blouses, returned to their seats shrouded in black, draped from head to toe. I could no longer distinguish one Saudi woman from another. The men had traded their Western dress for the traditional Saudi garb. Each man fussed with his headdress and continued to rearrange it until the plane landed. At this point, I breathed a sigh of relief that I had heeded Terry's advice to pack a long skirt in my carry-on bag, to change into at the Riyadh airport. I longed to ignore the "Fasten Seat Belt" sign and bolt for the rest room to don my long skirt; instead, I obeyed the sign and sat tensely in my seat, becoming painfully conscious of my pants and uncovered face.

I was completely unprepared when we stopped in the middle of the runway and began to deplane. My arm was already sore from loading and unloading my heavy carry-on bag onto the wheels I used to roll the bag through the airports. I was now aware that there was no way that I could lug the heavy load, along with my purse, coat, and wheels, down the steep steps. An American man, one of the few other Westerners on the plane, came to the rescue, obligingly carrying my bag down the stairs, and on to what Westerners call "the cattle car," an open-air transport.

As I stood waiting for the transport to load, I watched the other passengers make their descent from the plane. To my surprise, the Saudi women not only remained completely veiled and shrouded, making me wonder whether they could see, but also carried all of the travel bags and supervised the small children. To my consternation, the Saudi husbands and older male children left the women to gather up all possessions while the men raced for the choice standing spots on the transport. This was my first introduction to the man's world of Saudi Arabia.

Because my checked luggage was to be cleared through customs in Riyadh, my final destination, the only inspection in Dhahran was of my forty-pound carry-on bag. I was surprised to see separate lines, one for Saudis and one for foreigners, and the Saudi line seemed to move much faster, with less luggage inspection. I'm not sure whether the customs agents discriminated because my bag was so heavy, because I was a woman traveling alone (which is frowned upon and not allowed on in-country flights), or because I did not speak one word of Arabic. The customs agent emptied the entire contents of my carefully packed bag, even looking inside cosmetic containers and zipped bags. When the entire contents of my bag were spread all over the inspection table, he motioned me out of the way so he could inspect the next person's luggage. Frantically, I began to cram things into the bag, sticking some under my arm and even under my chin. With people stepping all around me, I knelt down next to the table, repacking the bag and somehow refitting all of the contents into it.

At this point, I didn't have a clue about where to go or what to do. I had been so busy repacking the bag that I hadn't watched where the other passengers went. There were a few signs written in Arabic that I could not read. I searched the remaining faces in the crowd, but I couldn't spot an American- or English-looking one. I was in a small room, with several exits, one of which I must have come in through. For the second time in an hour, I blinked back tears, feeling so nervous that I could have been sick. I took a deep breath, determined not to allow myself that option. Timidly, I entered one door, only to find myself in the middle of the uniformed airport authorities' supper break. The men were squatting in a circle on the floor with a large platter of rice and chicken, eating with their fingers. They looked at me in disgust as several of the men jumped to their feet, motioning for me to leave.

I made a hasty retreat into the customs inspection room. The thought entered my mind that I might go out a wrong door and be on the streets of Dhahran without a notion of what to do. Panic almost overwhelmed me. I didn't speak the language; I didn't know anyone to call, and Terry was on a farm ninety miles from Riyadh without a phone. I took a deep breath, looked at the custom officials, and tried another door that opened into some type of storage area. I immediately backed out, thinking of the harems that once existed in Arabia.

I stepped through another door and realized that I must be in the right place. I was standing in a huge room with benches that were crowded, mostly with young men. The overflow lounging on their luggage on the floor. The stares that met me made me feel as if I were nude. I didn't recognize any faces from my previous flight. Many of these people were of Oriental or Asian descent; I would learn later that most were Filipinos and Thailanders. None of them looked to be over eighteen years old. Perhaps they were looking at me because they not only missed their wives and girlfriends back home, but also realized that it might be a long time before they saw very many uncovered women's faces. Most had probably never seen an American woman in person.

As I stood inside the entrance, I heard an Arabic voice in plaintive singsong over the loud speaker. The Saudi men in the crowd walked to a large area covered with a dusty Oriental rug. The men lined up in a long single line, with an older man out in front with his back to the group, so that all the men were facing in the same direction. After standing there for a few minutes and repeating some Arabic words softly, the men placed their hands on their knees and swayed up and down. I couldn't restrain myself from staring at the fascinating ritual that ended with the men prostrate on the floor. As if they all knew exactly when to stand, the praying ceased. The men ambled back into the crowd as if they had done nothing more than order a soft drink at the concession stand.

The Asian men carefully kept their eyes down, avoiding any eye contact with the Saudi men. As the Saudi men returned to their seats, I took this opportunity to cross to the opposite corner of the room to the ladies' rest room where I could change into my long skirt. I could feel every eye in the room watching me as I walked.

I was completely unprepared for what I saw in the ladies' rest room. There were several Saudi women inside, all standing in puddles of water. The odor in the rest room was terrible. There were no mirrors, and the sinks were filthy and without soap, towels, or air dryer. I went inside a stall to put on my skirt; in the stall I found that instead of a Western-type commode or bidet, there was a concrete-ringed hole. The women had not taken careful aim; there were spots of urine and even a feminine napkin thrown on the floor. The reason for the water all over the floor was that, instead of toilet paper, the rest room was equipped with water sprayers. I held my breath, tried to step into my long skirt without anything touching the floor, and slipped out of the rest room.

When I reentered the large room, I created another commotion; it seemed that everyone noted that I had changed clothes. Because I had at least two hours remaining before my plane left for Riyadh, I had to find a seat. All of the benches were taken, but I noticed some empty seats around what could be called a concession stand. As I sat down in one of the seats, the man behind the counter glared at me, and I decided that I needed to buy something in order to have the use of the seat. I went up to the counter, thankful that I had traded some U.S. money with a man on the airplane for some Saudi Arabian currency, called *riyals* (SR or Saudi Riyals). I saw what looked like water in a sealed blue plastic bottle. I pointed to the bottle and the man put it on the counter saying, *"Moya"* (water). I wondered how to say "How much" and the man stuck out his hand and said, *"Toleta"* (three). I had no choice but to hold out a handful of money to the concessionaire and allow him to pay himself. He chose a ten, and I supposed that I had been swindled. I turned to go back to my table without arguing. The man called after me, "Sister" and handed me seven riyals. I learned later that "sister" is used as a sign of respect in all the Arab world when addressing an adult female. A man is addressed as "brother" and an older man as "father." The drink was bottled water from France; and I made a note in my journal to tell my family back home that my first drink of water in Saudi Arabia was from France.

I continued looking at the men in the room, and they continued watching me. An announcement in Arabic caused a mad dash for a door on the opposite side of the room. A line began to form, and I decided that it must be the line for my flight and that I didn't want to be the last person left in the waiting room. I stood in line, wondering as the line inched forward if I were the only one in that room who did not understand Arabic and if everyone else had understood the announcement. As I approached the front of the line, I readied my passport, my airplane ticket, and my shot record for inspection.

I created another round of confusion when the airport personnel examined my ticket and began a discussion that I did not understand. One man in broken English asked, "Where is husband?" When I said "Riyadh," the men began to confer again. I feared that they might want Terry to come and get me, and I knew that there was no way I could get in touch with him. Again I could envision myself alone in Dhahran. Little did I know that women are not allowed to stay in any hotel in Saudi Arabia, without a male,—husband, father, or brother.

After more discussion, the man waved me on. I walked outside on the airport runway and loaded onto another "cattle car" with a large group of the Asian men. As we pulled up to our airplane, my adrenalin must have been flowing; I heaved my heavy bag up the steep stairs to the plane. A stewardess, this time an Indian-looking woman, showed me to my seat, in the midst of a group of Asian men. For the first time in all the flights I'd made since Lubbock, the stewardess recognized that my bag wouldn't fit under the seat in front of me and allowed me to place it in another location.

Because Terry had told me the flight from Dhahran to Riyadh took only about fifty minutes, I relaxed a little, knowing that I was at least on a plane to my final destination. The Asian men around me talked in subdued tones to one another. I wanted to know what they were saying, but their conversations weren't in English.

After a quick nap, I felt the plane descending, and I knew that I soon would set foot on the tarmac of the Riyadh airport. I began hoping that by some chance Terry would be standing on the runway to meet me! Yet it would be another two hours before I'd see him. I deplaned and went through the "cattle car" ritual to the airport building. I stood beside the revolving luggage carrier, waiting to claim my baggage. I noticed many of the Filipinos had packed their belongings in large cardboard boxes, bound with tape. A few of the boxes had split, and the contents were exposed.

I wondered what Terry would think about my four big bags. The airline had allowed only two sixty-two-pound bags, but I had paid an extra two hundred dollars to bring two extra bags. I knew he would joke about my having to have four bags, but I felt as though I had packed for a trip to the moon and had not known what to take. There were men from Pakistan in airport uniforms, waiting to put each passenger's luggage on a cart and wheel it up to customs. My Pakistani porter and I proceeded to customs as he sized up my potential as a tipper.

As I stood in line, I saw the customs officials randomly pulling items out of other passenger's luggage. I knew my purse and carry-on bag were safe from another inspection, because the man in Dhahran had drawn a big X with chalk on both to signify that they had already been inspected. Terry had told me that when he went through customs with his bags six months earlier, the official dumped everything out of both bags, even the socks and underwear. I knew how skillfully I'd packed and that it would take me forever to repack, so I watched with horror as the officials randomly chose bags to dump. Terry wasn't allowed in the customs area, and I was glad he couldn't see the four overstuffed bags with the custom official ready to pounce on them.

Perhaps because the man didn't want to take the time, or because I was the only woman in sight, or because I was wearing a long skirt, I was spared a total dumping of my luggage. The man dug down several layers, creating a small mess in each bag. He began pulling out book after book, many of them Christian books. I understood it was permissible to have one Bible, but not more than one. I was thankful that he discovered only one, because I had brought several copies that Terry had requested for some of his Filipino workers. Most Filipinos were afraid to risk bringing in a Bible because the custom officials seemed to be much stricter on the Asian people coming into Saudi Arabia. Yet several had asked Terry if I'd bring them a copy, and my local church members had sent quite a few with me.

It felt odd to be so nervous over such an inspection when I knew I really didn't have anything illegal by Western standards. A few stations over, a customs official discovered a video tape in one man's luggage and immediately confiscated it. Later, I learned that all video tapes are taken and viewed for any pornographic material and are occasionally returned, but usually become the property of the government. We always joked that they used those tapes as entertainment during the government meetings. In future trips into Saudi Arabia, I smuggled in such things as vanilla extract (unavailable because of the alcohol content), pork jerky that I had purchased during a layover in Frankfurt, and women's magazines that might contain a picture of a swimsuit or mini-skirt. Most of the custom officials were checking for drugs, alcohol, pork, any pro-Israeli material, or any magazines or videos that were sexually suggestive.

Finally the customs official took his marker and put a big X on each of my bags, completing the inspection. My bags were once again loaded on the porter's cart and wheeled toward the entrance of the airport and to Riyadh, and to Terry.

If I had known the havoc that had gone on with Terry before I arrived, I would have been a basket case. Terry had waited for me at the international section of the airport because my flight had originated in New York. When the last person at the international section cleared customs and I hadn't appeared, Terry became frantic. Fortunately, an airport custodian worker suggested that Terry try the domestic section where another flight from Dhahran was coming in. It seems that the commotion about my ticket back in Dhahran had been because I was actually getting on the wrong flight. But because I was going to the right place, they let me get on the plane. I had wondered briefly what happened to all the people who had been on my flight from New York, but had decided that they all must have left the plane in Dhahran. I felt relieved that despite the language barrier, I had arrived in Riyadh. When I stepped through the customs door, Terry was there waiting, standing a head above the robed Saudi men, an expression of relief on his bearded face, and wearing his large cowboy hat.

Under these strange circumstances it was hard to know what to say first to my husband, whom I had not seen in six months. Terry had already warned me that no public physical contact between opposite sexes is allowed. An affectionate kiss or hug between husband and wife would not be tolerated; however, many men held hands and kissed each other on each cheek. Some men continued kissing over and over from cheek to cheek. I learned later that this is not only an act of friendliness, but a sign of respect. The more pecks on each cheek, the more noble, respected, or loved the person. Again I was almost the only woman present, a distinction I soon learned I would have to get used to. It became evident in the ensuing weeks that Saudi women are not to be seen regularly in public.

I was shocked by the appearance of the airport, noting the poor construction and the bare walls, devoid of the general advertising posters, snack bars, and small shops. This seemed more like an airport in a poverty-stricken Third World country than in prosperous Saudi Arabia. The Saudis finally constructed a new, modern airport that opened in 1984.

Chapter Two

Outside the Riyadh airport, Terry's first surprise was to tell me that Sheikh Latif had suggested that we spend the night in Riyadh at the Oasis Hotel rather than make the ninety-mile drive to the farm that night. In hindsight, I decided the next day that it might have been better for me to have traveled to the farm in the dark. As exhausted as I was from my trip, I would have slept most of the way to the farm and the darkness would have obscured the barren desert landscape. For the moment, I was elated at the prospect of a night out on the town with my husband from whom I had been separated for six months. We felt like newlyweds, going alone to a hotel for the night.

We fitted my luggage easily in the back of Terry's Toyota pickup for our drive to the hotel. When we arrived at the Oasis, we decided to place the luggage in the cab of the pickup rather than haul it to our room. This proved to be an act of sheer organization and push. In a major city back home, we would not have left luggage locked in the cab of our pickup for fear of theft; however, we felt quite safe in this country because the Saudis punish such crimes severely by cutting off the right hand of the thief.

When we registered in the sparsely furnished hotel lobby, we were somewhat surprised and amused that we had to show our passports and visas, to prove not only that we had proper identification, but also that we were man and wife. Terry also had to produce a travel letter from Sheikh Latif's company. Terry explained that a noncitizen traveling in Saudi Arabia must have a travel letter from their place of employment legitimatizing their presence outside the area of their work. Since Terry's residence was ninety miles from Riyadh, he had to have a travel letter.

Because I had been in flight for two days, with only quick cleanups in airport rest rooms, I wanted to take a bath. Terry explained to me that much of the plumbing and construction in Saudi Arabia had been done in great haste during a period of rapid expansion and that I would probably have to run the water for quite awhile before it became warm. I might even have to face the possibility of a cold instead of hot bath. We were delighted to feel warm water flowing from the dated hardware after only five minutes.

After I became acquainted with Riyadh, I understood what Terry meant about hasty construction. When the Saudis built a structure, they contracted with foreign firms to do the labor. The Koreans might contract to do the plumbing in a building, and the Germans might contract to do the concrete work. However, communication between the companies involved was usually nonexistent. The German company might pour the concrete for a structure before the plumbing had been installed. Then the Korean company would tear up the concrete to install the plumbing. This do and redo way of construction made Riyadh look like a city that was constantly under siege.

The hotel offered room service, so we ordered the fruit plate with cottage cheese listed on the menu. When our food arrived, I discovered that what was described as cottage cheese was really feta cheese, a firm, slightly salty cheese made from goat's milk. It seems that much of Saudi life has Western influences, even the names of foods on the menus.

That first night in Saudi Arabia, my body suffered from jet lag and refused to sleep. It thought the time was about 4:00 P.M. instead of midnight. As I lay awake, I remembered Terry's description of his first night in Saudi Arabia. I had been fortunate to arrive in January, one of the coolest months of the year, when the normal temperature at night is around fifty degrees Fahrenheit. Terry had arrived in August, when daytime temperatures soar to 120-130 degrees, and nighttime temperatures drop very little. When Terry arrived near 9:00 P.M., the temperature was still well over one hundred degrees.

Upon Terry's arrival, no one appeared at the airport to meet him. There happened to be an American man, Arty, at the airport who had some dealings with Sheikh Latif's company; he generously offered to take Terry to eat and to spend the night at Arty's home. He chose a Lebanese restaurant on a back street, where they could get chicken and rice for the equivalent of only two dollars.

Terry recalled that the old linoleum floors of the establishment were dusty, and the plastic tablecloths on the five tables hadn't been washed in days. The owner was honored that these Americans had chosen his place of business. Because he did not have printed menus, and he doubted that the foreigners would know what to order anyway, he took the men into the kitchen to make their selections. The chickens were quartered and roasted. A portable cook stove sat on the floor, heating a huge pot of rice and sheep's broth. On a cabinet sat a platter of fresh onions, tomatoes, and cucumbers with lemon wedges. Flies swarmed over all of the food, everywhere. In Arabic, Arty ordered chicken and rice and a salad. Terry declined the salad. The chicken quarter was served on a mound of rice with a huge round of Arabic flatbread. Terry watched Arty use his bread to scoop the rice to his mouth. Terry tried to eat a little, but the heat was unbearable. The propped-open front door of the restaurant proved to be the only source of air. Perspiration poured from Terry as he attempted to eat the food.

After the meal Arty drove at breakneck speed (there were no speed laws in Saudi Arabia at that time) to his villa, a housing unit in Riyadh that was surrounded by a concrete wall. Although the villa was new, the construction was so shabby that it looked old and haggard. The wall had been broken and shabbily patched in several places in an effort to install the plumbing correctly. The men stayed awake late into the night, discussing how each came to be employed in Saudi Arabia.

Because Arty had been in Saudi Arabia for a year, he played the role of veteran travel guide. Highlighting the heat, the wind, the sand, the unavailability of alcohol (at least legally), pork, and even chewing tobacco, he began to paint a bleak picture of life in this Arab country. None of these things bothered Terry until Arty began describing the wildlife on the farm where Terry was soon to be working. Arty, with skillful detail, described large and vicious snakes of all types, scorpions, and camel spiders. At this point, Arty proclaimed that they needed a good night's sleep so that they could drive to the farm bright and early the next morning. He showed Terry to a little room containing a twin bed with a thin, lumpy mattress. There was no other furniture in the room and in keeping with most Saudi housing, there wasn't a closet.

Terry flung himself on top of the blanket that was being used as a bedspread, not bothering even to remove his boots, determined to block the heat and Arty's creepy creatures from his mind. He began to perspire, and there seemed to be no air conditioning. Terry glanced at his watch; it was already 1:00 A.M. He heard a kind of scratching or scurrying noise, which continued off and on for several minutes. His mind recalled every detail of the snakes and scorpions and tried to imagine what a camel spider could be. Suddenly, something ran across his leg and Terry bolted up in bed. Jerking on the string that turned on the only light bulb in the room, he saw a huge rat scurry into a hole in the wall. He left the light on to discourage the rodents from leaving their holes. He fell into a fitful sleep, dreaming of camels with spiders crawling all over him.

At 4:30 A.M. Terry awoke with a start to the slow wailing of the faithful at their first prayers of the day. He lay on the uncomfortable bed and listened to the moaning noise, wondering if Arty wanted him to get up. When he heard no other noises, he fell back into a half-dozing sleep.

By eight, the Americans made their way down the street in the bustling morning traffic of Riyadh, the capital of Saudi Arabia. Before going to the farm, Arty said it would be a good idea for Terry to go to the company's head office to let Sheikh Latif know that he really had made it to Saudi Arabia.

When the car pulled up to a shabby three-story building that contained several stores, some apartments, and a couple of offices, Terry was puzzled. He had envisioned Sheikh Latif in an elegant, modern office. Instead, the entrance to his office was located between a small grocery store and a brass trinket shop. The office was on the second floor, and after making several attempts to use the old style elevator, the men took the stairs. The office was musty, dark, and smelled of stale cigarette smoke. In the front room were a green vinyl couch and an oversized desk with a small man perched behind. The man, a Sri Lankan named Francis, smiled from ear to ear when he realized this must be the new American. He jumped up and shook hands with the men, grinning all the while. He quickly informed Arty that both Sheikh Latif and Hafeez, the Pakistani general manager, were out of the country. He gave Terry an advance of riyals so that he would have money to buy soft drinks, soap for washing clothes, or to use the pay phone to call home in the town of Al Kharj, which was thirty-five miles from the farm. Everything else, including food, housing, vehicle, gasoline, and medical care, were furnished by Sheikh Latif's company. Terry left the office wishing he'd seen Sheikh Latif, if for no other reason than to reassure himself that this person he'd met almost six months before, eight thousand miles away, actually existed.

Sometime while reflecting on Terry's first night in Saudi Arabia, my first night there finally dissolved into deep sleep. I awoke to light streaming into the hotel room through the paper-thin curtains. Because of the sparse lighting the night before, I hadn't really seen the room. Now, I saw twin beds with bright red, threadbare spreads, and a shabbily patched wall where an electrical outlet had been positioned and then moved to a lower place on the wall. Thick dust filled the corners of the room, and the thin carpet appeared to have been swept with a broom.

When I peered out a window, I saw an already crowded main street. I watched as scrawny looking men and boys went from car to car selling boxes of Kleenex, sun visors, and other small items to people stopped at the traffic light. The behavior of the traffic on the street was incredible. Traffic was stopped in three directions, with only one section at a time allowed to proceed through the intersection. In spaces allotted for three cars, five to six cars tried to squeeze into the position of number one car at the light.

Long before the light changed, the cars behind the front cars began honking. The light changed and a man driving a car in a far right lane began honking and gesturing to all the cars to his left. After several minutes of dodging cars, he finally succeeded in turning left from the right-hand lane! I was aghast. Few drivers seemed to adhere to the traffic laws, and no one seemed concerned by the constant, flagrant violations. Traffic could not have been allowed to flow from more than one direction at a time in the intersection without a mass accident. I suddenly felt sure that women did not want to be allowed to drive in Saudi Arabia. Although there is no official law banning women from driving, no driver's licenses are issued to women. According to the Saudi Interior Ministry, it would contradict Islamic traditions for Saudi women to drive; therefore, all other women are also forbidden to drive.

From my hotel window, I could view several mosques in the city. The dream of Saudi Arabians is to be able to stand at one mosque and see another mosque in all directions. From where I stood, it appeared they were well on their way to realizing this dream.

After we checked out of our hotel, Terry took me to shop for a vacuum cleaner. Our company had asked Terry if I needed anything in order to be comfortable at the farm. Terry requested a washer and dryer and a vacuum cleaner. The washer and dryer had been installed a few days before my arrival, but the company suggested that Terry and I search for the vacuum cleaner together. Before the installation of the washer and dryer, Terry had washed his clothes by hand in the bathtub and hung them over chairs in the house to dry. In the arid desert climate, even socks dried in a couple of hours.

I am an avid breakfast eater, and I began to look for a fast-food place where I might order a take-out breakfast. Although I saw several fast-food restaurants such as a Hardees, a Herfeys, and a Dairy Queen, they did not serve breakfast. There were no drive-in windows, and parking seemed to be a real problem. We decided to forego breakfast and look for a place to buy a vacuum cleaner. Terry had directions to a section of Riyadh that would probably have vacuum cleaners. Otherwise, we would never have known where to go. His directions were based on landmarks: "turn right at the corner of the Saudi American bank and then turn left at the second bread store on the right." At that time, streets were not named or numbered, and all store names were in Arabic.

We found a parking place and wound our way down a crowded street. I was transported into a far away and mysterious culture as I viewed the dark faces of women shrouded in black, only their faces and hands exposed, sitting cross-legged on the sidewalks with large baskets of packaged snack items and many with babies or small children on their laps. Some of the women had tattoo-like scars and markings on their faces, and a few women had several teeth covered in gold. Terry explained that these women were from Ethiopia or Sudan and didn't have their entire faces covered because they weren't Saudi, even though they were Moslems.

We passed rows of shops containing electrical equipment such as stereos, cassettes, and TVs, all from Japan, Taiwan, and Korea. The Third World laborers loved to buy electrical items to take with them when they returned home on vacations. Finally we happened upon a shop with vacuum cleaners. It offered several older models of sewing machines and a few small vacuum cleaners. The shop owner was from Syria and became very animated when Terry spoke to him in Arabic. He became even more animated when he realized that we were not just looking, but buying a vacuum cleaner. Normally, we would have shopped around before making such a large purchase, but Terry said the rule among foreigners was that, once you found something you wanted in Riyadh, you'd better buy it right then because it might not be there when you return. I embraced this philosophy religiously. In the years to come, I bought twelve boxes of shredded wheat, a whole case of canned corn tortillas, and a dozen packages of chocolate chips when I finally located these items in Riyadh. The rule held true because after purchasing these items, I rarely, if ever, saw them again.

The little Syrian man motioned us to sit down while he scurried into the back of the store. Terry acted like this was all normal procedure, so I sat back to watch. The man soon reappeared with a small silver tray with two tiny clear glass mugs of liquid. Terry whispered to me that it was hot tea. It tasted almost like hot chocolate because it was so smooth and rich and sweet, but it really was hot tea laced with much sugar and canned milk. Throughout Saudi Arabia, the tea ceremony is practiced in all areas of business as well as society. It tasted good, I couldn't imagine drinking it during the steaming summers; however, I found it is consumed year-round. I learned later that the Saudis drink their tea without milk, but this man enjoyed the rich drink, as did Pakistanis and Indians.

The man brought all of the vacuum cleaners in the store to where we were seated. We tried to stand up to follow him around the store so that he wouldn't have to move all of the vacuums to us, but he insisted that we stay seated. We settled on a vacuum cleaner made in Taiwan. Later, I regretted purchasing this model because the handle was made for a person much shorter than I. All the while I was in Saudi Arabia, I bent over to vacuum.

With our vacuum cleaner and all my luggage in the back of the pickup, we raced to a nearby Hardees, as Terry quipped, "To beat prayer time." He explained that all shops closed from twelve until four in the afternoon, but the restaurants closed for only about thirty minutes for the noon prayer time. They closed again for thirty minutes at approximately three-thirty, six-thirty, and eight. The entire country comes to a stop at these times as men make their way to the mosques to pray. The other two prayer times are early morning and late evening. There is little fear of a shop's being burglarized because of the strict enforcement of hand chopping as the punishment for stealing.

Luckily, we made it into Hardees and placed our order before prayer time. We were careful to sit in the family section of the restaurant, which is isolated from the remainder of the establishment. Women were allowed to eat only in places that had a separate family section.

However, once prayer time had begun, signaled by long wailing, all the blinds were drawn and the lights were turned out. We were left alone to eat in the dark. After we had lived in Saudi Arabia several years, the *Mutawwa,* or religious police, stopped restaurants from allowing patrons to stay inside during prayer time.

After what could almost be called a good 'ole American hamburger, we drove to the farm. Terry had to wind around and backtrack, avoiding blocked intersections and impassable areas, as we drove through Riyadh. To my surprise, Terry had taken on the driving characteristics of the Saudis, squeezing in and making lanes where there really weren't any lanes marked, and honking his horn more in those few minutes than I'd ever known him to before.

As we left the bustling city, there was no question that we really were in the desert. The highway seemed to stretch forever into the flat, sandy terrain. Cars raced down the highway at unchecked speeds, and an occasional gas station dotted the desert landscape. There were a few signs containing only a written message in Arabic and no pictures of humans. When the Prophet Mohammed introduced Islam to the land of Arabia, many of the people worshipped idols; therefore, even a photograph or drawing of the human face is regarded as a form of a graven image in Saudi Arabia.

Traveling at a speed of seventy-five to eighty miles per hour, we reached the little town of Al Kharj, with a population of approximately twenty thousand. I was struck by the sight of a tall water tower at the edge of the city. Water is a precious commodity in Saudi Arabia, even today. In the 1930s, when the oil companies wanted to begin drilling, they had to ask the nation's founder, King Abdul Aziz ibn Abdul ar-Rahman al Faisal al-Sa'ud, for permission. He thought at the time that surely they must be drilling for water because it was needed so desperately.

Al Kharj is a pretty, quaint town with date palm trees planted down the center of the divided highway. There were row after row of little shops, closed for prayer time. We passed a large fruit and vegetable market, also closed. Some of the stall owners had thrown a piece of cloth over their produce, but most produce was left uncovered and all the stalls were unattended. As we made our way to the far side of town, we passed pens built around a camel market where the Bedouins brought their camels to buy, sell, and trade once a week.

I noticed the divided highway had become a narrow two-lane paved road. The thirty-five miles of desert between Al Kharj and my new home seemed desolate and bleak. A short distance out of Al Kharj, we passed a large dairy, and Terry remarked that he had heard there might be some Western women living there. As we continued to drive, we came to a lone gas station, our closest link to civilization. We stopped to purchase a Pepsi at a run-down building with two gas pumps. Coca Cola was not allowed in Saudi Arabia in the 1980s because there was a Coca Cola plant in Israel, and Saudi Arabia was boycotting products produced in Israel. Two young Egyptian men working there looked at me as if they'd never seen a Western woman in their lives, and I studied them with the same intensity. Terry had become friends with them, and they exchanged greetings.

As we began the last fifteen-mile leg of our trip to the farm, Terry became anxious to check on the farm after his less than twenty-four-hour absence. I was anxious to see the place where I was supposed to live. I tried not to think how far I was from town, and that I couldn't drive myself if I wanted to go somewhere. At that moment, I wouldn't have had the nerve to drive myself anywhere anyway. I thought it ironic that Sheikh Latif had named his farming enterprise "Green Sands" because I could see no evidence of green in the ocean of sand. I didn't realize the wheat that had been planted was about to burst forth, pushing its bright green shoots through the sand.

As I studied the desolate scenery, I thought back to Terry's account of his own first trip to the farm. The temperature in August had already soared above 120 degrees. As Terry drove to the farm with Arty his self-appointed guide, in a Dodge pickup, the wind blew so hard that the pickup swayed from side to side. When the wind blows in Saudi Arabia, the sandy terrain is whipped into dust devils, making visibility almost impossible. Motorists traveling the lonely stretch of highway to the farm this particular day were using their headlights, but not slowing their speed, even though they couldn't see ten feet in front of them. Arty assured Terry that he didn't fear hitting another car because there was little traffic on this road during midday. He was concerned, however, that a camel might be allowed to wander freely across the highway. A camel, if struck, could completely roll a car, and the driver usually had to pay the owner the price of the camel. Arty related horror stories about foreigners who had traffic mishaps with Saudis and had been taken off to jail, without notice to their employers. Arty's stories encouraged Terry to strain to see either cars or camels, lost in the sandy wind. The men were miserably hot, but grateful to be in the shelter of the air conditioned vehicle.

I was jolted back to reality as we reached the turnoff for our farm and was pleased to see a small grove of trees marking the entrance. Terry explained that there were some Palestinian farmers at the front of the farm who had probably planted the trees years ago. I didn't realize at the time how few trees and birds there were around our farm. As we drove the last mile from the highway to what Terry called the camp, all I could see was flat ground and a few center pivot irrigation systems, but no evidence of wheat or green. The irrigation systems were Valley electric-drive center pivots, with either eight or nine tower spans. Caterpillar diesel irrigation engines with six and eight cylinders were alongside each pivot.

We pulled into a fenced area that looked out of place in such rough terrain. The five-foot chain link fence seemed to be there just to section off a part of the desert, rather than for protection or privacy. There were several pieces of farm equipment around camp, and I spotted what I knew was our house. There were two identical mobile home units and about fifty yards away were several small campers. Terry explained that he lived in one of the mobile homes, called containers. The small campers were for the eleven workers who lived on the farm, called Project 2 (which everyone shortened to P2). The canteen where we ate, the farm office, workshop, and living accommodations for all the other workers were about nine miles away at Project 1 (P1), where Sheikh Latif had begun farm operations the year before. At first, under the umbrella of Green Sands, the two farm projects were kept almost entirely separate, with different managers, assistant managers, and laborers. This system didn't work, and after that first year, Terry became the farm manager for both P1 and P2, and the same laborers worked both farms.

Terry told me of his first glimpse of his container sitting in the middle of the desert. It consisted of two units joined down the center and had been split in order to be moved to the farm. Even though the container had been moved several weeks before, the two halves were sitting open, both collecting sand and desert creatures seeking refuge. Terry wondered how the sand could be removed from the two halves before they were hooked together, while the sand continued to blow.

Eventually, though all the sand wasn't removed, the two halves were joined together and plumbing installed. The plumbing was defective, and the container flooded, creating a muddy mess. I was thankful to arrive after these problems were remedied.

Terry wanted to take me to the house to unload my bags and allow me to start unpacking while he checked out the farm operation. A sudden and unusual panic gripped me, and I didn't want to be left alone. I told him that I'd just go with him after we dropped off my luggage. Because I had no idea in which of the four bags my clothes were packed, I remained in my long skirt. According to what I'd seen in Riyadh that morning, I felt I'd probably never be able to wear any of the pants or shorts I'd brought. I was convinced that I would be confined to the two long skirts.

As we drove around the farm, I was amazed at the progress Terry and the others had made in six short months. The untamed desert had been cajoled into cultivated farmland. Terry introduced me to three Filipinos, Rolando, Victorian, and Efren, who looked much younger than their actual ages. All three had wives and children at home. Efren had left his wife in the Philippines one month after marrying her and had never seen his new baby, born while he was in Saudi Arabia.

I also met two Sri Lankans, Perera and Mitrisena, both dark skinned and Buddhist. I had never heard of Sri Lanka, once called Ceylon, off the coast of India. The five men were all tactfully reserved, but I could see that they were just as curious about me as I was about them. None of the men had ever seen an American women except in pictures, and I learned later that they thought I was about sixteen years old (I was actually twenty-three). Immediately, I sensed a camaraderie among Terry and these five men, as if the harshness of the desert, the homesickness for family and country, and the incredibly long hours and hard work had somehow bound them together, breaking down barriers of culture, race, and position.

The last person I met at the farm that day was Midwess Dowas, from whom I gained much of my knowledge about Saudi Arabia. Midwess was Bedouin. *Bedouin* denotes the nomads of Saudi Arabia and refers generally to all tribesmen who live in the desert and herd camels, sheep, and goats.

I liked Midwess immediately because of his big grin and uninhibited interest in an American woman. Midwess had camels and sheep, but he had been employed by our company to drive a bulldozer. It was unusual that a Bedouin would know how to drive a bulldozer. He explained that when he was fifteen years old, he left home and took the railroad that stretched from the tiny country of Qatar across the eastern side of Saudi Arabia. He got off the rail line at Harrad, a tiny town about two hours east of our farms. He worked there on a new farm project with a hand shovel, excavating the land. A German man liked him and trained him to drive a bulldozer. Midwess was also one of the few Bedouins who had a passport, because when his father had heart surgery, he went to Qatar to visit him and was required to have a passport to leave Saudi Arabia.

Midwess had never been to school and didn't know how to read or write. He signed his receipt for his paycheck with an X. Before I arrived, he invited Terry to his tent to eat every night of the week. Although Terry declined to go quite that often, he did spend many nights under the desert stars conversing with Midwess, even though neither knew much of the other's language.

Terry recounted to me the first time he and Frank Baggerman went out to Midwess's tent. There were several other Bedouin men sitting around the campfire with Midwess. Terry noted that the women, Midwess's wife, mother, and sister, carefully concealed themselves behind the flap of the tent, peeking at what was going on and listening to the men's conversation. Because it was already dark and the campfire was dim, it was hard to see exactly where everything was located.

Midwess called the traditional Arabic greeting "Peace to you," and Terry and Frank responded, "And peace to you, also." In their haste to get near the fire so they could see better, Frank stepped in the bowl of dates from which the men had been eating. The dates flew in every direction, much to the delight of the Bedouin men, and the hiding women. Most of the dates landed all over the mat on which the men were sitting. They were gathered up and eaten over the course of the night. Frank was skilled at playing a guitar, and he entertained the group by playing and singing a few Texas songs. Midwess stood up and swayed to the music, dancing with his sword the national dance of Saudi Arabia.

After Terry had shown Midwess my picture and told him I was coming, Midwess had asked, "How much did you have to pay for her?" A man in Saudi Arabia provides a substantial dowry to the family of the bride. On one of our many visits to Midwess's tent in the years to come, we discussed the price of a bride. Midwess told us that Prince Turky ibn Saud al-Kabir (one of the many members of the royal family) had just taken a new wife and had to pay SR 300,000 ($85,714). He added that, including the cost of the wedding and gifts to the family, the bill might have totaled SR 1,000,000 ($285,714). I asked Midwess about the cost of a virgin bride when Saudi Arabia was still a desolate, poor country. Smiling, Midwess turned to Mama, his mother, and said that her family asked only one camel for her, which was the going rate at the time.

Midwess's first wife had left him to go back to her family. In keeping with Saudi Arabian custom, Midwess kept their child, a son. He had remarried, this time to his uncle's daughter, a woman much younger than he. It was from Rashmi, his present wife, that I was to learn much about the life of a real Bedouin woman in Saudi Arabia.

Chapter Three

Terry's first days on the desert farm had been very different from my initial days. After the shock of the heat, sand, and incredible remoteness, Frank, the manager, and Terry, as the assistant, began making plans to divide and conquer Sheikh Latif's second farm, P2. Sheikh Latif had rented the forty-five hundred-acre area from Prince Saud bin Mohammad bin Abdul Aziz in hopes of developing both a wheat farm and a dairy. On one small section of the farm, Palestinian farmers, who were squatters, grew vegetables, using flood irrigation from wells that had been dug years before. Much of their labor was done by donkeys. Terry felt a little like an American pioneer cultivating the land of American Indians. Using his own broken Arabic and Midwess as an interpreter, Terry approached the farmers and tried to explain that the land was rented, that they would have to move. The Palestinian farmers were always quick to offer hot tea and thimble size cups of the traditional Arabic coffee, but they did not move. The head office eventually sent someone to explain in detailed Arabic the sad fact that the small farmers must move.

Some of the squatters, clinging to what they believed were their rights, refused to move. Because the land needed preparation for planting wheat, Terry eventually had to confront one stubborn Palestinian farmer who had a fifteen-acre vegetable plot in the center of a planned major road. Terry visited the Palestinian daily for several weeks and left each time with promises that the man would move. Finally, Terry hooked a big land plane (level) behind a tractor and drove right through the middle of the vegetable plot. The man stood off to the side, shaking a hoe and cursing in Arabic. Terry had to assuage his guilt by reminding himself that the man could go to the government and get a new tract of land for farming, at no cost.

Our farm was located in the middle of a floodplain, called a *wadi*, a low lying area that holds water during a heavy rainfall. They reminded me somewhat of the playas of West Texas. Most wadis in Saudi Arabia have towns built around them, because of the importance of water in earlier times. We were located close to the *Al Rub' al-Khali*, or the empty quarter, a bleak area with almost no rainfall, where nothing grows. No towns had built any closer to this wadi than Al Kharj, thirty-five miles away.

Although P2 had been surveyed and mapped, it was easy to become lost on the huge patches of sand that stretched as far as the eye could see. Terry and Frank went out each day, trying to decide which areas of land needed the most groundwork. Some of the areas were so flat that they could drive 70 m.p.h. across the sand plane, but other areas were so rough with holes and breaks that three bulldozers required six months to level them into tillable fields.

Terry and Frank spent much time walking across the foreboding sands in the 120-degree heat because their two-wheel drive pickup often became stuck in the sand. Terry had been raised on a farm in West Texas where he had to drive himself out of muddy roads many times, but being bogged down in sand was a different experience. They walked to the nearest tractor, sometimes very close, but more often painfully far away and used it to pull the pickup from the sand. Their work became easier when Sheikh Latif purchased a pickup with four-wheel drive for the farm.

The most important and most difficult task was breaking the ground, much of it virgin soil, to prepare it for planting. Purchasing equipment to accomplish this work was not easy for Terry. Because high-tech farming was new to Saudi Arabia, there was little, if any, farming equipment available, especially the size equipment needed to farm many sections of land. Unassembled farm equipment was brought in by boat from America and Europe. Terry had to put the machinery together before any other work could be done. Often, the machinery came without all the necessary parts and many times without users manuals to show the finished product. Terry particularly remembered struggling to assemble a disk harrow that came unassembled down to every last separate nut, bolt, and bearing. To further compound the problem, some of the workers assisting Terry in this complicated task were hardly experienced mechanics; they had never even sat behind the wheel of a car, let alone serviced one. Now they were assembling large, modern equipment that most of them had never seen. Moreover, the thought of teaching these unskilled but willing men to drive the monstrous John Deere 8640 four-wheel drive tractors gave Terry nightmares.

To complicate things further, the farm's visas for Egyptian laborers were canceled, and new visas took a long time to obtain. Terry faced the task of creating a farm with either labor borrowed from surrounding farms or workers who could be picked up on the road. By putting in long, hard hours, inexperienced laborers, on loan from another farm, and Terry were able to do most of the work themselves.

The large equipment was finally assembled and after a series of operating lessons, the tractors began to roll, breaking up the earth and molding it into tillable farm land. Following the bulldozer work, the land was deep ripped and plowed with the disk harrow, creating a fine, mellow seed bed.

I don't know if it was the bright green color of the tractors, or perhaps the smell of freshly turned earth that attracted the sheep and camels that slowly wandered out onto the freshly plowed ground only to halt in front of the tractors. Their Bedouin owners were either nowhere in sight or sitting on the sidelines watching the animals with delight. The Bedouins were as curious about the new farming operation as the Americans were about the Bedouins. Yet, curiosity didn't lead the Bedouins to help remove the animals; they did little to budge them by waving their arms or throwing clods of dirt at the animals. In their own good time, the camels and sheep would amble off to other parts of the desert. A herd of sheep could delay work for quite awhile.

A group of Syrian men had been contracted to drill for water. Thirty-eight out of the thirty-nine wells drilled the first year produced water, each averaging 850 gallons per minute; however, the pumps Terry ordered to go into the wells didn't arrive. Unable to wait any longer for the pumps to arrive, Terry had to begin dry-planting the wheat in mid-December. Finally, the first pump arrived in January and was pumping water on January 15th. The six-inch Peerless pumps were set about 350 feet underground. Ironically, the water had always been available underground for desert use if only the Saudis had possessed the technology. To add to the confusion, on one of Sheikh Latif's out-of-country visits, he hired fifteen Mexican laborers to set the pumps. The Mexicans spoke no English or Arabic, so communication consisted of body language and picture drawing. Terry continued to plant and "water up" the wheat as pumps arrived and could be set until February 26th, even though normal planting season for wheat in Saudi Arabia is from November 15 to December 20. The Saudis were skeptical about the undertaking. Some of the surrounding farmers figured the shortened growing season would not allow the wheat time to ripen adequately.

Pumping irrigation water created a new problem. Although much of the land appeared to be sandy, almost half of the thirty-five circles planted the first year had areas of heavy clay. As the center pivots made round after round, spraying water on the young wheat, the tires dug deep ruts, eventually becoming stuck in the muddy clay. During the first year, seventeen of the thirty-five pivots stuck every day. As a safety measure, when the tires were stuck, the pivot itself stopped; however, the water continued to pour for a few minutes, creating a muddy bog. Terry and the workers had to watch the pivots constantly. When one of the seventeen sticking pivots stopped, one man on the switch box walked the pivot out of the bog while a crew shoveled the tires from the mud. The only consolation, if there could be one, was that the water coming out of the ground in Saudi Arabia was warm, which helped in some small way to wash away the layers of gooey mud.

In the midst of the frantic efforts to establish a farm, Sheikh Latif purchased several thousand dollars worth of supplies and equipment from an Argentinean company that had been contracted to build a pipeline across Saudi Arabia. When the company finished the pipeline, rather than ship their equipment and remaining pipe to Argentina, they sold all that was left to Sheikh Latif. Terry's job was to move the equipment, located 150 miles away on the highway that went right through the heart of Riyadh, to the farm. Terry had reservations about hauling the equipment through traffic in Riyadh, but soon gave in to necessity and gained confidence at the wheel of a huge Kenworth truck, pulling a flatbed trailer many times through the middle of the city.

The flatbed trailer carried big pieces of equipment such as graders, bulldozers, and housing units, and large quantities of items such as wrenches, thousands of dollars worth. There were also several lifetime supplies of abrasive pads and a kind of bath soap that didn't lather. The assignment not only gave Terry confidence in driving in Saudi, but also educated him as to just how much equipment had to be imported into the country in order for a company to complete a job.

Because he was born and raised in West Texas, Terry was familiar with sandstorms; however, a Saudi Arabian sandstorm was a completely new experience. One of the worst occurred when the crew was readying the land for planting. All the tractors were working on a couple of the pivot circles at the back of the farm. It had been windy all day, and the sky had been a strange grey color. Without warning, the air filled with dirt, enveloping them in a sandstorm, the likes of which none of the newcomers to Saudi Arabia had ever seen. They were experiencing a mild form of what is known to the Bedouins as a shamal. Shamal is actually Arabic for *north*, but the word is used by the desert dwellers to describe a violent, one hundred-mile-wide sandstorm. The shamal is a rare occurrence that causes winds of more than 50 m.p.h. and haze as high as eighteen thousand feet.

The poor visibility disoriented the tractor drivers. Sensing their predicament, Terry went in his pickup to each tractor driver, and led each one from the field. The drivers could barely see the tail lights of his pickup when they were only a few feet behind him. As the last of the six tractors took its place in the line, Terry yelled for them to stay in sight of each other, as he led them slowly to what his usually good sense of direction told him was the highway. Dust flew around him and visibility was zero. Terry glanced at his watch, surprised that they had been traveling for more than an hour. After an eternity of inching forward, the storm eased, and Terry searched the landscape around him. To his dismay, he discovered he was on a neighboring farm; he had led his caravan a long distance from the highway.

It would have been unthinkable for Terry or any of the workers to work in the desert without a jug of water. Even if the water became lukewarm during the day, it still tasted wet and hydrated the body. Once when Terry and several laborers were working on a tractor, an old Bedouin approached, walking alongside a herd of camels. The man wore the traditional *thobe*, or long, caftan style dress made from white linen or gray wool. His had once been white, but was now dull with wear and grease. His hair caked with sand, the old man flashed a toothless smile. He asked in Arabic for water to drink. Hypnotized by the man's filthy appearance, Terry and the workers wondered who would offer the man a drink from his jug. Thinking no one understood Arabic, the man spotted the water jug of Mitri, one of the workers. With a deliberate stride, the old Bedouin walked over, picked up the jug, opened the spigot, placed it directly in his mouth, and drank long and hard. Then he set the jug on the ground, nodded his thanks before striding off into the desert accompanied by his camels. The men looked at Mitri, relief in their eyes that it hadn't been their jug. With a determined move, Mitri picked up the almost empty water jug, tossed it as far as he could, and began working again.

Because the daytime temperatures were so hot, work began at the farm at 5:00 A.M. Breakfast was served between 4:00 A.M. and 5:00 A.M. at Pi, nine miles from where we lived. Work continued from 5:00 A.M. until noon. Because the heat was so intense at midday, work ceased from noon until 3:00 P.M. when the heat became more bearable. Terry and the laborers worked long after dark, trying to make up for the time lost at midday.

As soon as the tractors began to run, a problem developed that could not be ignored. It was almost impossible to locate spare parts to repair the equipment when breakdowns occurred. Terry became terribly frustrated when one of the tractors broke down and a part that was needed could not be located. The replacement part might have cost only sixty cents in the States, but no amount of money could have bought it in Saudi Arabia, because it wasn't available. Al Emar began to airfreight critical equipment parts into the country, but in those early years it was difficult to anticipate which parts might be needed. The company purchaser usually took care of acquiring necessary parts, so Terry was rarely involved. Nonetheless, during our first harvest, an interesting incident occurred in the John Deere dealership in Riyadh. The dealership was much like those in the United States, except the men drank either Arabic coffee in thimble-sized cups or sweetened hot tea. Replacing the American boots and jeans were the Saudi *thobe* and *ghatra,* the traditional Saudi headdress consisting of a tight-fitting skull cap, covered by a piece of material that looked like a red-and-white-checked tablecloth. Holding the *ghatra* in place was a heavy cord, called an *'agal* and once made of goat hair, which looked like a curled fan belt.

Terry had driven in to the John Deere dealership for a special part that he needed immediately, and, of course, I went along for the ride. Terry went onto the yard and removed a part from a new combine because it was the only part available in Riyadh for his combine. Moreover, because it was Ramadan, the religious month of daytime fasting, the mechanics were working fewer hours and were not on duty.

I sat inside the dealership while Terry removed the part. I was probably the first and last woman in a dealership in Saudi Arabia. While I was waiting, two men, one behind the counter and one a customer, began arguing in Arabic. Suddenly, a fight erupted. They grabbed each other's *ghatras* and hit each other with their *'agals*. Everyone in the store shouted "Ramadan, Ramadan," reminding the others that it was not right to fight during the holy month. I interpreted it to mean, "Remember, neither one of them has had anything to eat or drink all day; their nerves are on edge." The fight was over almost before it started. I found out later that the customer was angry because he thought the spare part prices were too high. He probably had a good case because many spare parts in Saudi Arabia were sold for double their cost in the U.S.

I knew little about Ramadan before coming to Saudi Arabia, but quickly became familiar with it. Ramadan is a month when Moslems throughout the world are required to fast from sunrise to sunset. The month of Ramadan always begins and ends with the sighting of the new moon and varies from twenty-nine to thirty days. Also, because the Arabic calendar is based on the lunar year, and the lunar year moves a few days faster than the solar year, Arabic months, including the month of Ramadan, gradually move back . One hundred years of the Islamic calendar equals approximately ninety-seven years of our Gregorian calendar. Many Moslem women prefer to give their ages based on the Gregorian calendar rather than the Islamic calendar!

Fasting during Ramadan prohibits not only eating, but also drinking (any liquid!), smoking, and sex. The religious leaders carefully watch the moon to signal its beginning and then carefully watch each morning for the beginning and ending of a day. The rule: if a hair can be seen when it is held in front of the face, then it is light, and fasting begins. If the hair can't be seen, then it is still dark. People who are traveling, pregnant women, and those who are very ill are allowed to forgo the fasting, but the number of days of fasting that are missed have to be made up during the year before the next Ramadan.

After our trip to the John Deere store and because of the spare parts problem, another operation developed on the farm. It was the company store, or The Store. The Store housed all tractor and equipment parts, all of the parts that Terry had transported from the Argentine company and anything else needed to keep a farm running. Al Emar hired a precise Korean, Mr. Park, to run The Store.

Along with The Store, Sheikh Latif brainstormed another venture into being. The goal of the farm was to grow the absolute best wheat crop possible. To do so, farmers had to apply nutrients such as nitrogen, phosphorus, potassium fertilizer, and micronutrients such as iron, zinc, and copper to the virgin desert soil. To distribute these chemicals quickly, Terry needed a fertilizer injector tank to disperse the chemicals through the pivot system. Because of the shortage of these tanks, our company began manufacturing them right there on the farm. The orders for the tanks were filled so quickly that all the tanks were sold before any were allocated for our own farm. When our wheat turned yellow because it lacked nitrogen, Terry documented the deficiency with photographs that convinced Sheikh Latif of the error of selling all of the tanks. Steps were taken to remedy the situation, albeit a little late.

In later seasons, most of the chemicals and fertilizer came in bulk. At times, the enormous quantities created problems and accidents. One season, the fertilizer was delivered in trailers from Dammam, on the east coast. The Saudis had plenty of urea fertilizer because it is a by-product of the petroleum industry that is located on the east coast of Saudi Arabia. This time the fertilizer had become wet in shipment and hardened to a rocklike state. Terry devised a fertilizer crusher to pulverize the shipment. A group of Sri Lankan laborers operating the crusher pushed the fertilizer in with pieces of pipe. Unfortunately a piece of pipe fell inside the crusher and a Sri Lankan was hit in the head with a piece of flying metal. After a trip to the hospital in Al Kharj, he returned with eight stitches.

The exorbitant price of wheat constantly confirmed that we were in Saudi Arabia, and we kept a close eye on the market. In the early part of the wheat season of 1985, we had several days of uncertainty about the stability of the market. The Saudi Arabian Grain Silos and Flour Mills organization moved from the Ministry of Commerce to the Ministry of Agriculture by order of King Fahad. The King, it seems, wanted a viable solution to the glut of wheat on the Saudi market. Within a three-year period, Saudi Arabia had gone from a wheat importing Kingdom to a country with wheat reserves totaling 1.5 million metric tons. At that time, the annual consumption was only 800,000 metric tons of wheat per year.

In short, the King hoped that the Minister of Agriculture might be able to find a solution to the problem. The Minister of Agriculture, who also was the first cousin to Sheikh Latif and a graduate of Texas Tech University in Lubbock, Texas, thought he had found a solution. The Minister's proposal appeared in the 18 November edition of *ARAB NEWS*, stating that the government would pay only thirty dollars per bushel for the first two thosand metric tons of wheat production, then eighteen dollars per bushel for any wheat produced above the two-thousand-ton bench mark.

Realizing the need to diversify to offset some of the lost income, we started growing forage crops. Terry had noticed a few farms in the area growing Rhodes grass, a type of forage native to the former country of Rhodesia. The Rhodes grass added a different green color against the ocean of sand. These farms were producing for the most part only enough to feed their own animals, so Terry was convinced that only extra production would turn a profit. Sheikh Latif and Hafeez weren't readily persuaded to diversify until Terry located some low germination seed at Al Khorayef farm that could be purchased cheaply. After a quick phone call for approval to make the purchase, the first Rhodes grass was planted. The venture proved lucative, providing the farm with enough operating capital throughout the year to withstand the deferred wheat payments.

We added other hay crops such as alfalfa and baled wheat straw, which proved quite a profitable cash crop in a country where raising camels and sheep was common and dairying was frequent. Our farm averaged four to five thousand dollars daily on the sale of these crops the first year. The sale and production of the hay crops improved, and in 1987, we sold almost five million dollars of forage. Clients ranged from a Bedouin with a small herd of sheep, to buyers from the United Arab Emirates and the Ministry of Defense and Public Security, which bought the hay varieties for their horses. After the first year, the company imported the Rhodes grass seed from the United States and the Sudan, and alfalfa seed came from Riyadh.

Sometimes there was time for recreation in the desert. On the nights the men finished working early enough, they either watched videos or played ping pong or basketball. Because viewing videos was the main form of entertainment in the country, there were many video rental shops. However, the main video trade was on the black market because the Saudi government censored the films so rigidly. Movies that were considered too risqué for public distribution were brought in from Europe, the U.S., or the Orient, and distributed illegally. When we first arrived in Saudi Arabia, we sent someone the ninety miles to Riyadh to rent videos, but as the farms around us began to develop and more English speaking people came, the business boomed for videos that were delivered to the farms. It didn't matter if they understood English, the workers loved to watch American films, perhaps because it was a chance to glimpse life on the other side.

Most of the films were copied from videos belonging to American Airborne Warning and Control System (AWACS) groups. Rick, our supplier, was from England, and he worked as an airplane mechanic for Boeing by day and peddled movies after hours. He was unreliable, sometimes skipping up to six weeks at a time before returning to trade movies. On the weeks that he didn't appear, tempers flared among the workers who watched the movies. Our arrangement was that we paid him about thirty dollars a week for ten videos. Because our company furnished a video player for each farm, it also paid for the videos. Usually, when Rick brought the videos, he stayed for a cold drink and updated us on any news that he thought we'd like to hear.

On one occasion Rick arrived in a terrible mood. He had been stopped coming from Riyadh, on his way through Al Kharj, for not stopping at a red light and the police had confiscated ten boxes of videos, each containing twelve videos. We never knew what was done with the confiscated videos.

As time progressed and workers saved their money, individuals began buying their own video systems and keeping them in their rooms, planning to ship them home when they left. Many of the workers from such countries as the Philippines and Sri Lanka would never have been able to purchase a video in their home countries.

Although Saudi Arabia had one TV channel, we could not receive it on the farm. No other TV channels were allowed, and a satellite dish was illegal. For a short time, Sheikh Latif, along with twenty other Saudi families in Riyadh, owned a satellite dish. Sheikh Latif detailed to us all the different channels that were available. Within a month, the government enforced its law against satellite dishes because they were allowing communication into the Kingdom that was beyond censorship. The law, based on the Koran, is interpreted by the Ulama, the Islamic scholars in Saudi Arabia who also play a significant part in many other areas of Arabian life, including supervision of mosques and religious education, the education of girls, and scientific and Islamic research. According to the royal family, the Koran, divinely interpreted, carries greater authority than a constitution for Saudi Moslems, and is the equivalent of our law. Even when a member of the royal family installed a satellite, the Ulama demanded that he get rid of it.

It might be said that modernization was itself channeled into Saudi Arabia. In 1966, after much heated debate over the issue of introducing TV, King Abdul Aziz called a special conference in Jeddah, inviting all prominent royalty and Sheikhs. Once they were inside the palace, the King promptly removed the vehicles of all the guests from the premises and told them that if they didn't approve of the use of television, they couldn't have the use of cars. King Abdul Aziz brought Saudi Arabia abreast with the twentieth century through his introduction of modern technology and support of education. Sadly, in 1975, at the height of his reform, he was shot to death in his audience chamber by the son of a much younger half-brother. The nephew, who opposed reform, fired three shots over the shoulder of the Kuwaiti Oil Minister, whom the King was receiving.

Radio was accepted only after the founding King read the Holy Koran across the Kingdom via radio. When Ibn Sa'ud introduced the radio into Saudi Arabia in the early 1950s, he encountered great opposition from most fundamentalist religious leaders, who chose to believe that in some way a demon was controlling the airwaves. Because he knew that Moslems do not believe that a demon may speak the word of God, Ibn Sa'ud arranged for a radio station to broadcast a reading from the Koran for the skeptical religious leaders. The group was convinced, and radio came of age in Saudi Arabia.

Even though we had videos, one of the things we missed most the entire time we were in Saudi Arabia was live television. After we'd been in Saudi Arabia almost three years, the government allowed a second television channel to be added that was labeled the English channel. Although this channel only operated from 6:00 P.M. to midnight, it broadcast some live news. We watched the channel occasionally when we visited Sheikh Latif or friends in Riyadh. Most of the television programming consisted of Moslem talk shows that discussed the virtues of being Moslem or shows that had run in the U.S. about twenty years earlier. At each of the two evening prayer times, there was a break in programming, during which the viewer saw religious pilgrims walking around the holy city of Mecca.

Ironically, although virtue and integrity were touted above all else, the most popular shows on the Arabic channel were soap operas that originated in Egypt. I watched quite a few of these soap operas with Jewaher, Sheikh Latif's wife, who would condense the plots for me.

Because we were ninety miles out in the middle of the desert, I had never dreamed that it would be possible for us to receive channel 2; however, when we were at the gas station a few miles from our farm, we were shocked to see that the television there had an almost clear black and white picture of channel 2 by using a small antenna. We were ecstatic and could hardly wait to begin receiving channel 2. We were able to purchase a fairly powerful television antenna, and Gunisekera, one of our Sri Lankan electricians, mounted it on a tall pole. Cash, an American working on the pump crew, hoisted the antenna into position with the pump rig. We were able to hear a great deal of static when we turned on the TV, but could get no picture. Gunisekera, or Guny as we called him, was undaunted and refused to give up. For days, he experimented with the antenna, turning it in all directions, while I stood watching the television screen, shouting out the window when the picture improved. In Guny's home country nothing is thrown away, and everything is repaired. Long before recycling became popular in the States, Sri Lankans made their own sacks and bags from old newspapers. Guny was furious that he couldn't make the antenna work. The gas station continued to receive channel 2, but our picture never improved. We even bought another antenna and adjusted every knob on the TV.

Chapter Four

As I had done every morning since I arrived on the farm, I awoke in the dark long before the ring of Terry's alarm. Even though I had been here almost four days, jet lag continued to disturb my sleep. I wondered why Terry had thought this was a place

I could live. I was afraid to make a move alone, afraid to stay by myself as if I didn't know what steps to take next. I felt alone; in the early morning hours, I promised myself that I would become independent and brave so that I could handle this new life in a strange land.

I decided to occupy my hands, thoughts, and time with some house cleaning. Although Terry and a couple of his employees had cleaned the house before my arrival, the dust had blown since then and everything looked dirty. I didn't want to sit down anywhere for fear I'd get dirty. Although the container in which we lived was only twenty feet wide and thirty feet long, and the kitchen area was tiny, I spent all afternoon scrubbing the kitchen floor. A large, wool rug covered the small den, that was furnished with an ugly, brown, vinyl couch and a large wooden desk. Mustering all my strength, I pulled and tugged at the heavy rug until it lay in the dust, outside my front door.

Once I had the rug outside, it was too heavy to heave into the air to beat. I thought of dragging it the twenty feet to the chain link fence surrounding the camp and throwing it over the fence to beat out the dirt. My idea was useless because I couldn't lift the rug. At this point Terry and Rolando, a Filipino farm worker, drove by the house and saw me outside. They each took an end of the rug to shake. Each time Terry shook his end, the small Filipino lost his hold on the rug and fell to the ground. With each shake, a smoke-like billow came from the rug, and the air soon became thick with dust. They were able to wrestle the rug back into the house, and somehow I felt comforted that a bit of dirt had been shaken from the rug.

Sheikh Latif had promised us that everything that we needed would be furnished, including food. I had assumed that I would have food supplies from which to prepare our meals. Yet for the first year and a half, our food was prepared and served at the canteen at the other farm, where all the farm workers ate also. It was dirty, by Western standards, but in the hot temperature in the middle of the desert, the canteen seemed to be appropriate.

The cook was a Sri Lankan who was accustomed to cooking hot and spicy curries and rice. Preparing foods for Westerners, Filipinos, and even Middle Easterners was quite a challenge. The first year that we were in Saudi Arabia, our daily diet consisted of a piece of grilled beef with French fries for lunch and a grilled quarter chicken with boiled potatoes for supper. At one point we noticed the box of frozen beef was imported from India, which seemed strange since we knew that the

Hindus consider the cow sacred and do not butcher it. After closer examination, we discovered we were eating water buffalo. Each meal was accompanied by four slices of white bread. A worker brought our lunch to us from the canteen, but at night, we went to eat there with the other workers. The first night we walked in, more than fifty dark, male faces turned to look at the American woman coming to eat in their canteen. For a long time, I did not feel quite comfortable eating with the men, because I always sensed that someone was watching me.

I loved to cook before I moved to Saudi Arabia, so I missed not only the activity of cooking, but also the time it occupied in my day. For some reason, the logic that we would buy our own food and cook our own meals didn't occur to me for quite some time. I didn't know what food items were available and where to go to buy them, so I just fit into the already established farm system.

I did prepare our breakfast and an occasional treat for some of the workers. The treats became a standing tradition on the farm, and I was soon making a birthday cake for each worker on his birthday. Many of the men had come from such poor circumstances that these birthday cakes were the first ones they ever had.

During one of our phone conversations before my arrival, Terry had told me that there were utensils and pans in the kitchen, but since he hadn't cooked anything himself, he hadn't checked them very carefully. To my dismay, there were only two huge frying pans, a huge tea kettle, and a few plates and forks. Terry also neglected to tell me that the farm furnished no towels; he had purchased two towels and two washcloths. I had great difficulty coping with only one towel and one washcloth to call my own.

Another aggravating deprivation: toilet paper and napkins were not common on the farm at the time. We were furnished a type of Kleenex tissue that we used for toilet paper and table napkins, although I think we were the only ones using napkins. These tissues weren't the soft American variety. They were made in Lebanon, and even though they were micro thin, it was evident that paper is a wood by-product.

Frustrated with the little I had to work with in the kitchen, I obtained from the farm store more adequate cooking utensils. I began my cooking career in Saudi Arabia by baking cookies for some old Egyptian men. The task occupied my time, and I could see that the cookies brought joy to the existence of the men who were far away from home and family. These six men had been hired because they had been small farmers back in Egypt. The recruiting agent assumed that they would be ideal employees for a Saudi wheat farm. Most of the group had never driven a car, not to mention a tractor, and it was evident that they were not going to be able to learn the skill. These men were assigned the task of unloading the fifty-pound sacks of seed and fertilizer to be distributed to the fields. For this reason, they were usually in camp. When I came out of my house with my cookies, they stopped what they were doing and eagerly waited my approach.

One of the Egyptians was a kind, gentle man everyone called Pop. After I got to know Pop, whenever he saw me, he would give me an Arabic greeting that meant that I was just like a daughter to him. Of all the old Egyptian farmers, Pop stayed on the farm the longest time. In his last years with our company, he enjoyed practicing his old farming techniques on a plot of flood-watered watermelons that he tended. He became aggravated when a group of Saudi men from the city, or Bedouins "stole" some of his prize watermelons. To the Saudis, taking the watermelons wasn't stealing because everything in the desert had been placed there for man's survival regardless of whether the watermelons had been planted. When it came time for Pop to return home, we invited him, along with Jamal, a younger Egyptian man, to our house to eat, and I made an attempt to prepare authentic Egyptian food from recipes in my Arabic cookbook. I am not certain that the food was anything that they recognized or enjoyed, but I do know that the thought was appreciated. Pop repeatedly invited Terry and me to visit him in Egypt.

When we first moved to Saudi Arabia, the closest phone was in Al Kharj. I was always pleased when Terry had some urgent farm business that sent him into town to civilization and a phone. I wore pants on the farm, but I donned one of my two long dresses when we headed into town.

On one of our trips to Al Kharj we ate in one of the local restaurants. When we entered, the owner seemed very surprised to see a woman in his shop. I seemed properly attired, so he smiled and welcomed us. In Riyadh, women eat only in restaurants where there is a separate family section. In my first years, however, in Al Kharj I was always allowed to eat with the men because there was no family section. I think they opted to take the risk of serving a woman because it might be their only opportunity to observe an American woman.

There were no menus. The owner gestured for us to go into the kitchen to peer beneath lifted lids and inside steaming pots, simmering on an old black stove. One pot contained something that looked like spaghetti and meat, another a kind of green bean soup mixture, and a third contained a white bean soup with pieces of lamb. Although the place wasn't spic and span, it didn't look too bad. Perhaps I was lowering my standards and eager for a meal out, regardless of the hygiene.

In Arabic, Terry asked for chicken or lamb kebabs, which he thought I would enjoy. The kebabs were chunks of chicken and lamb that had been grilled on an open fire with pieces of purple onion and lots of Italian parsley. The mixture was served on top of a large flatbread, garnished with fresh tomatoes. The proprietor also served us rice, the white bean mixture, and a salad made of leaf lettuce, tomatoes, olives, and lemons. The salad, as was customary, was served without dressing. The meal was served family style, and we ate directly from the serving bowls instead of individual plates. Ice, one of the things I missed most, was nonexistent except by request in five-star-hotel restaurants in Riyadh. Unless specifically requested, drinks were served chilled but without ice.

We purchased a bottle of water to drink with our meal, and when we were finished, the owner offered us a tissue, gesturing for us to go behind the beaded partition to wash at the communal sink. The whole meal, served in the large quantities common to Saudi Arabia, cost thirty-five Saudi riyals [SR 35] or about ten dollars.

After our meal, we visited a grocery store, searching for more variety than the jars of jelly and peanut butter and the white bread that the canteen provided for our breakfast. In the three stores we visited, cleanliness was no priority. We went to three stores because each one had items that the others didn't have. I discovered later that some of the bigger stores in Riyadh looked much like the stores in the States, but in Al Kharj, I once again wondered what I was getting myself into. The shelves were lined with items that were covered in dust. Everything seemed to be in small sizes, including the tiniest box of Tide I had ever seen. Being a health conscious person, I hoped to find skimmed or low-fat milk, but it was not available. Even the powdered milk was full fat, although it tasted great when reconstituted. I discovered a Saudi version of buttermilk called *laban*. The stores sold butter, but margarine wasn't available at that time. I purchased oatmeal in a can, probably packaged that way because of the long import route and extended shelf life. Terry told me that he had once bought potato chips in a sack that he discovered were several years out of date. I noted an abundant stock of Lipton tea bags, necessary for the huge quantities of hot tea consumed in the country.

The sugar was coarsely ground, resembling little rocks and was available in a twenty-pound burlap bag. It did not make light, fluffy cakes.

During our early time in Saudi Arabia, we enjoyed many experiences in Al Kharj. On one of our trips, we happened upon a restaurant that claimed to serve Eastern and Western food. After living in the desert awhile, we began to fantasize about an American hamburger. We ordered cheeseburgers and mushroom soup. The cheeseburger proved to be a lamb patty topped with feta cheese and a side order of limp, over-boiled vegetables. The soup was a thin broth that tasted of powdered milk. I couldn't figure out how it had rated the word *mushroom* in its title. We had a relish plate with green onions, olives, lemon wedges, and a kind of parsley that looked like cilantro, but tasted bitter. I didn't complain about the meal, because at least I was off the farm for awhile.

I soon realized the significant roles that other Westerners on surrounding farms would play in our life in Saudi. We needed them for moral support, to assure us that we were not all alone in this strange land. On a farm only a few miles from us was a short, friendly fellow Texan, named Charles Vasek. He always carried fruit or candy in his pickup on which to munch, and he always shared very generously. Charles was on a farm much smaller than ours. He worked for Sheikh Saleh, who had named the farm Riyadh Farm. Charles's chief assistant was a happy Pakistani named Haneef, who idolized his friendly American boss. Haneef, invited Terry and his newly arrived wife for lunch. Hungry for both a change of diet and companionship we gladly accepted the invitation.

We were seated at a table with a plastic cloth. The flatware was placed on the plates with a Kleenex atop, serving as a napkin. The drinking glasses were turned upside down, probably to prevent flies from alighting on top. There was a Pepsi, a 7-Up, and a large bottle of water next to each glass. The Indian cook must have perceived that Americans like large quantities and many varieties of food. He served each item in salad-sized bowls, so in order to serve a bigger quantity, he brought out perhaps four bowls containing the same item. The menu included a plate of fresh onions and bell peppers, a type of pizza, fried canned lunch meat, fish sticks and fried fish, boiled eggs, canned corn with lots of sugar, fried potatoes, macaroni with meat, English peas, boiled cauliflower, sliced beets, and buttered bread. For dessert we had chocolate ice cream, an unheard of treat in the desert, coconut cookies and an Egyptian sweet. Almost all of the items were certainly prepackaged American food, but they all tasted good and reminded me of American school cafeteria food.

After we had eaten, several of Charles's Filipino workers dropped in to meet the American woman. One of the men had a camera, and each man posed next to me to have his picture made. They agreed that I looked just like Julie Andrews. I knew I didn't look a bit like her; she was probably one of the few Western actresses whose name they could remember. The Filipinos were very disappointed that we didn't have our camera so that we could reciprocate and take their pictures, something that I learned was an important gesture. Earlier in the day Charles had picked a large leaf from a date palm in Al Kharj and to ham up the scene, he sat in a chair, eating a banana, the Indian cook fanning him with the large green leaf. The Filipinos took several pictures and seemed relieved to see that Americans also had a sense of humor.

Also offering diversion from the mundane life on the farm were Sheikh Latif's parties for friends, family, and business associates. Before a party, the farm was thrown into a frenzy of mad preparations. Although by the time we left Saudi most of his parties were catered from Riyadh (a sign of Sheikh Latif's growning prominence there), during my first years there, the entire meal was prepared on the farm. During those years, one of Terry's jobs included going to a farm nearby to purchase a lamb or goat for each party. We Westerners termed this party highlight the "goat grab," because the goat or lamb was served whole, and the men sat around the animal, grabbing off pieces of meat with their right hands.

Once, before a party, I was able to accompany Terry to the sheep farm. Sheep in Saudi Arabia are very different from any that I've ever seen before. Because of the enormous amount of thick, matted wool all over their bodies, the animals seem much larger than their counterparts in the U.S.

When we approached the farm, the Palestinian sheep herder ran to meet us, anticipating some long-needed conversation. He and Terry spoke a few words of the traditional Arabic greeting and began bargaining and bickering over the price of the sheep.

Bargaining is a way of life in Saudi Arabia. Except in grocery stores, no items are marked with a price; the price is almost always subject to negotiation. The seller sets the price outlandishly high, knowing that the buyer wants the price to go extremely low. The bickering sometimes continues for hours and is flavored with such propaganda as "you're my friend," and "only for you will I make this price." Many Westerners, un-skilled in the art of bargaining, accept the high prices and although the shopkeeper is happy to make a good profit, he always appears disap-pointed at the absence of bargaining.

When the sheep transaction was completed, the man approached Terry, and talking very fast, invited us to stay for coffee and tea. Because Terry was always in a hurry to return to the farm, he declined. I would have enjoyed the adventure of sharing tea with the old shepherd, al-though I might have questioned the cleanliness of his utensils, a prob-lem I soon learned to ignore. Terry secured the sheep in the back of our pickup, despite a bleat of protest, and we drove back across the desert.

Fridays were much like our Sundays in the U.S. Although the men on the farm worked on Friday morning, Terry released the men early enough in the afternoon to wash their clothes. Brightly colored clothes decorated our camp fence; underwear and socks dried in only a few minutes. It was somehow discontenting and difficult to have only one free afternoon a week and to adjust to the monotony of every other day. I worried about the laborers who did the same thing day after day, with no variance. In my last years in Saudi, most workers had the entire day off on Fridays, but before then, there was too much work for anyone to take off more than one afternoon a week. I longed for two-day week-ends, to go to the movies and dine out, or just to be lazy and irresponsible.

My first Friday in Saudi Arabia, Terry treated me to a break in the routine by driving us to the far side of the farm. I discovered a beauty about the land that I hadn't known to exist. Our farm was actually in a valley, surrounded by a caprock similar to that in West Texas. With our four-wheel-drive pickup, we climbed the seemingly sheer rock hill to reach the top of the caprock. From the top, we had a beautiful view. We could see clearly for miles, all the way to the shining steel fence of our camp. The pivots looked like green circles, neatly positioned in a row. Farms surrounded us, and to the back, we saw small camps of Bedouins, who were probably the owners of the camels and sheep that wandered in front of the tractors. On the rocky caprock across from us, two Bedouin men alighted from their old Toyota pickup to begin the afternoon prayer, kneeling on the ground, careful to face east towards Mecca. I wanted to capture this moment, a moment when I was catapulted back to Biblical times. The sights eased my anxiety over the impending weeks of the monotony and Terry's almost ceaseless labor on the farm.

Despite our distance from civilization, the farm was part of a sophisticated Saudi company, Al Emar. Although Sheikh Latif owned Al Emar, the actual power force behind it was Hafeez Khan, from Pakistan. Hafeez was tall, handsome, and had been born to rich and influential parents in a country where ninety percent of the population is illiterate. We couldn't understand his subtle aloofness, nor his blatant arrogance toward the workers, until we came to know the caste system that existed in Pakistan, separating the wealthy and extreme poor by a gulf of disproportionate benefits. While the poor struggled to survive, the rich lived in opulence with servants who were members of the poor class, doing such tasks as driving, cleaning, cooking, and watching the children. In Pakistan, many of the poor worked for room and board.

Being an aristocrat in a caste system, Hafeez expected the same treatment in Saudi Arabia that he received in Pakistan, and he received it. It was hard to comprehend, especially in a country where almost everyone was a foreigner. Yet the camaraderie among the foreign population in Saudi Arabia, regardless of affluence or position, did not touch Hafeez's cool exterior. Terry realized that despite any feelings Sheikh Latif had for him, Hafeez ultimately controlled whether Terry had a job. Hafeez had such charisma that although there were times that I longed to give him a piece of my mind, the minute I was in his presence, I melted under his gaze. Yet he was always friendly to me, perhaps because I was an American.

Having heard about Hafeez from Terry, I was apprehensive about meeting him, especially when I heard that he would be accompanied by his wife. We were invited to eat with them one evening soon after I arrived at the farm and the food was to be prepared by the canteen staff. I wasn't sure whether Hafeez's wife might speak any English. Terry had never met her or heard anything about her. I also wasn't sure whether to dress in Western clothes or to wear one of my two long dresses. At the last minute I opted to wear pants.

Dhahara Khan, Hafeez's wife, was the first woman I met after my arrival. Dhahara spoke fluent English, and was intelligent, warm and friendly. She explained that she was from a wealthy Pakistan family and despite being a Moslem, had attended a Catholic Convent school for ten years. I learned later that most of the wealthy send their children to Catholic schools in Pakistan, specifically to learn English. Unlike most Moslem women, she wore her dark, thick hair very short and uncovered. She dressed in a typical Pakistani outfit. The midcalf-length dress was split up to above the knee, covering a coordinating pair of loose pants that tapered and fit at the ankle. She wore tall, high heels and her toenails were painted a bright red. I noticed that Hafeez was dressed in pajama-like, loose fitting clothing, similar in style to Dhahara's clothes. Later I learned that all Pakistani men like to lounge in this attire, and many wear it to work because it is so comfortable.

When the dinner arrived, we sat on a worn carpet on the floor in a room in the management quarters at P1. As we drank hot tea and conversed, Hafeez and Dhahara seemed to know much more about America than I would ever know about Pakistan, probably because one of Dhahara's sons was studying in Atlanta, Georgia. I learned later that Dhahara was several years older than Hafeez and that she had three children from a previous marriage—not uncommon, but surely not the norm for Moslem women. As I had never seen him do before, the cook took on an air of complete submission, entering the room with head bowed to announce that dinner was ready. We ate in the next room where the food lay on the plastic tablecloth on the floor. No amount of practice ever taught Terry what to do with his long legs when sitting on the floor.

I had looked forward to this meal because I hoped to vary our staple diet of beef and French fries for lunch and a chicken and boiled potatoes for supper. When I saw the food on the tablecloth, I realized that the cook had no special food with which to work. Carrots were the only novel addition to our meal of chicken and traditional boiled potatoes. With our four slices of white bread, we had a half a stick of butter per person. For a treat, our dessert was canned pineapple. During the meal, we discussed typical Pakistani food, which our guests described as very hot and greasy.

As the traditional hot, sweet tea was served, with the milk that the Pakistanis favored, I listened with incredulity as Dhahara asked if I would like a cigar. She then proceeded to smoke one herself. Hafeez watched for my reaction, and somehow I was able to mask my surprise. Dhahara was not the quiet, submissive Moslem woman whom I had envisioned. She graciously offered to take me shopping in Riyadh, suggesting that we be friends in this lonely country. She seemed sincere at the time, but it didn't take me long to realize that her offer reflected the practiced cordiality that the moment and her upbringing called for. Our shopping trip never occurred in the five years we were in Saudi Arabia.

Chapter Five

By the middle of January, I decided
Terry had been crazy for suggesting that I bring a winter coat and warm
clothes. Daily temperatures had been mild. Then one morning we awoke
to a cold, stiff wind. We had always taken for granted the television
weather report that was available with the flip of a switch. Lacking this,
we became Bedouins, reading the sky and the changing wind, guessing
when the weather was about to change. The wind and cold and a pivot
catastrophe occurred at about the same time, although the two were actually unrelated.

All the pivots of wheat were numbered to make identification easier,
and on this windy morning the Filipino electrician, Efren, was on his
rounds checking and servicing the pivots. He discovered that number 28,
a half pivot that was next to a neighboring farm, had not stopped running as programmed and had crashed into a pivot on the next farm. The
two pivots appeared welded together. The water continued to run, and
Efren got stuck in the muddy mess. We happened along in time to see
Efren with his pants rolled up, standing in the mud, surveying the predicament. Terry's pickup became stuck when he tried to pull Efren
from the mud. After a nearby tractor happened on the scene and pulled
us out, we headed for Al Kharj, with mud flying, to use the phone to report the pivot accident. However, in incidents to come, Terry learned
that the Head Office, Sheikh Latif and Hafeez, didn't really want to be
involved with the daily farm problems. They wanted to hear about the
problems after they were solved.

The trip in to use the phone provided another opportunity to sample
a lunch that came to be one of our favorites in Al Kharj. On the highway
outside of Al Kharj, we passed a small bakery next to a tiny grocery
store: the bakery made *khubz*, Arabic flatbread. The bakery also made
a roll shaped like a hotdog bun but pointed on each end. The yeast
dough had been formed into the cylinder shapes and was rising on huge

metal pans, ready to be baked. Since it was almost lunch time, the bakers were baking and the fresh aroma permeated the air. The Turkish baker slid the pans into a round opening in the wall, where a brick-tiled oven with roaring temperatures baked the bread. The oven held quite a few of the large pans. When the bread had baked, the loaves were turned upside down and allowed to cool on long, uncovered wooden tables. When we arrived, there were at least two hundred of the rolls, already baked and packaged. We took a package that was still warm. The baker charged us one riyal (29 cents). We walked next door to buy a can of cheese from France, a popular item in a country where refrigeration hasn't been around very long. Our drink was an orange juice from Japan that had bits of real orange in it. I felt that the meal was superbly intercontinental and quite delicious.

I hadn't been on the farm two weeks before Midwess extended an invitation to dinner. He assured Terry that I needed to eat with the men rather than sit in seclusion with the women. In keeping with Bedouin tradition, the men ate from a large platter of either lamb or chicken and rice. The women and children ate what was left, from the same platter. Handicapped in a world where I didn't know any customs or speak the language, I felt secure in sticking next to Terry and eating with the men.

I wore one of my long dresses for the occasion. Midwess's three tents were at the back of the farm, farther than the newly constructed roads extended. After bouncing over dips and bumps across the sandy desert, we came upon his camp. I feared that Terry would lose his way in the dark once we had left the security of the pivot landmarks, but he and Frank had visited the camp many times and had no difficulty locating it. As we approached, the men around the campfire stood and greeted us in the typical Arabic greeting, shook our hands warmly, and motioned us to sit on the carpet next to the fire. Grouped around us were Midwess; his two brothers; Tamime and Abdallah; his two sons, Mohammed, about nine, and Abdallah, about three; and Mama, Midwess's mother. Mama had the privilege of sitting with the men because she was the oldest in the family and seemed to be greatly respected by the others. The males, including the boys, were all in traditional Saudi dress.

Because I had never been this close to a Saudi Bedouin woman, I took careful note of Mama's attire. A bright red, long dress peeked from under her floor length, black shawl, called an *abaya*, and when she sat cross-legged, I noticed a pair of brightly colored long pants showing beneath her dress in the dim light of the camp fire. Also, I could see her weathered and toughened feet clad in rubber thong sandals. Her head was completely covered and she wore the typical Bedouin black veil, showing only her eyes. Although the Saudi women in the cities completely covered their faces; Bedouin women, who actually work at herding sheep, choose to wear the veil that shows their eyes, affording them better vision.

Mama kissed me on each cheek through her veil. On later visits, after we got to know each other, she would lift it up to touch her lips to my cheek. The men motioned us to sit down and lean on two arm rests constructed of vinyl-covered oblong blocks. Terry and I leaned on one, and Frank shared another with Midwess.

After we were seated, Midwess began the coffee ritual. With his right hand he swished tiny, handleless cups in a small brass bowl filled with water. Then he poured some green coffee beans into a tiny aluminum skillet and shook them over the fire to roast them. Next he pounded the roasted beans in a heavy brass mortar with a pestle, called a *neggar*, invading the silence of the lonesome desert with his musical clanging. He closed his eyes, swaying to the music and opening them on occasion to grin at us. At last, he poured the crushed beans into a large brass coffee pot with a long, pointed spout. He poured water into the brass coffee pot from a metal teapot with a blackened bottom, which magically passed at exactly the right moment from behind the tent flap. At this moment I realized that there were other people present besides those around the fire. From the direction from which the hot water appeared, I glimpsed a pair of eyes peeking out from a veil.

My interest returned to the preparation of the coffee. Setting the brass vessel next to the fire, Midwess took a few cardamom seeds, pounded them in the mortar, and dumped them into the coffee mixture. After pressing a piece of palm leaf fiber into the pointed spout, he began to pour coffee into the tiny cups that he had swished in the water. I read that in the past the Bedouins used camel hair to strain the coffee, but now they used palm leaves. Only Frank, Terry, Midwess, and I were given coffee, probably because there were only four cups. The coffee had an herbal taste, that I later learned to identify as cardamom.

Midwess insisted that we have three cups of the potent mixture. After the third cup, Terry and Frank handed their cups back to Midwess, shaking their cups in the exchange. I learned later that it is proper to drink at least three cups of coffee and to signal enough by jiggling or shaking the cup.

Midwess placed the cups in the original washing water, adding four tiny glass mugs to the water, and washed each one individually in the now crowded bowl. I knew that these little cups would be used for the hot, sweetened tea. After we were served our steaming tea, Midwess quietly passed cups of coffee to the others gathered around the fire. There was little conversation during the coffee and tea ceremony. The silence was reflective, a time for each of us to be lost in his or her own thoughts, perhaps to imagine what life might be like if we traded places. We shared a communal bowl of delicious dates from local date palm trees. The natives tossed the seeds out into the desert.

Prompted by a signal from behind the tent flap, Midwess ushered us from around the fire to inside the tent. A plastic tablecloth lay on the ground, with food already assembled on it. The rice was still steaming, so the food must have just been placed there by the unseen hostess. Mama did not eat with us. I wondered what the other men thought about this American woman, whom they had never seen before, eating with them.

A large platter piled high with rice and large pieces of boiled lamb sat in the middle of the cloth. Scattered around the edge of the tablecloth were cans of Pepsi and Mirinda, an orange soda similar to Orange Crush. The cans retained a slight coolness; Midwess had driven to the gas station prior to our arrival to purchase them for this special occasion. Smiling, he pulled out three large tablespoons and handed them to us. Terry had always eaten with his right hand when visiting Midwess before, so I decided that my presence was the reason for the spoons. We shook our heads, choosing instead to eat with our right hand, Saudi style. The three Bedouins skillfully pulled the meat from the bone in a quick motion, and tossed it to the section of the tray where we were gathered. I watched as they expertly pressed the rice into a small ball in their right fist and popped it into their mouths. I was less skillful at this task, an art I decided must require lots of practice. The lamb was rather tough, but the rice had a pleasing flavor, having been cooked in the lamb's broth.

We ate the meal in great haste with little discussion. It was as if the men thought a vulture was going to swoop down at any minute and devour the food. I barely had the hang of getting some rice from the platter to my mouth when the men began to rise. I discovered later that it is the norm for Saudis to eat fast. We followed Midwess outside the periphery of the camp where he had a small box of Tide and a kettle of warm water. With a big grin, he said, Tide, having been told by Terry that this box also was called Tide in America. He poured a small amount of the soap powder into our hands and as we rubbed them together, he poured a stream of the warm water from the tea kettle over them. We shook our hands in the air to dry as we returned to the edge of the fire. In keeping with tradition, we had the coffee, followed by the tea once again.

As if on signal, Abdallah, Midwess's brother, went over to the four hobbled camels that Midwess owned and milked the largest of the four. He brought the milk back in a large blue plastic bucket. Two inches of foam covered the top of the milk. Taking two metal bowls similar to what the cups had been washed in, he poured the bowls full of the foamy milk. Midwess passed the bowl first to me, even though I was a woman. It was thoughtful of him to allow me to sample the milk first, even though tradition dictated that a woman should be last. Terry told me to drink right from the bowl. I had decided ahead of time that I was going to drink the camel's milk if for no other reason than I wanted to tell people back home that I had tasted it.

Perhaps this decision gave me the enthusiasm to put both hands around the bowl, turn it up to my mouth, and drink heartily. The liquid was slightly warm with a rich taste, almost like evaporated milk. As I lowered the bowl, all eyes were on me to read my reaction. I smiled and using one of the few Arabic words I knew, said, *"quayis"* (good). The three Saudi men breathed a sigh of relief, happy that one of their favorite drinks had been accepted by this American woman. Midwess passed the bowl to Terry and then to Frank. Midwess took a long drink, and said in Arabic that camel's milk gives you lots of brains. The other men drank, and although Mama had once again joined our circle, she did not drink from the bowl. I guessed that it wouldn't have been possible to drink and keep her face completely hidden. After everyone had a drink, Midwess took a date and smiling, dipped it in the foam from the milk, popping it in to his mouth. After observing Midwess partake of several foam-dipped dates, we all followed suit and were pleasantly surprised by the tasty combination of flavors.

As the evening progressed, I discovered how much Arabic Terry spoke and understood. Midwess loved playing the role of the teacher, pointing out an object and asking Terry whether he knew the Arabic word for it. We all laughed when Midwess said the few English words that he knew, Tide being the most understandable. Glancing up into the starry night, Midwess pointed and said, *"Aqrab."* Terry's face registered surprise because

Midwess had pointed to the constellation Scorpio and had said the Arabic word for scorpion. Terry had already learned this Arabic word since the insect was in such abundance in his new desert home. We hadn't suspected that these isolated Bedouins would know the names for the constellations and how to identify them. Of course, the Bedouins have probably spent a lifetime under the stars in quiet contemplation of the heavens, perhaps using the stars to traverse the oceanlike desert.

After exchanging a few quiet words, Midwess and Mama decided that I should be taken behind the tent flap to meet the yet unseen women. Mama had a firm grip on my arm, steering me behind the flap. There I found two women, both dressed similarly to Mama, both wearing the traditional Arabic veil. They kissed me on each cheek, somewhat more hesitantly than Mama had, yet with what I sensed to be genuine hospitality. We exchanged the traditional Arabic greeting, and they launched into a one-sided conversation in Arabic while I pretended to listen intently.

I guessed that one woman was Midwess's wife, because little Abdallah clung to her skirt. She was short and seemed tiny even with all the layers of clothes. The other woman, Midwess's sister, was much larger and taller. Although we never knew the complete story, this sister had never married and was doomed to a life as a spinster. She lived with Midwess and his family and herded his flock of sheep. Most educated Saudi women marry at least by age twenty; most Bedouin women are married much earlier. After an exchange of words that I did not understand, Mama steered me out of the tent to the camp fire. As we prepared to leave, Midwess tried to persuade Terry that we should spend the night. The dialogue continued several minutes, Terry and Midwess both knowing that we would not stay, but both enjoying the thought of these Americans sleeping out in the desert with the Bedouin family.

On the ride home, I reflected on our evening in the desert, amazed at the depth of communication between members of two such different cultures who barely spoke the other's language. After my visit behind the flap of the tent, Mama had whispered something to Midwess and he spoke for her, repeating her words to say that she would make me a long dress. I smiled and told Terry to ask her if I might come some day to visit her and the other women. I sensed that my request produced smiles on the all of the veiled faces, because Mama repeated loudly and rapidly, *"Aiwa, aiwa"* (yes, yes). I'm sure the women were happy that I wanted to know more about them and learn their culture, and that they also wanted to find out more about this strange American woman who ate with men and covered neither her face nor head.

Mama also had asked how long we had been married. When she discovered we had been married more than three years, she was aghast that we didn't have at least one baby. She even wondered whether we had left our babies back in America with my mother. "Baby" and "Mama" must be universal because I clearly understood her asking about my baby and my mother.

I understood her question because the Saudi woman's main purpose is to produce children, and failure is legal grounds for divorce. Most Saudi women have a baby at least one year after marriage. The entire time that we were in Saudi Arabia, the local population thought it was very strange that we had not produced a child in several years of marriage. When I explained that we had delayed having children because I had been starting a career, I was met with uncomprehending stares. Most Saudi women accepted no excuse for being childless. When I tried to explain that we were going to wait to have a baby until we returned to the States, they once again shook their heads, amazed that I would delay fulfilling my most important purpose in life.

After the baby discussion, Midwess insisted jokingly that Terry get himself a Bedouin wife as men are allowed to have four wives in Saudi Arabia. Later, I often heard Midwess teasing his wife, Rashmi, that he was going to get another wife; I saw that she was not amused by the joke.

Chapter Six

Although daily I felt somewhat more comfortable in my new home, there were several things that I felt might make my life more pleasant. About this time, I learned of a Saudi-based American who was on vacation in the United States in a town very close to my hometown in Texas. I immediately called my parents to ask them to assemble a care package for me, and transport it to this gentleman to deliver to me on his return to Saudi Arabia.

To contact my parents, I had to go to the phone center in Al Kharj. I had become accustomed to going with Terry to the villa of Saeed al-Doussary, a Saudi friend of Sheikh Latif, to borrow a phone to call the office in Riyadh. Placing an international call was another matter, and one of my most memorable early experiences in Saudi Arabia. We traveled to Al Kharj to a small building from where Terry had called me during our six months apart.

Terry approached the desk manned by three Arabic men and began carefully writing in Arabic my parents' phone number. We had both learned Arabic numbers so that we could price items in the grocery store and read critical signs. One man grabbed the piece of paper and quickly repeated the numbers, much too fast for me to understand, but Terry nodded his agreement. We were then instructed to wait. I was sent to the women's waiting room, and Terry joined the men.

Inside the women's room I sat among several older Saudi women, completely veiled, who had several children surrounding them. Because I knew very little Arabic, we exchanged only the obligatory greeting. There were several phone cabins, each containing a receiver that hung on the wall. One of the three men, after he had placed the call, would shout the number in Arabic and the number of the booth where the call would ring. The caller would make a mad dash to the booth to catch the phone as it rang. While these announcements were made, other Saudis were talking on the phone, shouting loudly into the receiver, as if their party could only hear and understand if the message was transmitted loudly. When my number was called, the man thoughtfully added the word, "Sister," a sign of respect for an adult female. I flew to the booth and began yelling, "Hello, Hello," praying to be able to hear my parents eight thousand miles away. To my delight, I could hear them above the low roar of the crowd in the phone center.

Shouting along with the rest of the callers, I explained that a man by the name of Karl Kemp would soon return to nearby Riyadh Farm from vacation in Kress, Texas, a town about two hours from my parents. I wanted items that were probably available somewhere in Saudi Arabia, but I didn't know where to find them or who to ask. I needed a fly swatter, my own pillow, a couple of nonstick pans, a muffin pan, towels, and soft toilet paper. My mother packed the items in a duffel bag, and she and my father drove through a hazardous snowstorm to deliver the items to Karl the day before he was to fly to Saudi. When the items arrived, I felt it was Christmas. I realized how the simple life in the desert could make even the smallest of what I had deemed necessities seem luxurious.

We soon became good friends with Karl. On the first Friday evening after Karl returned to Saudi, we decided to go to Riyadh to dine in a restaurant and experience a bit of urban luxury.

In Riyadh we searched for a Chinese food restaurant where Karl remembered eating once before. Riyadh had no street signs; the landmarks all looked the same; many streets were torn up, and the detours were often impossible mazes. We searched for the Chinese place for two hours, all the time becoming more confused. Karl could not locate the restaurant.

After the long drive and the two-hour search, I was in desperate need of a bathroom. I knew from experience that public toilets are few in a land where, not too many years before, the desert had been an open bathroom. Several times in Al Kharj, I had used an obscure vacant lot during an emergency, but felt that Riyadh was a little too sophisticated and populated for such an undertaking. Luckily, we passed a long shop area and I spotted a sign that said TOILET. Inside the rest room the stench emitting from the typical hole, flush with the ground, was sickening. There was no toilet paper, only the traditional water hose, but the relief was worth the discomfort.

When our hunger compelled us to abandon our seach for the Chinese restaurant, we tried to find a pizza restaurant Terry had once seen. Only then did we stumble onto Karl's Chinese food restaurant. Once inside, I felt as if I were in another world. The Oriental waiters were extremely polite and friendly, and the other patrons looked to be either British or European. I discovered that Chinese food is a specialty in Riyadh, an expensive specialty, with our meal totaling forty-five dollars. I learned though that the meal wasn't expensive compared to those in hotel restaurants in Saudi Arabia. Most hotel buffet meals cost more than thirty dollars per person.

After a sumptuous meal, Terry suggested a stop at what he called the best grocery store in Riyadh. Having only visited the dusty grocery stores in Al Kharj, I was elated at the prospect. Eura-Marche, the grocery store, was patterned after a European supermarket, stocking mostly European brands. The large building contained varieties of groceries and was surrounded by stores selling clothes, pets, plants, bakery goods, and crepes made on the premises.

I wanted to buy some curtains to replace the old towels I had nailed over my windows. When I discovered that one long panel sold for one hundred dollars, I changed my mind. Later, I learned that most curtains within the Kingdom are handsewn by tailors from India. I did buy a dustpan and dish drainer, which I had been unable to find before. Karl bought some beef for $8.30 per pound. After living in the desert awhile, price becomes secondary to craving. In this crowded store, full of Saudis buying foreign goods, my last purchase was powdered skim milk from France.

Unable to find everything we wanted in Eura-Marche, we went to Panda, a Saudi grocery chain that was much smaller and more friendly. We hoped to find pinto beans or other Mexican food products but decided such goods hadn't yet found their way to Saudi Arabia. I was happy to find cornmeal, an item not in demand in Saudi Arabia. The Saudis never cook with cornmeal, and only a small percentage of the American working population there uses it. When thoughts of early work hours entered our minds, our adventure ended all too soon for me, and we returned to the farm at 12:30 A.M.

Each day on the farm began to seem identical to the previous day, and although I had been hired to work on the farm's computer, the computer hadn't yet arrived. I began to wonder if my entire stay in Saudi Arabia would be spent riding with Terry in the pickup from task to task. At this time, I inherited a job from Terry, who was required to keep records of how many hours each man worked.

From the beginning Terry tried to convince our company that paying a man a basic salary, rather than an hourly rate, was best in farming because the long hours and work tend to be seasonal. However, a couple of years passed before the concept caught on. The task of recording and making receipts for all the hourly wages fell to me because I had no other job.

In the beginning, the men were paid for a basic eight-hour day but were glad to be able to work extra hours for overtime pay. That first year, Terry felt that they were always behind, so he worked the men overtime almost every day. Everyone shared in the consternation when January's payroll arrived, but failed to include any overtime pay for the month. The oversight united managers and workers. The management decided to go in force to Riyadh to protest.

When the men were ready to depart, I noted the absence of several managers. The only ones braving the encounter were the four Americans and Robin Branbury, from England. I suspected that the other managers didn't join because they weren't accustomed to a system that guarantees their right to protest, or they didn't really feel any personal connection to the problem because they were not eligible themselves to receive overtime pay. I didn't go inside the inner office with the group. Terry reported that the confrontation was curt, and although Hafeez finally agreed to pay the overtime, he intimated that if the management ever again chose to fight against the head office for the laborers, they would be fired.

We later learned that strikes or any kind of rebellion in Saudi Arabia is illegal. One farm did not pay their laborers for more than four months. But when the laborers refused to work, the management called in the police, who took the men to jail. I wondered whether we would have been quite so bold if we had known this earlier. Nonetheless, the incident seemed to convince the workers that management was their advocate.

In time, Terry convinced Hafeez to change several farm labor policies. Terry and Hafeez worked together to change policy regarding salaries, the number of people required for the farm work, vacations, and work schedules. Terry struggled to demonstrate that a farm runs more in cycles, requiring more hours during peak work seasons and fewer during the off season. It took another year of cajoling to convince the head office to give the workers a fixed salary that would be adequate to cover any overtime that they might work.

The change dramatically improved the work ethic on the farm. No longer did the men toil through a day, stretching out each job to receive the coveted overtime. The head office was afraid that the men would be lazy if such a policy was instigated. Instead, they performed more adequately, in much less time. The men knew if they completed their job for the day, they were finished.

I soon realized that there was a fair amount of free enterprise going on around our farm. One Filipino on Karl's farm made a sizable income from washing clothes during his afterwork hours. Telex earned the name Washington because he washed everyone's clothes. Telex liked to brag that he supported two wives and families back in the Philippines. Because divorce is illegal in the Philippines, he explained that if a man and woman could no longer get along, then the couple could simply stop living together and start living with someone else. Quite a few of our Filipino workers lived under this arrangement. Telex contracted to do everyone's laundry, washing it by hand in a bucket with a brush. Surprisingly, the finished product looked pretty good, considering the conditions. I was thankful that I had a washing machine, the only one for miles around at that time.

At the end of January, I was invited to meet some "city Saudis" who were vacationing in the country. They were Karl's boss's family, who had arrived to spend the two-week period between school semesters called "spring vacation." Karl's boss, Sheikh Saleh, a relative to Sheikh Latif, extended the invitation to me when Terry visited him at Riyadh Farm to discuss fertilizer.

Because I finally had somewhere to go, I got up extra early to go out to jog around the pivots. When I first arrived in Saudi Arabia, Terry and I had decided that I should not jog because I might become lost in the desert. Nonetheless, because the new wells and pivots required many hours of maintenance the first year, I was able to improvise a risk-free jogging routine that earned me a reputation throughout all the farms in our area. While Terry and some of the laborers worked to maintain or repair a pivot, I would jog a track-like circle around it, developing blisters at first, because I was unaccustomed to running in the soft sand. If any of the workers passed me, they would stop to offer me a ride. Terry was asked constantly where was I running, why hadn't he given me a ride, and when was I going to get there so that I could stop running. I became known as the crazy American woman who ran around and around the pivots.

After I became familiar with the area, I began jogging on my own, early in the morning. My morning jogs gave me an opportunity to watch the daily progression as the sand turned to green with the emergence and growth of the planted wheat.

On the morning I was to meet the Saudi women, I returned from my run to discover that we were out of water and that instead of a shower, I would have to take a "spit bath," using our drinking water. We were always running out of water because our camp population had outgrown the small holding tank from which water was pumped into the housing units. If a large quantity of water was used before the well was turned on to fill the tank, then we would be out of water. This always seemed to happen to me when I was in camp alone. Now I wonder why I never learned to operate the well myself.

Actually, on this particular morning, I was lucky that I had to contend only with being out of water. Not only did we have to pump our own water supply, we also operated our own generator. And just as we had outgrown our water storage, we had also overloaded the camp generator. The air conditioners in our home were 220 volt, but the wall outlets were 110; therefore, I didn't have to replace my blow dryer or other electrical appliances that I brought with me. The first year on the farm, with all the air conditioners running on high during the day, the temperamental generator overheated and shut off. When this happened, I was always the only person in camp. Terry always knew when he approached our house if the generator had stopped because I would be sitting on the porch, fuming in heat and anger. The loss of my shower on the morning of my visit was, by comparison, only a minor setback.

As we neared the back of Riyadh Farm, I saw the campground of the visiting family. In order to "camp out," the visiting family had erected big, beautiful tents, complete with patterned material on the inside walls, along with Persian rugs, scattered armrests, and even generated power. Terry stopped to let me out a good distance from the tents so that he wouldn't risk seeing one of the women's faces. I climbed out of the pickup hesitantly, as Terry promised to return for me.

When I stepped inside the tent, I saw a huge brass pedestal containing hot coals. The women were grouped around the warmth of the coals because it was mid-January, and the winter temperatures were only nearing seventy degrees. There were four women in the tent, three of whom spoke English, but in the course of the day, I met about a dozen women. There also were several young girls and boys who wandered in and out. The smallest children were bundled up in such warm, tight-fitting clothing that I wondered how they were breathing.

One of the oldest women was berating one of the house girls in a long stream of Arabic. One of the women who spoke English felt compelled to explain to me that the woman was chastising the girl because after the dinner the day before, the clean-up person had dumped the leftover food in the garbage instead of feeding it to the sheep. My translator smiled and said that the older woman believed that Allah was going to be angry at them for being wasteful.

The women were friendly, and one of the three women who spoke English introduced me to each newcomer as she entered the tent. Once they were inside the tent, the women dropped their veils, feeling secure that no man would enter the women's tent without being announced. As the women exited the tent, they were careful to veil, even though they were well away from the camp.

The women kept scarves loosely wrapped around their necks, readily available if they needed to shield their faces quickly. They fidgeted constantly with the scarves, giving me ample opportunity to observe their hands. Most of the women's palms were stained a reddish-orange color. Later, I learned that the stain came from henna, which they put in the palms of their hands when they went to bed. In bed they would clench their fists together tightly all night, and the henna would stain both their palms and the tips of their fingernails. The women wore pantaloons underneath their long dresses and several wore flannel-like warm-up pants beneath their dresses. Before coming to Saudi Arabia, I had read that it was impolite to point the bottom of one's shoe or foot at another person while sitting in a chair with one foot crossed over the knee of the other leg. I had no cause for concern because everyone was sitting on the floor, so the rule obviously didn't apply.

Two of the three women who spoke English were named Nora, so I differentiated them in my mind as Nora-number-one and Nora-number-two. Nora-number-one was one of Sheikh Saleh's uncle's two wives. The second wife was in the tent also. She taught English at the women's university in Riyadh and had received her training in England. Nora-number-two was a sister to Sheikh Saleh and was pregnant. She had learned English when she and her husband lived in Denver, Colorado, where he had studied. Because women are not allowed to drive a car in Saudi Arabia, she was proud of the fact that she had driven a car from Arizona to California when they lived in the States. Her husband owned a supermarket between Jeddah and Mecca, and they were there visiting relatives in the Riyadh area.

The last English-speaking woman was a large, talkative woman, about twenty-five to thirty years of age, named Loaf. Her husband was one of Sheikh Saleh's brothers, who was studying to be an electrical engineer in Connecticut, and they were home on vacation. Perhaps her willingness to talk was because she had lived in the States for three years.

The women began to feed questions to Loaf to ask me. Also they commented on the whiteness of my skin, especially my hands. They were curious why I didn't have a baby after being married so long. The atmosphere was very relaxed as the women lounged around in their long dresses and bare feet, their sandals having been shed at the door. In front of us were bowls filled with sunflower seeds, pumpkin seeds, and pistachio nuts, all in the shells, and the women ate with nervous energy. There were also candy bars and bakery cookies. I was surprised when the hot, sweetened tea was served in the same little glass mugs that we'd had at Midwess's tent. Until this time I had supposed that Midwess had been using these cups because it was all he could afford and not because it was tradition. The tea was brought in by a Filipino girl who wore a long dress. I learned that the Saudis brought all their house servants with them to the farm to take care of the cooking, cleaning, and children—a real holiday.

I asked questions about Saudi food. They told me that rice was eaten at every meal and would either be white or red (flavored with tomatoes and tomato sauce). When I asked about sweets, they said they ate a mixture of brown bread, dates, and milk. Even after living in Saudi Arabia for five years, I never found a dish similar to what they described! They also said that camels milk was the most healthy of foods and that all Saudis drank it when they were sick. If ground lamb was mixed with rice, it would be flavored with cinnamon, cardamom, and pepper. However, if there were too many spices in the mixture, it would be termed "dirty." Often the rice was cooked with dried lemons from Yemen. Loaf commented that because she couldn't buy the dried lemons in the U.S., she took them back with her.

Most of the women had substantial abdomens and wide hips. The very young, unmarried women had very slender figures. A few of the women wore eyeliner and mascara, but most did not have on any makeup, perhaps because they were on holiday in the country. I wondered if the women didn't allow themselves to get larger after marriage. If they spent most of their time as they had here at the farm, sitting around munching on seeds, perhaps their physical states were inevitable.

At one point, a man shouted a warning outside of the tent. Evidently the women recognized the voice because a few quickly covered their faces, and the others remained uncovered as Sheikh Saleh's brother Mohammed and his uncle entered the tent. The uncle was the husband of two of the women in the tent, and I assumed that the men were either a husband, brother, or father to the other women who didn't cover their faces, in keeping with the Saudi stipulation. The men conversed in Arabic for a few minutes, glancing around as if to monitor the situation, and both men nodded ever so slightly at me. I guessed that they also wanted to see Terry's American wife.

I realized that they were talking about me in Arabic. Even though this happened to me many times, I always felt a little uncomfortable. Loaf told me that the men didn't think that it was a good idea to tell me that men could have more than one wife, but Loaf answered them that it didn't matter. I was surprised that they didn't realize that I already knew about Saudi Arabia's policy concerning plural wives. Another woman entered the tent. She was the other wife of Nora-number-one's husband, but she and Nora-number-one seemed to have a sisterly relationship. Before coming to Saudi Arabia, my concept of plural wives had been limited to what I'd read about the early Mormons who might have several wives. They and their children lived together as one, big, happy family, under the same roof. Still it was hard for me to imagine these women sharing a husband and being so close.

In Saudi Arabia the man is obligated by the Koran and the command of the Prophet Mohammed to provide separate, but equal living quarters for each wife. He is permitted to have as many as four, and each must have her own house or tent, in the case of the Bedouin. If one wife has a cook and driver, the other wives must also have them. The man is supposed to divide his time, as well as his love, equally between wives. Multiple wives become a very expensive responsibility. Modern-day young men usually do not have more than one wife, not because they don't agree with the practice, but because they can't afford more. Also, as more Saudi women become better educated, the practice of marrying a man who already has a wife is not as acceptable. Most of the previous generation did have multiple wives. Sheikh Latif and Jewaher both had fathers who had two wives.

I questioned Loaf about polygamy, and she told me matter-of-factly that a man could have four wives. She was quick to tell me that a woman could not be forced to marry unless she consented and that divorce was simple for a woman. All a woman had to do was ask for a divorce. She didn't even have to give a reason. In doing research later for my thesis, I discovered that to the contrary, divorce is almost always initiated by the man and is relatively simple for him, but not at all simple for a woman. I didn't know whether Loaf told me what she did because she thought it sounded better, or because she really believed it was correct.

Love is regarded as a strong emotion but not as the basis for a happy marriage in Saudi Arabia. Marriages are arranged by the family and occur between family members (now, usually no closer than second cousins) so that "the good blood will be kept in the family." In wealthy families, the parents may decide on a mate for their child as early as infancy. Most families decide on a match when the mother and sister of a male pick from the choice of women at women's gatherings and when the father and brother observe the available men for their daughters and sisters at gatherings of men.

Actually, divorce occurs when a man pronounces to his wife, "I divorce you," three times. These words may be stated once with an opportunity for reconciliation, and then the process repeated two more times, or the statements may be repeated three times in rapid succession. A man may not announce the last statement of divorce if his wife is pregnant. A woman may leave her husband to return to her own family, but she cannot initiate divorce proceedings, except in limited circumstances. If her husband refuses to divorce her, she may not marry again. It is not necessary for a man to obtain consent or permission from his wife before he acquires a second wife.

A wife may inherit one-fourth of her husband's property upon his death if he leaves no children; otherwise, she is entitled to only one-eighth. The chances of a man's dying without children are almost non-existent, since a woman's inability to produce children is grounds for divorce. A husband is entitled to half of what his wife leaves, unless she has one or more children. If she has children, the husband's share is limited to one-fourth of the estate. A daughter inherits from her father's estate only one-half of what her brothers each receive.

The Saudi women told me readily that it is disgraceful and unheard of for a woman to have an affair outside of marriage. As I visited with the women that day, I had no comprehension of the double standard that exists for Saudi men and women. After I had lived there for awhile, I learned that it is not unusual, but even sanctioned by society, for a Saudi man to have a concubine, especially when he is traveling outside the country. Paradoxically, if a Saudi woman is found guilty of infidelity, her head may be chopped off. A woman in Saudi Arabia would never be pregnant before marriage. The consequences are too severe, and she wouldn't even have the opportunity for a liaison with a male in this society, where she isn't allowed to meet beforehand the person she is to marry.

I pondered often in the years since, whether the women had wanted me to think that marriage and divorce rights for women in Saudi Arabia were the same as for women in the States, or whether they were simply living in a fantasy world when we talked, pretending that things were better than they actually were. I have talked to other Saudi women who lived in the States for several years with their faces uncovered and the freedom to exist on a fairly equal basis with men. When they returned to Saudi Arabia to live for the remainder of their lives, I assumed that they might feel a sense of loss. In contrast, the women said that they did not object to covering their faces because it is "the way things are in Saudi Arabia." All of these women did express a sense of loss in closeness to their husbands when they returned to Saudi Arabia. Men and women are separated in all aspects of Saudi society and even eating dinner with the husband and another couple, other than relatives, is not a usual part of life.

The women visiting Riyadh Farm were very inquisitive about my family, wondering if my mother and father were alive, if they were living together, and if I had brothers and sisters. Their questions indicated a need to know how they are perceived outside their own country. They wondered what I had thought about Saudi Arabia before coming and if my speculations matched my current perceptions. Because these women had no associations with oil, they laughed when I told them that I anticipated that every Saudi would own an oil well. These women promptly informed me that their families were involved in the government; therefore, they had the same benefits as the royal family.

I sensed a restlessness in the air, and once again, as if on cue, the ladies covered themselves for a walk around the farm. One of the younger women took out a bottle of perfume, and everyone, including me, applied the perfume before we ventured outside. They laughed and teased that if a person hadn't taken a bath, the perfume would make that person clean. Briefly, I wondered whether they knew about my early morning spit bath.

The group trudged slowly up a tall sand dune that was directly behind the circle of tents. From the top, I enjoyed the beautiful view of the ocean of sand. Two of the younger women raced down the hill, with the remainder of the group following at a slower pace. We all collapsed in the sand, as if the walk up and down the hill had tired us. Nora-number-two began to speak in Arabic. I believe that she was telling an interesting tale because the women clustered around, smiling and nodding. When she finished the tale, Nora-number-one repeated the story for me in English. The subject of the tale was a haunted house in the town where Nora-number-two lives.

In the story, a girl is invited to a friend's wedding. The celebration is held in a beautiful palace. After the wedding, the girls and boys dance together, and as the girl watches, the dancers lift up their clothes to reveal legs that are those of a donkey. The girl becomes so frightened that she runs out into the street and catches a taxi. She is telling the taxi driver the story when she notices that his legs are also like donkeys' legs! As the car slows down for a stop sign, she jumps out. She makes her way to the police station and tells her story. They return to the palace where the dance occurred. The place is completely empty except for the corpse of her friend, the one who had married.

As she finished telling me the story, she asked, "Do you believe in ghosts?" All the women watched as I replied that I didn't and asked if they believed in ghosts. Nora-number-one said that they did believe in ghosts, that it was part of their religion. They believed that the ghosts of people in the past tell them things, to direct them or warn them of danger. At the time, I hadn't lived in Saudi Arabia long enough to understand the significance of the story. To me it was just a crazy tale. Had I known more about Saudi culture, I would have known that men and women wouldn't be together at a wedding and most certainly wouldn't be dancing together in Saudi Arabia. The men and women dancing together illustrated the pagan past of the Saudis, from which the Prophet Mohammed saved them.

Saudi men and women spend comparatively little time together, as society dictates the separation of the sexes outside the immediate family and allows only the father, son, brother, or husband to see the woman's face. Men and women are not allowed to touch in public. The penalty of breaking these laws of modesty, passed down to women from generation to generation is severe beating by the *Mutawwa*.

We heard a horn honk, and I was brought from the ghosts of the past to the present reality. I saw Terry a safe distance away, and when I glanced at my watch, I was surprised that I had been visiting with the women for two and a half hours. They all insisted that I stay for lunch, to be served around 3:30 P.M., but I declined. Terry had too much work to do to repeat the trip to retrieve me later in the day. Besides, I needed some time to digest my experiences with these women.

Chapter Seven

Almost a week had passed since our visit to Midwess's tent, and he decided it was time for us to come again. This time two other American male friends accompanied Frank, Terry, and me. We had the traditional coffee, tea, sheep and rice, and dates. Then Frank produced for everyone candy that he had purchased at the gas station. It was so appreciatively received that we never went empty-handed again. From then on, when we visited, I baked chocolate chip cookies and took them to our Bedouin friends, who absolutely adored them. Frank brought his guitar and we sang "Home on the Range" and "The Eyes of Texas," which seemed quite appropriate in this desert setting. As we sang, Midwess held his long, gold-colored sword, which he said he had owned for nine years, and swayed to the music, first on one foot and then the other. I read later that the national dance of Saudi Arabia is the sword dance.

The sword is used in the emblem of Saudi Arabia, symbolizing the country itself. The lower half of the emblem is a pair of crossed swords, symbolizing how King Abdul Aziz unified the Kingdom into Saudi Arabia in 1932. Abdul Aziz did not complete the national emblem with the camel of the wandering Bedouin, whose armies had built the Kingdom, because the Bedouin had also come close to destroying it with his fighting. He chose the palm tree of the settled oasis dweller for the top half of the emblem. We knew Midwess was familiar with the history of Saudi Arabia from things that he had told us about the King and the almost trancelike way he swayed with the sword, as if in deep thought.

Saudi Arabia, located on the Arabian Peninsula, has a rich history that dates from the latter stages of the Nile and Mesopotamian civilizations. Residents in Saudi Arabia claim their ancestry from the Biblical strains of Abraham and Ishmael. The southern part of Arabia developed into a commercial center specializing in the production of frankincense and myrrh. This area became a trade center for silks, spices, and jewelry brought in from the Indies and East Africa for the eastern Mediterranean market. Two major cities in Saudi Arabia, Taif and Jeddah are on the opposite side of the country from where we lived and were important centers during the sixth century for the caravan trade between Egypt and the Orient. While Europe was in the Dark Ages from the fifth through the tenth centuries, the Arabs in the Arabian Peninsula were ruling a vast and progressive empire that made great strides in the areas of medicine, mathematics, and astronomy.

This era of prosperity was followed by three hundred years of silence under the rule of the Turks. Society moved no further into enlightenment. The land became a wasteland, a tragic decline from its early and medieval greatness. Nomadism became the dominant way of life for hundreds of years in most parts of the Arabian Peninsula because of the scarcity of forage and water for animals.

These nomads came to be known as the Bedouins in Saudi Arabia. *Bedouin* derives from the Arabic expression *bedawin* (singular *bedawi),* and is a general term for all tribesmen who live in the desert and herd camels, sheep, and goats. In 1965, the government estimated that more than fifty percent of the country's population was Bedouin. The first population census in 1962-63 counted a population of 3,297,657 and listed 20.8 percent as nomads. Yet after the census was completed, it was never published, because the government believe the 3.3 million population figure was too low. Naturally, the Bedouins practiced the teachings of the Koran that demands that man be "faithful, courageous, generous, and compassionate, proud before brutal force and humble before goodness," all consistent with survival in the desert wasteland.

The modern history of Saudi Arabia began with the recapture of Riyadh by King Abdul Aziz in 1902, the King that Midwess revered and who originated the sword symbol. For several decades after its birth, however, Saudi Arabia remained virtually unknown worldwide. The country itself was not actually organized until 1932. Abdul Aziz, later crowned King, traveled around the country marrying all the different warring tribal leaders' daughters, in an effort to unite the land. It is rumored that he was married to as many as 400 women at one time. Often he married the girl one night and rode out the next morning, never to return. With the marriages, he was able to gather enough support to recapture Riyadh and declare himself King. Yet he was the King of an extremely poor nation whose subjects survived on dates and rice, and were always in search of water.

Sheikh Latif, in his mid-forties when I met him, was a product of this harsh life, as reflected in his mannerisms. He occasionally dropped in on us when we were eating and usually joined us, as was the custom. One time I had prepared a spinach souffle and feared that he might think it was horrible. To my surprise, he not only ate the portion that I served him but also every bit of the amount remaining in the bowl.

True to his Bedouin ancestry that revered truthfulness and candor, Sheikh Latif always told me, unabashedly, that my desserts were too sweet. Saudis generally end their meals with fresh fruit. On one occasion he stopped by my house for a drink of water and took time to reminisce about his early years as a young Bedouin boy. He remembered when his father brought him to the desert and the water they drank from a sheepskin bag was filtered through their *ghatra* (the checked headpiece). He said the water was not cool, but was exactly the relief they needed on their treks through the desert. He said that at times he regretted that gas stations had spread to the desert, even though they were few and far between. He regretted that his sons would never know the feeling of being in the desert and drinking water from a sheepskin bag. Nonetheless, we both knew that he would never trade his wealth for any of these experiences that he recalled so nostalgically.

The barren land of Arabia was virtually ignored until oil was discovered beneath its dunes, and the Arab nations were transformed into rich and powerful bargainers in the world market. After five years of drilling on the Eastern coast of Saudi Arabia, oil was discovered on March 20, 1938. Because of its rich oil fields, Saudi Arabia built its wealth on the strength of the twin explosions in oil prices in 1973-74 and 1979-80.

Midwess roused us from our meditations on the Saudi Arabia of the past when he took Frank's guitar, laid it flat on his lap and discordantly strummed the strings while he sang his own rendition of "Home on the Range" in a tuneless chant. From the smile on his face, I think he must have thought that he was producing the same melody that Frank coaxed from the instrument. As Midwess serenaded the group, the American men took turns dancing with the sword, and the women behind the tent flap giggled with delight. Becoming nostalgic, we sang "Amazing Grace" and "How Great Thou Art," explaining to Midwess that we were singing to God. He smiled and pronounced an approving *quayis, good* in Arabic.

The novelty of the Saudi experience gave me the vitality to endure day after day of farm life that seemed to pass without variation. Sometimes, I got homesick and cursed myself that I ever agreed to join Terry. On the days when the waves of loneliness hit me and I longed for companionship, I found myself shadowing Terry. I became convinced that a couple marooned in the desert would become either the worst of enemies or the best of friends. Luckily, Terry and I became best friends.

One day when I was riding with Terry in the pickup, he and one of the electricians decided to change the nozzles on one of the pivots. The fastest way to accomplish this task was for Terry and Efren, the Filipino mechanic, to stand in the bed of the pickup while I drove. Because I had not driven for almost a month I welcomed the opportunity, but was a little nervous, also, when I remembered that the farm workers would be watching to see how the American woman would do. I decided this place must be playing strange tricks on my ego, if I was nervous about driving, a skill I had conquered by the time I was sixteen years old. I had driven a standard shift before, but hadn't realized how cantankerous Terry's pickup could be. There seemed to be a stall from the point of releasing the clutch and actually engaging the gear. Terry and Efren stood in the back of the pickup as I eased off the clutch and the pickup lurched forward, throwing the two onto the ground, much to the amusement of the curious onlookers. After several attempts, I finally maneuvered the pickup slowly and smoothly down the road. I pledged to myself that from that moment on I would drive some around the farm, just to prove to all those men how smart I was.

Although it was illegal for women to drive in Saudi Arabia, there was an unwritten law when it came to Bedouins. Because the Bedouins moved from camp to camp in pickups rather than on foot as they had done earlier, many times the women might have to drive in order to ensure there being a driver for each of a clan's old pickups or water tankers that were used for hauling water to the animals. If the women didn't drive, small boys, who had to look between the steering wheel and the dashboard to see, might have to take on the task. We met these illegal drivers on the highway on our farm or at the gas station near the farm. We rarely saw the Saudi police, clad in khaki uniforms and red and white headdress, out in our part of the desert, even though we were only about fifteen miles from a police station. However, we often saw the police at the gas station. The Bedouins looked at the police defiantly.

The police ignored them, in silent assent that their laws did not extend into the harsh desert where the Bedouins dwelled.

The Bedouin attitude that everything in the desert was communal property was prevalent on the farm. Bedouins set up camp in the middle or on the edge of a circle in hopes of grazing their sheep and camels on the lush, green wheat. The communal attitude extended to entering other people's homes without knocking or being invited inside. Terry warned me to lock the door when I was home alone, but occasionally I forgot. The first time a Bedouin, unannounced, yanked open the door to our container, I'm not sure who was more surprised. He looked as though he had seen a ghost, the ghost being me with an uncovered face. Using the little bit of Arabic I knew, I told him to go, as he jabbered to me in rapid Arabic, about what, I did not know. Once the news spread that there was an American woman on this farm, many of the Bedouins drove up to my door and sat out in their cars, honking, either as a warning that they were outside or as a ploy to bring me into view for their scrutiny. When a Bedouin walked around my locked house, pulling on the door and even trying the windows, but refusing to knock, I was frustrated, but tried to keep my perspective. After all, knocking on a tent flap made little sense, so the act of knocking probably seemed a useless gesture to these desert people.

We called our boss Sheikh Latif, but his last name is al-Sheikh. The al-Sheikhs are the largest family other than the al-Sa'uds, the royal family. The al-Sheikhs are the ruling religious family in Saudi Arabia. Superficially, the Kingdom of Saudi Arabia is an absolute monarchy, but the Council of Ministers, in which the king occupies the position of Prime Minister, plays a powerful and decisive role in the government of the country. Saudi Arabian citizens seem to revere their monarch more than citizens of any other country in the modern world. This strong attachment seems to be in part because the kings are direct descendants of the family of Sa'ud, the first king.

Although the royal family is incredibly rich, the oil wealth of the country is distributed among its citizens. Saudi Arabia learned an important lesson from the Shah of Iran whose government was overthrown by the Iranian people because he retained the country's wealth for himself and a chosen few of his followers, leaving the masses of his citizenry in poverty. Even though the Bedouins seemed to live a meager existence, they, too, could receive a stipend from the Saudi government.

At one time the government also paid the Bedouins a subsidy for the sheep and camels that they owned; however, it was rumored that some of the Bedouins passed the animals back and forth on the day the government inspector arrived, so the subsidy was canceled.

A Saudi man was even able to obtain dowry assistance from the government under certain conditions. The dowry is very important in a marriage in Saudi Arabia. It originated as the custom of paying money to the tribe or family of the bride in consideration for her reproductive capacity and to foster good will between the families involved. In 1987, the dowry might include jewelry, usually gold, for the bride. The groom also bestowed presents on the bride's family, with the bride's father often receiving several camels.

Current dowry rates appeared in the *Saudi Gazette*, the English language newspaper in Saudi Arabia. The following is a quote from the 21 November 1986 publication: "The maximum dowry payable for a virgin is SR 10,000 (US $2666) plus some jewelry and a gold watch, according to a decision taken by Sheikh of Rijal al-Ma'a region." The amount for re-marriage of divorced or widowed women was set at SR 5000 (US $1333). These rates seemed quite fair considering that in previous years, dowries had risen to SR 160,000 (US $42,666) for virgins.

Islamic scholars encouraged wealthy Moslems to contribute to a fund that helped the poor who couldn't marry because they were unable to pay *mahr* (bride money). A Saudi male citizen might qualify for SR 25,000 (US $6666) in dowry assistance if he could: 1) marry a Saudi girl; 2) have it confirmed by a *share'ah* court that he is unable to pay *mahr*; 3) demonstrate he had not been married before; 4) provide a document proving the marriage contract; and 5) produce a letter of documentation from the mosque that he regularly performs five prayers a day.

The Kingdom is purely Islamic; hence, no churches, synagogues, temples, or shrines of other religions exist, and no proselytizing by other faiths is allowed. The entire population is Moslem. Although there were underground religious groups that met in secret, to practice any religion other than Islam was a risky undertaking. Saudis have been known to spy on noncitizens on Friday (the Sabbath) or on week nights when there was a large group of people assembled together. Saudis have made video-tapes of non-Moslem religious meetings, to use as evidence of illegal gatherings. While we were in Saudi Arabia, a large group of Mormons was deported for gathering, as well as proselytizing. Although I was never aware of anyone's being jailed for illegal religious gatherings, the penalties of losing one's job and being deported within forty-eight hours were serious deterrents in themselves.

Because non-Moslems in Saudi Arabia are not allowed to go into a mosque or even to look inside one when passing by it, we were limited in our understanding of their religion. We did our best to avoid what is called the *Mutawwa*, or the religious police, who roamed the Saudi streets with long sticks. If a *Mutawwa* spied a foreign woman whose attire was inappropriate and didn't cover her elbows and ankles, he struck the exposed area with his stick. I was always dressed appropriately, so I was never chastened, nor did I ever witness someone's being struck, but I had friends who told of women who had encounters with the *Mutawwa*. The *Mutawwa* also made sure that men and women maintain an appropriate distance from one another and that stores closed exactly on time for obligatory prayers.

We missed the freedom to practice the religion of our choice and to attend church services. Although there were private gatherings of different religious groups, we rarely had the opportunity to participate in the meetings. Many of the foreigners were European, and we discovered that most of them didn't consider themselves religious anyway. Noncitizens from Third World countries were either Buddhist or Hindu, and did't have regular church services.

We did discover the Riyadh International Christian Fellowship, or RICF, consisting of many small, home groups. Each small group had a leader who met with the leaders of other small groups to compare notes. At one time the RICF got into trouble for publishing the meeting times and places of all the different small groups. The printed page made it into the wrong hands, and the groups had to disband until the smoke cleared, reassembling later at different times, in different places.

The closest we ever came to proselytizing was when one of the Pakistanis from the Head Office came to the farm with a General Electric parts representative, who was a Moslem from Pakistan. While we visited, the man studied Terry's Bible that had been lying on the table. At one point, the man pointed out a verse about what God did on the seventh day of creation. Much to our surprise, when they prepared to leave, the man handed Terry his card and asked Terry to buy him a Bible on his next trip to the States. We were never able to contact the man again. I wish now that we had just handed him one of our Bibles, although I'm not sure that he would have accepted it as a gift at that time.

Through the year, I supplied several of our Filipino employees, who were Catholic, with Bibles I brought each time I returned to Saudi Arabia from vacation in the States. Although every foreigner was allowed to bring one Bible into Saudi Arabia, the Filipino men were afraid to bring theirs in, even after they knew that I had brought them into the country without any problem. They probably feared they might have been dealt with differently than I, an American—even if I had been caught in customs with more than one Bible.

Moslems are taught from birth that Islam is the true religion. The first Islamic government began when the Prophet Mohammed and his followers fled from Mecca to Medina in 622 A.D. He delivered the people in the Arabian penninsula from the paganism of idol worship and frenzied unrest to a nation of strict stability maintained by Islamic faith and law. Mohammed guided his followers to adhere to Koranic rules called the Five Pillars of Islam.

The first pillar is the confession of faith that is stated at the beginning of each of the five daily prayers: "There is no God but Allah, and Mohammed is the prophet of Allah." The second pillar is prayer and requires that believers pray five times each day, facing Mecca, the holy city in western Saudi Arabia. Many Moslems carry a compass when they travel to determine the exact direction to face when they pray. The third pillar is giving the *takat* or alms to the poor. They are to share 2.5 percent of their wealth with the poor, although many give much more, and as in all religions, some don't give at all. Mohammed directs Moslems to fast during the ninth month, called Ramadan, as the fourth pillar. Fasting occurs from sunup to sundown, and only travelers, nursing mothers, and the very elderly are exempt. The fifth and final pillar requires that Islam's faithful make a pilgrimage to Mecca, where Mohammed was born. A follower is required to go to Mecca once in a lifetime, if possible.

Several religious ceremonies are associated with pilgrimages: a goat is killed, its meat is given to the poor, and believers walk around the Kaaba, the most sacred shrine of Islam. The Kaaba is a cube-shaped building that houses the Black Stone. The Black Stone, enclosed in a silver ring, according to Islam, was built by Abraham and Ishmael and given to Abraham by the angel Gabriel. Moslems walk around the Kaaba seven times. In Mecca, caring for the pilgrims is the city's chief industry. The industry continues to grow, with some two million pilgrims having visited Mecca in 1993.

It is important to note that tourists were not allowed in Saudi Arabia, and the only two types of temporary entry visas issued were for short-term business contacts or pilgrimages or specific periods of familial visitation. Not all workers in Saudi Arabia were allowed visits from relatives. There was a set salary amount that the worker must make before relatives were allowed to visit. I was able to come to Saudi Arabia as a spouse because Terry made above the required salary. The residence visa was for individuals entering Saudi Arabia on an employment contract, who had a Saudi sponsor; Terry was issued this type of visa. The residence visa was called an *'iqamah* and had to be renewed annually. None of these visas were easy to obtain. Non-Saudi pilgrims who visited Mecca for religious reasons were issued visas that did not allow them to leave an area surrounding Mecca. Police were positioned on the highway to stop traffic, checking to see that each person was a citizen rather than a stray pilgrim.

Islam establishes an ethical and moral code for its believers to follow. Because the Saudi ancestors worshipped idols before Mohammed introduced Islam, the representation of human or animal figures is prohibited in Islam. Road signs contain only written messages with no pictures of human or animal faces. Islam forbids games of chance; therefore, most Saudis have never played games that involve gambling. Video arcades were introduced into Saudi society, but they were removed because they were deemed a menacing influence and a form of gambling.

Although Sheikh Latif might be considered a modern entrepreneur, he clung steadfastly to his religion. One time on a trip to Dammam, a trip of several hours to the east, he discovered that one of the wheels of his car had been held in place by only one lug nut. Because he had been traveling at a speed of 180 kilometer per hour (108 m.p.h.), he could easily have been killed if the wheel had disengaged. To show his gratitude to God, he fasted for three days after he returned home.

The Koran is the basis for a number of taboos regarding food and drink. The following are forbidden: the flesh of animals that are dead before they are butchered, blood, pig's flesh, and alcohol or liquors. Islam advocates a strict practice of personal hygiene to attain purity of spirit and cleanliness of body. Ancient scholars encouraged the religious taboo on pigs because pork spoiled very quickly in the hot climate. Also, the nomads of the desert had no use for the pig because it did not have the stamina for traveling that sheep, goats, and camels did. They considered the pig to be cantankerous, ornery, and impossible to herd or milk.

Pork and alcohol may have been taboo in Saudi Arabia, but they were not unavailable. Pork existed on private compounds where only foreigners lived and could be obtained only with certain hard-to-get permits. Bootleg liquor was almost as much a part of life in Saudi Arabia as camel's milk. At the time we were living there, as many as sixty to seventy-five percent of the non-Moslem foreigners made their own spirits. Imported liquor such as whiskey was also available, selling for as much as $150 a fifth. The foreign-made liquor was smuggled into Saudi Arabia in trucks that came across the border from the Gulf countries that allowed liquor. Although the Saudi government levied stiff penalties, including fines and jail sentences, on individuals who were caught consuming alcohol, we knew of only a few people who were ever arrested.

We knew of one ironic incident on a dairy near us that involved homemade alcohol. Friends of ours from the dairy related an account of a German co-worker who was put in jail on Christmas Eve because of a minor traffic violation. The company's assistant general manager, a Saudi, went to pay the man's bail so that he would be out of jail in time for Christmas. The police wanted SR 600 ($171) for each of three traffic violations. After much bargaining, the police agreed to release the German for SR 600 and one bottle of Sadiki, the German's homemade brew, for which he was famous.

Not surprisingly, the prohibition of alcohol somehow made the quest for it all the more compelling. In the late fall of 1987, the opening of the long-awaited causeway between the Eastern coast of Saudi Arabia and the tiny island of Bahrain became the perfect route for this quest. When the highway opened, as many as forty people a day were caught smuggling liquor from Bahrain. People not only smuggled alcohol, but they drove from Bahrain into Saudi Arabia in an inebriated condition. The Saudi government remedied the problem by building a special holding room at the midway point of the causeway for those who needed to dry out.

One of our Mexican pump setters observed first hand the consequences of being caught partaking of alcohol, when he was jailed for two days for driving without a license, a crime committed by almost every foreign worker. Terry drove without a license for almost three years. A license was not that difficult to obtain, but the paperwork involved seemed not worth the effort. The Saudis didn't seem to check the licenses of the American and European drivers as often as the drivers of other nationalities. I also think that the Saudis were not as likely to do license checks when a woman was in the car. I often asked Terry what would happen to me if he were caught without a license and sent to jail. Thankfully, experience never answered this question for me. I learned that if a woman is caught driving, her husband is sent to jail.

While our the pump setter was in jail, waiting for someone from our company to bail him out, a wealthy Saudi man occupied the cell beside him. The man had been caught drinking and was given the choice of ninety days in jail or ninety lashes. According to Saudi law, the person administering the lashes has to hold a copy of the Koran under his arm while delivering the lashes. The wealthy Saudi chose the ninety days in jail. His food, which he shared generously with the other inmates, was brought to him three times a day during his stay.

Chapter Eight

Islam is the unifying force among Saudi citizens, not only as a religion but also as a culture, reaching into every area of life, including crime prevention. All areas of life come under a code of law called the *share'ah*, the way or path that the faithful must follow. Islam prescribes behavior for individuals and society: codifying law, family relationships, business, etiquette, dress, food, personal hygiene, and much more. It is under the *share'ah* that murder and rape are punishable by beheading, and stealing by amputating the right hand. Stoning is the penalty for adultery, but adultery is not easy to prove in modern-day Saudi Arabia, requiring a third party witness to the crime.

The severity with which a crime is punished is in keeping with Koranic stipulations. The punishment is public. The citizenry is given advance notice in the newspaper of the criminal, the crime, and the day and place of the punishment. Even though the punishment may seem barbaric, the crime rate is almost nil in Saudi Arabia.

If the sentence for a crime is beheading, the punishment is executed in Riyadh in the older section of town, next to my favorite shopping place. This area, called *Dira,* is near a mosque that Westerners call the Friday mosque because Moslems from all across Riyadh came to it for prayer on Friday. The mosque has a large clock tower, beneath which is the area that Westerners call "Chop Chop Square," where the beheading occurs.

Friends who had been in Saudi Arabia for several years advised us against witnessing the punishments executed in Chop Chop Square. The Saudis regard these public punishments as religious rituals in which they are carrying out justice as outlined in the Koran. For that reason, the crowds tend to be emotional, almost to the point of hysteria, and at times, in irrational frenzies, they push the foreigners (or non-Moslems) in their midst to the front of the crowd. Many times policemen have to restrain the crowds from attacking the criminal when he arrives for punishment. One story circulated that if the prisoner who is to be decapitated is non-Moslem and of some other nationality, the crowd may attack anyone of that nationality who happens to be in their midst. We felt certain that we would have no stomach for the gory sights of Chop Chop Square that were described to us.

Despite the warnings, many foreign workers were drawn to the square on Friday mornings. Two of our very good friends, both Americans living on nearby farms, attended the chopping one Friday morning. On any other day, the area near the Friday Mosque would have been crowded with shoppers and honking cars. On punishment day, police blocked off the streets from traffic and scrutinized the crowd for any infractions. Our friends, Barry Bigland and Rick Tolmie, arrived early to find a crowd already gathered.

At first the crowd seemed to be quiet and somber, but the air was tense with an electricity of anticipation. Barry and Rick saw only males at the square. They were surprised to see many male children, as young as five years old, standing eagerly near their fathers. As the crowd grew larger, a voice blared from a loudspeaker at the Friday mosque, chanting passages from the Koran at a deafening volume. In response, the spectators cheered and chanted religious passages, all in Arabic. Within minutes, a black van with a large, round light on top stopped in front of the crowd. At the same moment the van arrived, Barry and Rick felt themselves being pushed to the front of the crowd. Glancing around, they found themselves in close company with the other foreigners, mostly Filipino workers, who had chosen to attend. Rick was fortunate to be standing to the right of a Saudi man who spoke English and explained the proceedings to him.

All eyes were on the vehicle as the police pulled a young man from the van, apparently of Middle Eastern descent because he was dressed as a typical Arab in the long white *thobe* and traditional headpiece. Although the man's eyes reflected fear, he appeared to be sedated. His hands were cuffed behind his back. In quick motions, one of the policemen removed the man's *ghatra,* the red and white checked cloth on his head, and wrapped it around the prisoner's eyes. One uniformed guard roughly pushed him to his knees and held him by the shoulder with one hand. Another Saudi, dressed in plain clothes approached the kneeling prisoner from behind and stuck a three-inch-long needle into the back of his neck. Barry and Rick guessed the injection to be some type of muscle relaxant because the man's head dropped to his chest. The prisoner remained on his knees as a giant man approached with a two-foot sword that glistened in the hot sun. Rick was told that the swordsman was a Nubian, probably a former slave, as slavery wasn't abolished in Saudi Arabia until 1965.

The crowd swelled with emotion at the sight of the ebony giant holding the sword in his right hand, a large copy of the Koran under his left arm, and quoting loudly from the Koran. With one quick sweep the man swung the sword, severing the prisoner's head from his body. A one-inch stream of blood shot six feet into the air. The crowd exploded into a wild frenzy, clapping as the man's head fell to the ground. The executioner calmly and deliberately wiped the blood from his sword on the dead man's *thobe*. Rick's Saudi interpreter explained that the final act of humiliation was to wipe the prisoner's blood on his own *thobe*.

What first appeared to be a clean decapitation proved to be not quite the case. When a Saudi soldier kicked the dead man's head, it remained attached to the body by two tendons. The executioner returned with his sword, to the accompaniment of the crowd's cheers, to cut the remaining ties between the head and body. A soldier grabbed the *ghatra,* still tied around the man's eyes, and yanked it, sending the head spinning like a top along the asphalt. The frenzy of the crowd increased to even greater levels at the grotesque spinning of the severed head.

Without any ceremony or additional ritual, two men picked up the limp body and placed it in the black van. The head remained on the asphalt. The noise in the crowd had become a low din. The reader of the Koran resumed his shouting from the loudspeaker.

A second prisoner, of Asian descent, emerged from the van, appearing to have little or no sedation. Shaking like a leaf, his hands cuffed in front of his body, the man faced the crowd with terrible fear in his eyes. When the prisoner saw the severed head on the ground, he appeared about to faint. The handcuffs were removed, and a metal device was placed on the man's right hand. A soldier pulled on the other end of the apparatus, stretching and extending the man's hand from his body. Another black man appeared with a six-inch knife and a copy of the Koran under his left arm. After a quick recitation from the Koran, without even a pause, the executioner made four quick movements with the knife and the hand fell to the ground.

In earlier times in Saudi Arabia, (as late as 1943), the stump would have been dipped in boiling oil to cauterize the wound. On this Friday, in modern day Saudi Arabia, a man who appeared to be a doctor arrived on the scene and quickly wrapped the prisoner's arm, shoving him into the van. As the crowd roared, the van exited the scene. A soldier picked up the hand, tied a piece of rope around one of the fingers, attached the other end of the rope to a pole that was raised into the air, and waved the hand, much to the delight of the now delirious crowd.

Rick and Barry, along with the other foreigners, were pushed almost under the swinging hand. They suspected that the Saudis were trying to make the point to them that the Saudi system of justice worked, evidenced by the head and hand on display. The Saudi beside Rick explained that male children are brought to witness the punishments to teach them to obey the laws. If I were one of those children, it would be a lesson that I would never forget. Rick and Barry certainly recalled the lessons in dreams for many nights thereafter.

Surprisingly, once a person has lost his right hand, he was not regarded negatively in society. Society accepted that the offender had paid for the crime, and he could return to society except for eating with anyone else. The Saudis ate only with their right hands, saving the left hand for purposes of hygiene. The criminal who had no right hand had to eat alone, using his left hand. In the days before toilet paper or the Saudi water hoses were available, the left hand was used to clean oneself. It was not only frightening and painful to lose the hand but also very shameful, because everyone knew that the person without a right hand was eating and cleaning himself with the same hand.

Rape was not much of a problem in Saudi Arabia. Women were rarely in an isolated position in which a rape might occur; however, sodomy was a problem. Many times, Oriental men working on the farms were sodomized by men wandering along the highways. Terry chose to describe in detail such incidents, committed by lone men in the desert, one morning after I had gone jogging and decided to follow a different route. I had climbed over a hill and could no longer see the camp. Somehow I became disoriented and lost my sense of direction. Being completely turned around, it took me quite some time to recognize any landmarks and work my way back to camp. When I told Terry that I had actually been lost for a while, instead of laughing at me as I expected, he told me the stories of the lone men in the desert.

Saudi Arabia also dealt severely with those who possessed drugs. Persons convicted of dealing drugs were not put to death, but those found to be in possession of even a small amount of marijuana received long jail sentences. Jails in Saudi Arabia were cold in the winter, because they had no heat, and were very hot most other months, because of no air conditioning. They were dirty, and food was not provided. If a jail inmate wanted food, he either had a family member bring it, or he must purchase it from a local vendor who frequented the jail. A manager from a nearby farm told of one of his Taiwanese workers who had tried to smuggle some marijuana through customs. He was caught and sentenced to fifteen years in prison. Visitors reported that he was contemplating suicide because of the prison's conditions.

Although few of our workers spent time in jail, Arshad Hussain, a grandfatherly gentleman from Pakistan who managed the store after Mr. Park left, was arrested because he had forgotten to take his 'iqamah, his license to be in Saudi Arabia, with him on a trip to Riyadh. The 'iqamah is the most important document that a noncitizen possesses in Saudi Arabia. Men must carry it on their persons at all times, and wives carry a photocopy of their husbands 'iqamah. Females who are legally working in Saudi Arabia are issued their own 'iqamah.

Arshad tried to talk his way out of the conflict, but was hauled off to jail anyway. He was not allowed to make a phone call, so our farm didn't realize he was in jail until the following evening. Arshad was packed in a twelve-by-twelve-foot room with twenty other men. There was barely room to sit down. The policeman in charge made the prisoners remove their shoes, subjecting their feet to miserable February cold in the unheated cells. Arshad spent only one night in jail, but he developed a terrible cold as a souvenir of his stay. Many Pakistanis were sent to jail at this time because they had been were paying homage to the Holy Shrines in Mecca and stayed in the country illegally.

Many manual laborers on the farms in Saudi Arabia also found conditions quite oppressive. Our workers were allowed to go to town on Fridays if we weren't planting or harvesting. During planting and harvesting season, they worked continually, seven days a week. On some farms, there was no transportation to town, and unless a worker wanted to take the chance of hitchhiking the ninety miles into Riyadh and back, he remained a virtual prisoner on the farm. Living conditions were less than adequate, and the food was often very different from the workers' accustomed fare. A Filipino worker on a farm adjacent to ours committed suicide in his room after spending only five days in Saudi Arabia.

Laborers weren't the only ones who were affected by the desert solitude and long hours of work. In the end, when we gave notice that we would be leaving Saudi Arabia in a few months, Al Emar began the search for a replacement for Terry. One of the replacement candidates was an Englishman named Bill. He seemed the ideal person to take Terry's job. He had managed a similar-sized farm just down the road from ours a few years before. We had known Bill when he worked at the other farm, and we knew that he would do a good job. We were aware, however, that he had left his other job rather suddenly, even though he had been in favor with the company. When Bill arrived at P2, we sensed his tension. After only two days, he came to Terry to admit that he had left his last job because of a nervous breakdown. He couldn't handle the long hours and the solitude of the desert farm work. Within twelve hours, he was gone.

On the other side of the coin, we were often amazed at the conditions that some workers seemed to endure without complaint or discomfort. After we had been on the farm for several years, Sheikh Latif expanded the operation, adding more pivots to an area that was miles from camp and covered with rocks amidst the sand. The company hired three men from Yemen to haul rocks out of the field. The men lived in a tent with someone on the farm bringing them a supply of food and water once a week. These men were without a vehicle or contact with the outside world and were paid less than thirty dollars for a sixteen hour work day. Terry checked on them occasionally, and they never seemed to be stressed or unable to cope with the conditions of the job.

Chapter Nine

Paradoxically, the days in Saudi Arabia seemed to pass slowly, but in the long-term, our time there seemed to pass quickly. Because the day began at five or six, I often felt evening should be approaching when in actuality it would be only 11 A.M. Time passed more quickly when we made frequent trips to town, and I could anticipate dining out. I think that we did more exploring in the town of Al Kharj than almost any Americans who visited or worked in Saudi Arabia. Perhaps living out in the desert in this distant land awakened an instinct for adventure within us that we had never recognized before.

On one trip into Al Kharj with Frank, we spotted a restaurant with a primitive clay water fountain in the center of an otherwise traditional Arab establishment. Inadequate water pressure caused the fountain to trickle for several minutes and then suddenly spurt out enough water to wet the floor around it. The proprietor didn't turn on the fountain until we entered, so I felt a little guilty when the waiter had to keep mopping fountain water from the floor. The rice in this establishment contained pine nuts. It was my first time to eat this delicious combination, and it became one of my favorite dishes.

On our way home this particular evening, we passed what I guessed to be a men's club. My guess didn't prove to be too far from the truth. Out of curiosity, we drove slowly by the establishment several times, while I strained to see what was going on. Inside we saw rows of benches where men were perched, smoking tall pipes. Men in Texas gather for coffee at the local cafe or gin; men in Saudi Arabia go to these establishments to smoke water pipes, called a *sheesha*. The *sheesha* is designed with a container at the bottom that is half filled with water. Two pipes pass through a seal, one of which is immersed in water, and the other leads to the air between the water and the seal. The pipe in the water allows smoke from the tobacco to bubble through the water, leaving nicotine and smoke residues in the water; the other pipe leads the filtered smoke through a hose to the smoker. The men each put aluminum foil over the tip of the hose for sanitation, and smoke tobacco and drink tea far into the night.

On another trip to town, this time with Karl to buy parts for a piece of farm equipment, we happened upon a quaint shop that sold what we could almost call fast food. Outside the shop were two vendors, each cooking something that I had never seen before. One man had a large container of hot oil in which he fried little round patties that he allowed us to sample. The man took a spoonful of the mixture, mashed it into a press and pushed it into the hot oil. The patties came out round, and golden brown. They cost seven for SR 1 (35 cents) and tasted much like cornbread stuffing. I found out later the balls, called *falafel*, were made from cooked chickpeas, cracked wheat, onion, and spices. Next to this vendor was the strangest looking contraption I'd ever seen that produced what Karl called a chicken sandwich, or a *shawarma*. He said that these machines are common all over Riyadh. The machine had a tall skewer that held a one-foot-tall and eight-inch-wide tower of meat, created by layered pieces of boneless chicken or beef. On top of the skewer was a whole orange. The man ran his knife down the side of the tower causing slivers of the meat to fall into a pan below. He then took a small round of flatbread and pressed it, for just a few seconds, to an electric cooker with a mesh grill on the front that warmed and softened the bread. Taking a knife, he split the bread about halfway and filled the cavity with the pieces of chicken, sliced tomatoes, and a little bit of laban, much like buttermilk. The vendor laid the creation on a thin piece of paper, rolled it up like a crepe, and handed it to us. The *shawarma* cost SR 3, less than a dollar, and was delicious.

While we ate our appetizers outside, we peered inside the shop and saw its Lebanese owner gesturing for us to come in. Several chairs lined the wall of the shop that was no more than eight feet wide. As we watched the man prepare his delicacies, we decided he had invented a Lebanese hot dog. He made a slit down the side of a cylindrical bun, scooping out some of the bread to make room for a filling. He had several fillings from which to choose: scrambled eggs with green peas, ground lamb with chunks of potatoes, lamb with parsley and pepper, lamb with tomato, egg with tomato, oily-looking slices of eggplant, fried cauliflower, and French fries. He even served the French fries in the roll instead of on the side. After adding the filling, he put the roll into a waffle-type iron to heat for just a minute. Each "hot dog" was only SR 2, about 65 cents, and tasted very good.

At this shop we sampled our first glass of juice at a Lebanese juice bar. I am amazed that the Lebanese can put practically anything into the blender to make scrumptious juices. Behind the glass counter we saw all kinds of fruits that might be pureed and blended with either water or milk and some sugar. We visited the shop numerous times, becoming good friends with the unassuming proprietor. We were saddened when the man quit his business and returned to Lebanon to check on his family, whom he had not heard from in a long time.

Just when I thought I was managing the language barrier, I was surprised to discover that I wasn't quite as smart as I thought. On one of my morning runs, I passed a farmer's plot on the edge of one of our center pivots. The man was eking out an existence growing tomatoes. He was quite close to the path on which I was running. He walked quickly toward me with several tomatoes in his hands. At first I was a little afraid, but I stayed calm, hoping he wasn't using the tomatoes as a front. As we came closer to each other, he spoke rapidly in Arabic and gestured with the tomatoes. He seemed to be giving me the tomatoes. I waved my arms, gesturing that he should place the tomatoes on the ground and that I would run back to the farm and then drive back to retrieve the tomatoes. Although he never nodded to acknowledge my directions, I felt certain that after all of my crazy antics, which included motioning like I was turning a steering wheel and sputtering a "BURRRRR" car noise, he must have understood. When Terry came in for lunch I told him that I had talked to an old farmer who was going to leave me some tomatoes on the edge of his field. I explained that I was supposed to go pick them up. Terry was skeptical, but I convinced him to drive me back to the spot. I realized the man was gone, as were the tomatoes, and my Arabic was, to say the least, still limited. I had absolutely no idea what the old man really wanted or what he thought I had communicated to him.

My first *kabsa*, besides the meals eaten at Midwess's tent, was also an experience. An Arab feast, called a *kabsa*, is an elaborate affair. If the group is large and the guests important, the main dish may be a young camel, although it is usually one or more sheep. We never attended a *kabsa* at which a camel was served, although we did eat camel in a restaurant in Riyadh. Camel tastes somewhat like beef and may be tough or tender, depending on how it is prepared. The food at a *kabsa* is as much a part of the Saudi culture as the method of eating, the dress, or the segregation of men from women. Any deviation from traditional foods or means of preparation and serving are very rare. Whereas Americans try not to serve guests the same food the second time they are invited, the Saudis would never think of serving anything other than the traditional fare.

Before my first *kabsa*, Sheikh Latif parked his maroon Mercedes in front of our container and honked. At this time, I was too ignorant of Saudi custom to realize what an honor it was to have Sheikh Latif come to invite me personally to an all male *kabsa*, in a world where men and women have very little association. He qualified his invitation with the words, "if Terry wouldn't get too jealous." The group comprised men from the United States who were on an agricultural farm tour and men from Saudi Arabia who worked for the Ministry of Finance. Of course, I accepted the invitation. I was thrilled with the opportunity to talk to Americans and to experience an authentic Saudi *kabsa*.

Sheikh Latif entertained in his villa and tent on P1. It was on top of a hill overlooking the circles and behind the camp where the workers for that farm lived. Worn Oriental rugs covered the floor of the large tent. Saudi couches, which are really cushions resembling couches, rimmed the walls of the tent. In a far corner there was a Ping-Pong table that seemed out of place in this Arabian setting.

The *kabsa*, scheduled for 6:30 P.M., fit the itinerary of the tour, not Saudi custom. In urban Saudi Arabia, the largest meal of the day was taken ordinarily in the early afternoon, although the Bedouins ate their main meal in the evening. Anytime Sheikh Latif hosted a party for Saudi guests, the meal was served about 4:00 P.M. and was called lunch.

As we approached the group of approximately fifty men, I suddenly felt self-conscious about being the only woman present. The feeling passed quickly. I enjoyed the attention of the men, all surprised to find an American woman in such a remote area of the world. It was wonderful to talk to the ones who had just come from America with news from home. Several of the men who worked for the Ministry in Riyadh gave me their wive's names and phone numbers and encouraged me to call them. As the men conversed, several of the canteen workers circulated among them with the traditional tea and coffee. As dinner was announced and we entered the tent, I noted that the tent had been cleaned as much as possible, considering it was surrounded by sand, and plastic tablecloths had been placed on top of the rugs. At each place setting were two glasses, a can of Pepsi and a can of 7-Up, a quart of *laban,* as well as individual servings of salad, French fries, and the traditional baked custard. The French fries were an addition made by the Sri Lankan cook, not a typical food of the Saudis. If potatoes are served Saudi style, they are boiled in the rice.

Food was bountiful at the *kabsa.* Between every two or three places had been placed heaping plates of bananas, oranges, and apples. Boxes of unopened Kleenex, to serve as napkins, were everywhere. For the fifty guests who were expected, there were ten huge, round aluminum trays piled with rice and large cuts of lamb, including the heart and liver. There also were two or three whole chickens on each tray. Flatware was provided at each place, but the Americans tried to follow the Saudi tradition of eating with their right hands. I worried because apparently the men had never read or heard that using the thumb and first two fingers is considered to be in accord with the teachings of the Prophet Mohammed. One finger used alone signifies hatred; thumb and first finger, pride; and thumb and three fingers, gluttony. Yet my own attempts to follow these Islamic guidelines not only frustrated me, but also ensured that only a limited amount of food would reach my mouth. After several attempts of "balling up" the rice, I regretted that I did not choose to use the utensils. I agonized that my awkwardness would make me even more conspicuous. Not wanting to admit defeat, I continued to struggle. The lamb was very fat, dark, and tough, and the rice had a yellow color from the saffron flavoring, the raisins, and the browned onions. Few bites reached my mouth, and I wished that I was eating with a spoon. Fortunately neither the visitors' ignorance nor my ineptness seemed to disturb anyone else.

The men finished the meal quickly, and I was surprised to see that a great deal of food remained on the large platters. Most of the trays still held one-half to three-fourths of their original contents.

The men washed their hands at the back of a large water tanker used for well-drilling, because there was no water or plumbing at the hill top. A farm worker handed them Kleenex to dry their hands. Coffee and tea were served once again, this time outside the tent, as the men gazed across the wheat fields. I could see the amazement and wonder in the men's eyes as they looked upon the perfectly circular fields of green, magically emerging from the desert. The tiny shoots of green were just starting to grow and contrasted beautifully with the sand. The last round of tea and coffee was the final rite of hospitality and was a sign that the guests could take their leave. I had a wonderful time; visiting with so many Americans felt almost like a visit from home.

The stares of a young Arab were the only clouds on the entire evening. He had wandered in from a neighboring farm to join the event (to turn him away would have been unthinkable). Throughout the entire evening, he sat and stared at me. One time I got up my nerve and returned his stare for what seemed like an eternity, but he never broke his gaze. I soon became accustomed to the stares of these men who saw no more than a few different women's faces in their lifetimes. I think this acceptance of their stares as no more than curiosity helped me to adjust more easily to the country. I knew several women who were never able to adjust to the constant stares, wherever they went. They became hypersensitive to such scrutiny and allowed the staring to make their time in Saudi Arabia uncomfortable.

When I reflected on the evening, I pondered the similarities between the *kabsa* with the important Ministry representatives and Americans, and the *kabsa* eaten with Midwess. Both were served in the middle of the desert in a tent and on the ground, atop a plastic tablecloth. Both served basically the same menu, a menu of lamb and rice. Both served the traditional tea and coffee, and the same catering customs were observed. Perhaps these similarities contributed to Sheikh Latif's ability to feel as comfortable with a Bedouin as with a rich city dweller.

Sheikh Latif's party had included *laban*, and I was curious about the Saudi's love of it. I learned that survival encouraged early desert dwellers to invent a process to preserve fresh milk, which soured quickly in the heat and was difficult to transport. In the early years in the deserts of Arabia, when food was scarce, it was not uncommon for a man to drink four pints of milk at a time. No one knows when the thick milk of the ewe, the goat, and the camel was first stored and transported from campsite to campsite in a butchered animal's stomach. The fresh milk was boiled and set aside in these vessels to become *laban*, or fermented milk culture. The sour *laban* was the favorite drink of both the Bedouin and the city dweller and was available commercially in all supermarkets.

Although there had been a great deal of food leftover at Sheikh Latif's *kabsa*, I knew he hadn't been expecting more people because there were no empty places at the dinner. I soon learned the reason for the overabundance of food. Hospitality was considered a stringent duty in Saudi Arabia. "Offer the guest food to eat, even though you yourself are starving," was only one of many proverbs that served to remind Saudis of this duty. Sharing food and drink with strangers was a pleasure as well as a duty to the simple, close-knit tribes of the Arabian peninsula who roamed the desert with their camels, goats, and sheep in search of water and forage. All wanderers considered themselves brothers in the harsh struggle to survive. It was unthinkable to refuse sustenance to a guest, though it might mean slaughtering the last sheep. Equally unthinkable was for a guest to refuse such hospitality. Understanding the Saudi commitment to hospitality, I began to appreciate why it was the norm to see an incredible amount of food prepared compared to the number of people present for the dinner. The extra food was always prepared in case unexpected guests arrived and hospitality needed to be extended.

I noted that Sheikh Latif ate quickly and rose immediately from the carpet. The Americans quickly followed suit. I remembered how fast the meal had been eaten at Midwess's tent and decided that this also must be a custom in Saudi Arabia. Later, I learned that the habit of eating quickly is a carryover from earlier customs among the Bedouin tribes. Tradition dictates that if ten men are dining together and one gets up satisfied, the rest must get up at once also and wash their hands to indicate that they are finished. Because of this custom, Saudis and their guests learn to bolt their food in order to avoid having to leave the table hungry.

Although I accompanied Terry often when he was tending to his farming, I did spend some of my time in our house, especially the first year. When I remained home alone, a tape player was my constant companion. I had brought several music tapes from home and played them over and over, not only to obscure any loneliness but to break the absolute silence of the desert. When the tape player was broken, my world became very silent. When my tape player failed, it might be several days before an electrician had the time to repair it. I guess I was just thankful that there was an electrician in the middle of the desert who was able to repair almost any electrical appliance.

The electrician who serviced almost every electrical contraption in my home during the time that I was in Saudi was Amara Gunisekera, the same man who had tried to improve the television reception. He was a tall, thin Sri Lankan, who, like most of the other Sri Lankans, added some weight to his lean frame while in Saudi. The quantity of food in the canteen was more than the men had at mealtimes at home. He had a wife and tiny baby boy who grew to school age during the almost seven years he stayed in Saudi. Guny, as we called him, was a Buddhist, as most Sri Lankans are. After graduating from high school, he taught at an electrical training institute until he was hired to work in Saudi. Necessity had taught him to repair electrical equipment that most Americans would have thrown away. Because the average Sri Lankan earns only about one hundred dollars per month, and few will ever own their own automobiles, Guny would have felt wasteful if he had thrown something away before he made every possible attempt to repair it. Throughout my stay in Saudi Arabia, he coaxed music from my tape player.

Once when I answered a knock at my door, I discovered seven car loads of British men and women from a Riyadh hospital. They had been camping in the desert, near what is called the Turkish fort, thirty-six miles behind our farm, when they became confused driving out to the highway and happened on our camp. They were as surprised to find us living out on a farm in the desert as we were to find them at our door. Even though our farm was isolated, many foreigners spent weekends miles behind us, searching for other Turkish forts. The Turks had nominal trade off the coast of Saudi Arabia before World War I, but didn't have control of the interior, which was ruled by Bedouins. The Turks had a puppet governor of sorts situated in what is now the city of Riyadh. The port city of Al Uqair, on the Eastern coast of Saudi Arabia, welcomed the incoming boats and their goods. Watch towers, similar to forts, were built approximately every eleven miles between Al Uqair and Riyadh for the traders who transported goods across the barren desert. Most of the forts were very remote, and some have not even yet been discovered in the desert, so the fort behind our farm was a favorite for visiting. The fort itself was a basic mud structure in excellent condition.

My visitors were the first English people to whom I had ever spoken, and I loved their accents. They enjoyed hearing my Texas drawl. The men seemed friendlier than the women, but I immediately formed the opinion that the British are reserved. I was pleased that later I made some wonderful friendships with British women, who were warm and outgoing.

When the Brits returned to their vehicles to leave, I wanted to jump into the car and travel with them to Riyadh, back to civilization. But their visit had a positive effect on me. It made me realize that I had a wonderful opportunity, living out in the desert, to experience authentic Saudi culture as few foreigners could. Our British visitors had extolled our ability to transform such a barren wasteland into a lush garden of wheat, actually changing the sands to green. Somehow, their perspective changed my attitude toward my new home. Instead of thinking about the past and longing for all the things and people from which I was separated, I began to crawl from my shell of insecurity to appreciate and enjoy this strange new world around me. I thought of myself as an anthropologist who had been catapulted into the past, with limited time to learn as much as possible about a place that had its roots in ancient civilization. This is not to say that I didn't occasionally relapse into spells of homesickness and loneliness, but I didn't allow myself to wallow long in that state. I had a great deal to learn and experience.

Chapter Ten

One evening when we returned from eating at the canteen, we noticed that Sheikh Latif's Mercedes was parked at Frank's house. Terry went over to learn the reason for the visit. Soon the three men came to my house because Sheikh Latif had requested tea. I scurried around heating water and searching for my few unchipped coffee cups, wishing that I had some of the tiny cups in which the Saudis drink tea. As I worked, I determined to purchase the special tea cups.

While the men talked about the farm and rabbit hunts, a favorite sport of many Saudis, I was suddenly overcome by a feeling of embarrassment for the towels nailed over the window, the ugly vinyl couch, and the old mismatched furniture. Although I kept the house as clean as possible in the dusty climate, I dreamed of entertaining Sheikh Latif in my own house back in the States. I felt the need to show him, "this is the way I really live." I quickly recovered my perspective about the dinginess of our house in Saudi, but I still wanted to entertain Sheikh Latif at my Texas home.

Sheikh Latif had something in his hand that I had never noticed before, but Terry said he carried around with him all the time. It was a set of "worry beads." The worry or nervous beads looked like plastic, colored beads looped on a circular frame. Sheikh Latif rolled the beads between his fingers during the entire conversation. Most men in Saudi Arabia carry these beads, and we heard that the King and many of the men in the royal family have beads made of gold.

My trips to Riyadh in the early days on the farm were few and far between. Because I was not allowed to drive and had no hired driver, I was stranded on the farm except on the rare occasions when Terry had business in Riyadh. At least I was able to see quite a bit of Al Kharj on our trips to use the phone. Ironically, in my isolation, I became thankful there was no phone on the farm.

Living in Saudi Arabia taught me to be flexible. I remember when we had planned a trip to Riyadh, but as time approached for us to depart, I feared that problems on the farm might prevent us from going. My fears were realized when Terry came in to report a flat tire and tales of pivot disasters that demanded his attention. I guess Terry sensed my disappointment because we drove in to Al Kharj in the evening. After a visit to our Lebanese fast food shop, it was once again prayer time, and we began walking and looking as we had several times in the past. An older Saudi man approached us and began shouting and gesturing. Terry spoke a little Arabic to him, which seemed to have a calming effect, and the man began talking at an understandable pace. He told us that we were not supposed to be wandering around during prayer time, that everyone was supposed to be off the streets. I guessed this was not only out of respect for prayer time, but to deter any theft from the uncovered goods. From then on, whenever we were in town, we waited in the pickup, during prayer time. I had become accustomed to carrying a book with me because I spent so much time in the pickup waiting for Terry. Terry, however, became very agitated when he had to wait for prayer time to pass so that the stores could open. As we entered town, he always asked, "Is it about to be prayer time?" While we waited in the pickup, Terry remembered he needed to call the head office. To my delight, when Terry made the call, he was ordered to be in the head office the next morning at eight thirty. At long last, I would have my trip to Riyadh.

We left the farm the next morning at six thity. On the two-hour drive to Riyadh, we passed the time by watching automobiles flying past us and by counting the several wrecked cars on the sides of the road. I also observed the few farms between Al Kharj and Riyadh, as well as several large herds of camels. Most of the farms were well off the main road, but a few circles came close to the road, splattering green on the sandy canvas. Unexpectedly, a white igloo loomed along the roadside, beckoning in frozen relief against the desert. We stopped, and I was surprised to find inside the structure, which was actually painted concrete, a man selling ice cream bars, *laban,* and milk. Several Saudis drove up in cars and purchased *laban* while we were there. As we left, I saw several completely veiled women in the back seat of a Cadillac. I wondered if they would drink the *laban* purchased for them from the carton, leaving their faces shrouded by the veil, or if they would remove the veil. We passed on the *laban* and purchased ice cream. This igloo turned out to be one of three such enterprises that stood invitingly along the fifty-five miles between Al Kharj and Riyadh.

We reached the office on time, but weren't surprised when we were told the man we were supposed to meet would be late. While we waited, we met and visited with one of Sheikh Latif's brothers, Abdul Rahman al-Sheikh. He was as short as Sheikh Latif, only thinner and younger. He was talkative and spoke English, because he had studied in Washington state. We learned later that he hadn't completed his degree before returning to Saudi Arabia. He was quick to tell me that he had been married the first time for only one month when their marriage was annulled because she wanted to go back to her family. He had been remarried only three weeks and had just returned with his new wife from their honeymoon in Egypt. He boasted proudly that his wife was still in high school, and I was surprised that she was so young. I learned later that men in Saudi preferred to marry younger women, even as young as sixteen or seventeen years old, but patterns were changing, and some women were waiting until they were as old as twenty to marry. It was Sheikh Latif's brother's turn to seem surprised when I asked him whether both of his marriages were arranged; all marriages were arranged in Saudi Arabia.

The man we were supposed to meet arrived, and I was amused to learn that his name was also Abdul Rahman. He was a cousin to Sheikh Latif, as well as his brother-in-law, because his wife and Sheikh Latif's wife were sisters. We liked this Abdul Rahman from the beginning, becoming close friends with him during our long stay in Saudi Arabia. Abdul Rahman was working for Sheikh Latif, at that time, as a Saudi purchasing agent. He was not to be confused with Jamshaid, a Pakistani who actually made the purchases. That morning his intent was to go with Terry to Ziad Tractor, the John Deere dealer in Riyadh, to make purchases for the farm. The store was completely across town, so it gave me ample time for asking questions.

As Terry joined Abdul Rahman in the front seat, I slid into the back. He explained that he and his wife, Eman, had lived in the U.S. in the state of Washington for three years while he earned a degree in business. A son, Mohammed, was born while they were living there. He said that they missed many things about the United States, especially pizza and Mexican food, and that his wife begged to return to the United States because she relished not having to wear a veil. In actual fact, when I met Eman later, I asked her if she regretted having to wear a veil. She said that she didn't mind. She explained, "That is what we must do in Saudi Arabia." She did say that she missed the closeness she felt to her husband while living in the U.S. because there they went out in public together.

Abdul Rahman assured me, "Ask me anything you want to know about Saudi Arabia." I asked about the schools, and he said that they met five days a week from 7:00 A.M. to 2 P.M. with Thursday and Friday free from classes. Only elementary school was mandatory; however, the government encouraged education by providing tuition-free schools with free lunch programs. Students on the university level paid no tuition, lived in free dormitories, paid only twenty percent of food costs and twenty-five percent of books, and received three hundred dollars a month in spending money. Females had their own schools separate from males and were taught by female teachers, from elementary through the university level. Abdul Rahman added that if a Saudi Arabian wanted to study abroad on the university level, the government paid the bill, including clothes, food, and a monthly stipend. This arrangement is how Abdul Rahman studied in the States. When he attended college there, he received $750 per month stipend from the government. At one time, both Saudi men and women were allowed to study abroad, but about 1980, the government allowed females to study overseas only if they were with their husbands. There were twelve thousand Saudis studying in the United States at the time Abdul Rahman was there. He learned to speak and read English in the U.S. Even though English was taught in private schools in Saudi Arabia, it was taught only as a foreign language, not as a second language. Government schools gave little attention to teaching English to the students, and for this reason, many parents were sending their students to private Saudi schools so that they could learn English. A third type of schooling that was offered to Saudi students was strictly religious education; English was not studied in these religious schools.

I questioned Abdul Rahman about housing in Saudi Arabia. He replied that he had just recently acquired a government loan to build a house. The government made house loans at extremely reasonable rates in hopes of strengthening the urban structures in the country. The government offered up to SR 300,000 (US $85,714) to any Saudi who wanted to buy a house, charged no interest on the loan, and allowed 25 years for repayment of only 70 percent of the initial loan. He added that it wasn't absolutely necessary to pay back any amount. Saudi Arabians didn't believe in charging interest; they considered such charges usury. I question whether his information concerning repayment was factual, although I am sure some Saudis just "forgot" to pay back the loan, and the government might neglect to follow through on the collection process. I asked whether a woman had an equal opportunity to receive a loan, and he answered, "A woman has no need for a loan if she is married, because her husband can get one, and most women are married." He continued that if the government gave loans to married women, then the women might build houses and rent them, and then people would quit building, opting to rent. He boasted that while almost everything in the United States had a tax, nothing in Saudi Arabia was taxed, including income.

When we arrived back in the office after purchasing the farm parts, we were served the hot, sweetened tea, this time with milk, because the man preparing the tea was a Pakistani. It was filling to an empty stomach. I was given SR 3000 (US $860) to purchase the necessary electrical attachments to make the farm's computer function. The computer had been on the farm since before my arrival, but it was inoperable in its present state, and I had not been given any data to enter. I had to force a discussion of the farm computer. Surprisingly, they didn't seem in any hurry to have me start earning my salary. My salary was never dropped from our monthly check, even though the computer work was sporadic the whole time we were in Saudi Arabia. Although, my passport had been stamped, "Unable to work, with or without being paid," as was the custom for all wives who joined their husbands on a visit visa, I had been assured that I would have no problem working on the computer at the farm. I would be a safe distance from any authorities. In fact, Hafeez Khan had told me to settle in and then begin work. After I notified them I was ready, there was a lull of several months before I was actually able to work. I shouldn't have been concerned because they were paying Terry my salary for six months before I arrived, but I needed a diversion to occupy my time. With my fistful of riyals, I entered the computer store, resolving to fill my order and return to the farm to program the records.

Things did not work so simply in Saudi Arabia. After I assembled all of the necessary computer parts, Efren, one of the electricians, brought the last two plugs necessary to make the computer operational. I used a television set for a monitor, setting it on channel 33, as I had been told to do. I fiddled with the computer all one morning, trying to make the right connection for reception. I had no success. When Terry came in for lunch, he switched the monitor to channel 34, and it finally worked. The computer worked for only 30 seconds, and the generator died. I feared that the computer had caused the failure and in my frustration wagered that I would probably never be able to use the computer on the farm. However, the computer wasn't the problem. It was a dirty radiator instead. While I waited for the generator to be repaired, I began to see a little humor in the episode. I had waited all this time for the computer to be ready, and when it was finally hooked up and running, the generator decided to heat up and become inoperable.

While purchasing the computer parts in Riyadh, we experienced another first. We ran into a man whom Terry had already met, who flew back and forth as a free-lance agent between the United States and Saudi Arabia, buying and selling parts to many Saudi companies, including ours. He was Jim Gonsky, a big man from California, with a gift of gab. He invited us to join him for dinner at the hotel where he was staying. We were joined by Terry Jones, who once had worked for Sheikh Latif, but had parted company with him on friendly terms, and Terry Grimshaw from England, who worked with trace elements for the booming farming business. Not only was I famished, but I was anxious to visit a "real" restaurant, not just a street cafe.

The Intercontinental Hotel was fabulous. Jim gave us a tour of the elegant shops, the tennis courts, the bowling alley, the billiards room, and the swimming pool. The rooms were SR 330 (US $95) per night, but because the men stayed there for an extended period, they were given a discount and a room was only SR 280 (US $80).

As we entered the coffee shop, I was amazed at the desert decor, supposedly depicting the desert where I spent all my time. The decor simulated a desert island surrounded by all kinds of fresh fruits, pastries, and a salad bar. I compared it to our small camp surrounded by the lush green wheat in an ocean of sand. We were seated on the patio, over-looking Riyadh, and in the dark, the lighted cityscape resembled a city much like one in the States. For the moment, I forgot the honking, crowded, dusty streets I had traveled during the day.

Because Terry hadn't eaten beef steak since he had been in Saudi Arabia, he ordered a steak. The large steak was served with French fries, baby Belgium carrots, green beans, and an artichoke heart. The restaurant featured a different ethnic food every month, and I wanted to be adventurous and try the Thai food. The food was very hot and served in a variety of sauces. The salads looked exotic, and the Thai soup was a very hot broth with shrimp and Thai mushrooms. The mushrooms must have been very large, because a piece of a stem in my bowl was about two inches long. There were raw meats to be grilled Chinese style, a sweet rice, chicken livers in a curry sauce, a chicken and a beef dish, and sweet and sour fish. The fish also was served with chutney. One of the condiments was a sauce that was dark and very oily and had pieces of red chilies floating on top. I decided I probably wouldn't eat Thai food very often, but I had enjoyed the experience. Terry savored every morsel of the steak. There are a wide variety of foods offered in Saudi Arabia, probably because eating is one of the few vices that are legal.

The service in the hotel was excellent and to my delight the rest rooms were beautifully elegant, with modern commodes, a sight I hadn't seen in a public rest room since my arrival in Saudi Arabia. I felt like Cinderella at the ball. Even though our meal was SR 160 (US $50), I decided this was a place I wanted to frequent more often.

I looked forward to our last stop of the evening with great anticipation. One of the Americans visiting the farm had informed us that there was a Safeway supermarket in Riyadh. Before I came to Saudi Arabia, no one could have told me that I would actually get excited about going to a Safeway. The man had given us careful directions to the store, and Terry and I were both surprised that we found it without any problem.

From all appearances, the Safeway of Riyadh looked almost like a Safeway at home, except the aisle markers were in Arabic and the prices in riyals. The arrangement of the food was somewhat different. I found breakfast cereal on three different aisles, probably put out as a new shipment arrived. I gazed at the wonderful produce, much more artistically arranged than what I had seen in the Al Kharj market. There were items such as iceberg lettuce and celery, which I had not found before in Saudi Arabia. Most of the more unusual produce items were from Holland

and very expensive. I calculated that one of the small heads of lettuce would cost about $3.40, while I could buy local leaf lettuce in Al Kharj for about 30 cents a bunch. I refused to buy any iceberg lettuce on this shopping trip, but after living in Saudi for awhile I succumbed to the foreigners disease of "see it and buy it before it's gone." Because we ate in the canteen, I didn't really need any groceries. But I did want bar baking chocolate, nonstick cooking spray, and marshmallows, none of which were available. I did see quite a selection of interesting Oriental food, as well as crackers, cookies, cheese, and drinks, imported from France, that were reasonable in price. I hadn't seen many of these items even in the international section of the grocery stores back home. I looked forward to shopping here again and trying all of these unusual foods.

Chapter Eleven

We had an occasional humorous experiences on the farm, despite the long work hours and the confusion of workers of so many nationalities. One Friday night we ate in the canteen and tempers were a little on edge because we hadn't been able to take our usual Friday afternoon break from work. The kitchen had run out of the flatbread that the Egyptians, Pakistanis, and Indians ate at every meal. One of the old Egyptian workers shouted in Arabic that he couldn't eat without bread and that he couldn't work without eating. After listening to his ranting and raving for several minutes, Terry marched over to the man to offer the old man a piece of white bread from his own plate. The old Egyptian began shaking his head at Terry even before they were face to face. Terry insisted that he take the piece of bread, but he refused. Terry marched back to his table and proceeded to butter the piece of bread. He walked back to the irate Egyptian and offered him the buttered bread, but the man continued to shake his head. Terry went into the kitchen and liberally swathed the bread with jelly. Returning to the Egyptian, with the entire canteen watching, Terry extended the jelly and butter covered bread a final time. When the man refused to take it, Terry laid his arm around the man's shoulders and ate the butter and jelly sandwich himself. We were not sure whether it was Terry's touch or the sudden realization of the futility of demanding bread that was not available that finally caused the man to grab a piece of white bread and eat it, all the while grumbling loudly in Arabic.

Time and promptness are important in America, but are apparently not part of the Saudi way of life. Promptness was generally the exception rather than the rule. Sheikh Latif notified the farm that he was to have a dinner party for ten to twelve people about three in the afternoon. The farm made all of the preparations for the dinner, but the group never arrived nor did anyone send a message to cancel or postpone it. The table lay on the ground for hours, still spread and ready, with the fruit and the now spoiled *laban*.

About seven thirty that evening we were eating in the canteen when Sheikh Latif waltzed in and without a word of explanation, announced that he hadn't eaten all day and had a headache. The cook rushed out with a big, metal platter mounded with rice, a whole chicken, fresh *laban*, fruit, and cake. Sheikh Latif, not a big eater, ate a chicken leg, a few bites of rice and half a piece of cake. Watching him eat, I wondered if he even remembered the missed party and the wasted food. I don't think that forgetting to tell the farm about the canceled party was a characteristic acquired with wealth, but an element of a culture that long had lived in the desert without time clocks or schedules.

On one of my daily jogs, I encountered a large herd of camels, followed by two pickups, as they traversed our camp, on their way to the main highway. I hesitantly waved at a man who walked alongside the camels, and he returned my wave with great gusto. He motioned me to come closer, and although I was a little hesitant, my curiosity overcame me, and I made my way toward him. I gave the traditional greeting, which prompted a large grin and an outpouring of Arabic. I guessed that he was encouraging me to run along with the camels (although I may have been completely wrong). He asked if I'd like some camel's milk, and I told him that camel's milk was good, but that I would drink it later. I had learned that when an invitation is extended to drink tea, coffee, or camel's milk, it was polite to answer "later" rather than "no," even though both parties knew it might never occur.

A tiny boy, about nine years old, was driving the oldest of the two Toyota pickups. A completely veiled woman, the man's wife, was driving the last vehicle in the procession. The woman, eyes peeking through her veil, waved hesitantly, and I noticed that five children were crammed in the front of the vehicle with her. They were all younger than the boy driving the other pickup. There were metal trunks, which I guessed held their belongings, in the pickup bed. I wondered where they had packed their tent; I thought maybe one of them would be returning for it.

I asked the man where they were going and he replied, "Kharj." I had seen groups like this walking beside their vehicles beside the highway on their way to Al Kharj, with an occasional camel straying into the driving lane. I wondered how long it would take them to walk the thirty-five miles to Al Kharj. I walked along with the man and his camels for several minutes, and then I bade them good bye and jogged on my way. I wondered what the Bedouin woman thought of my running alone in the desert with my face uncovered, to no apparent destination.

Soon after my arrival, the farm management held its first meeting, and I was elected to take notes that were to be sent to the head office. Actually there seemed little to discuss, because this same group ate every meal together at a management table in the canteen, and talked about most problems as they ate. A meeting, however, had been requested by Hafeez Khan, so the group remained together at its table after the evening meal. The most interesting part of the entire meeting was observing the conglomeration of countries represented. There was Mr. Fida, from Pakistan, who was in charge of drilling the water wells. He was a quiet, silver-haired man who had worked in Saudi Arabia for years. His home in Pakistan was close to the Afghanistan border. He called me "Mrs. Terry."

Mr. Felipe, from Mexico, was the head of the Mexican drilling crew that Sheikh Latif had hired. He seemed to be a gallant, modern day Don Quixote who spoke excellent English.

Mr. Park, from Korea, managed The Store. He never really seemed to find his niche within the group, perhaps because he was the only member of the management from the Orient. He took great pride in being a Methodist. On one occasion Mr. Park and I discussed makeup. He was astounded at how much less expensive Estee Lauder makeup was in the United States than the exorbitant prices he had been paying in Korea for his wife's makeup. Estee Lauder had recently been introduced in Saudi Arabia, so Mr. Park had been buying a few items as gifts for his wife. The prices in Saudi weren't appreciably less than those in Korea. On my next vacation to the United States, Mr. Park entrusted me with a one-hundred dollar bill and the instruction to buy as much Estee Lauder makeup as it would buy. He was delighted when he saw the amount of makeup that I had purchased with his money.

My most comical experience involving Mr. Park was when I told Terry that we needed some new "jelly" cans in which to store our drinking water. Because we had to drive to Al Kharj to purchase water, we pumped water into a number of five gallon containers, so that we would have water for several days. I had overheard Mr. Park telling a driver to be sure to fill all the "jelly" cans with water. Terry had a good laugh at my confusion, because the containers were actually called "jerry" cans. I hadn't realized that Mr. Park was pronouncing the *r* as *l*.

Another man at the meeting was Robin Banbury, a thin, British man who managed P1 the first year that we were in Saudi Arabia. He spoke so softly that I rarely knew what he was saying. He hated the food and seemed to subsist on a diet of "chips" or French fries from the canteen and cookies from the gas station.

Jeff, a wealthy young man from Connecticut, seemed to be the most displaced person in the group. He was only in Saudi for a short time, representing his father's company. He seemed to be in withdrawal from his stateside life as a young, eligible bachelor.

Junior was a Filipino who had been promoted from the ranks of the workers to the management table. His job involved transport. He seemed to have a real identity crisis on his hands. The promotion had estranged him from the other workers, yet he really did not relate to the men in management either.

Samere, a talkative Egyptian, was also a member of the motley group. Samere had a story to tell about any topic and was conducting a strange experiment on the farm. He headed a honey bee project for Ciba-Geigy, an agricultural chemical company. Because the bees were never able to produce enough honey to sustain themselves, Samere fed them corn syrup and molasses. The project was soon abandoned.

Besides Terry and Frank, there was another Texan named Cliff Williams, from Kress, who was a tall-talking Texan, hired to operate the pump setting rig. A Sri Lankan cook served tea to this multinational group of company managers.

There always seemed to be a deliberate social and class distance between the workers and management. From the beginning, Terry and I were called Mr. and Mrs. Terry. Coming from West Texas, where farmers and farm workers call each other by their first names, we were unaccustomed to such formality. Hafeez Khan had instigated some policies that created a real gap between the two groups. Perhaps his intentions were to promote respect.

The management lived in separate, more attractive housing, and most drove their own assigned vehicles. They were at liberty to come and go as they pleased without reporting to superiors, as was required of the workers. The management sat at a table in the center of the canteen and waited for the kitchen help to serve their food and to clear their tables after they ate. The workers waited in line at a window to receive their food and bussed their own tables when they finished eating. The food for the management was Western with some variety, while the workers ate their ethnic food. In the case of the food, I think they probably preferred their food to that of the management.

From the beginning Terry attempted to democratize the system to some degree. He considered himself a worker who happened to be in charge. We showed genuine interest in each worker as an individual, taking the time and effort to learn the name that each worker was called in his own country, a practice that had been neglected before. The workers were appreciative when we asked about their families, commiserated with them when they had problems, and inquired about what they did in their own countries before coming to Saudi Arabia.

The first work force on P2 was not as nationally diverse as the management; four were Filipino, and two were Sri Lankan. With these six men we had, perhaps, the closest relationship that first year. Not long after I arrived, Terry invited all of these farm workers over one night after supper. I cooked several American desserts, and they seemed to enjoy the brownies, peanut butter cookies, sugar cookies, and chocolate cake. We requested that each worker tell us a little about himself and to autograph our atlas next to his home country. We became well acquainted with many of the workers on our farm, our respect for them growing as we learned their personal histories.

Rolando had worked for the Filipino government before moving to Saudi Arabia. He had a degree in agriculture. He owned a three-wheeler with a passenger seat, that he rented for twenty pesos a day to a man, who used it as a taxi in the Philippines. He was thirty-seven years old and had two children, one of whom he'd never seen because he had been in Saudi Arabia since before the child was born.

Efren was a maintenance electrician for the Filipino Explosive Plant before coming to Saudi Arabia. His wife, Amy, taught English and Physics, and soon became my pen pal. He had been married only a few months before coming to Saudi. He, too, had a child he'd never seen, a little girl. His grandparents had belonged to a sect of Moslems in the Philippines, but his parents had converted to Catholicism.

Vic was a truck driver in the Philippines and had three children. He played Frank's guitar and sang American songs that had been popular about ten years earlier.

Ed was a very bright and well-educated Filipino with a bachelor of science degree in Agronomy, but ironically, had one of the dirtiest and most intellectually unchallenging jobs on the farm. While visiting the Philippines, Sheikh Latif had personally hired Ed as a soil technician because of Ed's degree. Yet before Terry's arrival, Ed was assigned the job of ticketer at the gravel and sand dump on the farm. Syrian truck drivers hauled in loads of sand and gravel to use in the construction of roads on the farm. The roads allowed quick access between pivots. Every time a trucker dumped a load, Ed issued him a ticket. The trucker's pay was based on the number of tickets in his possession. Ed spent all day, every day, standing in the blowing dust, created by the dumping of the sand and gravel, issuing tickets to truckers.

While Terry's workers munched on the sweets I'd prepared, I observed the two Sri Lankans whom I especially admired, perhaps because of their humility and gentle mannerisms. Unlike the Filipinos who had seemed very much at ease in our house, Mitri and Perera sat stiffly on the edge of their seats and ate the cookies very slowly and thoughtfully. Mitri, at forty-one, was much older than Perera, who was about twenty-five years old, but the pair lived together, separate from the Filipinos. Although the Filipinos wore Western clothes, the Sri Lankans, when they weren't working, wore a type of male sari, a long piece of cloth tied around the waist like a long skirt. Mitri worked in Saudi Arabia to pay for a grocery store back in Sri Lanka. His wife, son, and daughter lived behind the store, along with his brother and his family, who were running the store in Mitri's absence. Mitri ended up working in Saudi Arabia for more than eight years. He spoke very little at my house that night, possibly because his English at that time was very limited.

Perera had worked in a tourist hotel in Sri Lanka before coming to Saudi Arabia. He worked not only as what he called a "room boy," but also as a bartender in the Intercontinental Hotel in Colombo. He spoke with pride of Sri Lanka, a beautiful tropical island that grows bountiful crops of bananas, pineapples, and mangoes. Perera soon became Terry's right-hand man on the farm because he was so efficient. Little did I realize that night that one day Perera would be our tour guide in Sri Lanka when we visited the country to hire more laborers.

As the group prepared to depart, I gathered up a parcel of sweets for each of the men to take with him to his quarters. I thought of them more as boys because they acted so shy around me. It took me several years to convince any of the fifty plus workers to call me Martha, instead of Mrs. Terry. Outside our door, the men stopped to put on their shoes. According to custom in their native lands, the men had left their sandals and shoes outside the door. They never wore them inside my house or their own quarters.

While cleaning the kitchen after the men left, I thought how different Ed's work in Saudi was, compared to what he had done before. In the Philippines, Ed had worked on a research project, raising fish in flood water from rice fields and testing to see the effects of chemicals on the fish. Somehow, when he arrived in Saudi Arabia, he ended up with the menial position of ticketer. Ed had signed a subject to placement contract with the farm when he accepted the job in Saudi Arabia. If he had failed to honor this contract, he would have been unable to get another job in Saudi Arabia.

Moreover, Ed had spent all of his savings securing this job. Because he didn't live on the mainland, he had to use his savings to buy an expensive plane ticket to Manila, where the interview with Sheikh Latif took place. Even though Ed had a confirmed interview with Al Emar, he had to tip the employment agency on his arrival to make sure he was admitted to his interview. The tip, too, was paid from his savings.

It was not uncommon for the employment agencies to forge credentials and experience on a perspective employee's resumé, for a price. We had several workers who arrived in this predicament, unable to perform their assigned duties. Although it was frustrating and time-consuming for Terry, he tried not to send the employees back to the Philippines because they needed the jobs so desperately and had spent everything they had to obtain them. These people usually agreed to work as laborers and take a pay cut, just for the opportunity to remain in Saudi Arabia. Most foreign workers, especially those from Third World countries, earned four to ten times as much in Saudi as they made at home. A general laborer on our farm was paid from three hundred to five hundred dollars per month, plus room, board, and health care.

We became good friends with Ed in the five years that we knew him. Terry recognized Ed's talents and promoted him from giving tickets to working in the farm office and farm experiment programs. Ed became acquainted with a Filipino nurse in Riyadh through his cousin. In the beginning, they corresponded by letter, and Ed was able to see Beth occasionally in the lobby of the hospital where she worked. They had to be very careful because meetings between unmarried men and women were not allowed. Beth was not allowed to go out alone in Riyadh. If she even went to the store on a hospital bus, she and the other nurses were carefully watched.

Ed and Beth talked occasionally on the phone, and through their correspondence and their rare, illegal meetings, they fell in love. They were married one summer back in the Philippines while both were on vacation. After they were married, they returned to their jobs, ninety miles apart, but with the privilege of seeing each other any Friday that Ed could travel to town from the farm. Beth soon became pregnant, and luckily, the baby wasn't due until their next vacation so that she and Ed were able to be together when the baby was born. I guess I shouldn't have been surprised when both Ed and Beth returned to Saudi Arabia for another year's work, leaving the baby girl at home for Beth's mother to raise. Until this time, I hadn't fully realized how important a job in Saudi Arabia was to these people.

Chapter Twelve

W ord of my cakes soon reached the workers at P1, and one night at supper, Abisinger, the Sri Lankan cook, approached me timidly to ask if I would make a cake for the party scheduled for the next day. I was excited that Abisinger had requested one of my cakes for the party. It was to be the most important social event since we arrived on the farm. Both Sheikh Latif and Hafeez Khan cultivated associations in important social and political circles as Saudi Arabia grew and became more diversified. When Sheikh Latif had been introduced to the American Ambassador, Richard Murphy, he had invited him, along with other political figures, to a dinner at the farm. It was for this party the cook requested that I bake a chocolate cake. As I prepared to leave the canteen that night, he handed me the ingredients I would need to prepare it and a pan in which to bake it. The pan, as wide as my oven, was the biggest one that I had ever seen.

Early the next morning I began baking. I mixed a double recipe of Chocolate Dream Cake. As I began to pour the batter into the pan, I discovered that the double recipe didn't begin to fill it. Continuing to mix, I finally filled the pan with six recipes of batter, using eighteen cups of flour. Mixing the batter was quite a feat in itself as I was mixing it by hand. The cook wanted the cake by 11:00 A.M., but at 11:15, it was still in the oven. I decided finally that it was fully cooked; Terry rushed it over to Pi, and Abisinger set it in the freezer to cool before he cut it. I quickly dressed in my denim skirt and cowboy boots for the party, deciding that I should play the part of a Texas cowgirl.

The event was held at the tent party area, and I was delighted to see about ten women in attendance, including the Ambassador's wife and her mother; Sheikh Latif's wife, Jewaher; Abdul Rahman's wife, Eman (also Jewaher's sister); Dhahara, Hafeez's wife; and several other women. There were also several Saudi children running in and out of the tent. I joined the women who were visiting in the tent, while the men stood in small groups outside. I was surprised when cold drinks were passed around instead of the usual hot tea and coffee, but I suspected that one of the Westerners had requested them, because the day was already quite warm.

We gathered in one end of the tent for lunch, which was served on the usual plastic tablecloth on the ground. Neither Jewaher or Eman covered their faces because there were no other Saudi men present besides their husbands. Although the men and women ate together, the two sexes ate at opposite ends of the tablecloth, with the children joining the women. Hafeez, the last to be seated, chose a place next to his wife so that he might be a liaison between the men and women.

The traditional Saudi fare was served and next to our three canned drinks, bottle of water, and quart of *laban*, was a large piece of my chocolate cake. One of the women asked the Ambassador's wife whether she had tasted the chocolate cake. She answered that she had recently lost two pounds and was trying to keep it off. The woman turned and commented to me that the cake was good. When I replied that I had made it, the Ambassador's wife said that she must taste it. She not only tasted it, but ate the entire piece. I was relieved.

While everyone left the table to wash their hands, Sheikh Latif quickly organized a farm tour. Everyone participated in the tour except Jewaher, Eman, and me, not only because there wasn't enough room in the vehicles for us but also because we had already seen the farm many times. I enjoyed visiting with the two women as the three of us walked around in a small area near the tent. They spoke English and were very gracious about answering my questions.

For the first time, I was able to get a close look at Sheikh Latif's wife. Jewaher had married at the age of nineteen, and she was just a little older than I. She and Abdul Latif, as she called him, were second cousins, and of course, their marriage was arranged. At the time, they had two sons, and she was studying for a degree in English from a girls' college in Riyadh. She had beautiful, thick, dark hair and a smooth olive complexion. She was very short, less than five-feet-tall with a buxom figure. Her fingernails and toenails were painted a bright red. She spoke softly and quickly. Being sisters, Jewaher and Eman looked much alike, although Eman was thinner and a year younger. Eman spoke less than Jewaher, although her English was also good. At the time, she was three months pregnant with her second child. Both women covered their heads as we walked, ready to drop their veils at a moment's notice.

I wore my hair short at that time, and I asked them where I might have my hair cut. They both informed me that there were beauty shops for women, but that they couldn't be advertised or be visible in public. They assured me that one just had to know where they were located. Also, many Filipino maids and cooks were quite skilled in hair styling and would fix the hair of the women with whom they lived and worked. I was disappointed that they didn't tell me exactly where a shop was located.

When I asked them where they bought their clothes, they said that all their clothes were hand-tailored by male tailors from India and Pakistan. Women select fabric and a picture of a dress, and the tailor copies the design without the use of a pattern. The tailor is not allowed to take a woman's measurements and never fits the garment to the woman or sees it on her. They explained that all their clothes are hand-tailored because they can't find appropriate long dresses in stores. All of the ready-made clothes in Saudi Arabia are imported and generally considered inferior by Saudi standards. Moreover, the standard long dress was not readily available from other countries.

Because women in Saudi Arabia belong to a private world, veiling before strangers is an important custom. Although foreign females are not required to veil, they must observe local standards of dress and are required to wear clothing that covers the neck, arms, and legs. Saudi women are heavily veiled and shrouded outside the home. Few observers realize that beneath the veil and black cloak, the Saudi woman wears the latest fashions in Western-designed clothes, only in a longer-length version. The black cloak, called an *abaya,* is floor length and is worn in public at all times.

Women began covering their faces when Arabia was a land of warring tribesmen, roaming about stealing women and camels. The theory was that a bandit would be less likely to risk stealing a woman whom he couldn't see because she might prove to be ugly.

Although all Saudi women veiled their faces, veiling is not a religious requirement, as most people believe. The Koran, verse 59 of Surah 33, allows a woman to reveal her face and the lowest part of her hands. A. Zuberi, a writer for the Arab News, interpreted verse 59 in "Women's Dress," Nov. 17, 1986: "If a Moslem woman wants to cover her face or her hands, she is free to do so, but if she does not, then she is not violating any teachings of Islam." Yet despite many modern innovations and technological advancements within the country, the veil had not disappeared in Saudi Arabia. It was used by all Saudi women. The only males allowed to view a Saudi woman's face in Saudi Arabia were her father, her brothers, her husband, and her sons.

Saudi Arabian children looked like small men and women, differing in costume from their parents only in size. Except when playing soccer, male children began at a very young age to wear the *thobe.* The boys wore warmups when playing soccer, although we saw boys out in vacant lots in Riyadh playing in their *thobes* and holding them up as they ran. The girls wore long dresses, although occasionally a young Saudi girl with a liberal mother and father may have worn Western jeans in the privacy of her own home. A girl veiled her face when she reached puberty, but many girls started covering their faces at about twelve years of age. As I studied Eman and Jewaher, I tried to imagine them as young girls, before they began wearing veils.

When the farm tour returned, the visitors prepared to go back to Riyadh. They commented with admiration on the wonderful transformation of the sands to green. I discovered that Sheikh Latif had a sense of humor when he told me boldly that he had heard me complaining to the Ambassador about how long it had taken the company to get my visa so that I could join Terry. I jokingly replied that yes, I had complained, and that the Ambassador hadn't even liked Sheikh Latif until he found out that I had made the chocolate cake and that my husband worked for him. We both laughed, glad to discover each other's sense of humor.

The Ambassador's wife, Mrs. Murphy, told me that they had lived in Jeddah from 1965 to 68, and had thought Saudi Arabia much more liberated for women than on this visit. Although we never saw Richard Murphy again, we were pleased to have met him. After serving as the American Ambassador to Saudi Arabia for several years, he was promoted to a position in Middle Eastern affairs.

Before long I discovered that there were other farms near us that maintained a greater level of creature comforts. Al Rafia was a farm about fifteen kilometers down the road toward Al Kharj and about ten kilometers off the main road down a terribly bumpy path. We had a chance to see the farm firsthand when Terry was instructed to take a look at a piece of equipment they owned.

The camp at Al Rafia was surrounded by a tall cement wall, and as we neared the closed gate, a Sri Lankan man came out of a small building to check our credentials. Inside the gate, I was transported out of the desert; we were surrounded by a beautifully manicured lawn, flowers, trees, and even a man-made waterfall. Al Rafia, we learned, is a hobby for one of the princes in the royal family and is supposed to be a model for other farms.

We had only about seven workers that first year for a farm with thirty-five pivots, whereas, Al Rafia employed seventy Sri Lankans for a farm with the same number of pivots. The employees on this farm were furnished not only food and housing, as our workers were, but also uniforms, coats, boots, laundry and bath soap, and two cans of Pepsi a day. I could imagine that working here was every laborer's dream. I had assumed that we didn't have a telephone because we were too far out. I learned, however, that the real reason that we didn't have one was because we were in a military protected zone. Because the owner of this farm was a prince, the farm was able to get a permit to have a radio phone system to enable the prince to communicate with Riyadh during the four to six times a year he visited the farm.

We spoke with Bob Norris, the English manager, and Mark, the field manager from Pennsylvania, who had a gift of gab. He'd acquired his job on the farm through his sister, who had met and married a Saudi in the States. The couple then moved to Riyadh.

His brother-in-law was half Saudi and half Egyptian and was becoming rich in the air conditioning installation business in Riyadh. Mark's sister had a job as a secretary to the business manager of the prince who owned Al Rafia. Because she wasn't supposed to be working, she had been surprised when she was offered twenty-five hundred dollars a month. She discovered that part of the reason for the offer was the prestige of having (albeit illicitly) an American secretary in Saudi Arabia. She was able to get her brother his job on the farm. We enjoyed visiting a comfortable farm camp, a stark contrast to our own.

One day, during a particularly bad dust storm, I looked out the window of my small container onto the camp and was frightened to see a brick wall that stood next to the generator begin to weave and suddenly crumble. I knew the sandstorm was severe because I could actually feel the dirt blowing into my house, through the cracks in the wall. Rain, the first I had seen in Saudi Arabia, followed the dusty day, pouring all one night and into the next morning. I was amazed at how hard and fast it fell. The average rainfall in our area of the country was three inches a year, and we received two inches during this one rain. Water stood in big puddles all around the farm, and the edges of some of the wheat pivots were completely flooded. The mud brought the farm work to a grinding standstill. Amazingly, the water seemed to stand on top of the sand and not be absorbed by the dry earth. Karl joined us, and we took off for some rest and relaxation in Riyadh. Between the farm and Al Kharj, the rain had created little lakes of water in low spots. To our fascination and amusement, large groups of Saudis frolicked in the water, as Texans might do in a rare snow. The men tied up their *thobes*, revealing white shorts underneath. The veiled women tromped through the water in their long dresses. Children ran in and out of the puddles, splashing and having a wonderful time. Cars and pickups were parked on the shoulder of the highway, creating an occasional traffic problem. Sections of the highway were completely under water, and when we entered the outskirts of Riyadh, we saw some areas were flooded, causing cars to stall and block traffic.

We intended to take the trip for pleasure, but made the mistake of taking a typewriter to the office for repair. The result was that we spent two hours there while Terry reported on farm matters. On this trip, we also had business with the Saudi postal system because Karl had a package ready to mail to his wife, Sue. We searched out Riyadh's main post office, which looked much like our post offices in the States. After a lengthy discussion, we realized that we were not allowed to mail a package from this particular post office where only letters were accepted. In order to mail a package out of the country, we had to take the unwrapped item for mailing to a customs office at the airport, where it would be inspected and then mailed.

We threaded our way through the crowded city, at last locating the customs office, which was open five days a week. We were disappointed to learn that even though this was the only place in Riyadh where a package could be mailed, it closed at 1:00 P.M.

This was not our first encounter with the complexities of the Saudi postal system. Terry wore into Riyadh that day a brand new pair of Wrangler jeans that had arrived only a few days before in a package from my parents for his birthday. They had to pay sixteen dollars in postage to mail the package, but it made the trip in a record ten days. The man in our office who picked up the farm mail daily explained that there had been a few other items in the package including a small book, a voice tape, and a birthday card. He had to leave these things overnight while the post office inspected them, then return the next day to claim everything that was approved. This was my first encounter with Saudi censorship. Almost two weeks later, I received the items that had been retained and noticed that they had been treated roughly.

Although the Saudi government subsidized many of the social systems, including medicine and education, we didn't qualify for most of the benefits. Yet anyone in Saudi could enjoy the low postal rates, which until 1987 had remained constant for twenty-three years. Before the 1987 hike, we mailed a letter within the country for as little as 20 hilalah (7 cents). In 1987, the in-country mailing cost did increase to 1 riyal (36 cents), but foreign mailing rates were still a bargain. Before the hike, I mailed a cassette voice tape to the United States to my parents for SR 3 (86 cents). After the price hike, the cost of mailing a tape doubled to SR 6 ($1.60), which was still less than the rate from the U.S. to Saudi Arabia.

We turned our attention from the post office to the gold market. The main purpose of the trip was to locate the market or suq. Terry, who had been to the market before, had described it to me, but it was not until I actually saw it that I realized how breathtaking row after row of shops containing all kinds of 18 and 21 karat gold can be.

Litter cluttered the sidewalk that led us to an area that resembled a narrow alley. We gazed ahead at a long line of shops selling gold. Along the way, black women sat on the sidewalk selling nuts, packaged cookies, and canned drinks from baskets or metal tubs. We stepped from one world into another when we left the crowded, dusty street and turned into the tinsel world of glitter and gold. The sight was breathtaking. Shop after shop dazzled us with its wares, hanging all over the walls and lying inside glass cases.

Jewelry was important to Saudi women. Because the gold jewelry was actually a Saudi woman's sole property, women, particularly Bedouin women, kept all of their gold jewelry with them at all times. It was not uncommon to see as many as twenty gold bracelets on each arm of a Saudi woman. If a Saudi woman was divorced by her husband, she was allowed to take all of the jewelry she had acquired.

Gold jewelry was a real bargain in Saudi Arabia because one didn't have to pay for craftsmanship. The cost of gold jewelry varied according to the daily world market price for gold. Any gold item, no matter how intricate, was placed on a scale to be weighed so that the price could be calculated. Because the world market price was based on 24 carat gold, and the gold jewelry sold in Saudi Arabia was 18 or 21 carat, the cost of the gold was slightly inflated. Nonetheless, compared to that in the United States, the jewelry was still quite inexpensive.

We walked into several shops and asked to see different pieces of jewelry. The male owners left several pieces of jewelry with us, while they waited on other customers. They seemed to have little fear that we might steal from them. We selected a 20-inch serpentine chain of 18 carat gold. The market price for the day was SR 45 (US $12.86) per ounce so the cost came to SR 164 ($47). Terry was acclimated to the custom of bargaining. He bartered with the shop keeper and paid SR 150 (US $42.85) for the chain.

Facing a two-hour drive home, we piled into the pickup and headed out of town. Not too far out of Riyadh, we were stopped by a long line of cars in front of us on the highway. We asked a passenger in one of the last cars the reason for the delay. It was a driver's license check. Because neither Terry nor Karl had a license, and I, a woman, was with them, we turned around and headed back into Riyadh.

Hoping to give the driver's license check time to conclude, we decided to eat. Cruising the streets of Riyadh, we passed the Merryland Restaurant and decided to try it. A smiling waiter welcomed us to his Syrian establishment. There were no printed menus; the waiter recited the selections that were available. Karl and I chose asparagus soup, and Terry selected the chicken soup. None of us recognized any other foods on the menu, so Karl selected a dish that contained the word Oriental in its title. Terry chose a Syrian entree. I ordered only the soup. Karl asked the waiter the cost of the Oriental food that he'd ordered, and he replied, SR 15 ($4.30).

I needed to go to the ladies' room and rather hesitantly asked the waiter if the restaurant had a toilet, the English word used in Saudi Arabia. He studied me for a minute and said, "No, but you can use my villa." He told a young Syrian busboy to take me to his villa. Terry accompanied me. We followed the young man out the back exit of the restaurant and down a dirty alley where we stopped in front of a tall metal fence. The agile guide jumped onto a pile of old tires and effortlessly jumped over the fence and opened the gate from the inside. His explanation was brief, "No key."

The gate led into a courtyard, common in most homes in Saudi Arabia. Whereas an open-concept plan within the home is popular, seclusion from the outside world is preferred. Most houses have high walls around a small courtyard in front of the house. Smaller homes have virtually windowless walls exposed to the street, with a sheltered courtyard in the center of the house. Because all houses, called flats or villas, are surrounded by high walls, it is very difficult to locate a particular house without the aid of a posted address.

Our guide led us to a closed door, just inside the front door. He tried opening the door and found it locked; we waited. In a minute, a man opened the door and passed by us without a glance. The toilet, a typical hole in the floor, was dirty and smelly.

Terry waited for me. I kept the door partially ajar because the light bulb inside was burned out and I could not see when the door was closed. I also could not tolerate being enclosed with the odor. Our guide left us to find our own way back to the restaurant.

When we returned to the table, our soup had already been served. My asparagus soup was surprisingly thick and creamy, with pieces of white asparagus floating on top. Before we had finished our soup, the waiter brought a relish plate of two different kinds of sour pickles, pickled green chilies, black olives, and fresh mint leaves. He also brought three bowls of dip. I asked him the ingredients in each. One dip contained mashed chick peas, garlic, onion, lemon juice, oil, and yogurt. The second bowl was a mixture of eggplant, lemon, oil, yogurt, garlic, and parsley. The last bowl was identical to the eggplant dip, but with the addition of tomatoes. The main course was served on an oval platter with a large piece of flatbread, topped with "soft meat," or ground lamb, and pieces of grilled lamb and chicken. This mixture was covered with another large round of flatbread topped with parsley, tomatoes, onion, and a few whole chick peas. Terry and Karl thought they ordered different things, but the waiter brought nothing else. We had plenty to eat, but we never figured out what we had ordered. Our bill came to 109 riyals, ($32.70). We had no idea what the waiter had meant when he told Karl that his food cost SR 15.

Although the Syrian restaurant had been a good diversion, we had not succeeded in outwaiting the license check. As we headed out of town again, approaching the check point, we saw a steady stream of cars turning off into the desert to skirt the check. We fell in line with them and found ourselves following a well-trodden camel path. We were fortunate to have four-wheel drive, because the rain had created sandy mud. Several cars were stuck along the way, but it wasn't long until the path found its way back onto the main highway. As we crept along portions of the road that were underwater, we also had to contend with fog, a weather condition that rarely occurs in Saudi Arabia. We arrived on the farm at 1:30 A.M., feeling like criminals who had outwitted the law.

Chapter Thirteen

Terry learned Arabic rapidly and was able to speak fluently with the Bedouins. During the first year that I was in Saudi Arabia, Terry began instructing me in Arabic, teaching me a new word every day. Although I continued to learn an occasional word in the following years, I never learned as much as I did on our trips back and forth to the gas station. During the first years in Saudi Arabia, we traveled fourteen miles for gasoline before a gas station opened closer to our farm.

The Bedouins didn't mind our crude grammar. We might omit the verb in a sentence and say, "Tomorrow Friday." The Bedouins loved our attempts at speaking in Arabic, and they drew meaning from our stumbling efforts to communicate. Terry often played the role of mediator between the Bedouins and our head office, composed mostly of Pakistanis, translating messages and grievances between the two.

On one particular Thursday-Friday weekend when Sheikh Latif was at the farm, several Bedouins approached him, very agitated and distressed about some graves on P2. Terry followed the Bedouins to the supposed grave site, and I went along in case anything exciting developed. We followed the two Bedouin pickups to the back of the farm. Stopping near pivot 59, about ten miles behind camp, the oldest man jumped out in the middle of an area where the road was to be built and began pointing at the earth. He claimed that there were many Bedouins buried there and that if cars drove over their graves, they would cry out. We were doubtful about the veracity of this story because the area looked no different than any other desert spot. According to Sheikh Latif's directives, however, the road should detour around the spot of the alleged graves, and dirt should be bulldozed around the graves to insure that they remained covered. After Terry explained our efforts to protect the graves, the men became friendly. One of the men asked Terry if I was his only wife and extended us an invitation to join them for tea. As etiquette dictated, we responded that we must decline until later.

It was unusual for the men to know about the graves, because burial places were not prominent in Saudi Arabia. We never saw a grave that we recognized as such. Saudis were buried in unmarked graves, and even the founder, King Abdul Aziz, was laid to rest in a spot marked by a few plain, flat stones. Only men took part in burials, and women never went to the grave site, or even knew its location, in most cases.

When we returned to camp from the graveyard, we met Sheikh Latif and his family touring the farm in his Mercedes, followed by Abdul Rahman and his family. They informed us that they would come by our house a little later. This announcement sent me into a panic, even though I kept our tiny house clean. Remembering we had little drinking water we grabbed one of our jugs, ran to pivot 17 and quickly filled it with water. At last the group arrived and crowded into our small living room. As I poured the tea, I noticed it had turned black from sitting so long. Our guests ignored the fact, adding several spoonfuls of sugar. The women also seemed oblivious to my nailed-up towels and the mismatched cups. I showed them pictures of our two dogs back home and a rubber camel that a friend of mine had given me as a going away present. Both were ridiculous items to have shown. Saudis don't have dogs for pets; they believe dogs are unclean and intended for herding only.

Thinking back, I'm sure their impression of this American farm couple was quite the opposite of what it might have been had they visited us in the States. Our guests stayed about fifteen minutes, but the conversation seemed to have reached its end by this time anyway. Both sisters invited me to go shopping with them in Riyadh, and even though this was not the first time that I had received this invitation from them, it was the first time I actually felt as though they were sincere in asking.

As we watched the Mercedes leave camp, there was a group of Egyptians standing at the fence waiting for a ride to P1. Because vehicles were limited, most of the workers hitched rides with vehicles that traveled between farms. The Egyptians had been working at P2 all day and were waiting to return to P1 for supper. We usually took a group of workers with us in the evening when we went to P1 to eat. We loaded up the workers in our pickup and started for the canteen. When we reached the highway, a Palestinian farmer, who lived in a stone-block house on the edge of the farm, ran out of the house and waved for us to stop. The man's possessions were rolled up in two pieces of plastic that resembled the bags that contained the urea for the farm. He asked if we'd mind taking him about three kilometers in the opposite direction from P1, and we agreed. He jumped in the back and rode with the farm workers. At the destination, he alighted at the door of a tent we guessed would be his new home!

Because most of the wells had been drilled, it was time for the Mexican drillers to leave. When we told friends back home that we had well drillers from Mexico, they always assumed that we were drilling for oil. It must not have occurred to them immediately that water is as precious in Saudi Arabia as oil is in the United States. It was always exciting to test-pump a new well that the Mexicans drilled and to determine the amount of water flow. However, it took some patience to handle the water situation on the farm.

Upon arrival in Saudi, we were told that the water was too salty to drink, and we would have to purchase all of our water for drinking and cooking. Yet during the first year, because we were farm kids accustomed to drinking well water, we drank the water that came from one of the wells on our farm. We couldn't drink the water that came from our faucets because it was stored in an old, rusty tank before it was pumped into our homes. We took five-gallon containers to one of the wells, filled them, and transported them back to our house to use for drinking and cooking. Eventually though, we began to hear about people who developed kidney stones because of the salt content of the well water. We had our water tested, and whereas the World Health Organization recommends 800 parts per million of salt, the salt content of our water tested to be 1100 parts per million.

We began to buy our water in Al Kharj, hauling the five-gallon jugs in the back of our pickup and filling them from a spigot that was identical to the one in which gasoline was dispensed. During those first few years in Saudi Arabia, drinking water cost twelve cents a gallon, two cents more per gallon than we paid for diesel. I felt like a pioneer hauling water back to the covered wagon from the creek; however, the water trips provided a good excuse to leave the farm and drive the thirty-five miles into town.

On a Friday afternoon, with their laundry washed and hanging on the farm fence, a crowded pickup load of Filipino workers went into Al Kharj with us to get water. They planned to eat at this strangely named little restaurant, the Blue Wave, whose specialty was fried chicken. We decided to patronize the Blue Wave, also.

We arrived just as prayer time began, and the doors were closed. Terry had been tipped by the Filipinos to go around to the back door, where we discovered a black market entrance for non-Moslems who wanted to eat illegally during prayer time. There were no menus because the choice was either chicken or fish, each represented by a picture. On each of the tables covered with plastic cloths was a little water cooler and a dirty plastic basket for the flat bread. I was excited to see a small TV, but I soon discovered that the only station was running a feature about religious pilgrims marching around Mecca. Yet we joined the other patrons who were staring at the tiny TV.

Our salad arrived first, along with the traditional relish tray containing olives and green onions. The tomatoes in the salad were green, but everyone else seemed to be eating them. I followed their example. The smiling Asian who operated the Blue Wave also brought us a small bowl filled with what looked like sand dissolved in oil. The mixture had a strong garlic flavor with a smooth, almost pasty texture. We dipped the flat bread into the unusual dip, that I would someday learn to call hummus, made from ground chick peas and tahena (sesame seed paste). The chicken arrived underneath another piece of flatbread. I could not help noting the strange way the small chicken, fried without batter, had been cut. Our bill for all the food, a pleasant change for our taste buds, was SR 36 (about $10).

The Blue Wave in Al Kharj was near the suq, or market, and after our meal, we walked through the rows of small shops. In the more modern area there were several electronic shops with TVs, cassette players, and black market cassette tapes. When I noted the many barber and tailor shops that were for men only, I realized once again that I was in a man's world. Dressmakers and beauty shops were not visible, but as I learned later, were available if you knew where to find them. Wealthy Saudi wives who imported Filipino women to clean house or take care of the children soon discovered the talent of the Filipinos in hair design. It was not unusual for these house girls to operate hair styling businesses on the side.

The older area of Al Kharj contained more traditional Saudi items such as coffee pots, incense burners, and the beans, seeds, and spices used in traditional drinks and foods. One young boy sold wristwatches that were draped over his arm. A man pulled his pickup into the area to sell clothes from the pickup bed. Several vendors peddled their goods in wheelbarrows. I purchased two real treasures from one vendor, a hand-cranked beater and a hand-operated can opener.

I was disappointed that I saw only one woman who had her face uncovered. She spoke a language that I did not recognize, and she was not receptive to the smiles I sent her way. She obviously was not as deprived as I of female companionship.

Eventually, we no longer had to go into Al Kharj to buy water. When the population around our farm increased, a friendly man from India, with a water truck, operated a thriving business delivering water directly to the farms. Although I relished the luxury of having a constant source of drinking water, I missed the excuse for our frequent forays into Al Kharj.

We hated to see the Mexican water well drillers go, but the Mexicans were thrilled to be leaving. They had never known a land such as Saudi Arabia and were anxious to get home to drink some beer and eat Mexican food. We invited the group of nine Mexicans over for chocolate cake the night before they were scheduled to leave. Three of the nine men brought cameras and took picture after picture of Terry and me with them and with all the other men. Although two of the men spoke a little English, the remainder enjoyed conversing in Spanish with Terry. The men showed much interest in the television and VCR that Al Emar had recently purchased for us, so we played the *Rocky II* video. The entire group became engrossed in a movie whose dialogue most could not understand.

Chapter Fourteen

As time passed, we decided it was time to visit Midwess again. We had a standing invitation to his tent. I believe he would have loved for us to call on him every night. Midwess sang as Frank strummed his guitar. I'm not sure if I was just accustomed to the sound of his voice, or if the moaning noise had become melodic. For the first time, all three of the women—Mama; Midwess's wife, Rashmi; and Midwess's sister—sat with us while we drank tea and coffee, although they didn't take any themselves. When we moved inside the tent for the meal of the usual chicken and rice, the women didn't join us, but they returned for the coffee and tea ritual after the meal. Frank helped Midwess milk the camel. After several futile attempts at milking, the camel tried to kick Frank; Midwess thought this was hilarious.

During the evening, Mohammed, Midwess's oldest son, brought a Rubik's cube from the tent. I had no idea how they had obtained one. I don't think the family knew what to do with it, but after Terry scrambled the parts and showed Midwess how to align one side of the cube, Midwess repeated the process on another side.

The Bedouin family was barefoot while they sat around the fire. Frank grabbed one of Mohammed's feet and counted his toes as he recited, "This little piggy went to market, this little piggy stayed home, this little piggy had roast beef, this little piggy had none, and this little piggy cried, 'Wee, Wee, Wee,' all the way home!" Even though they had no idea of the meaning of the words, the rhyming and cadence of Frank's voice and his playful tugging on the toes created a mood of camaraderie and joviality. It was hard to imagine that this giggling little boy had driven Midwess's bulldozer. It also was sobering to remember that neither he nor his mother or father could read or write.

At one point during the evening, Frank dozed off to sleep, prompting Mohammed to watch Frank intently and giggle. When Frank awoke, he and Terry decided that Frank should act as though he were asleep again and Terry would encourage Mohammed to sneak up on Frank. The entire scheme was planned in English without our hosts understanding a word. As Mohammed crept up on the apparently sleeping Frank, Frank scared him. The women squealed with delight; I pondered whether their lives were filled with much laughter or gaiety. As we bid our friends goodbye, Midwess reminded Terry that earlier in the evening I had promised to visit the women the next day.

When I awoke the next morning, a sense of dread overtook my enthusiasm. Being unable to speak to the Bedouin women scared me. I forced myself to dress and forgot at the time that my desert friends might find my jeans very unusual for a woman.

Terry took me to the Bedouin tent at the back of the farm. I arrived at 9:30 A.M., and Terry promised to return about noon. The two and a half hours seemed to loom like an eternity. Upon my arrival, four women emerged from the tent, completely covered. It was the first time I'd seen them in the daylight, so I felt as though I were seeing them more clearly. I was able to distinguish between the shrouded figures: Mama, Rashmi, Midwess's sister, and a new member whom they said was the wife of Midwess's brother, Abdallah. Each woman shook my hand and brushed each of my cheeks with her lips, beneath her veil. A little boy I hadn't met before, Hidi, stood beside Mohammed and Abdallah. He was a doll with dark eyes and dark curly hair. Mohammed left in his pickup to check the sheep and camels that were grazing off in the distance, and I was surprised to see that Abdallah went with him. I guessed that perhaps the women were taking a holiday from herding the sheep because I had come to visit.

We went into the tent where we usually ate dinner and sat down on the sandy rug. Everything seemed so bleak and bare in the daylight, without the campfire and shadows to create illusions of The Arabian Nights. The women motioned for me to take off the coat I'd worn, and Rashmi shyly brought out a dress for me.

The authentic Bedouin dress reminded me of Jacob's coat of many colors. It was of a sheer fabric because the Bedouin women wear several dresses at a time, with a type of warm-up suit underneath. The orange material was adorned with embroidered flowers. Many of the threads were loose, and there were several torn places. The dress had a square, black yoke with a tiny purple stand-up collar and tie. The yoke had two bias pieces on either side, one red and the other blue. Most of the dress was sewn with a bright green thread. There was a narrow blue bias strip at the bottom of the sleeve and a snap at the cuff. The dress was obviously worn, and the selvage of the material served as the hem. I guessed that the dress belonged to Rashmi. As I pulled the dress over my head, on top of my other clothes, I noticed how tightly the bust fit. Then I remembered that most desert women do not wear bras. The sleeves were very fitted, and I couldn't fasten the snap on the cuff. I smelled all the Bedouin camp smells in the material, the cardamom coffee, fire smoke, sheep, and dust. The women told me that the dress was called a *thobe,* the same name given to the long white "dress" a Saudi man wears.

Mama pulled me to my feet and, holding both my hands, danced me around the tent a few minutes, as the women squealed with delight. The sister-in-law dug deep into a nearby trunk, pulling out a large jagged piece of mirror, about 9 x 12 inches, and held it up for me to see myself. Mama brought a long piece of sheer black netting that she skillfully wrapped tightly around my head, completely covering my hair. The end hung down in front and she called it a *shal.* Next, they put the traditional Bedouin veil over my face, and I was glad I wasn't wearing the veil that the Saudi women in the city wore that had no slits for the eyes. They called the veil a *burqa.* Last, a pink and white shawl was draped over my head and around my shoulders. Again they brought the mirror, and we all said *quayis* (good). They noticed that my eyebrows were showing so they adjusted the *burqa* to cover my eyebrows, indicating that eyebrows are not to show either. They gestured that Terry might have to take a picture of me dressed up as a Bedouin, and I said "Yes, and can he take all of our pictures?" They replied, "No."

When they were dressing me, Mama noticed that I had pierced ears. She pointed to one of my earrings; I took it out and they all passed it around. I was wearing an imitation gold earring, but by the way they looked, I knew they thought it was real. I wished I'd known the word for fake, because it would have somehow made me feel more honest. Mama raised the side of her veil, revealing her ear with a hole in it, but without an earring. All the women raised the sides of their veils, showing their ears, but only the sister had a pair of earrings in her pierced ears. Her earrings were very heavy looking and gold. I think the women were trying to explain why the other women didn't have their earrings in their ears; I didn't understand.

I tried to explain in my few Arabic words that I wanted to take off all that I had on around my head and face and put it back on by myself so that I would know how to do it. When I repeatedly lifted my veil and put it down to indicate that I wanted to practice, Mama must have thought that I wanted to see their faces. In a very quick motion and for only a few seconds, she lifted her veil, allowing me to see her face for the first time. Originally, Terry and I had thought that she was very old because of her aged hands and feet and the slow pace at which she moved. But her face, except for her wrinkled eyes, was very smooth and fairly young. It was several shades lighter than her hands and feet. Her hair was braided in a long thin braid that had probably never been cut. She was the only woman who wore shoes, a pair of old rubber thong sandals. The bottoms of her feet looked as worn as the old rubber. I finally dropped the subject of practicing putting on my new attire. All their veils remained in place over their faces.

They made signs to ask me when Terry would return, and I just pointed to the 12 on my watch and was able to say 12 in Arabic. They wore rather worn and weathered watches, and from then on they kept a close watch on the clock. We sat for a moment in comfortable silence, comparing and contrasting our two worlds. Then I suggested that when Terry came for me that we act as though I was one of them, and we'd say that Martha had already gone. I suppose that I communicated my thoughts accurately because they were highly amused, and when Mama frequently recalled our little plan, they giggled with delight. I decided that Mama assumed the role of official spokesperson. They spoke to each other in Arabic. Then Mama turned to me and said the same thing to me in a slower, more deliberately enunciated Arabic, none of which I understood!

Feeling more at ease, I asked where they slept. Mama took my arm and directed me to one of the four tents. I guessed it was used as a bedroom when I saw a thin, brightly covered mattress propped against one side of the tent flap. This was the only sleeping quarter that I saw.

I learned later that in the Bedouin tents, men and women sleep separately, with the children sleeping with the women. The Bedouin couple's sex life lacks intimacy and privacy. The man enters the tent from the back side, and in a secluded corner of the tent, in a very short period of time, he has sex with his wife. Many women do not even remove their veils.

Even though the floors were dirt, each tent had some kind of dirty rug on the floor. In the women's sleeping tent, the women brought out two sewing machines, one that belonged to Mama and one that belonged to Rashmi. The ancient machines had a wheel that turned to generate the power to run them.

Mama announced coffee, so we entered the kitchen tent. The kitchen was sectioned off from the remainder of the tent by a partition made of blankets hanging on a bench made of tree limbs. The branches were precious commodities because I had seen very few large trees in our area, other than the palm trees that had been planted in Al Kharj. Beneath the rack were several large burlap bags, and I could see canned goods and rice poking out of the top of a couple of sacks. The tea and coffee were kept in a metal trunk. The stove consisted of two propane burners that were lit with a match. The only cooking utensils that I noticed were a big spoon, two big pots with lids, and two big kettles. Turning up the propane fire, Rashmi put some coffee beans in a little black can with a handle and shook them over the fire to roast. Placing them in a heavy brass mortar, she ground them with a pestle. Pouring the powder into a kettle of boiling water, she repeated the grinding process with cardamom seeds. We hunched around the propane burners, but when she finished, they motioned me to walk to the other side of another partition made of an old wool blanket hung from the top of the tent. We sat down, drank our coffee, and ate dates. Mohammed returned and dropped Hidi off at the tent; he was probably tired and ready for a morning snack.

Except for the epidemic of flies, which worsened as the morning progressed, I realized that I was actually enjoying myself. When Hidi and Abdallah ate a date, the flies landed on the sticky remains around their mouths. It didn't seem to bother any of the other women, so I tried to restrain myself from shooing the flies from their mouths. If I had lived in the desert all of my life, as they had, I supposed that I'd get used to the flies and wouldn't even notice them.

While we sipped our coffee, I studied the women's hands. I observed that each one of them had the trace of color from henna on each fingernail and on their palms, as the city visitors had at Riyadh Farm. When I pointed to the color, they brought out some henna powder in a tiny cloth sack. Mama put some in her hand and mixed it with water. She then made a tight fist with her fingernails, touching the mixture in her palm and pretended to sleep. Then she acted out waking up and looking excitedly at her palms, indicating that the color would be on her fingernails. Her animation in explanation entertained not only me but the other women as well.

I supposed that Mama felt confident leaving me for a few minutes because she walked outside and busied herself with the few newborn lambs that were still in camp. One of the tiny lambs wandered in and out of the tent on its spindly legs, and I was the only one who acted surprised at its entrance. At one point, Mama went into the kitchen, returning with a piece of the hard, rock-like dried sheep's milk. The group, especially the two children, acted as though she had brought candy, and I pretended to be as thrilled about it as they were.

After I'd had the required cups of cardamon coffee, tea was next on the agenda. I asked them to show me how they made tea. I was surprised that they used loose tea leaves and about three fourths cup of sugar for each little six-cup pot. They had the same hard, rock-like sugar, which looks like our ice cream salt, that I'd found in the market. They kept smaller amounts of coffee beans and tea leaves in two oatmeal cans, and the sugar was kept in a tall can that once had contained powdered milk. They showed me that the larger sizes of these items were kept underneath the board that served as a table for holding the smaller items.

Their system of washing the cups made perfect sense for people who had no sink or washing machine, nor any ready source of water, running or otherwise. As each one finished with a cup, whoever was pouring the tea or coffee took the glass and swished it around in a small bowl of hot water, just as Midwess had done.

The most important subject on their minds was babies. Even though we'd discussed the subject the night before, they asked me how long I'd been married and why I didn't have any babies. When I tried to explain about my working in the States and then not wanting to start our family here in Saudi, I was met with blank stares. I thought that they seemed to have some comprehension when I said that I didn't want to have a baby in Saudi Arabia. My thoughts of such understanding were short-lived because Rashmi asked me if I had a baby inside. When I told her no, she shyly revealed to me that she was pregnant. They approved when I showed excitement for her. I didn't understand whether she said she was due in four months or whether she was only four months pregnant. It was impossible to recognize that she was pregnant because she was very small and wore many layers of clothes. I wondered if the women continued to wear the cotton underclothes and the several layers of dresses, in addition to all the veiling, even in hotter months, and even when they were very pregnant. I soon learned that their dress never changed from season to season. I didn't mind wearing all of these clothes at the time, but the veil seemed hot, even in February.

Groping for conversation, I pointed to the makeup on my eyes and asked them if they wore makeup. I didn't understand the answer to my question, but later I learned that Bedouin women rarely wear it, except during the marriage ceremony. I discovered later that Saudi women who are not Bedouins usually wear makeup daily. I tried to tell them that I would return to put eye makeup on them, but the meaning seemed to be lost in the translation, or they weren't too excited about the idea. I realized that eye makeup probably made little sense to these women who lived in such harsh, remote conditions. I couldn't even imagine when or whether they'd bathe to wash the makeup off their faces.

I invited my Bedouin friends to come to my house to visit me, but Mama shook her head. They never came to visit while Mama was on the farm, but after she went to live with one of her other sons and Midwess moved his tent closer to our camp, Rashmi occasionally came with her children for a visit. Even so, she would keep a tight grip on the children, stay only a few minutes, and leave. I always offered them a cold soft drink that I'm sure seemed strange to them, as the traditional offering would have been coffee and tea. But I continued the nontraditional hospitality because the children loved the cold soft drinks.

After we finished our tea, they began preparing what I assumed to be lunch. Rashmi seemed to be the one who was assigned to cooking. In one big pot, she put some oil and a purple onion that she chopped expertly in the palm of her hand. Next, she added a tiny can of tomato paste, a can of whole tomatoes, and a can of green beans and carrots. Without measuring, she added hot water from the kettle. She scooped a large handful of rice from a big sack and put it in another bowl, rinsed the rice with water, and discarded the rinse water. She added the rice to the simmering mixture, and covered it with a lid.

I noted that she tossed the empty cans outside the tent flap. One behavior of the Bedouins that we observed is that any trash, whether it be a can, the rinse water, or tea left in a glass, was just tossed out the flap of the tent. With this practice, I was surprised that the area around the tent wasn't more littered, but in retrospect, it seemed to be fairly clean. I decided that one of them must occasionally pick up all the trash that hadn't blown away or been scavenged by the sheep, yet I never saw a collection of trash of any kind in their camp.

As Rashmi cooked, she used a pair of fingernail clippers with attachments that were tied to her shawl. All of the women had a pair of these clippers, attached in some way to their garments. Rashmi used the clippers to pop open a lid or to pry open something that needed opening.

While Rashmi busied herself at the stove, I observed the two little boys. They both had on white *thobes* like the men wear, but I could see that neither had on any underwear, perhaps because they were both being potty-trained. They were both barefooted, and their feet must have already been toughened by desert life, because they walked painlessly and effortlessly around the camp grounds. I saw no toys, but the boys seemed content to play with whatever had been thrown out of the tent flap. One boy played with an old shawl that he was holding up in the air, watching the wind blow it. The other boy chewed on an old, dry piece of flatbread. The flies continued to perch on their sticky mouths and hands, but the boys seemed oblivious to them.

Mama had been gone for quite a long time. Turning to the sister, I asked about Mama's absence. Taking me by the hand, as she had done between tents, she led me out to the lamb's pen where Mama was working with the animals. The lambs had been tied on a single rope, one right after the other, and Mama was untying them for the rest of the day. As if on cue, the older sheep, presumably the mothers, wandered toward camp. The camels remained a good distance away, and I could see Mohammed in the pickup watching them.

About eleven o'clock, a man drove up. The women said he was one of Mama's youngest sons and Midwess's brother. I disliked him immediately, and he impressed me as being very different from the rest of his family. With adoration in their voices, as if to say he was one family member who made it out of the desert, they told me that he lived in Al

Kharj. As he walked up to us, he pretended to tousle the two boys' hair, and shoved them down to the ground. He laughed, but the women didn't make a move or say a word. He kept shaking his keys at the boys, but when they came close to get them, he'd hide the keys and wouldn't let the boys have them. Mama came back into the group when her son arrived. After several attempts by the young boys to get the keys, Mama pounced on her son and tried to wrestle the keys from him. For a moment I thought she was going to be successful until he bit her on the finger. She and the others laughed at his craftiness.

I guess in celebration of his visit, they brought out warm soft drinks that were probably left over from our visit the night before. The two boys clamored for their share and were each given one. It took me five minutes to convince them that I didn't want one. Not only did I not really want one of the warm drinks, but I also wanted to avoid the need to relieve myself, because I wasn't sure exactly where, or how, it would be appropriate. While they quickly drank the canned drinks, flies alighted on the cans each time they put them down, but they didn't bother to shoo them away.

As they visited, I picked up a few words, especially Terry's name, and decided they must have been telling him the events of the previous night. They laughed several times, and he joined in. Soon, Rashmi rose from the carpet and headed for the kitchen. I followed to watch as she cooked another dish similar to the first one she'd made, but to this one she added more tomatoes, less water, and no rice, creating a sort of soup. She told me they ate this with the flatbread and suggested shyly that I cook this recipe at home for Terry.

At 12:15, Terry's pickup could be seen approaching in the distance, and we quickly assembled. I agreed that I wouldn't speak. As Terry walked toward the tent, the women said that Martha wasn't here, that she'd already gone. I remained motionless, and for a split second Terry seemed baffled. Then he began to grin and point to me. He told me later that my white hands and blue eyes showing through the Bedouin veil had revealed my identity.

The secret revealed, Mama began talking very rapidly and pounding her hand on the carpet, telling Terry to sit down and have tea and coffee. He begged off until another time, and we left the group, waving good-bye. I had begun removing their clothes, but they shook their heads to indicate that they were giving me the clothes.

They must have thought I was staying for lunch, because I learned from them later that they normally cooked only one meal a day and that is in the evening. Breakfast and lunch usually consisted of dates, tea, and bread. They had prepared the noon meal because the relative came, and they must have thought that we would stay to eat too. The soup was also a special preparation, because the normal fare for the evening meal is lamb and rice.

Because I was all dressed up in local costume, we decided to take advantage of the situation. We drove into camp where we knew the workers on our farm would be eating their lunch brought from P1. We decided to test the authenticity of my appearance. We went first to where the two Sri Lankans lived, Mitri and Perera. They came out while I remained in the pickup, careful to hide my hands under my shawl. The men seemed surprised that Terry would have a Bedouin woman in his pickup. The Filipino workers walked over, but none recognized me. Terry told the men that I was Midwess's wife, and Efren asked why I was with Terry. After a few more moments of suspense, I spoke in English, surprising them all, and they seemed embarrassed that they hadn't recognized me. Before we left camp, some of the Syrian dump truck drivers saw me and said, "Good" and *lazim;* this meant it was "necessary" that I dress that way.

We continued on to P1, where we were pleased to see several of the management, including Frank, Robin, and others. When we pulled up, the men walked over, keeping a safe distance from the Bedouin woman in Terry's pickup. Terry told them that I was Midwess's sick wife who needed someone to take me to the hospital. They discussed who should take me and the ramifications of an American man driving a Saudi woman to the hospital.

The men decided that two of the Egyptians who spoke Arabic and fairly good English should talk to me to find out what was wrong with me. I tried to respond to the Egyptians' questions, but with my limited Arabic, I could do little more than "Yes" and "No," and to hold my stomach and groan. The men did lots of talking and turned to the group to describe in English and in great detail the symptoms of my illness. I waited until the men had given all the information and then said in English, "Well, let's get going." The men, except Terry, turned white, looking as if they'd seen (or heard) a ghost. After the initial shock wore off, they were able to laugh, but it was evident that they were embarrassed that they hadn't been able to recognize me. We took some pictures before I removed the garb.

Chapter Fifteen

My jogging around the pivots had become a common sight among the workers. I was particularly surprised one day when a Yemeni driver, Faizel, appeared at my door early one morning with a large, dead snake. In Arabic, and with lots of body language, Faizel relayed to me the importance of being careful when I was out jogging because there were lots of snakes. It flattered me that he cared enough to pick up a dead snake to make his point to me; however, during the entire five years in Saudi Arabia I never saw a live snake, and I saw very few dead snakes that had been run over by vehicles. I guessed that they did most of their prowling at night when the desert was slightly cooler.

Just when I felt I was becoming acclimated to, and a part of, my new home, I was reminded that the desert can be a very ominous place. One morning, as I headed out of the camp gate, I decided to be adventurous and jog in new territories. Ignoring Terry's earlier warning, I decided to risk the unforeseen danger for a little adventure. I felt a little more confident because I had my two companions, Cocho and Ban Ban, two dogs that Terry had adopted when the Argentinean company disbanded its operation. Cocho had been named for one of the men in the company, and we could only guess where the name Ban Ban originated. Once the dogs got to know me, they went out with me for my morning runs. It was nice to have their companionship, and they appreciated my always bringing them plenty of scraps from the canteen.

As we turned in a new direction, the wind picked up. I saw dark clouds on the horizon, but supposed nothing more than that the weather would probably be changing in the next few days. Terry had recently pointed out some unplowed, but relatively smooth land that would be the site for additional pivots next season. I decided to run in that direction for awhile, with the dogs following happily. In a matter of a few minutes, the sky turned dark and rain fell in hard pelts. I had worn my Windbreaker, and when it began to rain, I unzipped the collar, thankful for the hood tucked inside. As the rain beat down at a harder pace, the dogs began to whimper and then to howl loudly. They had probably never been in the rain, exposed without a shelter to crawl beneath.

To compound the problem, because I had read recently adding weight when jogging increases the heart rate, I had loaded a backpack with about ten pounds of rocks. The weight of the pack hadn't bothered me but my left elbow kept hitting the rocks, and I was quickly developing a bruise. I was in such a hurry to get home before the downpour that I didn't take the time to dump the rocks.

As the rain became harder, I turned, thinking that I could make a shortcut back to camp. The dogs cried at my heels, the three of us tripping over each other, as they tried to use me as a shelter. Without warning, Ban Ban turned on his heels and ran in another direction. I called after him, but he kept running. I was thankful that Cocho stayed with me. I couldn't see the camp, even though I felt that I'd been running and walking for a long time. The ground became slippery and muddy, and the more I hurried, the harder it was to make any progress. Although I was thankful for the companionship, every time Cocho's wet hair touched my bare legs, I shivered. The wind blew, and I could barely see through the pelting rain.

When I saw a small hill in the distance, I assumed it was the mound of dirt near camp. I whisked to the top, but still couldn't see the camp. Cocho continued to cry, and the hard rain felt like blunt darts. I spotted a pivot nearby. I knew that Terry had numbered each pivot at the end of the towers and figured that if I could read the number, I could get my bearings and find my way to camp.

The arm of the pivot was on the opposite side of the field from where I stood, but I ran the extra distance in an attempt to discover my location. I gained confidence the closer we got to the end of the pivot. The rain continued to beat against us, and we hurried toward our compass.

The closer I got to the pivot, the more disillusioned I became. The nozzles seemed to be lower to the ground than I had noticed before, and they were shaped differently. To my dismay, I discovered that not only was there no number, but it was a different brand of pivot than our farm operated. I realized that I was on another farm.

A few feet from the edge of the pivot, Cocho spotted a scraggly bush that he cowered underneath, refusing to come when I called to him. I gave up calling him and crouched by the bush with him, putting my arm around his shivering body. We probably sat there for only a few minutes, but it seemed like an eternity. When the rain let up some, Cocho wiggled out of my arms and away from the bush and looked at me as if to say, "Where do we go from here?" I knew he was wishing that he'd gone with Ban Ban instead of sticking with me.

My legs felt like rubber, and for the first time I became aware of the soreness in my elbow. I stopped long enough to remove the 10 pounds of rocks from my backpack. I looked in all directions. In the distance I could make out a drilling rig with a tent next to it. Feeling that this was my only option and wishing that I'd listened to Terry about not wearing shorts, I ran toward the rig. After only a few yards, I realized that I was walking across a wet, plowed field. My feet sank into the muddy ground, and several times I lost my shoes. Finally, I removed my shoes and socks to walk barefoot across the oozing ground. After carrying the muddy socks for several minutes, I threw them down in disgust.

The closer I plodded to the tent, the more I wondered if I were doing the right thing. Bedouins would not have a drilling rig next to their tent. More than likely some other nationality of laborers lived here, probably without any women. I was thankful for Cocho's companionship, although I was dubious that this bony, wet creature could serve as my protector.

By the time I was within a few yards of the camp, the rain had almost stopped, and I could easily see the drilling rig and canvas tent through the drizzle. Several pieces of trash had washed around the camp, standing in puddles of water. I hollered out, "Hello," in a cracked voice that sounded strange in the barren, wet desert. A man stepped to the entrance of the tent, motioning me to approach. I hesitantly walked over to the tent, and as I stepped into the entrance, I was surprised to see six Arab men sitting on the floor of the tent, drinking tea. I'm sure that they suspected that I had come from another planet.

Wearing my soaked yellow Windbreaker over my mid-thigh shorts and walking in bare feet with mud halfway up to my knees, I'm sure I looked like something they'd never seen or imagined. My dripping wet companion probably furnished no familiarity to the sight. Finding my voice, I asked if any of them spoke English, and they all shook their heads. I broke down in sobs, telling them in English that I was lost and didn't know how to find my way home.

They didn't know what I had said, but they sensed my urgency, and they jumped to their feet, talking at once. They motioned for me to sit down and have tea, but I shook my head at the invitation. After a brief moment of silence, one of the men was able to convey to me that he would take me in the pickup, the only vehicle in camp, to find my house. I motioned that I would have to take Cocho with me, and he reluctantly nodded his head in agreement.

Cocho wasn't as willing as I to ride in the pickup, and I chased him around the camp. Finally, catching him, I picked up the wet mess and dragged him over to the pickup. The minute I climbed into the vehicle, I realized I'd made a mistake because the seats were red fur and the dashboard was covered in matching red fur with several plastic flowers tied to the mirror. I tried to make Cocho crouch on the floorboard, but as soon as the man boarded, Cocho stood up and shook. Water not only went all over the two of us, but sprayed the red fur.

I looked at the man, trying to convey with my eyes that I was sorry for the mess. The man drove, and I stared at the landscape, looking for familiar landmarks. All I could think to say to him in Arabic was "train," because I felt that I could orient myself if we could locate the tracks. The train ran near the road that was in front of our farm. He nodded as though he understood. To complicate matters, P2 was the only title that I could remember to identify where I lived. At that time, I didn't know *Rimal al Khizra*, the Arabic for Green Sands, and knew he couldn't recognize the name anyway. If I had thought to name Sheikh Latif, he might have recognized the farm.

As we met a diesel truck, my rescuer stopped the driver, and the two talked for several minutes. The driver stared at me while I clung tighter and tighter to Cocho. Because all of the pivots ran on diesel, the gas station sent a truck out to the farms to fill the diesel tanks with fuel. I'm sure the driver would have known my farm if I could have identified it properly. Both men shook their heads every time I repeated P2. As I sat, my imagination ran wild. The two men were plotting to take me wherever, to do whatever, and then kill me. Before I could flee, the two parted, and we continued on our way.

I breathed a sigh of relief when we saw the highway and then the railroad. I figured out that we were west of our farm and I began motioning for the man to go east. He nodded and turned west, driving alongside the railroad tracks. I motioned again that it was the other way, and he continued to nod and say *badain*, "later." The fear returned, and I knew that I couldn't jump from the pickup as fast as we were going. I decided that at the first opportunity I'd fling open the door and run. If I'd been thinking clearly, I would have realized that there wasn't a person or car in sight to help me.

Soon we came to the entrance to another farm. The man drove onto the road, across the railroad track, turning east and smiling at me. I realized that he had been driving this direction, to reach a road to pass over the railroad tracks. I felt even more foolish, but relieved that I hadn't attempted my escape plan.

I began to worry about how frantic Terry must be. I imagined that he had the entire farm crew and the police out looking for me. Even though we were only a few minutes from our farm, I had to resist the urge to tell the man *hamy-hamy*, "hurry, hurry." He was driving slowly, enjoying this novel experience, even though Cocho had made a mess of his pickup.

As we neared the entrance, I motioned him to turn north. When he saw our camp in the distance, he nodded. Passing some of the first circles, I saw two of our men working and waved at them, confident that they must have been the only two men who Terry left working while the remainder searched for me. The man let me out at the gate. When I opened the door Cocho bounded out, running to Ban Ban, who was curled up near a puddle of water. I repeated the Arabic word for *thank you* over and over again. If I'd been in the States, I would have offered to pay the man, but since I didn't have any money with me, I let him drive away with only a thank you.

I walked to our container, but there was no sign of life. When I went inside, I looked in the mirror and gasped at how awful I looked. I had mud spots all over my windbreaker, and my legs were streaked with mud. My bangs, hanging out from under my hood, had dried against my forehead. I wanted to bathe, but I decided I'd better make my presence known in camp in case Terry or one of the workers drove in. After standing out in the mud for several minutes, I finally saw Lando approaching, and I waved at him. He rolled down his window to stare, his face showing shock at my appearance. I excitedly told him that I'd been lost, but that I was okay now. He nodded his head and mumbled, "Yes ma'am," hastily driving away.

Feeling extremely conspicuous, I returned to the container, wondering why Lando hadn't been looking for me. Before I reached the door, Terry entered camp and drove over to me. Karl was with him, and they both laughed when they saw me. I couldn't believe that they were laughing until I discovered that Terry had never known that I'd been lost! When it began to rain, he just assumed that I had not jogged and that I'd been safely inside our house during the storm. I tried to relay to them my harrowing experience, but they could hardly keep straight faces in front of this muddy, barefoot woman. When I got to the part about the tent, the six men, and finally riding with one of them, Terry became a little more serious. He didn't like the idea that I rode with a stranger, but conceded that there wasn't much else that I could have done. We all laughed together about Ban Ban's knowing the direction home.

The rain had caused problems also for the two Sri Lankans, Mitri and Perera. Terry had assigned them to night duty, to check and make sure that all of the pivots were functioning properly, as they ran on twenty-four- to forty-eight-hour rotations. Mitri and Perera went out for their scheduled night duty, even though the pivots had been shut off by another worker after the rain. Terry had taken it for granted that they knew that the pivots wouldn't be running. The night after the rain, the two found themselves stuck in the mud at one of the pivots furthest from camp.

Feeling a great sense of responsibility for company property, they thought that it would be unwise to leave the pickup out in the desert during the night while they walked to camp. They spent the night with the truck, and, in the morning, they walked to camp. Terry brought them to our house for breakfast, because they were cold and wet and had missed breakfast in the canteen. I fed them pancakes and fried eggs, noting that neither poured the maple syrup on their pancakes. When I asked them what they ate for breakfast back home, they replied, "Curry," which was a generic name for most of the Sri Lankan dishes.

Chapter Sixteen

After I'd been in Saudi Arabia for almost three months, I heard of a regular gathering in the capital city for foreign women, The Riyadh International Women's Group (RIWG).

The group met once a month, and even though it would be a hardship for Terry to take me to the meetings, he thought I needed the company of other women. The meeting began at 10:00 A.M., so we left home at 6:00 A.M.

We reached Riyadh by 8:00 and began following directions to the Grand Festival Palace, where the meetings were held. After almost one and a half hours of searching, we had not located the palace. I was almost in tears. We stopped at a travel agency and called one of the men who had come to the dinner for the Ambassador at the farm. He gave us a different set of directions.

Before we left the agency, the manager, who had allowed us to use the phone said politely, "Please excuse me madam, but I feel I need to tell you something," and he continued to tell me that I should not be wearing my cross necklace in Saudi Arabia, at least in public, because the Saudis punished people for displaying this symbol. Because the travel agency was connected with Swiss Air, he cautiously pulled out a map of Switzerland, showing me that their flag had a cross in its center, and telling me that they weren't allowed to display anything that had the Swiss flag on it. He went on to say that one travel agency had displayed a large map of Switzerland, that had a large flag on it, and that the *Mutawwa* had ripped down the map. He quickly returned the map to the drawer as a Saudi man entered the travel agency. His sudden secretive manner prompted me to quickly grab my cross and thrust it down my high-buttoned dress.

With this disquieting information, we left in search of the Grand Festival Palace, following the directions from the man on the phone. After following his instructions precisely, we were not at the Grand Festival Palace. We stopped to ask for more directions from a Sri Lankan walking down a side street, who most graciously climbed in the pickup with us and led us the last few turns to the Grand Festival Palace.

The building was sandstone, shaped somewhat like a palace. A doorman dressed in crisp white pants and a red jacket and hat stood at the entrance. Asian drivers stopped at the entrance allowing women to get out of their cars. I felt conspicuous in our farm pickup and considered returning to the farm without stopping. Near the entrance, I recovered my nerve, and Terry dropped me off.

The grandeur of the palace took away my breath. There were beautiful Oriental carpets hanging on the walls and along the exterior walls were Saudi "couches," the flat floor cushions with matching back cushions.

A waterfall with a reflective mirror behind it was at the end of the long room. I registered, paying SR 30 ($8.60) to enter the meeting. I also purchased a *Newcomer's Guide to Riyadh* for the same price. There were several tables with information, including a table where women were soliciting volunteers to work in different areas of the club. As I stopped at each table, giving a brief explanation of where I lived, the women were incredulous at the distance I'd traveled and the isolated conditions in which I was living. Several women wrote down their telephone numbers for me when I told them how long it had been since I'd talked to other women. Most of the women did not even realize that there were farms in Saudi Arabia.

I visited the rest room in the palace; it was just as elegant as the other accommodations. Each individual stall was a separate room with two individual compartments, a commode and bidet in one and a sink in the other. In the main area of the bathroom were more sinks, each with a gold tray with a gold-colored pitcher in the shape of a Saudi coffee pot containing water. On the walls hung gilded mirrors.

Following the other women into the main hall where the meeting was to take place, I was astounded at the tremendous size of the room. I should have known that the building would be large because many of the Saudis have either the male or female ritual of the wedding ceremony in the Grand Festival Palace. The room was almost as long as a football field with a large stage and row after row of huge chairs. The chairs were at least three feet wide with deep mahogany backs and covered in beautiful brocade. I was equally awed that the entire place was packed with women. Until this time, I had seen only a few foreign women in Al Kharj, and none of them seemed to speak English. I had the idea that I was probably one of the few foreign women who had been allowed into Saudi Arabia to live with her husband.

I wandered up and down the aisles looking for a seat, but found no empty spaces. I noticed several women sharing the wide seats, but I had no offer from any of them to share. I felt as though every woman in the place was looking at me like I had come from another planet, and I wanted to flee because I was almost in tears.

About the time I gave up finding an empty seat, I saw a group of women congregating on the floor in front of the stage. I took my place on the floor with these who also couldn't get a seat, then spotted the Ambassador's wife and her mother, who were seated near the front. Mustering all the courage I had, I decided to risk sharing a seat with this important woman. Climbing over several legs to get to her, I said, "Oh, I finally spotted someone I know. May I sit with you?" I half perched on the edge of her chair, and she looked at me as if to say, "Who are you?" Breathlessly, I explained, "You probably don't remember me, but I met you at the farm . . ." She seemed to think for a minute and, to my relief, smiled and said, "Oh, yes, the chocolate cake." She then moved over to let me share her chair. We made light conversation for just a few minutes until the meeting was called to order.

The president of the club was a soft-spoken British woman, and the first order of business was to give a Saudi coffee pot as a prize to the woman who had been in Saudi Arabia the shortest time. I was surprised that one lady had been in the country for less than two days and had come to this meeting. A few other door prizes were given away, mostly dinners for two that had been donated by hotels and local restaurants. A serious announcement followed, advising all women that in order to attend the International Women's Group each woman had to wear a long dress with long sleeves. I glanced around, noting many didn't conform to either stipulation. Many had on Western clothes, with an abaya, like the Saudi women wore, covering the Western attire underneath.

The program proved entertaining. A Syrian-born fashion designer who was married to a Saudi man and who owned a boutique in New York City, showed slides of some of her designs. The slide presentation was followed by a fashion show, using four women who attended the meet-ings as models. The fashions didn't follow the Moslem dictate of long dress and long sleeves, but they were not in any way risqué or offensive. The meeting ended all too quickly, for me, at 11:15. Although a luncheon followed at a cost of SR 50 ($14.30), I decided not to remain for it.

I had asked Terry to come for me at noon, so I left the meeting room and walked around to several of the tables set up in other parts of the building where women were signing up for various activities. Most of the women I met seemed to be British, and each asked me if I played bridge. Besides bridge clubs, there were all kinds of activities in which women might participate, these groups meeting surreptitiously in dif-ferent women's homes, away from the eye of the *Mutawwa*.

I walked outside to wait for Terry. There was general bedlam as ap-proximately one thousand women congregated to wait for their drivers. I surmised that the biggest percentage of women did not remain for the luncheon. The drivers had no organized parking. Cars were blocked everywhere. Many of the drivers had left their vehicles to find the women for whom they were driving, adding even more congestion to the flow of traffic. I took the opportunity to observe the women. There were women of all nationalities represented, most dressed in their native costumes. There were many Pakistani women who kept their heads covered and dressed in knee-length dresses with matching balloon pants underneath. There were also quite a few Oriental women.

I was Cinderella without her ball gown because I had worn a long simple brown dress that buttoned up to the neck and had long sleeves. I had made the dress before I came to Saudi Arabia, hoping it would be what Terry had described to me as acceptable to wear. There were many elaborate long dresses, although many of the women wore the caftan style of dress. Many of the hair styles looked much too modern for this conservative desert country.

My general impression was that most of the women attended the meeting as part of a group, and they remained within the confines of their groups, leaving me to stand by myself. I missed that good ole "Howdy. How are ya?" Texas hospitality. If I'd been more aggressive, I would have met more people, but I felt a little bit overwhelmed among all of these women after living in a rural, male world for three months.

Terry pulled up in his pickup, and although I relished the thought of leaving in an elegant car, I was glad to see him. I raised my skirt and climbed regally into the pickup. We headed for the office, while I described my first meeting of the International Women's Group. I continued to attend the RIWG, but after the first year Terry no longer had to take me, because I had a driver.

One of the constant topics of discussion among the workers was that they all disliked the food. Although we had workers from as many as fourteen different countries on the farm, the two major groups were Sri Lankans and Filipinos, followed by quite a few of Arab descent. The Sri Lankans' food choice was curry made with coconut milk, which was available in cans in Saudi Arabia, and so hot with chilies that they perspired while they ate. The curry tended to be rather greasy. After finishing a meal, we'd see the Sri Lankans blowing air in and out, trying to cool their mouths and throats. Terry and I enjoyed hot Mexican food, but the Sri Lankan curry was too hot for us.

On the other hand, neither the Filipinos or the other workers liked hot food. The Filipinos liked many vegetables, with a small amount of lean meat, all cooked together in broth. It seemed that the only common ground the two groups could enjoy was plain, boiled rice. But the Sri Lankans preferred fluffy rice, whereas the Filipinos insisted that their rice be cooked to a gummy state. The Arabs wanted rice cooked in sheep's broth, served with Arab flatbread. The cook for this assorted group was Sri Lankan. Not only did he try to please all of the seventy-five workers, he also prepared for managers the same type of Western food day after day, which unfortunately, we tired of quickly.

The monotony of our diet was a problem, but we had an advantage over the workers in that we could cook for ourselves to add some variety to our diet. We Texans craved Mexican food, and we tried to prepare our own Mexican dinner. We all had been on the lookout for any Mexican food products and after shopping at five different stores, we'd collected quite an assortment. Karl received a care package that contained three cans, one with a *queso* dip, one with jalapeño pepper slices, and one with nacho sauce. I made tortilla chips out of the flatbread by carefully separating it into two thin halves and cutting them into triangular shapes like chips. We then baked the triangles in the oven until they were crisp. We used canned cheese imported from Australia. The chicken and fresh tomatoes were grown locally, and the meat for our tacos was the minced water buffalo from India. Using the chicken and canned corn tortillas, we made enchiladas. We also fried the canned corn tortillas to make taco shells. We even found a can of enchilada sauce and refried beans that had come all the way from El Paso, Texas. Our dinner tasted quite authentic and quenched our Mexican food craving for awhile.

The workers seemed to have little opportunity to enjoy their special foods. Abysinger's solution to this problem was to take all of the different ingredients from the Filipino and Sri Lankan food and mix them all together, creating a product that none of the men found desirable. He made the curry mildly hot, but it was too hot for the Filipinos and not hot enough for the Sri Lankans. Although they could add chilies at the table, the Sri Lankans claimed that the chilies had to be cooked in the curry for the taste they wanted. On a seven thousand-acre farm, such problems seemed trivial when we discussed them with Hafeez in the head office in Riyadh. But, in a country where most of the laborers were on foreign soil, away from their home and families, food becomes a priority. The problem took on serious proportions as more food was being discarded than eaten and dysentery among the workers became chronic.

Because the workers had come to regard me not only as Terry's wife and secretary but also his confidant, I soon became the crusader for the workers' rights. Depending on the situation, I might negotiate with Hafeez for more time off on Friday, a salary increase, improved housing, or better food. With my list of grievances, I sat in the office with Terry and Hafeez, feeling a little like a union representative. Hafeez listened intently, making a few appropriate remarks, such as, "Yes, they need a fruit every day because vitamin C is water-soluble." It was at this moment that I realized I was dealing with a Pakistani who had a knowledge of nutritional needs that I hadn't recognized before. I also mentioned the tremendous food wastage that resulted from foolish food buying and food preparation. The quality of the meat purchased for the workers was inferior, and even though they were given a large portion, it was so tough, most of it was later fed to the dogs. Also, the kitchen used a tremendous amount of tomato paste, but it was purchased in cans containing only about four ounces. Hafeez, a quick decision maker, decided that I should form a committee consisting of representatives from all nationalities of workers to discuss ways to improve the food in the canteen. I was to work with the cook to develop menus, as well as to approve and sign the weekly purchase orders for food.

Hafeez also approved my request for uniforms for the workers. He requested that I take the workers' measurements to use in ordering uniforms that fit each worker. I was elated with my new job. Not only would it give me something to do in my spare time, but it also would provide an opportunity to learn more about the workers and their cultures.

Now that I was involved with the food for the canteen, we soon made a startling discovery. The food was sent on a flatbed truck from Riyadh, once a week, without refrigeration. This wasn't a problem during the winter, when the temperatures remained relatively cool. During the hotter months, the frozen chickens had thawed by the time they reached the farm. They were refrozen upon arrival. Morever, because we ate beef, either ground or minced, as they called it, or in chunks once a day, we soon grew tired of the strong tasting meat of the water buffalo. Eventually, we found another source of beef to replace the water buffalo, and the frozen food was purchased and transported only at night.

After enacting the food improvement committee, the workers began to see some subtle changes. The workers, like the managers, were able to get ketchup. At this stage, even a simple bottle of ketchup, or a stick of butter made the workers feel more considered and improved their morale.

As part of our plan, I took Roger, the Filipino mechanic, who also was an excellent cook, to the kitchen to teach me and the two Sri Lankans to cook some Filipino dishes. We had decided to start with Filipino food first, because the Filipinos seemed to be the least satisfied. Roger had quit eating in the canteen. He bought what food was available at the gas station and cooked in his room. Although cooking in the rooms was against company policy because of the fire hazard, the management had been looking the other way because Roger swore that the food from the canteen made him sick, and he couldn't come to work the next day if he were sick.

I instantly liked Roger, both as a chef and as a comedian. He laughed after each explanation of a cooking step, as if to say, "I can't believe you really don't already know this." The two Sri Lankan cooks were very serious, acting as if they were going to be tested after the lessons ended. We learned to cook sticky rice, the way the Filipinos liked it. We also made a dish using mung bean noodles and chicken. The Filipinos are very resourceful in their cooking, wasting little, if anything.

A Filipino friend whom I met in Saudi Arabia once watched me eat an entire apple. When I was about to throw away the core, she grabbed my arm and said, "May I have that. It is my favorite part of the apple." She then ate the remains, seeds and all, except for the carefully discarded stem.

Roger took a small amount of meat off the chicken bones for the one dish. He placed the skin in a bag, explaining that once enough skin had been accumulated, he would teach us how to fry it, making excellent eating! He placed the bones in a pot of water, using them to make broth. I couldn't imagine that one chicken was going to make more than two meals for ten Filipinos. For the evening meal we prepared *Nabaha* and *Nilagang Baka,* or boiled beef with vegetables. I noticed that Roger used many vegetables, using the meat more as a flavoring than a main ingredient.

The Filipinos were so thrilled with the improvement of the food that they began to eat immediately after work, instead of showering first, as was their normal practice. I was surprised what a difference in attitude a little sticky rice and a change in cooking technique could make in the men.

Another of my job assignments from Hafeez was to create at P2 a liaison office to serve as a bridge between the farms and the head office. He instructed me to make a list of the supplies I would need to start an office. Because I had no idea where office supplies might be located in

Riyadh, Terry and I accompanied Jamshaid, Al Emar's Pakistani purchaser, to shop for the items. He was a delightful man, always wheeling and dealing to turn an extra profit to supplement his regular salary. He had begun by importing Pakistani spices into Saudi Arabia. He was working in Saudi Arabia to save enough money for dowries to ensure the marriage of his three sisters. As the only son in his family, he was responsible for providing the finances for his sisters. Unlike Saudi Arabia, where the man furnishes money and gifts for the bride and her family, Pakistan is similar to India, where the bride furnishes the dowry items for the groom and his family.

Jamshaid became a close friend. Only a few months before my arrival on the farm, he, his wife, and daughter had lived on the farm. Jamshaid and his wife, Jasmine, were a wonderful Pakistani couple, as round as they were tall. They had been very friendly to Terry while they lived on the farm. Their daughter would visit the canteen every day because the cook always gave her a plate of French fries. In the early months of farming, Jamshaid drove into Riyadh almost every day to purchase spare parts and other supplies for the farm. Just before I came, a driver was hired to take the list of necessary items into Riyadh, and Jamshaid was transferred to Riyadh in order to purchase the items for the farm. I was very disappointed when I learned that. I missed having another woman on the farm by just a few months.

Jamshaid, who knew every store in Riyadh, had a talent for spotting a bargain. We couldn't find everything we needed at the first office supply store, so we went to another one. I enjoyed the opportunity to tour Riyadh with Jamshaid, because I was discovering that Riyadh was a fascinating city, with countless stores and shops of all kinds. After we'd made our selections in the second store, we were almost to the check out stand, ready to pay for our purchases, when the call for prayer began. Jamshaid talked very fast to convince the clerk that he could check us out quickly and we'd be on our way. The man remained adamant about not letting us go, and by that time it was too late to exit the locked doors. We stayed in the darkened store for thirty minutes, waiting for prayer time to end. I pondered how strong a deterrent to crime the punishment of hand chopping must be—the shopkeeper seemed not at all concerned that we might stuff our pockets and my purse with small items while we were left completely unattended.

Jamshaid invited us to eat Chinese food with him. Even though it was getting late and we still had a long drive ahead, we agreed because we enjoyed Jamshaid's company. We seated ourselves in the secluded family section and ordered chicken corn soup and spring rolls for appetizers. We each ordered a different entree, to share with each other. Jamshaid insisted on treating us; I didn't realize how generous this gesture was until I learned later that his salary was less than one-tenth of Terry's. Jamshaid insisted also that we spend the night with him. We declined because Terry had to be at work at six the next morning. With the new office equipment loaded on the bed of the pickup, we arrived at the farm at 12:30 A.M.

Chapter Seventeen

I enjoyed every opportunity to break the normal routine on the farm. My most frequent break was to make the fifteen-mile trip to the closest gasoline station to fill up with gas. When we arrived at the gas station, I always went inside, much to the surprise of other patrons. They were puzzled to see an unveiled, white-skinned woman in the middle of the desert. The gas station was somewhat of an oasis to me because the shelves looked like a miniature version of the convenience store in my hometown. The proprietor stocked the shelves with canned fruits and vegetables, flour and sugar, fresh bread, toothpaste, and even diapers. Terry and I always treated ourselves to a package of cookies that were delivered fresh from a bakery in Al Kharj.

Another opportunity to leave the farm arose when Ciba-Geigy invited us to an information meeting at the Intercontinental Hotel in Riyadh. Although I seemed to be the only woman among probably two hundred men, I was no longer inhibited by the lone woman syndrome and thoroughly enjoyed the meeting. The elaborate buffet afforded my first opportunity to taste Saudi "champagne." The mixture, served in cut glass pitchers, contained equal parts bottled water, apple juice, and non-alcoholic beer.

Our first celebration for all the farm workers occurred soon after I'd been appointed to oversee the food preparation. The cook hesitantly approached me one night after supper, asking if the farm might be permitted to celebrate Sri Lankan New Year. The Sri Lankan New Year, April 13th or 14th every year, was the new year for the country once known as Ceylon. I boldly completed a special purchase order to be submitted as a request for special provisions. To my surprise and delight, the food was approved, and the party was scheduled.

The cook worked laboriously to prepare a menu that would please all of the workers yet still reflect the Sri Lankan culture. The menu included fried rice, fried chicken, French fries, eggplant curry, potato curry, canned and fresh fruit, and cake. I arrived early in the afternoon to assist the cook and was surprised by the enormous quantity of food. Because the workers were normally served a specific amount, I assumed that the large platters were to facilitate the serve-yourself food bar that we would set up for the party.

The canteen had been scrubbed, and someone had strung tiny Christmas lights around the ceiling. As we worked in preparation for the party, we listened to Oriental-sounding Sri Lankan music. With the food spread out on several tables, the freshly washed faces of the workers began appearing at the canteen door.

Everyone had a wonderful time. The main entertainment was taking pictures. There were five or six cameras clicking throughout the evening, taking hundreds of pictures. The workers expressed their gratitude for the celebration again and again. Those of us at the management table posed for pictures with every worker on the farm. My picture was taken no less than fifty times. I knew these men wanted a picture of a Western woman. The photoshoot became comical when someone brought out the Saudi headgear and each worker took a turn wearing the headgear for a picture.

A trip to Sri Lanka to recruit farm workers enabled me to wear a typical Sri Lankan sari at subsequent Sri Lankan New Year parties. It made the Sri Lankans very happy to see an American woman dressed in their native costume. My only problem was that a sari is very difficult to assemble. I heard one of our Sri Lankan workers say that he had to tie his wife's sari every day when at home, so from that time on this worker had to tie my sari for the annual party. I stood in my blouse and slip and he wound the yards and yards of fabric around me with great expertise.

The end of harvest was marked by yet another party in the canteen. The men who worked in the head office were invited to attend, and they apparently enjoyed visiting the country and many of their own countrymen who worked on the farm. Festivities were to begin at seven. Both Sheikh Latif and Hafeez planned to attend, but were late, so we all waited until their arrival to begin the party. Terry and many of the workers played ping pong to pass the time. The mounds of food, that the cook had worked for days to prepare, sat on the tables becoming cold.

As Sheikh Latif and Hafeez made their grand entrance, the men rose to their feet to show respect. As the only female, I felt it appropriate to remain seated. Sheikh Latif shook hands with everyone and gave the traditional kiss to the few Bedouins who had attended the party. When Sheikh Latif reached me, he bent down to whisper in my ear, "I'd rather be kissing you than those Bedouins."

The first Christmas party that was held before I came to Saudi Arabia had been a disaster, with food actually flying because of the rush and general bedlam of a crowd unused to buffet service. This time Terry took charge and everyone moved through the line in an orderly fashion. We sampled a variety of curries and dishes from Pakistan, Sri Lanka, and the Philippines. I had been in the kitchen all afternoon helping the cook and making my chocolate cake recipe, with fourteen times the normal ingredients. Evidently the cake did not bake long enough, because it tasted more like fudge than a chocolate cake, but everyone seemed to enjoy it simply because it was a Western treat.

The ping pong matches continued, and Frank and a Filipino worker played their guitars. I joined Frank in traditional songs such as "The Yellow Rose of Texas" and "The Red River Valley." Cliff, another Texan who worked on our farm kept insisting that we dance. Finally, I consented, noting that Terry had walked outside with Sheikh Latif holding his hand. As Cliff and I attempted to two-step and finally to waltz to Frank's guitar music, the crowd went crazy. I decided that they hadn't seen a lady dance in a while, but I should have known also that many of the workers came from countries where men and women don't dance together at all, let alone with someone other than their husband. Cliff and I sat down. Terry returned, and the crowd roared for us to dance together, so we did a quick two-step and sat down. We also had a wonderful man from Switzerland, Jack Meiser, on our farm who persuaded me to waltz with him. I knew that he was an experienced dancer as we spun around the canteen floor. Sheikh Latif and Hafeez reentered the canteen as we were ending our dance, and Sheikh Latif proclaimed, "That is the luckiest man in the world!" I realized that Sheikh Latif saw me as a person and not just the wife of someone who worked for him. During our years in Saudi Arabia, I always felt comfortable with Sheikh Latif and enjoyed the company of this man whose world was so different than ours.

While Terry and Sheikh Latif were outside the canteen, Sheikh Latif had offered Terry a new position. He asked Terry to be the overall manager of both P1 and P2. Franklin, who had been the manager on P2 with Terry, was going back to the America. If Terry took the new job, Sheikh Latif assured him that I would have my own driver so that I could be free to travel away from the farm whenever I wanted.

I knew nothing of Terry's new position as the party continued, and Hafeez asked me to organize a singing contest. We had entries from Sri Lanka, Pakistan, Switzerland, America, Egypt, Mexico, and the Philippines. Each singer took full advantage of the microphone, crooning hysterically in his native tongue. The winner, decided by a panel of appointed judges, was Jamal, the Egyptian. He took Frank's guitar, turned it around, using the back of it as a sort of drum. With his eyes closed, he tapped the guitar with his fingers keeping time as he sang an Arabic tune.

We could not return to Texas for Christmas because the wheat had to be planted, so we always had a Christmas party on the farm. Technically, we weren't suppose to call the celebration Christmas because of government directives, but we still managed to celebrate. It was interesting to spend our holidays in the canteen with about ninety people of different nationalities: Sri Lankans, Egyptians, Filipinos, Pakistanis, Yemenis, Koreans, Europeans, British, Australians, Saudis, Turks, and Americans.

I always made each worker a little package of assorted cookies, candies, and cakes. On several Christmases, I made as many as forty-eight dozen cookies to fill the seventy-five plus Christmas packages. On three different Christmases, we gave our workers caps that we brought from the States when we returned from summer vacation. This was probably the best gift we could have given them, since these caps symbolized everything they dreamed about America. Usually, our Texas John Deere dealer, Hurst Farm Supply, along with the world's largest cotton gin, Associated Cotton Growers, furnished the caps when they learned who would be receiving them almost eight thousand miles away.

We were very humbled when we realized the tremendous respect the workers from the various countries had for America. We had seen the protests against America on the nightly news, so we had the impression that America was not highly regarded in other countries. Among our workers, we found a sense of respect and awe for our homeland. Many of the workers talked of some day going to America in the same terms many Americans talk of going to heaven.

Being around people from Third World countries made us realize what Americans take for granted. Once we employed a Sri Lankan who stole a toilet seat from the farm and shipped it home when he left for vacation. The irony of the situation was that he lived in a remote section of Sri Lanka that didn't even have running water. Evidently he wanted to be ready with a toilet seat in case the water and a toilet ever became available.

Because I made each worker a birthday cake on his birthday, the workers regarded me not only as the boss's wife but also as a friend. Many of the workers' wives and girlfriends wrote to thank me for remembering their sweethearts with a cake on their birthdays.

One letter that I will never forget came from the wife of one of our Filipino workers. Bert was a shy, quiet man who worked in the workshop. I would have guessed that he was in his twenties and was astounded when his wife wrote that she and Bert had eight children. She went on to say that Bert had come from a very poor family and had never had a birthday cake. We continued to correspond. In one letter, the wife asked what I did all day out in the middle of the desert. When I answered her question, I told her that I did aerobics and I described my aerobic dance videos. In her reply, Maria said that the only aerobic exercise she received was scrubbing the floor on her knees with coconut shells. That humbled me.

Despite the several parties, most of my days were spent in solitude, especially during the early years. It was on one of these usual days during our first season in Saudi Arabia that I received some information that made me feel both jubilant and much less remote. One fall evening in 1983, Terry and I, along with a pickup load of workers, were headed out on the P2 road on our way to P1 for supper. As we were about to pull onto the highway, a pickup coming from the other direction turned in on our road. I didn't look closely at the vehicle because we had lots of traffic down our farm road, mostly Bedouins going behind the pivots of wheat. I took a quick glance at the occupants of the pickup and felt like rubbing my eyes because I thought I had seen a woman without a veil; maybe several women. I told Terry, who had been lost in thought, to turn around to check. When we caught up with the pickup, we discovered, not one female, but a family of three. The family, a husband, a wife, and two daughters, was from Ohio. They lived on a farm eight miles down the road. We talked briefly because we had to deliver the men to P1 to eat, but we did learn that the man was working for a Saudi on a farm called Basil-Salmia and had been only eight miles away for eight months. John Zielske had been in construction work in Ohio, but they had moved to Florida not too long before coming to Saudi Arabia. Patsy, his wife, was really friendly, but the two daughters, Lesli, age twelve, and Sherri, age eighteen, were rather reserved with us, as most teenagers are with adults. The Sheikh for whom John worked owned a small piece of land near P2, which explained why they had been on our road. We got directions to their farm and promised to visit them the next evening. They had not been aware of our presence either.

That night, I hardly slept knowing there was an English-speaking woman only eight miles away. I could not wait for work to end the next day so that we could drive to their farm. I was amazed that as many times as I had been down the main road into Al Kharj, I hadn't seen these Americans before. When we turned into their farm, we were extremely impressed with the paved road that spanned the entire distance from the highway to the camp. Our bumpy sand path didn't begin to compare.

There was an official gate with a gatekeeper, a little, old Egyptian man, who stopped us to investigate our presence on the farm. When Terry greeted him in Arabic, he offered a wide, toothless grin. We told him that we wanted to visit John, and he grinned again, shaking his head and saying "Amerikey." He invited us to have tea with him first, but we asked for a rain check and persuaded him to open the gate. There were no awkward gaps in the conversation when we arrived at John and Patsy's home. We talked and talked, as if we were old friends, catching up on lost time. John and his family lived in a trailer house that was a little bit bigger than our container.

As we entered their house, we were surprised to find two young Saudi men reclining comfortably on the couch. We were introduced to Tariq and Khaled; later we learned that they were sons of Sheikh al-Salem, and that they practically lived with John and Patsy when they were visiting the farm. A little romance was occurring between Tariq, about twenty years of age, and Sherri. Tariq had even flown to the United States to escort Sherri to Saudi Arabia, because she traveled separately from her family. At that time, she disliked Tariq so much that she wouldn't even talk to him. A few lonely days in the desert made his companionship a great deal more desirable.

The Zeilske trailer was furnished with real curtains, American carpet, and a refrigerator that had an ice maker. Patsy took me outside for a tour of the camp. As we walked, she explained that John worked for a Sheikh who was married to a member of the royal family, a close relative of the Crown Prince, with the title of princess. Today, the royal family of Saudi Arabia encompasses a large group of individuals. The privileged are direct heirs of Abdul Aziz ibn Saud, creator of the Kingdom. King Fahd was proclaimed, fifth in the present dynasty of Saudi Abrabia 13 June 1982. He, along with his three reigning brothers before him, are all sons of Abdul Aziz ibn Saud. As we continued through the compound, I was enchanted by the sight of trees. Up until this point, I hadn't realized how much I'd missed green trees. Patsy said that the Ministry of Agriculture gives Saudi farmers trees to plant, and if the trees live, they pay the farmers a subsidy. Around the gravel yard in front of the trailer house were large stones, forming a border. Patsy explained why the rocks were there. When the Zielskes first arrived, Bedouins and Saudis visiting from the city walked right up to their windows to peer in at the American females they'd heard were on the farm. Although the rocks hadn't discouraged all of the Peeping Toms, it had reduced their number.

Their trailer sat in front of a long group of white stone villas, all connected. We peeked in the window of one of the rooms that the Sheikh used when he came to the farm. The thick, blue shag carpet and mirrored walls looked out of place in this desert setting. Patsy described the splendor almost begrudgingly, and I learned later that they had been shown pictures of the villa back in the States when they were interviewing for the job. The pictures had been used to describe John's and Patsy's housing if they took the job, when in fact, they weren't allowed to live there and the rooms were kept locked, except for when the Sheikh visited the farm.

As we passed through a six-foot-tall concrete fence, the sight ahead almost took my breath away. I couldn't have imagined the Garden of Eden to look any differently. Amidst the green grass and trees and legions of flowers, was an elaborate swimming pool, shaped like a figure eight with a bridge suspended in the middle where the two circles met. There wasn't any water in the pool, and Patsy said that it was rarely filled. However, when it did have water and a group of Saudis came out to the farm from Riyadh, the women waded into the shallow end, still clad in their long dresses and veils. She suspected none of the women knew how to swim, because they never ventured to the end with the fourteen-foot-depth. A diverse array of trees enhanced the garden area, including a large grove of date palm trees. In one corner stood a sanctuary for birds, and on the opposite end, a large tent for the men, when visitors came to the farm.

Patsy suspected that I'd had little contact with Saudis and knew very little about the customs. She explained that her two Saudi "sons," as she referred to them, didn't mind her asking any kind of question about their country or their people. They were beginning to prefer her American cooking to the food the Indian cook prepared for them on the farm.

Patsy revealed that their boss, the Sheikh, was a tyrant for whom to work. John tolerated working for him only because the Sheikh rarely came to the farm, but left most of the responsibility of running it to John, and supposedly, Tariq and Khaled. The princess, to whom the Sheikh was married, was not the mother of these two sons. The princess was the Sheikh's second wife. Tariq had told Patsy that if a Saudi woman realized that her husband no longer had any interest in her, she might select another wife for him, which was the case when Tariq's mother selected the princess for his father. I knew that it wasn't necessary for a man to obtain consent or permission from his wife before acquiring a second wife, but a wife's selecting another wife for her husband was a slant that I'd never heard.

According to Tariq, his father spent one night with his mother, and then stayed about a month with the princess. I wondered if this princess lived in an opulent palace, luring the Sheikh to spend more time with her. It wasn't long before Tariq's mother tired of the unbalanced arrangement and sought a divorce. Tariq told Patsy that when a Saudi woman divorces, it is her sons' responsibility to take turns taking care of her. Tariq's mother alternated living with each of her two sons. I knew that in an arrangement of plural wives, the children of each wife live with their own mother, even though they refer to each other as brother or sister, rather than stepbrother or stepsister. If one of the women divorces the father, any children that she has in her next marriage are not considered related to the children she has from the previous marriage.

As Patsy talked about the princess, I envisioned a young and beautiful Cinderella. Patsy dispelleded this vision, relating that both wives sometimes came to the farm for a party. Tariq's mother was pretty, while the princess was plain. She added that the princess was not only plain but had atrocious manners. At one of the *kabsas*, where everyone ate from the communal platter with their hands, Patsy had seen the princess use both hands to wrestle the tongue from the head of the sheep and gnaw on the whole tongue. The two wives seemed to get along, appearing to be best of friends. At several family gatherings, both Tariq's mother and the princess would be together at the farm.

Patsy had strong feelings about the inequality of treatment of male and female Saudi children who had visited the farm. I had read that preference toward male children and discrimination against female offspring in the Moslem culture begins even before birth, with the blessings that are bestowed upon prospective parents—that Allah fill their house with *sibyan* (boys). Also, when a newlywed couple is congratulated by friends and relatives, they are wished a future full of "happiness and male children."

The father is the authoritarian head of the household, and the wife and children are obliged to submit to this authority. The physical care of children is totally entrusted to the mother's directives. The mother, in turn, in most wealthy households, has the aid of a servant. The father traditionally has little to do with the children until they are able to walk and take care of themselves.

Traditional Saudi society accepts without questioning the differentiation between the sexes from an early age. Boys are introduced to male occupations by their fathers, and mothers teach girls typical female tasks. (While I was in Saudi, home economics and related courses were not taught to boys, and girls did not study physical education.) Loyalty to a man's parents transcends that to his wife and children.

In Patsy's opinion, the children, especially male, were rarely disciplined. This may have been because much of a child's actual nurturing in the first few years of life came from a maid, or houseboy or housegirl, who might have been afraid to deny the child anything he or she wanted. In Patsy's case, the male children whom she'd observed enjoyed destroying property. For instance, they often threw rocks, much to their fathers' delight. When the mother tried to interfere in a male child's destructive fun, the father stopped her. The princess had a seven-year-old daughter, but had very little to do with her. A servant dressed the girl, hand fed her at meals, and carried her in her arms much of the time. The child was not only overweight and lazy, but also disrespectful of the servant, treating her as she'd seen her mother do.

As we concluded our visit with John and Patsy, we were thrilled to know that there were Americans close by. Yet, in a sense they were still as far away as if they had been in Riyadh, because neither Patsy nor I was allowed to drive. She and I could get together only when one of our husbands had time in their hectic schedules to drive us.

Chapter Eighteen

My first opportunity to visit Sheikh Latif's wife in Riyadh came after I'd been in Saudi Arabia for several months. Terry went to the office in Riyadh for a meeting, and I accompanied him into town. We arrived at the office after three in the afternoon. The minute we walked through the door, Sheikh Latif called his wife to tell her I was in the office, and she sent her driver to transport me to her house. While I waited for the driver to arrive, I became intimidated just thinking about what I'd say and do with the woman from whom I felt worlds apart. As I rode in the back seat of a luxurious white Cadillac, driven by a Sri Lankan, I fought off my apprehension.

The driver opened my door, and I stepped onto a paved side street lined with tall, concrete fences with iron gates. He motioned me to enter through the gate directly in front of us. As I stepped into the courtyard area, I caught my breath and gathered my confidence. Someone had made an attempt to grow grass in the courtyard, although it appeared to need water and care.

I knocked hesitantly at the door that was opened by a Sri Lankan maid whose face reflected surprise to see an American woman. She led me into a long marble hallway, relating shyly that Jewaher would be down in a minute. I wandered around, curious to explore a real Sheikh's house. On the left of the entry was a closed door that later I discovered opened into a beautiful living room with numerous overstuffed couches and chairs, all tightly fitted around the perimeter of the room. There were sundry pictures and decorations hanging on the walls. Hanging on one of the walls was an elaborately done family tree with both Sheikh Latif's and Jewaher's names on it, because they were second cousins.

Beyond the living room was a wide hallway with three ornate free-standing sinks. At the opposite end of the hallway was a bathroom, separated from the sinks by a curtain of hanging beads, reminiscent of the sixties era in the States. It seemed strange that they should have these three sinks in such a prominent location in their home. When I realized that the sinks were used for washing not only before prayer (Moslems wash their feet, hands, and forearms before praying) but also before and after eating, their prominence made good sense.

Although the house had three levels, I only viewed two of them. The second floor had a large open area, used for a sitting room with a couch and several large floor pillows. There was another bathroom, partitioned with beads, a large bedroom where the two boys, Ziad, six, and Faisal, three, slept, and the master bedroom. Jewaher's bedroom had a king-size bed, and although it had been made, there was no bedspread. A sheet served as a coverlet. I was surprised to see the sheet was the same as the one I had on my bed at the farm. It had come from the buy-out of the merchandise of the Argentinean company that left Saudi Arabia. Most homes in Saudi Arabia aren't built with closets in the bedrooms; instead of a closet, Jewaher had a long, mirrored cupboard. The bed had a cassette player in the headboard. There was an elaborate dressing table lined with a profusion of perfume and makeup bottles. In one corner of the room stood a table and chairs, along with a television and video player.

I had been ushered up the stairs by the Sri Lankan maid to sit in the waiting room outside of Jewaher's bedroom. When she emerged, she gave me a quick peck on the cheek, much like Mama had back on the farm, and explained breathlessly that because she had a party to attend at six, we could only shop for an hour. I had not realized before that we were to shop together that day. As I followed her down the stairs, she explained that the party was held at her niece's school every two years. It sounded much like our school recitals, but must have been somewhat more important, because she had been unsuccessful obtaining a ticket for me to attend the affair. I realized several years later that as a foreigner I was banned from attending any school functions in the country. No wonder she could not obtain a ticket for me.

As we walked through the house, she stopped occasionally to pick up a toy or retrieve an article of clothing that the boys had left in the way. Mary, the Sri Lankan maid, held Faisal, and Jewaher picked him up, giving him a series of kisses before leaving. She sent the driver next door to retrieve Ziad from Sheikh Latif's mother's villa so that he might go with us. After a few hasty instructions to Mary about the baby, Ziad appeared, and we prepared to leave.

Jewaher opened the front door, shouted the driver's name and expertly wrapped her face in the black veil, tying the two ends of material in a knot behind her head. She covered her head with another rectangular piece of black cloth, and draped her long, red dress in the black abaya. I stood there, pretending to straighten my hair, careful not to stare at her veiling ritual. She marched out the door, and I fell quickly in behind her. The driver opened the door, and I climbed in the back seat after her.

I couldn't decide whether to speak to the black shroud sitting next to me. I felt almost as if I were in the car by myself—I couldn't see her face to determine whether she was smiling, frowning, or daydreaming. She answered the few questions that I voiced, but didn't generate any conversation herself. We rode in silence for much of the trip, but for me it wasn't an uncomfortable silence. The veil, covering her eyes and facial expressions, made her almost nonexistent.

The driver deposited us in front of the store where Jewaher instructed him to wait. Jewaher remained completely shrouded during most of the excursion, showing her eyes only when she was in a secluded area of the store. Because we only had about an hour to shop, she had decided to take me to Eura-Marche, the grocery store that Terry, Karl, and I had been to before. I didn't want to tell her that I'd been here before because she seemed to think that shopping here would be a real treat for me.

I had mentioned to her when she visited me on the farm that I would like to buy a new long dress, so she showed surprise when I didn't pick out one of the dresses on the racks of clothes. I not only didn't really want to buy a dress in a supermarket, but I was aghast at the high prices on the plain dresses. I tried not to disappoint her by saying that I would buy some groceries. I spotted a rack of abayas, recalling that many of the women wore the abaya over pants when they went out in public. The abaya provided the appropriate cover so that it was not necessary to wear a long dress. When I suggested this to Jewaher that I buy one, she informed me without hesitation that the Saudi women didn't approve of foreign women wearing the abaya and that I should wear a long dress like the one that I had on. She stopped to look at the rack of abayas declaring that they were poorly constructed. She said that these abayas were not authentic, and that a true abaya should be made from silk, as was hers.

I was at once impressed with her decisive manner that refrained from arrogance. She even pushed the grocery cart that we were sharing. At one point, before we had anything in the cart, when we had walked away from it for a moment, someone took the basket. I offered to go for another one, but she insisted that she would get another one for us, so she walked to the front of the store for another cart. She waited until we'd gone down one of the aisles to fold back her face veil, just above her eyes. I selected a few items, but I was more interested in what Jewaher purchased. I suspected that the maid or driver did most of the shopping. Later I learned that they had a cook who prepared meals for not only them but also Sheikh Latif's mother and his brother's family. The three families lived in separate but identical villas connected to each other behind the walled fence. Jewaher bought bananas, mangoes, and a long loaf of French bread from the bakery. She also bought Ziad a small toy and an ice cream cone. Ziad was well-behaved and quiet in the store, never once straying from the side of his mother. I wondered if perhaps Patsy's boss's children were not the exception to the norm among Saudi children.

While I stood near the door of the bakery shop waiting for Jewaher, the Syrian shopkeeper asked me if I needed anything. Shaking my head no, but at the same time glancing over his shoulder into the bakery, I asked the name of a pastry item on the pan directly behind him. He gave me an Arabic name for the flaky pastry, and then picked one up and handed it to me. As I munched on the tasty pastry, he asked me where I was from and where I worked. I thought nothing of answering his questions, especially since he had just given me the pastry.

As Jewaher's veiled figure approached, I immediately sensed her feelings of apprehension and nervousness. I realized that women in Saudi Arabia are not allowed to have any casual contact with men other than family; I was probably violating acceptable standards. We quickly walked on, and I sensed that much of the store seemed to be watching us, a strange combination of two very different cultures. I couldn't detect whether Jewaher noticed the curious stares. The driver was waiting just outside the door of the store when we emerged. He first rushed over to remove the bags from Jewaher's hand, and then he took mine.

At the house, Jewaher dropped her purchases right inside the door and hollered, "Tea," as she continued her pace up the stairs. She gave me a hasty invitation to come up to her room while she dressed for the party. I sat on the bed watching her open the wardrobe to reveal a long row of Sheikh Latif's *thobes*, taking up about one-fourth of the closet space.

The rest of the space was filled with long dresses, long skirts, and blouses. There was a huge pile of high heeled shoes on the floor. She chose a bright blue, taffeta dress with full sleeves and a tight fitting bodice. While she went into the bathroom to dress, I sat on the edge of the bed and sipped the hot, sweet tea that the Sri Lankan maid served. I would have preferred a cool drink of water. As I sipped my tea, I studied my surroundings and was surprised to see the telltale signs of unskilled labor jarring amidst the opulence of the decor. The paint on the walls seemed to have run in places, even onto the pretty marble tiles on the walls along the stairway. The corners of the carpet had frayed where they had not been finished properly. These clearly evidenced Saudi Arabia's rapid development, which left even the wealthiest of families dependent on unskilled labor and visited flaws in construction upon homes of all classes democratically.

In a flash, Jewaher was out of the bathroom, gave herself a quick spray of perfume, and talked to me over her shoulder as she descended the stairs. She invited me to return in a week, promising to take me shopping again. She also explained that because the farm was so far, I should plan to spend the night, a proposition that had never entered my mind. She concluded her invitation with the traditional, *insh Allah*, meaning "if God wills," a phrase that most Saudis use after they have made any kind of plans. I enjoyed my time with Jewaher and determined to keep the overnight invitation if I had the opportunity.

Terry came for me not long after Jewaher left for her party. He surprised me with a dinner invitation from our Pakistani friend Jamshaid. After living in Riyadh only a few months after leaving the farm, Jamshaid's family had returned to Pakistan because his wife Jasmine was allowed in Saudi Arabia only to perform her Hajj, the religious pilgrimage to Mecca, which is one of the Five Pillars of Islam, properly made between the eighth and thirteenth days of Dhu'l-hijja, the twelfth month of the Islamic calendar. Once this act was complete, she was supposed to leave. Moslems who come to Saudi Arabia for the pilgrimage are able to obtain only a restrictive visa that limits the amount of time that they may remain in the country.

Jamshaid had obtained only a three-month visa for his wife for the Hajj. She had lived on the farm almost three months past the time she was supposed to depart, making her, to some degree, an illegal alien. She and Jamshaid had been very careful whenever they left the farm. When they were moved to Riyadh, she felt she had to leave and was fined SR 2000 ($571) at the time her exit visa was processed. I felt some apprehension knowing that we couldn't just drive to the airport and leave the country whenever we wanted, because no one leaves Saudi Arabia without an exit visa. Our exit visas should have taken only twenty-four hours to process, but generally we had to allow three days.

Jamshaid now lived with a Pakistani family whom he called his relatives, although the term was only a measure of respect. When we visited with this family, the children were instructed to call us "uncle" and "aunt" as titles of respect. The head of the house was a short little man named Zetti, who worked for Sheikh Latif in his tile factory, from which Sheikh Latif's family had made part of their fortune.

When we arrived at the home of Jamshaid's "relatives," we were introduced to Zetti's wife, Ai, pronounced I. Ai's mother was visiting in Saudi Arabia to perform the Hajj. The mother spoke only Urdu, the language of Pakistan, but Ai spoke perfect English, explaining that she had been a science teacher in Pakistan before coming to Saudi Arabia, four years before. At the time I couldn't imagine living in Saudi Arabia for four years, never realizing that I would eventually reside there for five. Both women dressed in the typical Pakistani knee-length dress, split up the side, over matching baggy pants. Both women covered their heads with a sheer scarf through which I could see long braids of hair. I inquired whether the women ever cut their hair, and Ai told me that they cut it only an inch or two, when they go for the Hajj. The mother had a white cloth wrapped tightly around her neck as treatment for a cold. Ai was very pretty, with olive skin and jet black hair; she wore a stud in her pierced left nostril that somehow seemed to add to her beauty.

The family lived in a flat on the third floor of a building. Each unit had a balcony overlooking Riyadh. The men, including several neighbors, migrated to a room with large cushions on the floor and a television that was tuned to American wrestling, dubbed with Arabic. I joined the women in the kitchen.

I watched Ai patiently remove the meat from the neck bones of a chicken that she had boiled. As she worked, she told me she was on a diet because she had gained ten kilos (twenty-two pounds) since coming to Saudi Arabia. Her husband enjoyed a big meal when he returned from work in the evening, and they had been eating much more than they had eaten when they lived in Pakistan. In Pakistan, they ate rice only once a week, but in Saudi the rice was so cheap that they ate it every day. Turning to her mother who spoke in Urdu while mixing up what appeared to be bread dough, Ai smiled, then translated what her mother had said: "If you eat rice more than one day a week, it will give you a cold."

I continued to watch Ai as she added a can of corn to the chicken broth. She was making chicken and corn soup, and I wondered if it would be similar to what I'd eaten in the Chinese Restaurant. We came to the table, and Ai ladled out the thick delicious soup. I took a second bowl of soup when she offered it, thinking that the soup was our total meal. After the meal, the men returned to the television, and we went into the kitchen to make the flatbread dough into a bun called a *chapiti*, which is much thinner and softer in texture than the Saudi flatbread. The dough is a mixture of wheat flour and water. The mother and daughter skillfully and quickly worked the mound of dough into small balls about the size of a large lemon. The balls were then placed on a large tray of flour that had been stored under the cabinet. Placing the balls directly on the board, the mother shaped the balls with a rolling pin. With skill that came with years of practice, the women pounded, turned, and coerced the balls into perfectly round, flat pieces of bread that were then placed on a black iron pan that looked like an inverted skillet. They set the pan on top of a burner. The bread cooked for about a minute on each side. Ai explained as she worked that girls in Pakistan begin making the *chapitis* at the age of five, and when they reach a marrying age, sometimes as young as fourteen, they are skilled at the art of bread making.

I took my turn at one of the balls of dough. To my dismay, no matter what I did to the ball of dough, it remained just that, a ball of dough. The mother-daughter team had made shaping the dough look so easy, but I knew now, from experience, that it was quite an art. The *chapitis* were quickly cooked and placed in a white towel to keep warm. Ai filled bowls with food from the oven. As if on cue, the men assembled at the table again to finish their meal.

Ai had made a simple, but artistically arranged salad, using locally grown Romaine lettuce, the cheapest and most common lettuce in Saudi Arabia, sliced radishes, and tomatoes. She had garnished the salad with lemon wedges. The cooked vegetables were a mixture of green beans, carrots, and green peas, all chopped very small and served with vermicelli noodles. She boiled rice with pieces of lamb and served another lamb dish cooked with tomatoes and black pepper. They teased us, saying that if we had not been their guests, the food would have contained many chilies. After eating with several Pakistani families, we realized that it is customary to serve company more than one meat dish, normally even three or more, at a dinner. Yet because meat is expensive in Pakistan, many families can afford it only once a week or in small quantities mixed with rice. It is a symbol of not only wealth but also hospitality to offer several meat dishes.

The final course was a most unusual dish that Ai called *gajeraila*. It was made with shredded carrots that had been boiled until tender in milk sweetened with sugar. It tasted strongly of cardamon, added as the dish chilled.

When we left the table, I joined the women in the kitchen despite their insistence that I sit with the men. I sensed their shy approval that I insisted on helping with the dishes and remaining in the kitchen. We came to realize that owing to our ignorance of, and disregard for, the age-old caste system that they had lived by rigidly in their own country, we were overwhelmingly accepted by our Pakistani acquaintances, even though we were not Moslems.

While we cleaned the kitchen, I admired the string of six or eight bracelets that Ai wore on her wrist and arm. They were the exact color of her outfit and fit tightly around her arm. She quickly exited the kitchen, returning with a large ring of bracelets tied together on a piece of cloth. There were several different colors and patterns, each set containing six or eight bracelets.

As Ai showed me the different sets, she explained that the bracelets are not only for beauty in Pakistan, but also a sign that a woman is married. She said that a virgin—she did not use the term *unmarried woman*—does not wear the bracelets. She added that it was unheard of and would have been a disgrace for a family to have a daughter who went to her marriage bed without her virginity.

Ai removed one from a set of beautiful blue bracelets that she said were made of glass. She tried to put the bracelet over my hand, discovering that it was too small. She even placed a plastic sack over my hand to help her slide it on but was unsuccessful. I suspected that she wanted to give me a bracelet since she was going to such great lengths to fit the bracelet over my hand, onto my wrist. She continued to try different bracelets until she finally found a bright red and gold set that was larger and slipped onto my wrist. She sighed, regretting that the larger pair was made from plastic, but I assured her that they were still very pretty. I thanked her profusely that she would even consider giving me the set, and she seemed overjoyed that I considered the gift worthy of receiving.

While we washed the dishes, the topic of discussion was the reason Terry and I did not have any children, especially since we had been married more than four years. I explained, as I had to most other Moslem women, that we were going to wait until we left Saudi Arabia to have our family. I could sense that this answer was not satisfactory, especially to Ai's mother. To strengthen my argument, I elaborated on the fact that because we lived ninety miles from Riyadh and a doctor, and because it would be my first baby, I was afraid to deliver in Saudi Arabia. The mother nodded and smiled when Ai quickly said that I could live with them one month before my delivery date so that I would be near a doctor. I smiled and said I'd gladly consider their offer.

I lived in Saudi Arabia for several years before I fully comprehended that in a world where men and women are constantly separated, even within family gatherings, a woman's entire life and existence is entrenched in bearing children. Traditionally, in Moslem cultures, a woman's sole purpose in life has been to produce children, and it is from these children that she is to find happiness and contentment, as well as acceptance in society. I realized that the women's prodding me to have a child and offering to help me in any way if I chose to do so was their way of helping me to fit into their culture and to legitimatize my role as a woman.

We had a wonderful visit with this Pakistani family, who graciously opened their home to us. As we prepared to leave, they insisted that we spend the night. They even showed us the small bed on the balcony where the mother slept, explaining that she preferred to sleep outside. Warmly, they offered us her empty bedroom. After we returned to the States, we regretted never accepting one of the numerous invitations that we received to spend the night with one of these families of a different culture, with whom we had grown to feel such kinship. We did stay with Sheikh Latif our last night in Saudi Arabia, in order to catch a very early morning flight out of the country. Other than that the only nights in Saudi I ever spent away from the farm were the two that I stayed over with Jewaher. Neither time had Terry joined me.

It was near this clock tower in Riyadh, on Fridays, that the Saudis administered their system of justice. Murder and rape were punished by beheading; theft, by cutting off the right hand. Notices of crimes committed ran in the newspaper, and Saudi men and male children, along with a few foreigners, attended the punishments. The criminals were rarely Saudi, but usually foreign workers whose names and nationalities were published in the newspaper.

A popular suq in Riyadh where brass, gold, copper, fabric, sandals, spices, and veils abounded.

Spices such as cardamom, cinnamon sticks, and dried lemons were sold in bulk in the market.

Rachel Armstrong from New Mexico, who lived on the farm with the author for almost two years. She now resides with her husband in Grady, New Mexico. The two salesmen enjoyed outfitting her in the traditional Bedouin veil and abaya. The store sold the head attire for both males and females, and like all other stores had only male employees. The salesmen seemed not to be offended by the unveiled American women and enjoyed their attempts to communicate in Arabic.

Tariq Al Salem, a Saudi from a neighboring farm, at the first
birthday party he ever had. He was 18 years old. Saudi Arabians typically
do not commemorate birthdays with any kind of celebration. The
birthday party was hosted by Sherri, teenage daughter of John and Patsy
Zielske, the Americans who managed Tariq's father's farm. Tariq
entertained Sherri during her short stay in Saudi Arabia. Tariq refused
to marry the bride his family had chosen for him and remains single.

Since many of the nationalities living in Saudi Arabia were accustomed to eating flat bread twice a day, some of the larger farms had their own bakery. This oven was on the Al Salem farm and was manned by a Sudanese worker. The thin dough cooked quickly over the hot flames.

These children had been sent to a bakery in Al Kharj to buy fresh bread. The flat bread was warm and delicious and patrons had to bring a piece of newspaper on which to take the bread home. Children dressed as miniature adults at all times, boys wearing the long, white *thobe* and the headdress; girls wearing long dresses. Girls began veiling at puberty, sometimes sooner.

Midwess and his close friend Faizal leaning on a Saudi armrest. Faizal was from Yemen and drove a grader for the farm. He went with us to visit Midwess, who had moved to Al Flaj.

Driver Amine Khan and the van that the company provided to the author for excursions from the farm. The author had numerous drivers during her stay, but Amine Khan, from Afghanistan, was one of the most cordial, even though he spoke no English. The author would leave the farm at 6:30 A.M. and head towards Riyadh, stopping at other farms and compounds along the way to pick up other foreign women. These women formed fast friendships on the two-hour drives.

Midwess's children (Mohammed, Abdallah, Latifa, and Abdul Latif) visiting the author in her new house on the farm. They loved the cold canned soft drinks that she served them. Usually, they stayed just a few minutes before they were hustled off by Rashmi. Houseplants thrived in the author's desert home.

A woman drinks fresh camel's milk. Camel's milk, consumed at room temperature, tasted much like evaporated milk. The rich liquid was milked into a plastic bucket, then poured into a communal bowl that was passed around to the guests. Dates were then dipped in the foam on top of the milk. Midwess always told us that camel's milk promoted "good brains."

Saudi soldiers, in khaki uniforms with traditional Saudi headdress, outside the fence at the King's annual camel race. The camel race was one of the rare events at which foreigners were encouraged to take pictures.

Virgin, undeveloped desert. When Terry Kirk first observed the site, he couldn't imagine that the desert could ever be transformed into a workable farm, let alone the lush oasis that Green Sands became.

Two Texans, Franklin Baggerman and Cliff Williams, with a Filipino mechanic whom we called *Sadiq* (meaning friend in Arabic) test pumping a well. They are showing with their fingers that it pumped 1200 gallons per minute. As each well was test pumped, the crew responded excitedly to the gushing water, coming warm out of the ground.

Sheik Latif and his brother-in-law Abdul Rahman observing the test pumping of the first well on P2. The well pumped 1200 gallons per minute.

We had sixty-seven Valley eight- and nine-tower electric-drive center pivots. During the author's first season at P2, the pivot tires were always getting stuck in the ruts they made in the clay loam. Terry Kirk and the workers spent a great deal of time digging them out. After the first season, the pivots no longer became stuck because the tire tracks were filled and ridged so that the pivot could run on dry ground. The wheat grown under pivots would produce 100 bushels per acre.

One of the pivots at the very back of P2, which was surrounded by canyon walls. This pivot was 15 minutes by pickup from camp and produced beautiful wheat in the shadow of the canyon.

As the green fields turned golden and the full heads ready for harvest, the combines began to roll. The three International and three John Deere combines worked fourteen-hour days and could harvest a field (120 acres) in four hours, barring any serious breakdowns.

After two years of wheat production, the government silos reached capacity and had no place to store more wheat. Large farms, like the one on which the author lived, piled the wheat high on tarps on the ground, where it remained for seven months. Once the government started accepting wheat again, the wheat had to be augured into the air, and the dirt was blown out with a large fan. The little bit of wheat that was left on the ground was gleaned by Bedouin women, who went from farm to farm sifting the dirt for the wheat kernels, much the same as the Biblical Ruth.

The sale of rhodes grass provided operating money for the farm after the government delayed wheat payments. Terry Kirk proposed growing rhodes grass, and the rich fodder for camels and sheep attracted buyers from all over the gulf.

It usually rained only one time a year in the desert, in January. This three-inch rain created mud on the farm and at times tractors would get stuck. During the rains, the Saudi people would come out and play in the puddles of water that the rain had created in the desert. The man on the tractor is Kalapuhana, a Sri Lankan that came to Saudi as a common laborer making $215 per month. Terry Kirk realized his potential and promoted him through the ranks. Kalapuhana is now the farm manager, has brought his family to live with him, and receives a salary of $1200 per month. Few Americans remain in Saudi working in the agricultural sector owing to the drop in the price of wheat subsidies.

Tabinda, wife of Imod, a Pakistani employee of Al Emar, and her daughter Tabona would often visit the farm with their family and loved harvest time, when the combines combed through the golden fields of wheat. Imod's position with the company, in charge of international purchasing, enabled him to bring Tabinda and the children to live with him in Saudi Arabia, a luxury many laborers were not afforded. A large percentage, roughly thirty percent, of Saudi Arabia's labor force is made up of Pakistanis, partly because of Pakistan's proximity to Saudi Arabia, partly for religious regions. Many Pakistanis sought jobs in Saudi Arabia so they could make pilgrimages to Mecca (one of the Five Pillars).

It was not unusual to see Toyota pickups stacked much higher than this traveling down the highway. The Bedouin population was mobile, constantly searching for fodder and water for the animals.

Midwess's children, Abdul Latif and Latifa (both named for Sheik Latif, our boss) in the only home they have known, the inside of a tent. Rashmi used the hand-cranked sewing machine to sew all the dresses she wore. The maroon dress on the sewing machine was later given to the author. Since the Bedouins are so mobile, most possessions are stored for quick departure in suitcases, which are elevated from the reach of desert varmints and wandering baby sheep.

Midwess's only daughter, Latifa, is lost in a fantasy world as she plays with one of her mother's scarves. As a Bedouin, she faces a harsh life battling desert elements as she herds camel and sheep, cooks on a butane stove, marries young, and gives birth to many children. When the Kirks left Saudi Arabia in 1988, schools were beginning to spring up in the desert for Bedouin male children. Midwess grinned and shrugged when the Kirks asked about schooling for the Bedouin female children.

Midwess's oldest son, Mohammed, named for the prophet of Islam. Mohammed could look forward to a brighter future than what Midwess was afforded because schools were starting for Bedouin boys. Midwess, despite his great knowledge of desert life and skill in driving a bulldozer, could not read or write. Mohammed's real mother left Midwess shortly after Mohammed's birth and returned to her family. Midwess, in keeping with Saudi law kept the baby and soon married Rashmi, who had not yet reached puberty.

Inside Midwess's tent on a dark desert night. Midwess and two friends entertained us with the national dance of Saudi Arabia, the sword dance. Traditionally, the gray *thobe* is worn in the winter; however, the white *thobe* is worn year round by some Saudis. Men hold hands in public frequently, but touching between the opposite sexes in public is forbidden.

John Zelske, Midwess, and the author at a typical meal of fruit, Pepsi, and rice, and either mutton or chicken. Customarily, rice is served on a communal platter, but during this visit Midwess had placed large quantities in individual bowls. He had observed the use of individual plates in the author's home and must have purchased the bowls to make his guests feel more at home.

Dick Cates, an American from Wisconsin, worked at Al-Safi dairy, just outside of Al Kharj. Midwess was enchanted with Dick's fiddle and his ability to coax music from it. Midwess loved to bring out his sword to entertain any foreigners we brought to his tent.

A typical Bedouin meal on a communal platter. The rice and lamb, chicken, or goat are eaten with the right hand, without utensils. Midwess's two sons Mohammed and Abdallah (no head attire) are eating with their father and other friends. In the days before Saudi Arabia was a wealthy country, the men would eat first, and the women and children would then consume leftovers from the same platter. Today, men and women eat at the same time, but in separate locations. The reason for the separation is that only the father, son, husband, and brother are allowed to see a woman's unveiled face. If only immediate family are present, males and females usually partake of the meal together. During her first year in Saudi Arabia, when the Kirks visited Midwess, the author sat with her husband and the other men. Finally becoming at ease, she began to eat with the women on the other side of the tent flap. Even though only women and young male children were present, the women always remained veiled in the author's presence.

The author read about the process for preserving the fresh sheep's and camel's milk before going to Saudi Arabia, but could not believe it was still being practiced by Bedouins. The fresh milk was first stored in a butchered animal's stomach. After the milk thickened, it was poured into a large metal tub. The mixture was stirred periodically with a long stick and allowed to thicken further. When the mixture reached the consistency of dough, it was shaped into patties resembling sugar cookies and laid on plastic sheets in the sun to dry. The patties were then dried until rock hard and were called *nougat*. They tasted like hardened, soured yogurt, but when popped into the mouth along with a drink of the sweetened tea (a trick the author learned from the Bedouins), they were edible. The *nougat* was considered a delicacy, perhaps a reflection of its importance for preservation of milk in the absence of refrigeration.

Turkish laborers. These two were the only Turks the author ever knew to be employed by the farm, whose staff sometimes numbered as high as one hundred. During the first six months of the farm's inception, these two men drove bulldozers and leveled sand dunes in preparation for pivots.

Sheik Latif posing in the canteen with laborers from Mexico. The Mexicans set pumps and drilled wells in the early stages of farm development. The pumps were set at 400 feet and wells drilled at 600 feet. The Mexicans spoke no English or Arabic so communication with others was difficult. The biggest challenge for them was the canteen food, which bore no resemblance to their native cuisine.

A group of Pakistani workers gathered in the canteen during a party celebrating the completion of harvest. During the harvest party, the company, Al Emar, provided soft drinks and near beer. The standing man in the bow tie was a Sri Lankan cook, named Reganathan, who came to work for the company as a pastry chef, for which we had little need on the farm.

Camel in the back of a Toyota pickup. A common sight on the road in Saudi Arabia.

A camel being transported to market for sale in the back of a pickup was a common sight on the highways of Saudi Arabia. To get the camel into the pickup, the legs of the camel were first tied, bending back at the knee. A rope was then placed around the stomach and across the hump of the camel to facilitate lifting the camel into the pickup. If the owner of the camel was fortunate enough to have a tractor, the camel was scooped up into the pickup by the rope around the camel's hump. Many Bedouins used the tripod block and tackle or chain hoist, which required brute strength to crank.

Camels crossing the farm during the early years, when much of the area was still undeveloped virgin soil. It was unusual to see camels being ridden except at a camel race. Usually camels were herded with a pickup and rarely used for transportation, even by the Bedouins. Instead, the camels represented wealth and were traded, presented as part of a dowry package, or eaten as a delicacy on momentous occasions such as weddings. The author ate camel in a restaurant in Riyadh and thought it tasted similar to beef.

The two containers at Project 2 (the farm where the author lived), one of which (on the right) was her home for her first two years in Saudi Arabia. The structures looked like interlopers in the vast sands that encompassed them. When Terry Kirk first arrived, on a hot, windy August 13th, 1982, the 20 x 38 feet containers had not been put together properly at the seams, and sand had sifted in. Even with better alignment, the author could write her name in the sand on the kitchen table whenever the sand blew. As the wind was blowing, one could smell the dirt in the air inside the container. The metal containers were so hot from March through October that the Kirks had to eat lunch in front of the air conditioner in the bedroom to keep from dripping perspiration into their plates.

Two Bedouins who were part of a group that was camped for a time on the farm. They made friends with Terry Kirk and, when they discovered the author was pregnant, would bring her an old water bottle filled with camel's milk every day. The young woman had no inhibitions about having her photograph taken and even encouraged the author to take more.

Terry Kirk and Midwess standing in the Kirks' container. Midwess would often stop in during lunch because he knew that Terry would be at home and that it would be more appropriate to visit when Terry was there. Because Bedouins eat usually only two meals a day, at mid-morning and again in late afternoon, Midwess was surprised to see the Kirks eating during the noon hour when it was so hot.

The author, dressed in a traditional Sri Lankan sari, standing in the canteen with Sheik Latif at the Sri Lankan New Year's party. After the author was appointed as their advocate, the workers asked her to persuade the company to host a Sri Lankan New Year's party every March. The farm had a large population of Sri Lankans and the New Year's party became a popular event.

The swimming pool in the new diplomatic quarters in Riyadh. Mixed bathing (men and women) was permitted here. Whereas in public pools in Saudi Arabia, including hotels, it was forbidden. The people who lived in walled compounds provided by a company or foreign government rarely had occasion to mix with the locals, especially the Bedouins.

The author and her husband Terry with Prince Sultan ibn Salman ibn Abdul Aziz Al-Saud in his palace. (Ibn in a name is translated "son of.") The prince, who had been the payload specialist on (American) Space shuttle mission 51-G in 1985, had granted the author an interview about the future of education and employment for females in Saudi Arabia. Owing to the Prince's busy schedule, the interview was granted at 10:00 P.M. The author recalls the Prince as both gracious and optimistic.

The men's and women's living rooms in Sheik Latif's house. On weekends all the sisters in a family typically return to their mother's house for uninhibited, and unveiled, visiting and laughing, confident that no man would enter the women's quarters unannounced.

The black wool tent where Sheik Latif entertained everyone from ambassadors to Bedouins. The tent was carpeted with Persian rugs and the walls were lined with Saudi armrests. In one end of the tent was a Ping-Pong table, unusually modern in the Arabian setting.

The author standing in front of the black, wool tent that Sheik Latif used for entertaining guests. She is wearing the dress that Midwess's wife Rashmi made on the hand-cranked sewing machine. The fabric of the dress was lacy, but would not have been considered immodest by Rashmi (not pictured), as she typically wore several dresses, one on top of the other, even during the hot months.

Chapter Nineteen

The day arrived for the shopping trip and overnight sojourn with Jewaher in Riyadh. Terry was unable to leave the farm, so I rode with Roger, the Filipino mechanic and my cooking instructor. He was going to town to purchase a special part for a motor.

Although his name was Roger, we called him *Sadiq*, which means "friend" in Arabic. He kept us entertained with his lively stories of life in the Philippines. On one particular evening, he knocked on our door, excited about his idea for a new invention. As he described a special cooling jacket for an irrigation motor, Terry burst out laughing. Roger was disappointed to learn that such a piece of equipment had long been in use in the States, but delighted to know that his idea had proven substance.

I climbed into his nonair-conditioned pickup, careful to lift my long skirt above the floor board of a typical farm vehicle that had been driven in the middle of the desert. The ninety miles passed quickly as Roger told me tale after tale of life in the Philippines. One of his most amazing tales concerned the mountain people in the Philippines who live far from the civilized world. According to Roger, a mountain man shoots a pregnant monkey when his wife is pregnant. The umbilical chord from the monkey is saved and used ceremonially in the delivery of the baby to ensure good luck for the child.

We arrived in Riyadh, where Roger dropped me off at Jewaher's villa. After Jewaher gave me the formal greeting of a kiss on each cheek, we quickly embarked on our shopping trip. In the car, she explained that we had departed so quickly in order to complete our shopping before prayer time, which would begin at 6:20 P.M. When we reached the shopping area, I guessed that prime-time shopping must be from four to six because the town was very crowded. As we rode along in the back seat of her Cadillac, the Pakistani driver honked continuously as he threaded his way through the streets of Riyadh.

We went to three different shopping areas. Jewaher knew that I wanted a new dress, so she took me to the Kuwait Market. The market consisted of shop after shop of open-air stalls and endless rows of kitchen shops, each containing about the same goods. The male shopkeepers stood outside their shops, talking to each other and drinking the sweet, hot tea. There was also an abundance of fabric shops with brightly colored cloth selections.

We came to several clothing stores where Jewaher, in abaya and veil, searched through the racks of long dresses. She pulled out several selections for me to scrutinize. Sensing her urgency to complete this task, I chose a long black dress trimmed with gold-colored braid. The dress, imported from Morocco, cost SR 50 ($14.30), a bargain.

We visited another market where she quickly selected several items. I purchased a traditional Arabic brass coffeepot and a small brass camel. She seemed pleased that I wanted one of their coffeepots. I planned to use it for decoration, but I knew she was thinking I'd use it for serving Arabic coffee. I noted in my journal later that Jewaher was very cordial, treating me as her equal. Reflecting on this statement, I wonder now what I had expected our relationship to be.

We returned to her house to freshen up for a party at Jewaher's cousin's house. I envisioned a simple family gathering. The thought never entered my mind to change out of my simple long dress into something more formal. Actually, I had nothing more appropriate, but at least, I might have worn the new dress I'd purchased.

Waiting for Jewaher downstairs, I was shocked when she descended the stairs in an elegant red dress and tall, spike heels. I watched as she covered her new makeup and hairdo with the black covering. We quickly scrambled into the car as Jewaher told the driver our destination.

As we entered Jewaher's cousin's house, I stepped quickly to the side as the incoming groups of women removed their abayas and veils just inside the door. The house and furniture were very grand, and the women were dressed elegantly. I felt underdressed and homely in my simple cotton, high-necked, long-sleeved dress, next to the exquisitely garbed Saudi women, in their plunging necklines and gorgeous taffeta and silk fabrics.

Jewaher's cousin greeted me with the traditional kiss on the cheek and a soft handshake. I took my place in the huge, elaborately furnished living room on one of the many couches that lined all four walls. The women clustered in groups, talking until a new arrival appeared, at which time the conversation ceased and the women stood to extend the traditional greeting to the newcomer, as she circulated around the room, careful to miss no one. The women then resumed their conversation until another guest arrived and the process repeated. I was met with curious, but not unfriendly stares, and a few of the younger women even spoke a few words of English to me.

In the midst of this greeting process, a number of Filipino and Sri Lankan girls passed among the women, offering Arabic coffee in thimble-sized cups, and sweet, hot tea in tiny glass mugs. The tea cups were rimmed with gold, and the servants offered a choice of teas, one containing mint leaves. One of the older servants passed around a decorative incense burner emitting sandalwood odors. I discovered later that the beautiful container was called a *mabkhar* and is usually ornamented on the outside with gold and mirrors and a combination of flowing colors. Some of the women just smelled the aroma and let the container linger before them for a moment, but others, particularly the older women, wanted the scent to permeate their clothes. They pulled out their bodices, allowing the smoke inside, to be absorbed into their clothing. It is said that a festivity without burning incense in the *mabkhar* is no festivity. The purpose of the custom began in the early years of the wandering Bedouins when a frequent bath was impossible, and the aroma of the sandalwood was needed to mask odors. At some of the more important functions, frankincense is used instead of sandalwood.

Because I could only say little more than hello in Arabic, I spent the night observing the different groups of women. I was the only woman who said thank you to the servant girls for the refreshments. The other women stared right through the girls, as if they weren't there. Because I was accustomed to eating dinner early, and we continued to sit until almost 10:00 P.M., I took ample servings of the dates and hot tea.

At ten-thirty the hostess called us to dinner. Ironically, she had just received the last guest at her door. I wondered if that person had been told that the party began at seven.

Jewaher guided me into the garden area, where places were set among trays of food on top of beautiful Persian carpets. She insisted that I eat with the older women. It must have been decided that I would eat with the older women because I was a guest. I would have preferred to eat with Jewaher, the only person I knew, but I sensed that I shouldn't upset the plans.

Huge platters held the traditional whole sheep and rice, surrounded by several unusual vegetable dishes, stuffed grape leaves, and a beautifully decorated whole fish. In front of each place setting was an individual bowl of whole fruits, egg custard, and several soft drink cans. Some of the women had finished eating by the time I took my place on the floor. I was amazed to see the women eating so fast and furiously and that manners were abandoned. Even though they were dressed elegantly, the women lost their air of sophistication as they flew into their food, dropping as much as they ate onto the lovely carpets and the bodices of their dresses.

As each women rose to leave, one of the servants replaced the soiled plate with a clean one. I had hardly tasted any of the many dishes in front of me, when I was surrounded by a totally different set of women. I considered that the women might be eating quickly to allow for the second group, when to my consternation, I noticed that the second group of women was eating just as rapidly.

I followed the second group of women into a room with four elaborate wash basins, and everyone washed her hands. Most of the women had eaten with their right hands, even though a complete set of silverware was placed at each place setting. As we dried our hands, the servants poured perfume onto them.

Back in the original gathering area, tea and coffee were served for the final time of the evening. Servants passed around bowls of expensive chewing gum to freshen the breath. The gum, made from the sap of a tree, is sold in the markets. The final serving of coffee and tea was the signal to depart. The women seemed to understand this unwritten rule because there was little, if any, conversation as they sipped the hot drinks. One by one the women kissed the hostess goodbye, donned the complete black covering and exited into the night. As we left, I noticed many of the drivers parked in the exact spots as when we had arrived more than four hours earlier. Most of the drivers were of the same nationality, and I guessed that they visited together while they waited.

Because my normal bedtime back on the farm was about 9:30, I was very tired; however, the evening seemed to have just begun for Jewaher. She told me that she rarely went to bed before 2:00 A.M. because sometimes Sheikh Latif, Abdul Latif as she called him, didn't come home until midnight. I realized how separated the sexes are, socializing separately even in the evenings.

We removed our shoes and put our feet on the couch, while she showed me some of her photo albums. She had married Sheikh Latif, ten years her senior, when she was only eighteen. Because Jewaher asked me how old I was, I didn't hesitate to ask her how old she was. Although she was only twenty-six in what she termed American age, she was twenty-seven according to the Moslem lunar calendar, which gains eleven days every year. She laughed and said that she told people she was twenty-six. She told me matter-of-factly that Sheikh Latif was her second cousin, a common union in Saudi Arabia. She appeared much slimmer in her honeymoon photographs. They had gone abroad for their honeymoon, so she didn't have her face covered in the pictures.

Jewaher and I talked easily, sharing much common ground, although we were from very different cultures. She asked me very frankly what kind of birth control I used and when I planned to have children. Having lived in America for two and a half years, she accepted my answer about waiting to have a family, although she did offer that if I wanted to get pregnant, I could live with them in town during my ninth month.

One of her favorite subjects was weight loss. Posted on her refrigerator was a diet plan, written in Arabic, that she had torn from a magazine. She also enjoyed discussions that centered around shopping and told me that she loved the shopping in America. On one occasion about three years before, when she had visited in the United States, she had returned with twelve additional suitcases full of items from her shopping sprees. When I asked naively where she got the twelve extra suitcases, she replied that she bought them, of course!

Because Sheikh Latif and Ziad, the oldest son, were spending the night at the farm, I slept in Ziad's bedroom. Several years later Sheikh Latif's family would move into a house with many guest bedrooms, but for the present they had no guest room. The bed was purchased in the U.S. and was a twin, shaped like a car. I told Terry jokingly that I slept in a car at Jewaher's home.

We awoke about 9:00 A.M. the next morning to a traditional Saudi breakfast of Arab flatbread, scrambled eggs with tomatoes and onions, two kinds of olives, four kinds of cheeses, peanut butter, honey, and a sweet cake, all served with the hot, sweet tea.

Jewaher was a college student and was studying to receive a degree in English that would qualify her to teach English in the schools. When I met her, she had almost completed her degree and was to have finals in a few weeks. Before I left that morning, she asked me to read a section from one of her textbooks and to explain. Terry arrived to get me at 10:30. Jewaher explained that if I could stay longer, I might accompany her to her mother's house, where she and her sisters would congregate to visit. Because Terry needed to get back to the farm, I declined.

After being marooned in the desert for three weeks after my visit with Jewaher, without even a trip to Al Kharj, much less Riyadh, I would have resorted to anything to experience what I termed civilization. Because I hadn't called my parents in quite some time, phoning them seemed a legitimate excuse to go as far as Al Kharj. About this time, the head office sent word to the farm that both Mitri's and Perera's records for visa renewal needed an updated photograph. The request sounded urgent, so Terry allowed them to go into town. When I heard that Mitri and Perera were going in to Al Kharj, I convinced Terry that I should hitch a ride with them, in order to make my call.

I waited inside my container for the sound of their vehicle and bounded out the door when I heard the screech of the brakes on the sand. I was eager to get off the farm, but by the wide smiles on the faces of the two Sri Lankans, I was no more eager than they. Mitri drove, and Perera prepared to move to the center of the pickup seat. When I insisted that I would ride in the middle, their grins became broader.

Terry nor I felt any hesitation in trusting these quiet men on any mission or journey. This trust included driving me into Al Kharj. We learned later that we could all have been in serious trouble for allowing a lone woman to be in company with two single males. Luckily, our outing to Al Kharj went undetected, at least by anyone with authority. I wondered later if pleading ignorance would have exonerated us if we had been caught. I would have insisted that the men were merely my drivers, hoping the police or *Mutawwa* would not question my honesty, even though a pickup requires only one driver.

We went unheeded by the law or religious police, but we did cause quite a stir in several places we went. It was not unusual to see a Sri Lankan man driving a woman, but when we parked and alighted all together from the pickup, people stared.

We were racing the clock to accomplish our tasks before the afternoon prayer time. We went to two different pharmacies to locate asthma medicine for Terry. One good thing about Saudi Arabia was that we were able to purchase almost any kind of medicine without a prescription. After I placed my call at the phone center, we also made a stop at the fruit market and a grocery store. Of course, we also had to attend to current photographs for Mitri's and Perera's passports.

The men and I enjoyed the trip. We carried on a conversation easily, even though Mitri barely spoke English. He communicated with nods and smiles. Later, after Mitri had worked on the farm for five years and had practiced his English with Terry and other English-speaking employees, his conversational English was almost perfect. For the present, Perera served as the spokesperson.

I questioned them hesitantly about being Buddhist, a religion about which I knew nothing. Perera explained that they prayed to Lord Buddha in a Buddhist temple, but attended no regularly scheduled worship services. He explained several religious practices also. Buddhists are expected to take fresh flowers or food to the temple to place in front of Lord Buddha when they go to the temple to pray. If two Buddhists decide to marry, they go to a government office, sign a paper, and then have a party. Although divorce is allowed, it is very uncommon in Sri Lanka. The Sri Lankans refer to American marriages as "love marriages" in contrast to their marriages of arrangement. Long before I had asked about all I wanted to know, we arrived at the farm, ready to resume daily life.

Chapter Twenty

The bright green heads on the wheat began to yellow and deepen to a golden hue in the blazing temperature. Harvesting was upon us. I knew that soon thereafter we would go on vacation. I decided that I should visit my Bedouin female friends and watch carefully to see how they wrapped the long piece of sheer black cloth around their heads. I knew that my family and friends in the States would be interested in knowing all about the life and customs of my Bedouin friends. Early one morning, I donned the long dress that they had made for me, and Terry drove me to the back of the farm to the Bedouin tent.

I took some things along to show the women: my camera, snapshots of my family and U.S. friends, hard candy, a flute, and a small mirror.

The Bedouins were overjoyed to see me. They raced to the pickup and practically dragged me out of the vehicle. They kissed me warmly on both cheeks, and Mama even lifted her veil to kiss me. They quickly hustled me into the tent, raising the east tent flap, so that we felt the cool breeze. They could hardly contain their excitement and curiosity about what I had brought in the bag. As I pulled the items slowly from my bag, their excitement mounted. They loved the pictures of my family, identifying with the universal words *moma* and *daddy*. They attacked the hard candy, the women no less ferociously than the children.

When they saw my camera, I asked with gestures and a few words of Arabic if I might take pictures of their tent. I made it clear that there would be no pictures made of them. They must have misunderstood because they shook their heads no, but would later allow me to take pictures.

I also brought my flute because they had enjoyed Frank's playing his guitar so much. My friends were extremely curious about the flute, and they were especially attracted to the bright silver color. Because I am unable to play anything by ear and didn't have any sheet music, I just played the scale. Not surprisingly that didn't hold their interest long. They preferred to examine the flute, passing it from one set of hands to the other with great care.

Frank had said that he had seen Mama with a stick and some lamb's wool that she seemed to be spinning, and I wanted to ask her about it. After much motioning, Mama finally understood what I was trying to say and seemed excited that I was interested in watching her do something so mundane. She brought a simple device made from a stick of wood, for me to examine. From a mass of camel's hair, she pulled out a small piece of the wool and twisted it tightly into a length resembling yarn. She continued twisting the strand and as it passed through the device, it came together into a cord, and she turned and wound it around a ball. In Arabic she explained that it didn't matter whether the wool came from a camel or a sheep. She motioned that from the camels she pulled out a little of their wool with which to work. She pulled on my arm and pointed to the black flap that covered the opening of the canvas tent. She indicated that she made it from the camel's spun wool. As amazement registered on my face, I felt Mama's pride in her accomplishment. She pulled me into the tent and from a large tin box, she pulled a pretty brown and white pallet, about two feet by four feet, gesturing that she had made it from both camel's and sheep's wool. I couldn't imagine the amount of time it had taken her to spin the wool. To my absolute astonishment, she picked up my camera and made motions to indicate that I might take her picture spinning the wool. I grabbed my camera, snapping a few pictures before she could change her mind.

Although I couldn't see the women's faces because of the veils, I sensed that they were equally as shocked that she was allowing her picture to be taken. I think my attitude conveyed to her that I thought this was a tremendous accomplishment, even though she viewed it as a part of her daily life. In the years that I lived in the desert, I often saw her walking with a herd of sheep, in the middle of the desert, in the scorching heat, spinning busily with her fingers.

The women then showed me how to tie my black head covering. I used my tiny mirror and their large mirror to get a front and back view of what they were doing. I never understood the process exactly because of the swiftness and surety of their tying, but I felt as though I had the general idea. As they worked with the head covering, they expressed their disapproval of my short, then popular, wedge haircut. They scolded that I should let my hair grow long so that I could braid it like theirs. To make the point, each one pulled her long braid from under the layers; I was surprised at the length of their hair. I guessed that they had probably never cut it. I figured that they kept it tightly braided because they had little opportunity to wash it. Their hair was braided in four separate sections, two in the front and two in the back. The tight braiding made hair more manageable in the dusty, windy desert.

Shortly thereafter, both Mama and Amora, Midwess's sister, exited the tent, walking out toward the sheep. While they were gone, Rashmi and Abdallah's wife served me coffee and dates, and we all took a drink of water from the same aluminum bowl.

Mama and Amora must have released the lambs from their pen, because we were suddenly surrounded by the tiny lambs. They wandered all around camp and in and out of the tent where we were sitting. It was such a funny sight that I laughed aloud, provoking laughter from the other women. One of the biggest of the lambs was down on his two front knees, literally crawling around the camp searching for food. As the lamb continued to crawl and sniff, Hidi jumped on the lamb's back in hopes of getting a ride.

The commotion and noise made by the free lambs brought the mother sheep closer to the tent, away from the spot where they were grazing. I watched as Amora swiftly moved from sheep to sheep, collapsing to her knees in the sand, milking them. I indicated that I wanted to try my hand at milking a sheep, and Amora seemed surprised and pleased that I'd consider doing such a thing. Whereas Amora's pulls had produced hard, fast squirts of milk into her plastic bucket, my attempts rarely produced a trickle. As I struggled to pull the milk out of the sheep's teats, Mohammed, who was about eight years old, tried to squirt us with the milk from another sheep. Some of the mother sheep's teats were covered with a cloth bag that Amora expertly slipped off before she milked them. With great difficulty, she finally conveyed to me that the bags were to wean the babies from the mothers.

From the bucket, the milk was poured through a large metal funnel into a long leather pouch that was made from a butchered animal's stomach. This was the first step in producing the dried cookie that they called *nougat,* which was what I had eaten earlier with my tea. After several days the somewhat thickened milk is poured into large metal bowls and set in partial sunlight. The bowls are covered, and a large wooden paddle is left in the mixture to be used for stirring. After standing and being stirred occasionally for several days, the mixture becomes thick enough to shape into patties that resemble sugar cookie dough. The patties are then placed on cloths on a box outside in the sun. This process was especially interesting to me because I had read about the procedure before I ever came to Saudi. I noticed that when the women ate the sour, hard mixture, they popped a piece in their mouths and quickly took a swallow of the sweet, hot tea. I marveled at the Bedouin procedure to conserve the milk, a rich source of calcium, without refrigeration.

After our milking experience, they motioned me to sit down; we seemed to be resting. I had worn the long dress the women had given me, even though the wrist bands were too small for me to snap them together. They noticed that my sleeves were too small, and Rashmi quickly disappeared. She soon reappeared with a different dress. This dress was made from transparent maroon lace. The yoke was bright red, trimmed in several different colors of ribbons, some what like a clown's suit. They insisted that I take off the other dress and put on this new one. Feeling a little self-conscious because I only had a bra and half-slip on underneath, I pulled off the orange dress. The women cackled and laughed, examining my underclothes. I could understand their amusement; they wore something that looked like a sweat suit for underwear. I struggled to pull the maroon dress over my head. The neck was very small and had no additional opening. I was afraid that I was going to be stuck with the dress halfway on and halfway off. I could see myself standing outside the tent in the middle of the desert with a dress stuck on my head and my half-slip flapping in the wind. I finally pulled on the dress and to their delight, the sleeves fit so that I was able to snap them together. I tried to return the orange dress that they'd given me earlier, but they all shook their heads, saying that they wanted me to have both dresses to wear in America. "Amerikey," as they pronounced it, Mama asked me if I was going to have a baby while I was gone on vacation. I assumed that she meant to ask if I might become pregnant while I was at home. I just smiled; I didn't know the Arabic words to convey my thoughts and feelings on the matter.

As we talked, Midwess stopped by the tent for just a moment. In his haste he didn't notice the extra woman, maybe because I was dressed like the others. When Mama pointed me out to him, he really laughed. He then said that I should dress that way all the time and that I looked better that way. He followed the statement with a hearty laugh.

There was just time for me to play my flute for a few minutes before Terry came for me. They begged him to stay for coffee and tea, but he explained that he had a broken-down combine to repair. They watched as we drove off into the desert. The final comment that I wrote in my journal about the day was that none of the women spoke a word of English, and I spoke only a few words of Arabic, yet we had communicated beautifully.

In the five years that we knew him, our Bedouin, as we fondly called Midwess, became more and more attached to the trappings of a more stationary lifestyle. One of the first steps of progression into modernization occurred when we finished our first wheat harvest. Prior to harvest, Midwess worked as a bulldozer driver at a nominal salary. During harvest, he drove a truck after normal work hours, hauling wheat from the fields. With some of his extra income, he bought a refrigerator and put it in Terry's office on the farm. Not only were he and his family able to enjoy the luxury of cold soft drinks, but they began freezing portions of the slaughtered sheep.

One afternoon I noticed that Midwess stopped by the office to get something from his refrigerator and had Rashmi and Mama with him. I hesitantly walked over to them, observing that they remained seated in the pickup while he went inside. I felt that they probably were curious to see the refrigerator and even the inside of Terry's office, but believed that they needed to remain carefully secluded. Nonetheless, the women got out of the pickup as I approached and squatted down on the ground next to the vehicle as we "talked." Midwess came out, insisting that I take an orange and a soft drink. He tried to give me some frozen sheep, but I explained to him that I didn't know how to cook it. I realized later they probably thought I knew very little about anything if I didn't even know how to cook a piece of sheep.

We were harvesting the wheat with the biggest and best combines, including three 1480 rotary Internationals, two 7720 John Deeres, and one German-made 1085 John Deere. Yet the powerful state-of-the-art machinery ground to a halt each prayer time if its driver was Moselm. On one dark desert night, we were headed to the combines for Terry to do a quick check when we almost ran over one of the grain carts that had been parked in the middle of a pivot road. We were thankful for the full moon. During this time of the month, there was good visibility at night, but the rest of the nights were pitch black. The driver of the grain cart was a Pakistani Moslem who had stopped with a load of wheat at the designated late prayer time. He was down on all fours in the middle of the pivot road in a typical Moslem prayer position, oblivious to our having almost run over him.

At the field where they were harvesting, Terry walked from one combine to the other, checking progress. The six combines ran in a pattern, literally devouring the wheat, and were able to clean a 120-acre pivot in about four hours, barring any serious breakdowns. The remarkably efficient operation took on an almost magical quality as the combines combed through the golden heads of wheat. After a combine was full of wheat, it dumped the grain into a cart that pulled right alongside the combine in the field. The filled grain carts were driven to trucks parked outside the field, where they dumped their loads. The combines never had to leave the field.

I was sitting in the pickup, deep in my own thoughts, when I was surprised by a tap at the window. My visitor was Abdallah, a Saudi truck driver. He wasn't an employee of our company, but had been hired as contract labor to transport the wheat from the field. He liked Terry because of his attempts to communicate in Arabic. Now I realized that he was gesturing for me to come sit on a blanket he'd spread on the ground next to his truck. Only hesitating for a minute and realizing that Terry was in sight, I agreed. Abdallah had some camel's milk in a covered bucket. I didn't have the heart to turn down his offer to share, so I drank from the communal bucket, pretending to take long drinks. He continued to insist that I also share the meat and rice that he had in another pail. I kept pointing to my stomach, acting as though I'd already eaten and was full. I'm sure he loved the escapade and the "visit" with the American woman.

On another of our trips to the office in Riyadh, we were invited to supper with a group of four Pakistani men who lived together in a tiny apartment provided by the company and located above the office. One of the men, Omar, was married, but had to leave his family back home in Pakistan. During our early years in Saudi Arabia, the government did not allow many classifications of workers to bring their families into the country, even if the worker's company would have allowed it. In our company, I was regarded as a privileged person because I was allowed to live year-round in Saudi Arabia with Terry. Jamshaid was no longer living with the family we had visited and had joined the three men in this apartment. The other two men, Rafique and Owais, were not married, but their families had arranged suitable mates for them back in Pakistan when the time arrived for them to marry.

We went straight from the office to their apartment. There, the men changed immediately from the Western pants and shirts they were required to wear in the office to the typical male Pakistani attire, a knee-length shirt, split to the upper thigh, and full loose pants that were fitted at the ankles. I understood why they changed clothes. They had only one chair in the apartment, so they sat cross-legged on a mat on the floor, a position that was much more comfortable in the loose-fitting attire.

Jamshaid was always on the lookout for Pakistani goods that would turn a huge profit for him in Saudi Arabia. His latest venture was Pakistani menswear. He offered me a small size in one of the men's outfits, adding that modern women in Pakistan were starting to wear the men's outfits. I gladly donned it because I had on a long skirt and felt uncomfortable on the floor. The loose pants were perfect.

The men began assembling a meal, cooking on a single, portable burner hooked up to a propane tank. As I helped Omar snap the fresh green beans, he explained that we were making beef curry with green beans and potatoes. I couldn't believe my eyes when Omar opened the window and threw the potato peelings and remains of the green beans out the window onto the streets of Riyadh. I walked casually over to glance out the window and discovered it was a vacant lot, where construction of some type was in progress. Evidently, the practice was common, because the lot was littered with scattered trash.

Omar added ground beef to the curry sauce, prepared rice with mixed vegetables and fried some preformed hamburger patties. Each course was cooked in progression over the single burner. One of the other men prepared a salad. They spread a clear plastic sheet over the mat on which we were sitting and passed out plates. Unlike the Saudis who prefer to eat with their right hand, the Pakistani people like to use the flat bread as a scoop to pick up the curry to transport to their mouths. We enjoyed eating the spicy curry this way, turning down the utensils they offered us. For dessert, they served fresh mangoes that were grown in Pakistan.

Although we had left the office at 7:30 P.M. to go up to their apartment for a meal that they said would be ready in thirty minutes, we finally ate at 11:30. Nonetheless, we enjoyed our visit, and Jamshaid insisted that I keep my Pakistani outfit.

On the way home, even though women are not allowed to drive in Saudi Arabia, Terry finally suggested I drive the thirty-five miles from Al Kharj to home on the deserted two-lane road. He was dozing off to sleep and swerving off the road. I felt quite smug as I was finally driving down the highway in Saudi Arabia, even if it was almost 2:00 A.M.

Chapter Twenty-One

Perhaps some of the most difficult problems for Terry in Saudi Arabia were his allergies and asthma. He reacted to most of the allergens associated with farming, including wheat. With the help of medication, he was able to keep his problems largely under control most of the year, but once wheat harvest began and the air was filled with the dust and residue from the combines, Terry's asthma became nearly unmanageable.

Because almost all drugs in Saudi Arabia were for sale in the pharmacies without a prescription, we were confident that we had easy access to a more effective treatment for Terry. After Terry had a particularly bad day with his asthma, we headed for Al Kharj, hoping to purchase some medicine that would provide relief. We entered a pharmacy that we'd visited several times before. When the pharmacist heard the state of Terry's breathing, he suggested that Terry see the doctor upstairs for a shot that he claimed would cure Terry in just two minutes.

We had never noticed a sign for a doctor above the pharmacy, but the pharmacist followed us out the door and pointed to a small opening in the building at the top of a set of concrete steps. The steps were dusty and strewn with pieces of trash and debris. Terry barely had enough breath to climb the steep set of steps.

When we entered the door at the top of the steps, we were surprised to find a waiting room much like those in America. An older man in a white *thobe* controlled the room, telling each man when it was his time to go in to see the doctor. Because I had been the only woman in so many situations, it didn't disturb me to be the only woman in the waiting room. To my irritation, when I took a seat next to Terry on one of the green vinyl couches, the man jumped to his feet, motioning and explaining in a loud voice that I must move to an area behind him. I cautiously peeked around the corner to where he had motioned and discovered several women with children sitting in a separate room. Each woman was covered completely, although a few of them wore the Bedouin veil, revealing only their eyes.

I sat down with the other women, extending the traditional Arabic greeting. The women responded, and the oldest of the women immediately began to question me in Arabic. With my very limited Arabic vocabulary, I explained that I was from America and knew very little Arabic. The women seemed undaunted and continued to question me. I did understand a few words about "baby" and quickly explained that I didn't have a baby. One of the women asked something in Arabic, and when I indicated that I didn't understand, she motioned with her hands, wondering if I was pregnant. When I shook my head, the women seemed to sigh at once and fall silent, probably feeling uncertain if they should commiserate with me because of my barren womb. After the man loudly called an Arabic name, an obviously pregnant woman disappeared down the corridor, holding a small child's hand. The woman soon emerged and several others in the waiting room took their turns in the doctor's office.

Before long, I saw Terry go down the hall. I hadn't heard the receptionist shout his name as he had done the others, probably because he didn't know how to pronounce it. The man ducked into the women's waiting area to motion me to follow Terry. I realized later that he didn't know which of us was there to see the doctor, so he had sent both of us at once.

I was somewhat apprehensive about the type and quality of the medicine that we were about to encounter. The large, dark-haired man who rose to greet us was Egyptian. He made a deliberate effort to show us a diploma from Alexandria University in Egypt bearing his credentials M.B. CH. B., General Practitioner. The only problem was that we didn't understand what the initials stood for.

He spoke excellent English and recognized Terry's problem immediately. He quickly wrote out several prescriptions and told us to go downstairs to the pharmacy to have them filled and then to return to him. As we descended the stairs, we noticed several of the men and women who had been in the waiting room also buying prescriptions and returning to the doctor.

We only waited a minute before we were allowed to go back in to see the doctor. From the prescriptions we had purchased, the doctor gave Terry two different shots, one cortisone and one calcium. Terry felt the effects of the shot of cortisone immediately, first as a warm sensation in his heart, and next as an easing of his breathing difficulties. We learned later that cortisone is used in the States only as a last resort, under careful supervision. The doctor charged us SR 30 ($8.60) for the visit, and the medicine had cost only about a fourth of what it would have cost in the States, because all medicine is subsidized by the government in Saudi Arabia.

During the time we were in Saudi Arabia, we became good friends with this doctor, visiting him for all medical problems. On one of the last occasions that we went to him for Terry's asthma, he advised Terry to change careers because of the damage the asthma was doing to his lungs. The Egyptian doctor returned to his home country before we left Saudi Arabia. He had a prosperous practice in Al Kharj, but he preferred to live in Egypt because it is one of the more liberal Moslem countries.

When we left Al Kharj after our visit to the doctor, we saw something that we'd never seen before—a mill where wheat was ground into flour. Several Bedouin women were lined up with sacks of wheat, waiting to have it ground. Many of these women had gone to different farms after the harvest to glean the leftover grain, as women had done in biblical times. Some also gleaned from the already harvested piles of wheat on the ground, rather than from the stalks left standing in the fields. Many of the farms, including ours, dumped the wheat directly on to the ground after it was taken from the fields, because there weren't enough silos yet erected to house all that was produced. I am sure the bumper crops of one hundred bushels per acre had not been anticipated, nor the need for storing such bounty. Other women waiting in line at the mill had received their grain from wealthy Saudi farmers as part of the required gift to the poor.

The tiny operation milled and sold flour from both Saudi Arabian, and American wheat, with the flour from America costing SR 3 per kilo (39 cents a pound), whereas the homegrown flour was SR 8 per kilo ($1.04 a pound). It only made sense because wheat in America was selling for three dollars a bushel, while the Saudi government was paying their farmers thirty dollars a bushel for wheat.

The days were much slower, and work time was shorter once we finished harvest. We were in for another surprise at this point. The Bedouins, along with their families and animals, began to converge on the farm. The Bedouins were still nomads, as they had been for centuries. In the days before oil, the entire nation was nomadic, always searching for the water. Only very recently has the desert been used for farming. Before its cultivation, the desert outside of the towns was accepted as the communal property of all the citizens of Saudi Arabia. The Bedouins had little understanding of, or refused to accept the idea that they could not move onto and graze their livestock in any part of the desert.

Even though we had been told the habits of the Bedouins, we were unprepared for the number of them who moved onto our farm. Almost overnight, the families pitched tents, and the sheep and camels began grazing on the wheat stubble. Not only did the humans and animals hamper the process of plowing the land in preparation for next year's planting, but the camels walked underneath the pivots, breaking off the sprinkler drops.

When Terry had farmed in the States, he had never burned the wheat stubble off the land, as he saw being done on other farms in the desert. In our area in the States, the stubble was always plowed back into the ground for added mulch and soil enrichment. Terry decided that he would not burn the stubble. Instead, he plowed it into the ground. Many of the Bedouins, forced from other farms by the burning, took refuge on our farm. Terry spent much of his time issuing warnings to the Bedouins to leave. The tractor drivers found that they had to drive the tractors straight at the campsites before many of the Bedouins would move onto another area.

The fact that Terry did not burn the stubble would come back to haunt him the following year. The soil in the U.S. is rich in mulch and easily decomposes each year's stubble. In the Saudi desert, the soil is virgin, with no microbial activity to decompose the stubble. The fertilizer that Terry applied was consumed in deteriorating the stubble, leaving no available nutrients for the newly planted wheat crop. In the years that followed, Terry burned the stubble after every harvest.

After harvest, most of the workers were scheduled for vacations, but the head office had never told them their exact departure dates. The Sri Lankans had been told that any day now they would leave on vacation, but owing to the complications of securing exit visas and plane tickets, we didn't know the exact date. I was jogging one morning when Terry overtook me in the pickup to explain that the Sri Lankans had been summoned and we would need to leave for Riyadh in thirty minutes. I returned to our container to dress for the trip.

Five Sri Lankans rode in the pickup with us, while the remainder of the men filled two other pickups. Their luggage was stacked precariously in the bed of each truck. As we sped the ninety miles to Riyadh, one of the vehicles in our caravan was stopped by the police. We knew it couldn't be for speeding because at that time there were no speed limits in the desert where we lived. Later, a speed limit of 110 kilometers per hour (66 m.p.h.) was imposed, but was enforced only sporadically. When the policeman emerged from his car, the men in the three vehicles, including Terry, climbed out to ask what the problem was and learned that the vehicle had been stopped because the license plate was missing. It was common for many of our farm vehicles to be without a license plate, because the bumpy terrain often bounced the plate loose from the bumpers. The Sri Lankans were visibly shaken, and Terry had difficulty feigning calm because he didn't have a driver's license at the time.

The policeman, dressed in his brown khaki uniform with the traditional Saudi headdress, raved in Arabic that the vehicle had only a photocopy of the owner's certificate, not the original (which we knew was kept in the head office). The policeman tore up the photocopy and threw it on the ground, proclaiming that it was "no good." Terry asked the policeman if he could see his owner's certificate so that he would know how it was supposed to look. To our delight, the policeman stated quickly that he didn't have one in his car. Without any further comment, the policeman waved all the men back into the trucks, and we continued on our way.

We neared the outskirts of Riyadh and stopped at the first traffic light. We were the middle car in the convoy and when we stopped, the driver of the third vehicle, evidently still shaken from the incident with the policemen, failed to come to a stop behind us and slammed into our rear. Fortunately, we all escaped unharmed.

Although Terry knew the way to the office, he was following the lead pickup and decided to remain behind it, even though he realized the first driver had departed from the normal route to the office. We took a winding path down small dusty streets in a part of Riyadh I had never seen. Evidently, this route was the one used by most drivers who have no license.

To complicate matters, it was Ramadan, and I was hesitant about going to town during the holy month of fasting. We'd heard horror stories about foreigners who were caught taking a drink in public and who had been severely reprimanded. Foreigners are expected to obey the rules of Ramadan when they are in public. Little did we realize our first year that the country actually reverses day and night schedules during Ramadan to accommodate the resulting discomfort. Many Saudis sleep during most of the daylight fasting hours.

At the Riyadh office, I had an hour and a half to reflect on the Ramadan season, as we waited for someone to arrive who could assist the vacationers in their departure. The men were late because they stayed up for Ramadan the night before. While we waited, we were supposed to observe the fasting rules. A Sri Lankan young man, whose job it was to serve tea in the office, took a few of us at a time into a closet, so that we could have a drink of tea or water.

One of the head office staff, a Moslem who halfheartedly practiced Ramadan, arrived, and the server smuggled him a cup of tea into the office in a paper sack. He locked his office door to smoke a cigarette, also taboo during Ramadan. When the door opened, the trapped smoke escaped, but everyone pretended not to notice.

Sheikh Latif finally arrived at the office. When he saw me, he suggested that I spend the afternoon with his wife, Jewaher, and then Terry and I would break fast with them. The prospect sounded much more exciting than staying in the office, especially when Sheikh Latif's brother, Abdul Aziz, offered to drive me to their home.

While I waited for my ride to Jewaher's, a woman entered the office. She was dressed shabbily, draped in black from head to toe. I wondered why a woman would be in this second floor office. She surveyed the group and immediately approached Sheikh Latif's brother, Abdul Aziz, who must have looked the wealthiest and most responsible. We watched as she seemed to pour out her heart to him.

After the woman left the office, the men told me that her husband was killed in Lebanon in the war and her daughter was in the hospital. Sheikh Latif's brother offered her SR 15 ($4.30) but she countered that this amount was not enough. He ignored her request for more, pretending to return to the newspaper he was reading. She approached others in the office, and Terry gave SR 30 ($8.60). It seemed very important to Abdul Aziz that I understood that the woman who was begging was not Saudi, that all Saudi women are cared for by their families.

On the way to Jewaher's house, I felt very comfortable riding with Abdul Aziz. In his early twenties, he was home on vacation from college in San Diego, California, where he was majoring in business. His English was perfect, and he spoke quite openly with me. He claimed to like America much better than Saudi Arabia, adding that he didn't associate with other Saudis in America because they were interested only in partying. He confided that he had a girlfriend who was an American Indian. Though he said he liked America better than Saudi Arabia, several years after our conversation, he returned to Saudi to join the family business.

When I arrived at Jewaher's home about 2:00 P.M., she had just awakened. She explained that because they break fast at 6:30 P.M. and then eat again about 3:30 A.M., they wait until 5:00 A.M. to go to bed, as the sun comes up and fasting once again begins. She said that Sheikh Latif woke at ten or eleven to go into the office and then came home to sleep from four to six.

She was very open about Ramadan and explained a little bit about the fasting. She encouraged me to drink in front of her because she said it gave her "more grace." I asked about fasting for pregnant women, and she said that one of her sisters was two weeks beyond her due date and was fasting, but sleeping almost all day. She explained that if a woman is pregnant and finds fasting a hardship, then she is not to fast but is to keep an account of the number of days out of the month of Ramadan that she does not fast and make up those days at a later time. Jewaher had just ended her menstrual period two days earlier and had drunk water during her period because it was "necessary for women"; however, she did not eat any food.

The average age that a child begins fasting was thirteen or fourteen, but some begin as young as seven years old. The children begin by fasting for only a few days out of the month or fasting for one meal a day.

I had been nervous about spending the afternoon with Jewaher because it was Ramadan, but the time passed quickly, and I felt very relaxed. We played with her boys while we watched an Arabic television show that she interpreted for me. We also watched a program that she called "a family program" in which an Egyptian woman demonstrated preparing the recipe for stuffed cabbage leaves. Jewaher said that she often made the recipes demonstrated on the show. I was surprised when she changed the baby's diaper, because I expected a Sheikh's wife to have a servant to perform such a chore.

Although it was more than two hours before we would break fast, we set the table. I was surprised once again when she prepared the table on the floor. Although they had a dining table that they used occasionally, they preferred to eat on the floor.

I was excited that she wanted to prepare a few dishes to add to the cook's menu. We made the traditional triangular *sambusa* appetizer. The *sambusa* is made with a spinach and pine nut filling folded into a type of phyllo dough. She spread newspapers on the floor, and we sat cross-legged and rolled the triangles out on the newspaper. I could envision women centuries before in the Middle East, sitting crossed-legged on the floor in this same way.

We also prepared another dish made with purple onions and minced mutton. Jewaher said matter-of-factly that the cook would bake both dishes out in the kitchen, which was separate from the house, so that the cooking odors would not permeate the house.

Terry and Sheikh Latif arrived at four, after clearing the paper work for the Sri Lankans to leave; Sheikh Latif looked tired and thirsty. He immediately retired upstairs to take a nap until he could break fast. Terry sat with Jewaher and me while we watched Arabic television.

A few minutes before 6:30, Sheikh Latif returned, and he and Jewaher watched the clock. Sheikh Latif asked Terry and me how much money we were giving to Israel every year. When we replied that we weren't giving any money, he responded by saying that every American gives $2,700 each year to Israel in the form of U.S. aid. I asked him why he didn't like Israel and he replied, "How can you like someone who steals land and takes things from people and kills them?" He wasn't angry, but seemed rather to enjoy the conversation.

At exactly 6:30, we broke fast, first with the traditional coffee and a fresh date. I think if I'd really been fasting all day, I would have been less reserved, but they remained calm as we passed the dishes around. Actually, I hadn't eaten since a quick breakfast early that morning so I felt as though I had been fasting myself. Besides the traditional lamb and rice dishes, there were soup and three kinds of juice, to satisfy hunger as well as thirst. Both Jewaher and Sheikh Latif ate only soup and drank several large glasses of juice, convincing me that they really had been fasting. I admired their determination, but doubted that eating a meal right before sunrise and sleeping most of the day achieved the true emulation of the hungry and poor that the prophet Mohammed had intended when he instigated fasting during the month of Ramadan.

Because the shops were scheduled to reopen at 9:00 P.M., we visited until that time and prepared to leave. Jewaher asked what I wanted to buy, and I told her that I wanted an abaya. As before, her immediate reaction was negative. She exclaimed that the Saudi women didn't like Western women wearing the abaya over pants, but preferred their wearing long dresses. She had told me all this before, but I explained that I wanted to take one home as a souvenir. I said that I planned to purchase one at the grocery store. She gave me a look of incredulity and told me not to buy one there because the abayas at the grocery store were made of jersey. She went upstairs to her bedroom and returned with a pure silk abaya with a beautiful scalloped edge and presented it to me. I told her that I'd tell everyone at home that a real Sheikh's wife had given it to me. She seemed amused at the thought.

The city was alive as we took our leave, and it seemed as if everyone in Riyadh was out on the streets. Traffic was slowed to a crawl in the busy shopping districts as Ramadan celebrators emerged from their day of fasting. Even though it was midnight, the crowds reminded us of those that usually formed at midday, when a big sale was scheduled. Our main purchase was a twenty-five-pound sack of dog food for SR 61 (almost $18). It turned out to be a wasted purchase. The camp dogs had been raised on scraps from the canteen and refused to eat the dog food. After our purchase, we exited the bustling city quickly, ready for the quiet of the desert.

Terry soon learned on the farm that by law, during Ramadan in Saudi Arabia, Moslem workers are required to engage in only six hours of labor a day. The workers on our farm began their six-hour work days at 5:00 A.M. In the hot days of Ramadan, it would have been dangerous to do outdoor, physical labor for more than six hours without drinking liquid. The Moslems then retreated to their rooms and slept until thirty minutes before sunset, at which time they got up and prepared to break the fast and have the evening prayers. This prayer was followed by a full meal with plenty of food and drink. Watermelon was especially popular during Ramadan because it was not only filling but also thirst quenching. A breakfast was then served before sunrise to prepare the believer for the next day of fasting.

Towns and cities virtually closed during the day, opening after the breaking of the fast and staying open until nearly two in the morning. It was a time of celebration and shopping, eating and making merry.

The Prophet Mohammed instigated the time of fasting as a time for spiritual cleansing, and as an opportunity for the average person to experience the hunger of the less fortunate. Yet despite the reversal of night and day, we knew several Moslems who were unable to adhere rigidly to the daily schedule of fasting. They would sneak into closets to smoke or eat or take a drink of water.

Not unreasonably, Terry both marveled at and worried about the farm laborers who were not supposed to drink during their six-hour work days in the tremendous heat. And indeed, several seemed to find it difficult. One of these was a spindly old Egyptian with mismatched eyes and a toothless grin, whom Terry soon came to nickname *Insh Allah*, "if God wills." The old man's nickname was also his only response to Terry's shouts of "Get to work." That *Insh Allah* found it a hardship to go so long without water was evident when he alone among the workers asked that a camp well pump be repaired one day during Ramadan.

The Bedouins seemed the true yardstick of religious faith. During the time that we were in Saudi Arabia, Ramadan always came during the hottest season of the year. The lunar schedule caused Ramadan to start a few weeks earlier every year, but for quite a span of years Ramadan remained in the season of 120-degree temperatures. For the Bedouin, life had to go on. Sheep and camels wouldn't allow their masters to sleep in the daytime; probably, neither would the heat. I became careful not to visit the Bedouin women during Ramadan because they were always very lethargic, especially during the late afternoon, having gone without food and water all day in the scorching sunlight. They weren't able to drink, yet they would offer to prepare tea for me, hospitality still utmost in their minds. I always declined with a smile, saying, "Ramadan," at which point I could sense that the women heaved a sigh of relief.

The stories I heard of Moslems attacking foreigners who dared drink in front of them may have been legitimate. One of our Filipino workers had come to Saudi Arabia several years before we arrived and saw a foreign man buying a bottle of water at the lone gas station near our farm. The Moslems watched closely as the man drove away from the station, taking a drink as he drove. Irate, they followed him, taking away the water and shaking him up a bit.

We were always cautious when we went to town during Ramadan, being careful to lie down in the seat of the pickup to take a drink of the water that we'd secretly brought from home. The few times we went into town during Ramadan, some of the shops and the grocery stores were open, but no restaurants, so we had no place to buy our noon meal. The elite hotels in Riyadh did continue to offer room service during the day. We comforted ourselves that we could always rent a hotel room and order room service. Of course, if I had happened to be in town without my husband, I could never have rented a hotel room. In later years, when I occasioned to travel to Riyadh during Ramadan without Terry, I resorted to carrying a sandwich with me and ate it either in torn-off bites while lying on the pickup seat or hiding in an office closet.

Once, during Ramadan, Terry received word to call the head office. We headed for Al Kharj. As we made our way into town, we noticed that even though it was Ramadan, the fruit and vegetable market was open for a couple of hours so people might purchase what they needed for breaking fast in the evening. I was delighted to see cherries, plums, grapes, and even apricots, had been imported for Ramadan.

After we made the phone call, we walked through the market. The shopkeepers seemed rather grumpy and very sleepy. I knew that many hadn't been to sleep all night, staying up to celebrate by eating and drinking. They were counting the minutes until they could go home and sleep. The shops would not open again until 9:00 P.M. As we looked at the rows of watch shops, Terry decided to buy watches for the seven men who worked on our farm that first year. These seven had worked like Trojans, transforming the virgin soil into the green sands, and we had all become quite close. After much haggling, we were able to get seven watches for SR 700 ($200). We also spotted some of the tiny coffee cups that Midwess had used to serve us the Arabic coffee. We observed that if there were many people at his tent, they would drink in shifts, because he owned only a few cups. We purchased twelve more cups for Midwess.

I had read in the English-language paper that foreign and all non-Moslem women were to cover their heads during Ramadan, so I kept my only scarf around my head despite the 110-degree temperature. As it turned out, the first year was the only one in which I had to cover my head during Ramadan. The directive was not reissued in following years.

Around high noon, as we left Al Kharj and prepared to make our way home, we had an irritating experience that resulted in trying our hand at hitchhiking. After a few kilometers, we saw two young men who looked tired, hot, and, of course, thirsty. Terry slowed down and they climbed in the back of the pickup, and we started off. Picking up hitchhikers was common in Saudi Arabia, especially in the farming areas.

We were about ten miles from the farm when the pickup suddenly died and wouldn't start. We had just passed the small railway depot, where we knew that a person was stationed. Terry and I began walking back to the station. Without a word, our hitchhikers walked in the opposite direction. As we neared the station, a man came out. To our dismay, he jumped in his pickup and drove off in the opposite direction. We knew we were in trouble, because traffic on our road during those early years was minimal, especially during Ramadan and the hottest part of the day.

Soon, we saw a large diesel truck approaching, but Terry was hesitant to stop it because I was with him. I knew, however, that we could not stand too long in this heat. I stuck my hand out, signaling the truck to stop. They seemed very shocked to see a white man and woman hitchhiking. We all piled into the cab of the truck and started down the road. With the Arabic Terry knew, he talked to the men quite well.

The older man was the father of the younger man, and they were on their way to Dhahran. They were very friendly, nodding in agreement when Terry asked if they were fasting during Ramadan. They delivered us to our door on the farm and wouldn't accept any payment for transporting us.

Chapter
Twenty-Two

On yet another trip to Riyadh, in April 1986, to deliver workers to the office before their vacation, this time five Filipinos, we were invited again to break fast with Sheikh Latif and his family. After the traditional meal, Terry returned to the office to finish some work. During Ramadan the office reopened at 9:00 P.M. for a couple of hours. Jewaher had been invited to a jewelry showing in the home of Hafeez and asked me to come along.

I was surprised at the difference between Sheikh Latif's and Hafeez's houses. Although I assumed Sheikh Latif was much wealthier, Hafeez's house was elaborately furnished and carpeted. Sheikh Latif was also at the jewelry party. He was surprisingly frank in his explanation that he was here because of his fascination with the Pakistani woman who was selling the jewelry. Despite his worldliness and travels abroad, his captivation with this pretty, successful, and unveiled businesswoman was not atypical of his less-traveled countrymen.

After a quick survey of the twenty-one-karat gold jewelry with insets of rubies, emeralds, pearls, diamonds, and turquoise, I realized I was out of my league. Both Hafeez's wife, Dhahara, and the saleslady concluded that I was not a buying customer and turned their full attention to Jewaher. Every piece of jewelry that she tried, they cooed and complimented. Before any of the other women arrived, Sheikh Latif came in and surveyed the jewelry, telling Jewaher to pick out whatever she wanted.

After only a brief moment, Jewaher quickly made a selection. She chose matching necklace, earrings, and bracelets of gold and rubies. The earrings were so heavy that they had a chain that hooked into the hair for support. One of the bracelets was for the wrist; the other, for the ankle. The dealer managed to persuade Jewaher to buy both, even though

Jewaher confided to me later that the latter was of no use to her because Saudi women don't wear ankle bracelets. Back in the car, Jewaher told me that she thought she had made a good deal on the jewelry purchase. Although Sheikh Latif would pay for the items, she estimated that the total would be a little more than SR 24,000 ($6,857).

Possibly because men and women in Saudi Arabia lead such separate lives, women seemed to me very dependent on their mothers and sisters for companionship. After we left the jewelry showing, we went to Jewaher's mother's home to see her sister Eman's new baby. I recalled when Eman had come to the farm as the green sprigs of wheat were peeking through the ground. It seemed appropriate that her baby should develop during the same maturation period as the wheat and be born as the wheat matured into golden ripeness. The reason Jewaher called the house her mother's house rather than her parents' house was that her father had another wife who lived in a separate house.

We drove a short distance and pulled up to a gate in the center of a busy commercial district. Jewaher explained that her father had purchased all of the land in this area and built a house here years before the district was developed. The town developed around their home, tremendously inflating the value of the property.

To my surprise, a beautiful villa and full size swimming pool nestled inside the high walls. All of the office buildings around the home were one story to maintain privacy within the villa compound. Inside the home, we walked on lush carpet covered with beautiful Persian rugs. Much of the elaborate furniture was covered in fine tapestry.

When we entered the house, I felt as though I was in a modern day harem. Males never ventured into this part of the house. There were quite a few sisters and female relatives lounging on couches and on the floor, visiting and drinking coffee and tea. Jewaher's mother was very quiet and gracious. Although she appeared to be fifty-five or sixty years old, she had a two-and-a-half-year-old baby girl.

Eman, the sister, had been two weeks overdue but was still fasting for Ramadan when she delivered the baby. The baby girl, whom they named *Walah*, which means loyalty and friendship, was dressed in a white satin dressing gown, with a rather large, gold brooch pinned to the collar. Jewaher explained that they did not have baby showers, but that everyone brought a gift after the baby was born. Jewaher said that typically she would give the baby dresses and a gold bracelet, and the mother a watch.

She explained that it was the custom in Saudi Arabia for the mother and baby to go from the hospital to her mother's house, where she may remain for up to forty days. This allowed the mother time to rest, with someone else taking care of the baby. Visitors were received at the mother's house, and the father of the baby visited daily.

On the seventh day after the baby's birth, there is traditionally a family gathering at which the grandfather holds the baby, prays in its ear, and names it. The parents usually select the name, which they tell to the grandfather. Tradition holds that if the baby is a boy, the family slaughters two sheep; if the baby is a girl, they slaughter one sheep. The sheep are then either distributed to the poor, or served to family and friends.

After leaving her mother's home, we made one more stop. Jewaher had paid SR 100 ($28.60) to a video store to record cartoons for Ziad, her oldest son. She returned the tape because it had only about ten minutes of cartoons. I was amazed to see this short Saudi woman, completely shrouded in black, heatedly addressing the shopkeeper in no uncertain terms. He took back the tape meekly without any discussion. I guessed that even though women took a back seat in society, they still made most of the home purchases, and shopkeepers were cognizant of this fact.

After returning home, Jewaher prepared a snack for us, taking green powder that had sesame seeds in it and mixing it with olive oil. We took flat bread and dipped it into the oil. The mixture tasted of thyme and other spices. It actually wasn't bad, and I tried not to think about the fact that I was eating almost straight olive oil.

As we were eating the olive-oil dip, Terry returned. It was almost 2:00 A.M., and during the drive home, neither of us was able to remain awake, so we stopped on the side of the road between Riyadh and Al Kharj and slept for about an hour. I thought of how the topsy-turvy schedule of Ramadan had changed our lives, even though we weren't fasting. We had no fear of sleeping on the highway, as we would have had in the United States, because there was so little crime in Saudi Arabia.

Also, at this time, all restaurants were required either to have separate family sections for women or to refuse women entrance. We experienced the directive firsthand when we tried to eat in a Lebanese restaurant in Al Kharj. Terry and I had already entered the restaurant and had chosen our food by going in the kitchen, lifting lids, and pointing to what we wanted to eat. While we were waiting for our food, the Lebanese manager approached our table and requested that we leave, because he was afraid he would get in trouble with the *Mutawwa* for having a woman sitting among men in his restaurant.

Oddly enough, Jewaher's olive-oil dip caused me to remember a RIWG program presented in December 1985 by an American woman who was married to a Syrian and who had lived in Syria for a number of years. Her program was on food and life in Syria. Before the meeting began, she sold her autographed cookbook. Because I was collecting cookbooks, I purchased it. Her program was interesting, and I remembered vaguely that she said that the Syrians use quite a bit of olive oil in their cooking for flavor because many times meat may not be available. A few months later, we found out that several of the Syrian women who had been at the meeting went to the governor of Riyadh and complained that this American woman had degraded Syria. I believe that the government used the complaint as an excuse to repress the RIWG, because they were a little uneasy about such a large gathering of foreign women under one roof on a regular basis. As a result, the International Women's Groups in several of the cities in Saudi Arabia, including Riyadh, were closed by April 1986. They were never reopened during the two-and-one-half years I remained in Saudi Arabia.

This was a terrible blow to international women who depended on the meetings as their social lifeblood and connection to other women. After my first year in Saudi Arabia (with my own driver and having grown more accustomed to finding my own way) I had never missed the monthly meeting of the RIWG. In retrospect, I can see that its closing was foreshadowed by a pervasive governmental crackdown on the behavior of foreign women. To comply with new governmental restrictions, the International Women's Groups began fining women who came to meetings in dresses above the ankles or with sleeves above the elbows. The fine was SR 5 ($ 1.43).

We were never quite sure what brought on the tightenting of restrictions, but they became evident in several areas. Many of the video and cassette shops began refusing entrance to women. If I went to town with Terry and several of the management from the farm, I had to remain in the van while they went into these establishments. Perhaps my most stinging experience with these restrictions was in the fashionable Al Akaria Shopping Center, where friends and I were tantalized by exquisite shops that displayed the latest Paris fashions in both clothing and jewelry, with price tags to match. Eager to have lunch before prayer time, we found a small restaurant, but noticed that a sign above its door read Women Must Take Their Food Out Side. We tried to slide inside as if we hadn't seen the sign. After all, in such a modern mall, we couldn't imagine that the restaurant really wouldn't serve us. The manager quickly stopped us and asked to take our order. He explained that he wasn't allowed to have any women inside, because he had no separate family section.

Determined to be seated for our lunch, we headed to Herfeys, a Saudi hamburger chain with a separate entrance and eating area for women. We could barely view the menu from our segregated area, and the salad bar was strategically placed in the men's section. When we asked how we were supposed to get salad if we ordered from the salad bar, the waiter responded that he would select our salads for us. We ordered hamburgers.

Even though we were ninety miles out in the desert, we were still keenly aware of Ramadan. During Ramadan more than ever, Midwess insisted that we eat with him and his family. I had begun wearing a long dress every time we went to Midwess's because it seemed to please the women.

When we arrived, Midwess motioned us to sit on a mat outside the tent. I realized that we were sitting on this mat because the only light we had was a small one that was connected to the battery in the pickup. Even though it was 7:30 P.M., Mama was still out with the sheep. I sat down for a minute with the men, but soon went in search of the women.

Before long, Mama returned with the sheep. She took me by the arm and propelled me back to where the men were sitting. Midwess then served coffee, tea, and dates. For just a few minutes, surprisingly Rashmi crept around the blanket to sit down on the ground, just outside the circle of light. The men seemed to ignore her tactfully.

When it was time for the meal, Mama left the group while Midwess spread the plastic cloth over the mat. I noted that we weren't having the traditional rice. They served large noodles that had been cooked in the boiled lamb's broth and bowls of lamb soup with tiny pieces of potatoes. Midwess said that the Arabic name for the noodles was *macarona*, which sounded much like our macaroni. We all used spoons to eat the soup, drinking the last of the broth from the bowls. Soup is a common dish during Ramadan because it satisfies both hunger and thirst.

Midwess then produced two huge watermelons. He cut both melons, even though there were only eight of us, including the women. I guessed that the family would nibble on the remaining watermelon all night until sunrise came, and the next day's fast began. Midwess asked Frank to play his guitar, and he and his brother Abdallah each took turns singing as Frank played. Midwess kept pressing us to tell him who was the better singer, an answer that we jokingly avoided giving him. As usual, they asked us to teach them some English words, which they tried painstakingly to pronounce. Occasionally, we saw the women peeking around the blanket or heard a giggle as Midwess performed.

Without warning, Midwess, Abdallah, and Mohammed rose, walked to the side of the tent and prayed together. When they returned, I saw Mama go to a spot further from our vantage point and pray. As we drove away, I realized that in this country, where men and women are separated all the time, even their prayers to Allah must be offered separately.

Chapter Twenty-Three

As accustomed as I was becoming to the solitude of desert life, at times, I still found myself lonely. One morning, Terry brought me a tiny white kitten. Some Egyptians on a nearby farm had found the pregnant mother cat giving birth underneath their bed inside their house. Terry agreed to take one of the kittens. We christened her Pamper, and she became my constant companion during the remainder of our time in Saudi Arabia. I'd kept a cat before, for a brief period of time, but she lived outside and finally disappeared. The desert wasn't a healthy place for a kitten, so I decided Pamper would be a house cat.

When we went home during the summer, one of the workers stayed in our house to feed her and give her company. Because Terry always returned to Saudi before I did, he was the first one to greet Pamper after the separation. Evidently she missed us a great deal because at night she slept on Terry's chest. Once I returned, Pamper returned to her usual place at the foot of my bed. When we left Saudi Arabia for the final time, I was faced with finding a home for her. Fortunately, Camille and George Munk had just moved to Riyadh from Jeddah, didn't have children, and wanted a cat. They adopted and spoiled her as much as I had. When they decided to return to England, they flew Pamper home with them. In England, any animal coming into the country must stay in quarantine for six months, and she even survived that experience. Each year we receive a picture and Christmas card from Pamper.

Pamper was company, but she wasn't human. I grew lonely for female conversation and was constantly on the lookout for a woman companion who spoke English. On one of my many trips with Terry to the gas station, we met an American man from a nearby dairy. He told me about a group of women who met once a month, every second Thursday, in the Al Kharj area. He invited me to attend the next meeting that was to be held at the dairy where he worked. I couldn't wait for the meeting. I was excited that I was finally going to have permanent contact with the women in the area, even if it was only once a month.

When the date arrived for the meeting, I put on my long dress with nervous anticipation. Terry was too busy to take me, so he chose Mitri to drive me. Either Mitri was not accustomed to driving, or he was nervous and cautious about driving his boss's wife, because we crept down the road at twenty-five miles per hour. The man at the gas station had told me that the meeting began at 10:00 A.M. and I had allowed thirty minutes for the thirty mile trip, plenty of time because no speed limit was enforced. As we crept down the road, I wanted to scream, "Move over and let me drive." Yet I knew that Mitri was proud to be driving me and forced myself to be patient. We arrived at 10:45, only to be told by the man at the gate that the women had left for a meeting in Al Kharj. I had no idea where the women might have gone. Evidently, they had changed the meeting place.

If I had been in the car with Terry instead of Mitri, I would have burst into tears, but I didn't want to upset Mitri. As we started our snail's pace back to the farm, Mitri must have sensed that I was upset. Even with our obvious language and culture barrier, he somehow knew that I was in desperate need of female companionship. Hesitantly, and with great thought, he managed to convey to me that there was another woman living on a farm that we would soon be passing. I almost jumped out of the car when I heard the news. I quickly said, "Let's stop!"

Mitri had visited Al Rafia Farm several times before, because the farm's entire work force was composed of Sri Lankans. Terry and I also had been to the farm, but no woman had been there at that time. We bumped down the rough road, almost ten miles off the highway, to reach the beautifully groomed farm. We were directed to the boss's house, where I knocked timidly at the door. I was greeted by Judy Norris, a tall, blonde British woman whose cool demeanor was the exact opposite of my West Texas boldness. I talked to her for just a few minutes before we left, giving her my farm address. I left feeling a bit foolish, not realizing that most Brits take a while to warm up to a stranger. Mitri smiled all the way home after I complimented his wisdom in acquainting me with another female. Judy became good friends with Patsy Zielske, and we would visit Judy and her husband Bob several times in their home. Despite my first abortive attempt to join them in the months and years to come, the Al Kharj women's group became an important part of my monthly trips off the farm. It fostered a sense of community among all the different nationalities of women in the area.

We were excited when it was agreed in the summer of 1983 that new Sri Lankan workers would be hired, and we were chosen to recruit and interview them in Sri Lanka on our way home for vacation in the States. We had formed some close friendships with some of the Sri Lankans and looked forward to visiting their country. By air, Sri Lanka is about four hours east of Saudi Arabia, just south of India.

As the time grew closer for our annual vacation in the States, we discussed the options of side trips on our way. We assumed that the travel agent in the small town of Al Kharj would be comparable to the ones in Riyadh, which we thought should be similar to those in the States. We drove into Al Kharj one evening to see a travel agent. As we sat before the Pakistani man, we felt more like we were in a circus. The phone rang every few seconds and between rings, Saudis entered, approached the travel agent and began asking questions. In their minds, I'm sure their questions must have been much more important than whatever this American couple wanted. The agency had no information. It had only a few brochures, which were completely out of date. We left the travel agency tired and frustrated. On other trips that we made out of the country, we used travel agencies in Riyadh, which improved each year we were in Saudi Arabia.

By coincidence, it was during Ramadan that we headed for the island of Sri Lanka. It also was by chance that we were traveling on July 4th, spending our Independence Day trying to exchange some riyals for dollars at a bank, and sitting in an airport where we were compelled to observe the fast.

On our way, we had stopped in Al Kharj at the Saudi American Bank to exchange our money. While we worked in Saudi Arabia, we had very few out-of-pocket expenses, so we telexed our salary to the States every month. Because we didn't have a bank account in the country, we had very little contact with Saudi banks. The banks in Saudi Arabia became more efficient every year that we were there, but our first visit was a nightmare. There seemed to be little organization to the system. Every time a Saudi entered, he pushed to the front and was immediately helped. After observing how the system worked for the Saudi customers, Terry spat out some Arabic and pushed his way to the front of the line.

We made the mistake of asking for traveler's checks. The man who waited on us spoke only a few words of English. He had to call his supervisor for assistance. The supervisor spoke very little English, but was finally able to find the traveler's checks that were locked in the safe. The two decided that our name had to be typed, rather than written, on the checks, so the poor man waiting on us was assigned the laborious task of typing out our names on an ancient typewriter. After several vain attempts, the pair agreed that it would be permissible for us to write the checks by hand. After almost two hours, we finally emerged from the bank.

Our five days on the tiny island of Sri Lanka were financed by Al Emar because Terry was to interview and hire about thirty workers for the farm. On our trip, we also visited Singapore and Hong Kong. After such an interesting and thrilling vacation, I decided I could easily tolerate another year in Saudi Arabia just for the opportunity to visit such exciting places. Over the years we also visited India, Israel, China, Japan, Thailand, Austria, Denmark, England, East and West Germany, Italy, the Republic of Ireland, and Switzerland on our way home for vacation.

My most unusual experience during one of my vacations at home in the States was when Sheikh Latif visited me. He was in the States on business and managed to fly into Lubbock, Texas. Because Terry was already back in Saudi Arabia, my parents accompanied me to the airport to pick him up at 10:55 P.M. I had never seen Sheikh Latif dressed in any other than typical Saudi garb. As he entered the airport, I hardly recognized him. Hardly the picture of a rich Arabian tycoon, he wore double knit pants and a knit shirt. Instead of the usual red and white checked head garb, he wore a black beret. To our dismay and his, we discovered that his luggage had been lost. After a discussion with airport authorities, we took him to the Hilton Hotel in Lubbock.

I received a call from him the next morning, asking me to come to Lubbock to help him buy some new clothes, because his were lost. I was delighted to assist Sheikh Latif, but we wound up spending most of the day visiting in the Hilton. He had been instructed to wait by the phone for notification as to the location of his lost luggage, so we were not able to venture out. Fortunately, he had been in Lubbock while interviewing and had been able to see some of the city. He received a call about 3:00 P.M. that his luggage had arrived, so I didn't have the opportunity to take him shopping. He treated me to a late lunch in the hotel, and I enjoyed entertaining him on my own turf.

After another one of the annual trips home, my year in Saudi Arabia began with an exciting stopover in Bahrain, the tiny Arab island off the coast of the Arabian Peninsula. Because I had stayed several weeks longer than Terry in the States, I made the long trip back across the ocean alone. After a ten-hour layover in Frankfurt, Germany, I arrived in Bahrain at 3:30 A.M.

Before going to Saudi Arabia, we had discovered a Texas couple living in Bahrain, Bev and Jim Moore. Bev and I had become very good friends through correspondence. When she invited me to stop over in Bahrain on my way back to Saudi Arabia, I jumped at the opportunity to meet her personally and to see some more of the Middle East.

I had sent my passport number to Jim, but when I arrived in the tiny Bahrain airport, I was whisked off to a corner of the airport and subjected to a grueling several minutes of interrogation. This paranoia surprised me, because I had heard that Bahrain was much more modern than Saudi Arabia. Neither of my interrogators spoke English with any fluency and naturally seemed to be extremely grumpy at 3:30 A.M. After telling them repeatedly that my American friends lived and worked in Bahrain and were meeting me at the airport, they agreed to find Jim and bring him back to customs to verify my story.

I was relieved when I saw one of the custom's officials return with Jim. After several minutes of haggling, I was granted a temporary visitors' visa, which I thought had already been arranged. Both officers looked skeptical that I was coming for only a two-day visit. I had four oversized suitcases and an overstuffed carry-on bag.

I enjoyed my visit in Bahrain. On the surface, it looked like Saudi Arabia. The Arab men and women dressed in Saudi Arabian garb, but in fact, the tiny island was much more commercialized and modern. Bev explained that women were allowed to drive, and to wear pants, and that both liquor and pork were sold. Bev had a part-time job because women were allowed to work. She had the best of both worlds. Because most of Bahrain's labor is imported, as is the case in Saudi Arabia, Bev had a houseboy from India named Babu. Babu not only did all the cooking, cleaning, and ironing, but also catered to Bev's dog. My two days in Bahrain were restful and fun and eased me back into my solitary life on Green Sands.

Upon my return to Saudi Arabia, I wrote in my diary that I thought I had become accustomed to loneliness. How wrong I was. Although I returned from the States with an array of books and crafts to keep me occupied, I didn't seem in the mood to do anything. During my vacation, I had again become accustomed to watching the news and other programs on television. I suppose that I was going through withdrawal from American TV. The adjustment to being alone and isolated from the Western world was taking some effort.

In the ensuing years, no matter how accustomed I became to my isolation, after every vacation, I faced some period of readjustment. This was true even after I had been in Saudi Arabia for a little more than two years and the new, real house that Sheikh Latif had been promising since our first year became a reality. Although we had a contractor who was Lebanese, the laborers were from Pakistan, and communicating our Western ideas for a house was difficult. On several occasions, the work of the previous day had to be torn out, because major components, such as plumbing, had been left out. Despite the delays, after five months of work, our house was finally completed in September 1985. Not surprisingly, the company suddenly had no cash flow with which to furnish the house.

I happened to be on vacation at home when the house was completed and unaware of the lack of funds. Terry picked me up at the airport and explained the problem. He had no idea when we might move in. I moped all the way from the airport to the farm, thinking that I couldn't spend another night in that tiny container. Terry suggested that I at least look at the completed house, even though it was now after dark.

As we entered the new house, Terry explained that he couldn't turn on the lights because the house hadn't yet been wired for electricity from our generator. I was standing in the middle of our new bedroom, when Terry flipped on the lights to reveal all new furniture. I walked around the house in utter amazement, almost in tears at my good fortune. Terry related that only two days before my arrival, the house had been without carpet and furniture, and the company was unable to spend any money at that time. A newcomer to the company, a Saudi financier, Abdul Latif Abraham, heard about our plight and offered to finance the furniture himself until Al Emar could reimburse him.

It turned out that one of Sheikh Latif's relatives was recarpeting his house, and Terry suggested using his old carpet. Everyone in the head office scoffed at the idea, since they were unused to recycling anything. New is better seemed to be the prevailing idea in Saudi Arabia. Terry took the carpet, and some of the farm workers helped him lay it. Because the house was built on a concrete foundation, we regretted that we hadn't purchased a pad; nevertheless, everyone was delighted at how good the carpet looked, and no one guessed that it had ever been used.

Sheikh Latif visited the house soon after it was completed. We had designed a sunken den. He walked in the house, stepped down into the den, walked across the room, and stepped up into the entrance to the bedrooms. He looked around and came back, stepping down into the den, crossing the room and stepping up into the kitchen. After a minute, his only comment was, "Too many steps." This was a funny comment from a man who lived in a three-story house.

Since Saudis weren't accustomed to building closets, Sheikh Latif was astonished by the walk-in closet and walk-in shower we had incorporated into the plan. We designed a flat roof, much like those common in homes in the area. Even in Riyadh, it was common for a family to have a flat roof where they hung their laundry out to dry and kept a sheep for an upcoming meal. We had a spiral staircase that led up to the large thirty-by-forty-five-foot roof. On numerous occasions, we had large groups over for barbecues on our patio roof. Once the fish farm was incorporated, we had old-fashioned fish fries for our friends there.

The fish farm was yet another of Sheikh Latif's inspirations. It was probably the last thing one would expect to find in the desert. After a trip to Germany, Sheikh Latif returned to Green Sands excited about fish farming. He hired a German to make his dream reality. The Saudi government also entered into the new enterprise and in accordance with a government directive that Saudi Arabia was to become self-sufficient in food, the Ministry of Agriculture began providing fish for farmers to grow.

After almost a year of planning, three lakes were dug at P1, and canals and ponds were constructed. It was quite a site for Bedouins and city dwellers alike to see three small lakes out in the middle of the desert.

The bodies of water were like droplets of rain on the flat, sandy surface of the farm. Among the green pivots, they looked like diamond studs, glistening in the sun. The operation produced a bounty of Tilapia, a fish similar to a perch or blue gill. Only after several months did the marketing of the fish catch up with the production. With the glut of fish on the farm, the Filipino workers loved to eat those sent to the canteen. A recently hired Filipino cook could fillet a fish with such speed and precision that it was hard to see his hand move. The cook even dried fish on the canteen roof, because dried fish was a delicacy for the Filipinos. The smell alone would keep the rest of us away, but the blazing Saudi sun was perfect for drying them. We were happy to have an abundant supply of fish on the farm for our parties, where everyone who tasted cornmeal-fried fish for the first time enjoyed it. The whole fish brought a fantastic price at the markets in Riyadh, selling for $1.75 per pound live. The Saudis liked fish, inheriting their tastes from their ancestors who lived on either coast; however, the largest buyers were the Oriental labor force who worked in Saudi Arabia.

Chapter Twenty-Four

One way I survived the isolation of living so far from civilization for almost five years was through prayer and the friends we encountered in Saudi Arabia. With imported labor in the country, Saudi Arabia was a virtual melting pot, so we had friends of many nationalities. It would be impossible to recall all of the wonderful relationships and experiences we had during our stay.

In our second year in Saudi, I had just returned from my daily jog around the pivots of wheat and was stepping out of the shower when I heard a loud banging on the door of our container. As was my custom, I hurried over to the window to peek out to see who was there.

To my surprise, two white males and two white females stood on my porch. I quickly shed my towel and dressed, shouting, "Just a minute." I wrapped my hair in a towel and hurried to the door. I was met by four smiling faces, and the first words out of my mouth were, "Are ya'll from Al Kharj?"

With a hearty laugh, one of the women said, "We love hearing that 'ya'll,' and no, we aren't from Al Kharj, but from Abqaiq." I had not heard of Abqaiq before, but learned that it was about 170 miles northeast of us, near the coast. Without hesitation, I invited the group in and quickly explained that I had been in the shower after going for a jog. They were flabbergasted that a foreign woman could jog across the Arabian sands in shorts without causing a real sensation.

We introduced ourselves, and I found out that Mal and Jerry Stephens and Clair and Maureen Brustkern were all employees of Aramco (Arabian-American Oil Company) and were on their way back to Abqaiq, on the Eastern coast, from a camping trip in central Saudi Arabia.

They explained that almost a year earlier they had been going down the road on another camping trip and had stopped at the gas station we frequented. They had met Franklin Baggerman, the man who had worked with Terry the first year we were on the farm. Frank had suggested that they stop to visit me on the way back because I was so lonely. He drew a map to our farm on a scrap of paper. Frank forgot to relay the incident to me, and Mal explained that on their way back from that camping trip, they didn't feel they had time to stop.

Mal had saved the scrap of a map for almost a year and decided to take a chance that I was still in Saudi Arabia. Terry was alerted by various farm workers that I had visitors so he soon joined us. After a cool drink and some homemade chocolate chip cookies, the quartet left, but not before giving us their phone number and making us promise to visit them at Aramco.

It was almost a year before we took off to visit them. Harvest had been completed, and Terry thought he had time to take two days off. We first had to get a letter of permission from our company to travel from where we lived to the Dhahran area on the east coast.

When Sheikh Latif learned that we were going, he graciously offered us his Suburban so that we wouldn't have to ride in Terry's farm pickup. Needless to say this didn't leave Sheikh Latif without a vehicle. He still had a Cadillac and a Mercedes to drive. It was after 7:00 A.M. when Terry finished giving last-minute instructions to the workers and we were able to leave the farm for our long-awaited outing. The suburban was loaded with freshly picked sweet corn that we had grown on the farm and were taking to our friends at Aramco.

We clipped merrily along the highway, passing beside the edge of the *Al Rub' al-Khali* or empty quarter, where we saw nothing but sand to the horizon. The farms had disappeared abruptly, and we felt alone in the virgin desert. When we began to see oil pipelines, we knew we had run into the area that put Saudi Arabia on the map and created the wealth that turned the desolate country into a powerful force.

We had made only one stop at a lone gas station to get something to drink, so we anticipated arriving at Mal's and Jerry's before noon. We were running our air conditioner at full power because it was the end of May, and the daily temperatures were close to 120 degrees. Without warning, our temperature light came on, and steam poured from the hood. Terry pulled the suburban to the side of the road. The hood was already so hot that he had to clasp a newspaper in his hand to raise it. Terry discovered that the water pump was broken. We were stuck, and I suddenly realized we had drunk almost the entire bottle of water that I had brought along for the trip. We had violated the first rule of travel in the desert by not bringing extra water.

As it was Thursday, the start of a weekend in Saudi Arabia, the usual flow of business traffic, mostly truckers, was not on the road. We tried to remember whether we'd seen any other cars on the road since we stopped at the last gas station, but could only recall one vehicle. It was too hot to stand on the asphalt highway and too hot to sit inside the Suburban, so we stood to the side on the hot, white sand. The area was a stark contrast to the green sands of our farms. The seriousness of our predicament became increasingly evident.

After about ten minutes, a vehicle approached from the direction we were heading. My immediate thought was that if this car helped us, we would have to go all the way back to the farm, because we hadn't passed any towns during our two-hour journey from the farm. Also, the likelihood of this car's stopping was slim, because it was evident we were going the other direction. To our relief, the car slowed and came to a stop directly in front of us. Terry approached the car, and a lone Saudi man, dressed in the traditional male garb, stepped out. He appeared to be about forty years old and spoke only a few words of English. We were able to understand that he had been working a half-day in Udylliah, a town about thirty miles ahead of us and was on his way home to a compound located off the road. He offered to turn around and take us to Udylliah. We took our bags out of the Suburban and filled the man's pickup with the sweet corn.

The ride passed quickly as he and Terry exchanged small talk in broken English and Arabic. I sat listening, remaining silent. He never addressed me or looked at me, probably feeling uncomfortable in such close proximity to an unveiled woman.

Udylliah was a mere village with very few vehicle repair shops. All the shops were closed because it was Thursday afternoon and the start of a weekend. We found one shop that was a combination gas station and grocery store, and the owner was still in the grocery store. After a detailed explanation by our new found friend, we were dismayed to learn that the man did not stock parts for a Suburban. After more discussion between the man and our new friend, the former agreed to tow the Suburban into town. He knew where he could get a water pump, which he agreed to install the next day, for the right price.

Our new friend turned to Terry, saying he would let us take his car on to Abqaiq and would drive his company vehicle home. He also agreed to lead the shop owner to the Suburban. He explained that we could then return his car the next day when the Suburban was ready. Terry and I looked at each other in amazement and wondered whether we had somehow misunderstood our friend's combination of Arabic and English. Here was a man we had never met before, who was willing to let us drive off into the sunset with his car.

Surprisingly, the plan worked exactly as arranged. We took off in our new friend's car, and the tow truck followed him to the Suburban and brought our vehicle back to Udylliah. The gas station owner found a new water pump in a neighboring town and installed it in our Suburban. Terry and Jerry Stephens returned the next day and picked up the Suburban, leaving our new friend's car in a predetermined location. Neither Terry nor I could get over how kind this man had been—truly the Good Samaritan. We knew that the chances of this happening in the States were probably pretty slim.

Aramco turned out to be an Americanized oasis. We were allowed inside the compound through a checkpoint only after our visit was okayed by telephone with Mal. She gave us directions to their house, and we were speechless as we passed house after house, each looking as if it were plucked from suburban America. The Aramco compounds were designed to make the employees and dependents feel like they were at home, and the objective had most certainly been accomplished. They had their own grocery store (complete with pork), school, tennis courts, swimming pools, golf courses, and bowling alleys. Women were allowed to drive within the compound, and people dressed as they wished. We made several trips to Aramco during our five years in Saudi; each time we came away refreshed as if we had experienced a taste of home.

The Saudi long-range governmental plan included gradually replacing imported, foreign labor with Saudis, in specific areas. Especially important in this procedure was the replacement of Americans with Saudis in oil production, specifically at Aramco. With the phasing out of Americans, Saudis began moving into the compounds. In the beginning, the Saudi males came to the swimming pool, not for swimming, but only looking. It was suggested that pools be segregated for male and female, an idea most abhorred by Western families. The streets of the compound were crowded with young Saudi males whizzing around in their fathers' Mercedes, eyeing the young American girls. Switching American labor to Saudi labor changed the culture of Aramco dramatically. The pools remained unsegregated, but unmarried males were no longer allowed inside unless accompanied by their families.

Remembering our Good Samaritan, we had a chance to reciprocate several years later when Terry was able to do a good deed for a Saudi in Al Kharj. We had gone into town to use the phone and stopped off at one of the local hearth ovens for some fresh flatbread. There were quite a few Saudis gathered outside waiting as the Lebanese baker pulled the steaming flatbread from the oven. We took our place in line to wait for the next tray of bread to be ready. A short, round Saudi man passed us with several of the hot loaves wrapped in newspaper. When he reached his car, he began shouting loudly in Arabic. The commotion attracted quite a crowd in a matter of seconds. We joined the group of onlookers and discovered that the man had left his little girl in the car and his keys in the ignition. The little girl had locked all of the doors. The darling little girl looked to be about two and one-half years old. She seemed delighted to have agitated her father. The onlookers began pointing to the buttons on the four doors, gesturing for her to pull one up. She danced around in the car from door to door, pretending to unlock the doors, teasing the frantic father and the spectators. Terry went back to the baker and returned with a coat hanger. Now he was the center of attention, not only because he was the only foreigner in the group, but also because he appeared to be working on a plan to open the car door. They all watched in fascination as Terry slid the bent coat hanger in through the window and attempted to pull up the button. He even had the attention of the little girl, who watched the piece of wire slide up and down. After several minutes of intense concentration on Terry's part, he succeeded. In celebration, the crowd surrounded the father and little girl, completely ignoring Terry, which was fine with him. As we returned to the bread line, the father came back to thank Terry. The baker presented us with several pieces of flatbread and shook his head when Terry tried to pay.

One friendship lasted only one wheat season, but was particularly interesting. Harold Provence, a native of Kansas, worked for a cantankerous Saudi named Prince Turky bin Saud al-Kaabir, who was a distant member of the Royal Family. The Prince not only was difficult to work for, but held tightly to his money, even though he had plenty. The farm where Harold worked was about ten miles from our farm, so we saw him quite often.

Harold and the man he worked with, Larry Hottman, also from Kansas, entered Saudi Arabia on a thirty-day visit visa. This is not an uncommon practice for Saudi businesses if they are in a hurry to get employees into the country. The visit visa can be converted to a resident visa once the employee arrives in Saudi Arabia. To facilitate that process, Larry and Harold handed over their passports as soon as they arrived. Ironically, their passports were not returned, nor did they receive their resident visas, leaving them without identification of any kind. At that time, the police had positioned roadblocks all around the area, hoping to catch people who were in the country illegally, without resident visas. It was common for pilgrims to Mecca to drift off into the country in search of jobs. They hoped someone would hire them, even though they were illegal aliens.

The Prince told Harold and Larry adamantly that if they were caught in such a roadblock and taken to jail that he could do nothing to secure their release. Their assumption was that he was using fear to keep them working constantly on the farm. Nevertheless, they made weekly excursions into the small town of Al Kharj to buy groceries. They drove off the highway, into the sandy desert, whenever they saw a roadblock ahead of them. They spent their time making large circles in the desert, hoping the police wouldn't see them returning to the highway. At times they lost sight of the road and wandered around in the desert until they sensed that they were safely beyond the roadblock.

Harold recalled one incident when he and Larry were riding in separate vehicles with some of the Arab farm workers, and the vehicle in which Harold was riding was stopped by police at a roadblock. Abdallah, the Prince's assistant, persuaded the Saudi policeman not to take Harold to jail for failing to have any kind of identification. For Harold, that thirty minutes of persuasion seemed to last an eternity.

Harold joked that he not only had trouble getting into Saudi Arabia, but had a hard time getting out as well. To get to Saudi Arabia in November 1984, Harold flew from Kansas to New York City, where he boarded a Pan Am jet from New York to London. He changed airline carriers in London and flew to Jeddah, Saudi Arabia, on SAUDIA airlines. At this point he continued to Riyadh on SAUDIA and changed to a domestic flight. Harold was privileged on the last leg of his long flight to secure a bulkhead seat so he had more leg room and was next to an exit door. He had an aisle seat that faced the opposite seat where the stewardess sat during takeoff and landing. A normal flight from Jeddah to Riyadh takes a little more than an hour, so Harold settled back into his seat to doze after such a long day of flying.

He was awakened, after about fifteen minutes, by a voice on the intercom that asked for a man named Mohammed "Something" to come to the front of the plane. He thought this announcement was a little bit unusual but he returned to his nap. About forty-five minutes elapsed and Harold was again awakened when the stewardess strapped herself into the seat across from him, evidently in preparation for the descent.

At this point, the airplane circled a city that everyone assumed was Riyadh. After circling several times, the airplane continued to fly. The stewardess left her seat and returned shortly. Harold jokingly asked, "Do we know where we are going?" The stewardess nervously said, "No." Harold then nervously asked, "Have we been hijacked?" The stewardess gravely nodded her head.

The man who had been sitting next to Harold in the window seat suddenly came to life, peering out the window. Harold and the man agreed with the stewardess that it would be better not to say anything to the other passengers. After flying for what seemed an eternity but in actuality was only thirty minutes, the man next to the window said that he could see rivers and lakes down below. Harold replied that the presence of so much water was a good indication that they were no longer in Saudi Arabia.

Within minutes, two fighter planes appeared to escort the plane onto a runway below. When Harold looked out the window, he could see nothing but runway. Everyone on the plane remained calm, because few suspected that the plane had been hijacked. The pilot shut down all but one engine, and it soon sputtered and died. The captain later told the passengers over the intercom that the plane was completely out of fuel.

Because Harold and the others still didn't know their location, he scanned the map featured in the SAUDIA airlines flight magazine and tried to determine his whereabouts. He estimated the plane had flown for about three hours from Jeddah. It normally took about an hour to fly from Jeddah to Riyadh, so he used the distance on the map to figure a location where two more hours of flying time might have taken them. It didn't take long to realize that they might possibly be in Tehran, Iran.

As they waited, a glimmer of hope came when the plane began to move, but they soon realized that the plane was moving backwards. The brakes failed, causing the plane to roll backwards. A ten-foot chain link fence stopped the moving plane, directly in front of a ditch with a steep incline.

With the somber possibility of being in Iran still in their minds and daylight beginning to dawn, they could see soldiers on the runway not far from the airplane. After a whispered discussion with some of the flight crew, a woman on the airplane pretended to be sick. After a short while a ramp was brought to an exit door, and she was allowed to leave. The suspicions of the passengers were confirmed when they read Iranian Air on the side of the ramp.

After almost an hour of anxious waiting, the crew in the cockpit requested that pillows be brought to the front because they were tired. An Arab doctor who was a passenger, along with a flight attendant, agreed to take the pillows to the front. Once in the cockpit, the doctor courageously jumped one of the two hijackers. The other hijacker began shooting into the air and was quickly wrestled to the ground by a member of the crew. The hijackers had entered the cockpit by holding a gun to the stewardess's head. A third man pretended to have met the hijackers in the airport and was serving as an interpreter to mediate the problem. Actually, Harold was told that all three had planned the hijacking.

At this point, the doors of the airplane flew open, and rubber ramps were put in place. The cabin crew had quietly passed among the passengers, alerting them to prepare to exit and slide down the ramp, if escape were possible. The passengers were told to take off their shoes because the ramps were rubber. Harold recalled that many people, in their haste to exit, left their shoes on board. As the doors flew open, everyone raced for the exits and slid off. They were quickly hustled onto waiting busses by Iranian soldiers. When they were transported to the terminal, the passengers saw big signs: "Down with Israel, Down with America."

As the passengers entered the airport terminal, they were met with camera crews and reporters from all the major networks. The group was taken to a small room and held for about two hours without any contact with the outside. They were then escorted by soldiers to busses and taken to the former Hyatt Regency. After the takeover by the Ayatollah, it had been renamed Tehran Hotel.

In the lobby, all passports were confiscated, which gave every nationality a scare, especially the eleven Americans. The man in charge announced that everyone would be given the opportunity to make a phone call. Harold decided that he didn't want to attract any more attention to himself than was necessary, and he especially didn't want to phone the U.S.

After a few hours of rest, the group was again herded onto busses and returned to the airport. Passports were returned, after the passengers were searched twice. Then the group was flown to Riyadh. When they emerged from the plane, airport personnel and various embassy representatives presented the passengers with roses.

The group didn't learn until they were safely on the plane that the hijackers were from Yemen and had demanded SR 500,000 ($142,857), friends released from a Saudi prison, and Iranian citizenship. Two of the hijackers were not seriously hurt, but the man whom the doctor jumped injured his hand in the scuffle. The doctor hit him with the fire ax that was kept inside the cockpit. The American pilot told the group that the hijacker had kept a gun to the back of his head during the entire ordeal.

Ironically, when Harold's co-worker Larry Hottman returned to the United States, he sat next to an American in the London airport. They conversed, and Larry mentioned Harold's hijacking experience. The man he was talking to was the American pilot who had flown the plane with a gun held to his head.

Harold also enjoyed relating how he had left Saudi Arabia. Prince Turky had kept all identification, including passports, the entire eight months that Harold and Larry had been in Saudi Arabia. Also, he had failed to pay salaries each month, putting not only Larry and Harold in a bind, but their families back home, as well. On several occasions, the

Prince sarcastically offered Larry a wife as part of his payment; this was not quite the reimbursement that Larry was prepared to accept.

When finally the time came to go home, Harold and Larry were taken to town by one of Prince Turky's drivers. They were deposited at a villa, where they waited for an entire day. When the man returned with the salaries, they discovered they had been shortchanged by one month's wages. They protested to the delivery man, but the Prince was out in the desert with his camels, so there was little anyone could do.

They were taken to the house of a Saudi man, name Husni, whom they had met before, to wait for someone to do the necessary paperwork for an exit visa, a complicated process because technically they had been in the country illegally for the seven months since their visitor's visa had expired.

After many cups of Arabic coffee and hot tea and more waiting, Husni returned with the airplane tickets and exit visas. Husni's eighteen-year-old nephew drove his uncle's Mercedes to take the Americans to the airport. Driving through the busy streets of Riyadh at top speed was like a roller coaster ride for Harold and Larry. Once they were on the open highway to the airport, the nephew drove the Mercedes as fast as it would go. Both Harold and Larry saw a stalled car in the lane ahead, long before the nephew, but their screams were too late to slow the car enough to keep it from crashing into the back of the stalled car. The accident was compounded by two other cars that rear ended the Mercedes. Fortunately, no one was seriously injured.

Neither Harold nor Larry wanted to miss their flight and be forced to spend one more night in Riyadh with their host, so they stepped out on the highway, waving their arms in an attempt to catch a ride to the airport. The Saudis in the other cars, who had been involved in the accident, shouted that they were not to leave the scene of the accident.

After a few cars zoomed past, two Thailanders stopped, and at first, refused the men a ride. When Harold offered them two one-hundred riyal bills ($75), the pair quickly agreed. As Larry and Harold threw their luggage into the trunk of the car and jumped in, they could hear the Saudis yelling, "*Mafi imshi*," (Don't go away).

Harold never returned to Saudi Arabia after that eventful year, but Larry decided to give it another chance and returned with another Kansas native, Dick Frain. Dick and Larry were important friends to us in the lonely desert. Dick missed homemade ice cream, so I experimented constantly to perfect making ice cream without an ice cream freezer. He was always nice enough to eat my concoctions without complaining.

Because Prince Turky was unreliable, Dick and Larry had their mail sent to our farm. On one occasion near Christmas, Dick received a huge can with three flavors of popcorn, from an aunt back in Kansas. Terry and I had been to Riyadh the day it arrived, so we picked up the mail from our office in person rather than having it delivered to the farm. During the two-hour ride home, it was too much of a temptation not to sample Dick's popcorn, which had already been opened and examined in customs. After sampling and sampling we were embarrassed to see that we had eaten almost half of the contents. Grinning guiltily, Terry presented the package to Dick and commented that someone in customs must have liked popcorn. Dick had a long memory, because Terry and I took a short trip the following spring, and Dick snook into our greenhouse and ate almost all of our strawberries, a delicacy in Saudi Arabia. His only comment was that the strawberries tasted similar to popcorn.

We enjoyed a continuing joke with all of the men who ate a home-cooked meal at our house. Because pork is prohibited and not available except in private compounds, most foreigners were forced to do without it. Because we had connections at Aramco, we occasionally secured pork to serve our guests. Sometimes I had a big pot of pinto beans with pork for seasoning. Only Terry knew that I had put the meat in, and he intentionally put it in the bottom of the serving bowl. After all the men were served, Terry fished for the piece of pork, innocently showing his find to the others at the table. All the men seemed distressed that they had missed an opportunity for this treat. At subsequent dinners, all the knowing guests would dig deep into the beans, checking for pork. Usually Terry planted a decoy, such as a spoon, at the bottom of the bowl.

Pork wasn't supposed to be available, but there were substitutes, such as beef bacon, that were almost better than the real thing. Such luxuries carried a heavy price tag of about six dollars per pound. The whole issue of pork with the Moslems was interesting. Unlike alcohol, which was forbidden, yet drunk by many Moslems, pork was a different matter. Many Saudis enjoyed the luxury of drinking alcohol when they were out of the country, but they always regarded pork with utter repulsion. On our annual flights to the States, we noticed Moslem passengers would become hysterical if they thought they had been served sandwiches containing pork. Moslems are taught from birth that pork is unclean and remain adamant in this belief. One of our good Saudi friends com-mented with amazement that he had heard that in America we even eat the skin of the pig (pork rinds).

Dick liked to recall the time that he would have given anything to have his camera. Arab men not only exchange the traditional greeting of a kiss on each cheek, but also walk hand in hand. Prince Turky's right-hand man was a Saudi named Abdallah. Often Larry was angry at both Prince Turky and Abdallah for some problem on the farm that they had neglected to take care of, yet when they came to the farm, he was forced to hold hands with them. Once, much to his delight, Dick observed Larry and Abdallah walking across a wheat field holding hands. Larry had his free hand behind his back with the appropriate finger extended.

Larry was able to laugh more easily about the Arab idiosyncrasies in the remaining years he was in Saudi Arabia than during his first year. He spent that first year in even more rigorous circumstances than he had experienced with Dick. Larry recalled that the first time he arrived, he spent one night in Riyadh before he was taken to the farm. In Ri-yadh, he was jolted from a fitful sleep at 4:00 A.M. with the call to prayer, alerting the faithful to awaken. Yet after arising so early, for some un-known reason, Larry's driver waited to begin the drive to the farm until it was too late to get there before nightfall, so he and Larry spent several hours wandering in the pitch black desert, searching for a lone tent. Af-ter finally locating the tent, Larry wrapped himself in a blanket and col-lapsed on the ground in exhaustion.

In a few minutes, Larry was startled awake by someone or something beating on the outside of the tent. Larry realized that his only protec-tion was the small pocketknife he carried, so he crouched in the tent, knife ready. As the pounding on the tent continued, Larry imagined his wife Geneva reading of his death in a dark tent in the middle of this for-saken desert. With a big huff, the flap of the tent was thrown back by an American, Ron Cush, who was to spend the next eight months with Larry. Having arrived on another flight, Ron, had been groping his way around the tent, searching for the flap in the darkness.

Larry and Ron spent the next months together in true pioneer spirit. They never had lights; they cooked on a propane hot plate; food was de-livered so sporadically that many times they had only two cans of food and one jug of water when supplies were replenished; they didn't have a vehicle to drive off the farm that first year. They were really at the mercy of their Saudi employers.

Although conditions were difficult for them on Prince Turky's farm, the Americans developed a real camaraderie with farm workers from many different countries. Once, accidentally, Larry dumped diesel on an Egyptian worker; they both had a good laugh as the man stood there covered from head to toe with the fuel. This same Egyptian made sure that Larry rode on a camel before he left Saudi Arabia at the end of his first year of work. The group of Egyptians standing around the camel told Larry to jump on the camel by grabbing its neck and swinging his leg over the hump. After several foiled attempts, the men wrestled the camel to the ground, and Larry crawled on the large hump. Despite Larry's attempts to hold on, the camel easily bucked him off into a large pile of camel dung. The man over whom Larry had poured the diesel laughed loudest.

Larry and Dick never knew how Prince Turky came by all his wealth, but they knew that he had quite a sum of money invested in camels. Prince Turky, a confirmed desert dweller, delighted in racing his camels against those of anyone willing to race and was always urging Larry and Dick to attend one of the races.

Finally, they agreed to attend a camel race. Prince Turky furnished them with a rudimentary map to the race area. They clocked sixteen miles out into the desert before they saw the gathering of camels. It was a dusty day with sand swirling everywhere. The jockeys and camels were milling around, when suddenly they began running in the same general direction. Larry and Dick assumed that someone had called, "Go," but they never heard it. The camels ran wildly along the path of dirt mounds that the Prince had erected to serve as a track. Not to miss any of the twenty-kilometer race, most of the observers jumped into their vehicles to race along with the camels. The jockeys had to concentrate not only on winning the race but also on dodging the vehicles. The scenes could have passed easily for an episode of the "Dukes of Hazzard" set in the desert.

Dick's experiences in Saudi Arabia weren't limited to the area around our farm. He had been in the country the year before in an area in central Saudi Arabia called Wadi da Wasser. This area, clinging proudly to its Bedouin roots, sported no modern conveniences.

Dick recalled riding in a Nissan pickup truck with a Filipino and two Thailanders hanging on in the back. The roads around Wadi da Wasser were less developed than in other areas and really dangerous for night driving. The group drove along in total darkness until they saw a yellow light. The two Thailanders yelled out, "*Ei, Ei,*" meaning elephant. The group then struck a large object with a force that threw them forward.

When the group climbed from the vehicle, they were stunned to see they had struck a camel. After closer examination they realized that the camel had already been struck by another pickup that was overturned by the side of the road. The taillights of the overturned vehicle were the yellow lights they had seen. Both the camel and the driver were dead, so the group made a hasty departure, realizing that they could easily be blamed for the accident.

When the Saudis first began to farm the desert, some of the wealthier purchased large pieces of unclaimed desert land, where many Bedouins lived. The Bedouins and their ancestors had lived on these lands for centuries and had no comprehension of land ownership. Words on a piece of paper that they couldn't read meant nothing to them. Many of the land disputes, resolved in other areas of the country, were still raging in Wadi da Wasser when Dick worked there.

In Wadi, the police were often close relatives to the Bedouins, with whom they sided. Consequently, the police tried to force the farmers, including Dick, off the land. The raids on the farmers always occurred in the daytime, during working hours, because so much of the farm work had to be done at night. Occasionally, police surprised the farmers at the tasks that had to be done during the day. One particular day, a Filipino worker heckled the police, and a policeman hit him on the head with the butt of a rifle.

Usually, the police chased the farmers a few miles across the desert. Then they retreated. Dick began posting a watch guard. Once the guard warned the workers that the police were coming; the workers, all thirteen of them, would pile into the one pickup at the site where they were living. They would drive into the desert and hide behind a sand dune for several hours, until they thought the coast was clear.

Dick never seemed to mind the raids, because they were always a good excuse to return to the living quarters to drink home brew. Relations between the Bedouins and farmers improved, and the raids became less frequent. According to Dick, the Bedouins were more than likely paid a handsome sum of riyals to move further into the desert.

Despite its small acreage, the farm on which Dick had worked in Wadi had an office in the small town. Across from the office was a dilapidated sheep pen. One day when he left the office, Dick backed his pickup into the sheep pen. When he pulled away, he dragged the pen down the street with him. The usually deserted streets filled with veiled women, curious men, and grinning children, all staring at the American who was dragging a fence through town. The owner of the sheep pen demanded furiously that Dick's company repair the fence. Dick's Saudi boss sent two Thais to do the repairs. Dick was amused to see that the pair put the old fence in place and repaired it to its former broken-down state.

Often on Prince Turky's farm, Dick and his fellow workers would find themselves stranded without a farm pickup and dependent on three-wheelers to get from point to point, because another of Prince Turky's employees "borrowed" the pickup. Yet, whenever Dick's boss came to the farm, he would bring several young male family members. The boys would drive the three-wheelers until they were out of gasoline and then abandon them. Dick and the other men would have to search for the cycles, sometimes finding them two miles from camp. Dick became smarter. He learned to deflate the tires as soon as the family arrived and to tell the boys that they needed repair.

Larry told a story about a gas station in the tiny village of Aber that depicted traditional life in the desert of Saudi Arabia. The gas station had trench silos with above ground storage tanks for gasoline and diesel. Because the remote gas station didn't have any electricity, the only means of dispensing fuel was by gravity flow. Customers drove into the silos to allow for adequate pressure to fill their vehicles. However, the fuel wasn't dispensed directly into a vehicle, but was measured out first into a one-gallon olive oil can. Then the gas was siphoned into the vehicle. Filling one's vehicle with gas became an arduous adventure.

This quaint little gas station in Aber had a large chest cooler where the canned soft drinks were stored. Because the gas station didn't have any electricity, the owner raised the lid on the cooler at night to cool the drinks and closed it during the day to keep them cold. Despite temperatures soaring near 120 degrees during the day, anything wet tasted good.

Another friendship that sustained us while we lived in Saudi Arabia was with a couple who lived on a farm that was almost two and one-half hours away from us. John and Meredith McCleod lived on a wheat farm called Khafs Daghrah. John was a native New Zealander who had met Meredith, and American, while he was in South Dakota. Meredith recalled the time when one of the Filipino farm workers brought her a *dhub* (large lizard) to cook. The Filipinos had stoned the lizard in an attempt to kill it. The Saudi lizards grow quite large and are often seen running across the desert on short, stubby legs. The lizard was considered a delicacy by the Bedouins.

The workers left to take showers, while Meredith sat in her kitchen contemplating how to cook a lizard. After a little more deliberation, she decided to boil it in a pot of water as the Saudis cook their sheep.

John and Meredith joined the Filipinos in eating the *dhub*. Meredith described the meat as tasting like rich chicken, with a tough, chewy texture. The group eating the *dhub* decided the meat might have been tough, because the lizard didn't die for almost an hour after it was stoned.

While we lived in Saudi Arabia, we met a couple from Wisconsin in their late fifties who became some of our closest friends. Dean and Lorraine Greenwood weren't strangers to the Middle East, having lived in Iran immediately before the fall of the Shah. Dean contracted to set up dairies in Iran, and Lorraine, along with their son, Joe, accompanied him. As fate would have it, Joe fell in love and married an Iranian girl named Gholi, who was raised by missionaries as a Christian rather than a Moslem. Just before the fall of the Shah, the two families refrained from going out on the streets for fear that they might be killed because they were Americans. Dean and Lorraine finally left the country, leaving their possessions behind. Joe waited until the eleventh hour to obtain permission for Gholi, an Iranian citizen, to leave.

Despite this harrowing experience, the Greenwoods returned to the Middle East to establish dairies in Saudi Arabia. Eventually, Dean accepted a job as head of maintenance for the world's largest integrated dairy operation, only twenty miles from our farm. The Saudi Arabian Agricultural Dairy Company (SAADCO) was a showcase, complete with a palace owned by a member of the royal family. We often visited the dairy because it employed many Western families, who became our friends. After Sheikh Latif hired a driver for me, I went to the dairy once a week to play a piano that had been furnished by SAADCO.

One season, we joined a square dancing group that met at the dairy. The teachers for our small group were Mary and Stan Johnson from Sweden. They taught the dances to American square dancing music, with a decided Swedish accent, but because there were as many nationalities as couples on the dance floor, the distinctive Western music seemed unimportant.

Another square dancing couple who became our friends were Kim and Dick Cates. Dick was hired as the crop superintendent for the dairy.

We remember fondly the time that Kim and Dick went on a two-week snow skiing trip in Switzerland and allowed us the privilege of babysitting Eric, their six-month-old son. It was common for Westerners in Saudi Arabia to vacation in Europe, a mere six hours away. When Kim and Dick announced that they were taking Shannon, their five-year-old daughter skiing, along with Eric, their baby, we suggested that they leave Eric with us. The two weeks that we spent with Eric convinced us to forget about waiting for the perfect time to have a child and to forge ahead. After Kim and Dick left Saudi Arabia, they applied and negotiated for another job in Oman, a tiny Sultanate next to the United Arab Emirates. For more than a year, they actually had their bags packed, waiting for the call to go to Oman. Even the experience of living in Saudi Arabia did not prepare them for the incredible procrastination of the Oman company. Finally, they decided they had to go on with their lives. They abandoned the idea of a job in Oman and settled in Wisconsin.

Although most of our friends lived in the direction of Riyadh, we had a couple of wonderful friends who lived even farther out in the desert than we did. Neil and Genia Roberts were an interesting pair who had lived much of their married life in such places as Sudan and Kenya. Neil was from Wales, and although Genia held a British passport, she was born and raised in Kenya. After living in Kenya and Sudan, Genia knew the difference between luxury and necessity. For some reason, the farm where Genia and Neil worked in Saudi Arabia was much more heavily infested with scorpions and tarantulas than others in the area. Genia finally had to resort to sleeping under a mosquito net after several nights of waking up to a scorpion crawling across her pillow.

Al Sabar farm produced chickens as well as wheat. Saudis eat a great deal of mutton and chicken; therefore, chicken farms are common. Live chickens may be purchased in the market. I remember visiting Al Sabar and being overwhelmed by the flies. In the spring, flies are terrible in Saudi Arabia, especially on the dairy and chicken farms.

Neil had an encounter with his boss's brother, S'aad. Neil and S'aad discussed farm business, and S'aad accused Neil of a slight discrepancy in the accounting department of the farm. When Neil denied it, S'aad said, "Well, I must believe Fathi (another man), because he is a Moslem and you are a Christian."

My fondest memory of being with Genia is the time that in desperation to get off the farm, the two of us took off to Riyadh in a farm pickup because the passenger van needed repair. We had both longed to purchase several sizes of ornate copper pots from a market in Riyadh, having admired them on several of our shopping trips. The shopkeeper, sensing he could make a double sale, bargained with us until we reached a price we all agreed on. Piling both sets of copper pots in the back of the pickup, we started our return trip to the farm.

Our driver was pushing the pedal all the way to the floor, but the vehicle only limped along. Holding our breaths, we hoped the desert-worn vehicle would make it home before it died. We chugged through Al Kharj and with just under thirty miles from the farm, the car lurched and died. We were far enough from Al Kharj that walking would have been difficult, and I could only imagine the attention two Western women walking along with a driver would attract.

Mustering our courage, we hailed the first vehicle that chanced down the road. The driver was a middle aged Bedouin who hadn't seen a bath in weeks, and his pickup looked and sounded no less on its last legs than had our dead one. He glared at us as we took turns explaining in limited Arabic our final destination. Our driver chose to remain quiet, figuring our ability to garner sympathy was greater than his. With a disgruntled sigh, the Bedouin nodded that he would take us with him. Genia and I both knew that our purchases could not remain unattended in our pickup, so we quickly began transferring the mountain of copper.

Between trips from one vehicle to the next, the man's jaw dropped; we guessed he thought we had purchased the total copper available in Riyadh. With the transfer complete, the four of us piled into the tiny cab of the pickup and started down the road. After an eternity of closeness, we gestured where to turn toward P2. With the turn completed, we heard a loud explosion and realized we'd had a blowout. The Bedouin turned and glared as if to indicate the blowout occurred because of overload. We had no choice but to wait until one of the farm workers drove near us. Once again the transfer of the copper mine took place, and we were at last deposited at my camp. At my suggestion, the Bedouin's vehicle was taken to the workshop and repaired.

Another friend on our end of the road was Jack King, an Irishman who worked for Mastock, an Irish company in Saudi Arabia. We loved Jack's Irish accent and his polite manner. After Jack had been in Saudi Arabia several years, his family began coming to Saudi for Christmas and summer vacations. His family comprised his wife, Gladys; two sons, Allen and Paul; and twin girls, Jennifer and Nicola. We were able to visit them in Ireland on one of our vacations.

Twins were uncommon among the Bedouins, owing perhaps to the difficulty of such deliveries in the desert. Jennifer and Nicola looked exactly alike, each with very blond hair and very fair skin. The first time they arrived at the farm, a small group of Bedouins came up to the windows of the house where Jack lived and peered in, hoping to catch a glimpse of the twelve-year-old girls. By afternoon, quite a crowd had gathered, and as many as a dozen Bedouins encircled the house. When Jack returned from work, he herded them away as quickly as possible.

Jack's farm had a swimming pool, a real treat for the children during the hot summers. Once the pool was discovered by the Bedouins, it became a communal male bath for them. During lunchtime, the men took the plunge, fully dressed in even their headgear into the shallow end of the pool. To discourage the Bedouins, the children began to pretend that they were testing the pool water. They tried to look positively dissatisfied with the water's cleanliness, and then they added algicide and acid, which would ferment around the edges. Not knowing the true cause of the reaction and its effects, the Bedouins always left in a hurry.

Jack's Irish company sponsored one of the most interesting events in Saudi Arabia, the yearly Mastock Sports Day. We were privileged to be invited to the annual gathering. They not only sponsored various sports events but also fed the guests. Because Mastock is a large company with many farms under its auspices, representatives from the various farms competed in the sporting events. There were always Bedouins in the area who heard about the sports day and stood on the outskirts of the playing field, observing the crazy Westerners in competition. Many of the teams included female athletes in shorts, an unusual sight for the Bedouins.

Chapter
Twenty-Five

Because I rode with Terry in his pickup almost constantly the first couple of years in Saudi, I became acquainted with many of the workers. If Terry had to confer with one of the workers when we went to Pi at night to eat, another of the workers might ask me to accompany him to his room to look at pictures of his wife and family. Many times the men showed me pictures of new babies they had never seen in person.

On one such occasion, Javid, a Pakistani who worked in our farm store, invited me to his room to see his photo album. Besides the regular family groups, there were several pictures of Javid with his head shaved during his Hajj. His primary reason for working in Saudi was that it enabled him to go to Mecca every year. In some cases, Moslems in other countries must wait years to come to Mecca; only a limited number of pilgrims from other countries are allowed to come each year.

In the picture, he wore two white sheets, one wrapped around his waist like a long skirt and the other draped over his shoulders. Although he had been to Mecca before, Javid was planning to go again in the place of his father. Because his father had died at an early age from a brain hemorrhage, without making the pilgrimage to Mecca, Javid believed it was his duty to go in his place.

I questioned him about why the pilgrims throw stones when they pay homage at Mecca. He explained that there are three devils: a big devil, a medium-sized devil, and a small devil. To destroy these devils, each pilgrim must throw nine stones at each. A woman may gather the stones and request that a man throw them for her, but some women throw their own stones, because they want to see the devils themselves. He added that pilgrims are following the directives of the prophet Mohammed when they visit Mecca and throw the stones.

While we talked, a big camel spider ran out from under Javid's bed, on which we were sitting, and disappeared somewhere on the other side of the tiny room. I asked if he were afraid of being bitten by a spider during the night. He replied stoically, "We are not afraid of snakes or anything, because we each have a specific day when we will die. That only God knows, so we don't have to be afraid!" When I reflected on some of the Arab habits that I had observed, from their fast, reckless driving to their concepts of safety and death, I realized that this fatalistic attitude permeated their lives.

We had some Moslem friends who were not Saudis and were as Westernized as we were. One such friend was Mohammed Alam, who worked in our head office. He was a Pakistani, who had lived much of his life in either England or America. His family had spent most of their lives in Florida, but had joined him in Saudi Arabia. Although his eight-year-old son did not speak a word of Arabic, he had to attend a Saudi school because he was Moslem. King Fahad had proclaimed that Moslem children could not attend the International schools, even if they did not speak Arabic.

We were usually invited for a meal whenever we went to the head office. One particular evening, Imod, one of the Pakistanis who worked in the office, invited us to dinner. When I first met Imod, I was flattered by his obvious attentions, but soon became annoyed by his boldness. Later, Imod visited the farm several times. He always found a reason to come into our house before he had seen Terry. He always brought me something, if only a carton of melted ice cream. One time Imod even presented me with a beautiful picture frame.

I began to discourage his attention, because he was becoming very free with his touches. He always kissed me when he arrived and when he departed, and any other time he could get away with it. I would have become quite distressed at this attention, except that he seemed to kiss Terry almost as much as he did me. We decided that his attentions meant nothing. They were his customary treatment of people whom he liked.

On the evening that we were to dine with him, we followed Imod from the office. When we arrived at his home, we were ushered into the apartment by Yassir, his son, with the explanation that Tabinda, Imod's wife, would be out after she finished her prayers. Tabinda soon emerged, dressed in typical Pakistani clothes but with her head covered. Pakistani women always had their heads covered in public in Saudi Arabia, and I assumed she was covering it because of Terry's presence. Tabinda had a broad smile and soft-spoken manner that I really liked. I followed her into the kitchen while she prepared tea.

She served tea, Pakistani style, with lots of sugar and milk, along with a plate of Snickers candy bars. Yassir, the son, and Tabona, the daughter were very well mannered. At the time, the family was only visiting Imod, but later they came to live in Saudi with him, allowing us to know them better. Yassir was twelve, attended a boarding school in Pakistan and was allowed to go home once a month. Tabona, who was ten years old, attended a Catholic school, much to my surprise. Tabinda pointed out that they planned on Yassir's becoming an engineer and Tabona a doctor. Both children smiled and seemed perfectly happy with the decision their parents had made concerning their future.

On the wall of the living room were a huge picture of Imod and the two children, when they were younger, and another of a woman who was not Tabinda. Imod must have noticed my curiosity as I gazed at the picture, because he proceeded to tell me a tragic story. His first wife, the lady in the picture, and another child had been killed in a car wreck in 1979. Imod searched for another wife and met Tabinda. Without reservation he explained the reason that he married Tabinda: she could remain in Pakistan to finish raising his children while he continued to work in Saudi Arabia. Their relationship appeared platonic. Tabinda was an educated person, who served as a supervisor for a school district. All four family members seemed happy with the arrangement.

After we finished our tea, Tabinda and I went into the kitchen to prepare the traditional flatbread. We talked as she expertly rolled out the *chapitis,* the Pakistani flatbread. Our supper consisted of chicken curry, rice with vegetables, potato patties, *dal*—a thick soup made from lentils, and an Egyptian dish made with yogurt and diced onion rings. Although the food was hot with chilies, it tasted good. After I helped Tabinda with the dishes, we joined the men in the living room, and she presented me with a traditional female outfit from Pakistan.

I tried on the outfit, and Tabinda decided that I needed some Pakistani bracelets. After she tried to slide several of the tiny bracelets over my wrists, she and I both realized that my hand was too large. I recounted my experience with bracelets that Ai had wanted to give me.

With a two-hour drive ahead of us, we departed despite their pleas for us to spend the night. There was a small grocery store on the ground level below Imod's apartment, where we decided to buy something to drink. I had on my Pakistani outfit when I entered the store. Several men in the store seemed somewhat confused. One or two of the men voiced his approval, saying, *"quayis,"* which means good, in Arabic.

Our closest friendship with a Saudi grew throughout the years that we were in Saudi Arabia. Tariq, the young man who was the boyfriend of John Zielske's daughter Sherri, eventually became the manager for his father's farm. We were invited to Tariq's graduation party, given by the Zielskes, before they left Saudi Arabia. Tariq graduated from college with a degree in agriculture. The party was a surprise, and Tariq said that even his family would never have given him a graduation party. Birthdays or other landmark dates in a person's life are not regarded as momentous or celebrated in Saudi Arabia. For Tariq's graduation party, the Egyptian cook had prepared the typical chicken and rice, but added French fries, stuffed squash, and fried eggplant. Sherri presented Tariq with a chocolate cake that had fruit cocktail in it, because she knew that he liked fruit cocktail. I was surprised to see Sherri, who had obviously come in from the pool, dressed in a bikini. I was amazed at her nonchalance especially in this world, where Tariq was accustomed to seeing a woman clad in black from head to toe, with even her face covered. The Zielskes, having been blessed with a teenage daughter who happened to come of rebellious age in Saudi Arabia, were trying their best not to force any issue that might fuel the rebellion. It was evident that Sherri and Tariq were very close; they walked around with their arms around each other. Yet after Sherri left Saudi Arabia, even though Tariq stayed in contact with her, the relationship ended. At the dinner, we were served homemade wine, the first time we had seen served the illegal substance in the presence of a real Saudi. The substance was usually offered at non-Saudi parties.

Even though Tariq would one day manage his father's farm, as a graduate of a Saudi University, he had been given a government job. He was paid SR 6000 ($1,714) per month for three hours of work each day, five days a week. Because he had not been guaranteed the job when he started college and had graduated without that incentive, he received a SR 50,000 ($14,285) bonus. If he worked for the government for two years, they would pay all expenses if he wanted to get his Master's degree in the United States. While in America, he would be furnished with SR 12,000

($3,428) a month for spending money (Such an offer is fairly irresistible; Tariq began graduate studies in the U.S. in 1993.).

Although Tariq had been to the United States several times, he remained more or less a product of Saudi Arabia's rigid codes. Sometimes, it seemed hard to imagine this same Westernized young man who had kept company with a bikini-clad American girl in a world where marriages are still arranged, and the sexes are segregated. And, indeed, Tariq committed an unusual, almost unheard of act of defiance, by refusing the woman his parents arranged for him to marry when the time came for the wedding preparations to begin. He had been Westernized to the extent that he didn't want to marry someone with whom he had developed no personal relationship.

Yet despite the young man's apparent Westernization, my only matchmaking effort in Saudi Arabia—with Tariq—was a complete failure. I had met a charming young Saudi girl who spoke excellent English and seemed to embrace Western standards. I thought that she'd be perfect for Tariq, because he wanted to marry a Saudi woman of his own choosing. When I described LuLua to Tariq, he seemed interested until I told him her name. His attitude changed; he didn't want to meet LuLua because he recognized her last name as that of a Saudi family from Jeddah. He said that Saudis in Riyadh were different from Saudis in Jeddah, and his family wouldn't accept her. He refused to even discuss meeting her. He remains a bachelor to this day.

Because quite a few Bedouins camped around Tariq's farm, he had several proposals by Bedouin fathers for their daughters. Although he never considered marrying the daughters, he enjoyed driving up to the Bedouins' tents and catching glimpses of the daughters. At one time a bold Bedouin girl actually pursued him, hoping that her brashness might attract his fancy and eventually his wealth and hand in marriage. The plan backfired when Tariq seemed almost repulsed at her boldness. On another occasion, Tariq came in contact with a Lebanese woman who openly pursued him. Tariq came to us to ask advice in ways to rebuff her advances.

Even Terry was offered an arranged marriage. One season some particularly friendly Bedouins tried to set up camp on some of our pivots of wheat. Terry teased the old patriarch in the Bedouin camp who had many children, including several teenage daughters. On several occasions the old man persuaded Terry to drink tea with him. Because Terry frequently chased two of the daughters from several pivots, they felt that they were well acquainted with him. The oldest sister, who was married, asked Terry to get rid of me and marry her seventeen-year-old sister. She had seen me jogging around the pivots and probably guessed that I was crazy. Terry asked why he would have to get rid of me, when two wives were no problem in Saudi Arabia. The younger sister replied that she wanted to go to the States where more than one wife was not acceptable. When Terry asked the girl how old she was, she answered that she didn't know, but her married sister quickly responded that she was between seventeen and twenty years old. Terry told her jokingly that he would have to see her face behind the veil before he would consent to marry her. The father promised that Terry's only dowry obligation would be to allow the family to camp permanently on the farm. Eventually, they abandoned the prospect of marriage and moved to another farm. We decided they must have been no more serious than Terry, because it was illegal in Saudi Arabia for a Christian man to marry a Moslem woman, unless he agreed to convert before the marriage occurred.

Chapter Twenty-Six

The growing seasons (November through May) of 1984-85 were uplifting. For the first time, I was no longer the lone female on our farm. Terry hired Brent Armstrong, a fellow Texan, and his wife, Rachel, joined him two days before Christmas. After the hustle and bustle of Christmas activities in the States, I felt sure that Rachel was depressed by the absence of any Christmas festivities in Saudi Arabia. The King banned any references to Christmas, and the only holiday cards available bore the message Season's Greetings.

Rachel was only a year younger than I, and we shared many common interests. Best of all, she lived only thirty feet from me in an identical container. My options had been to spend my days alone in the house or ride with Terry around the farm; now I had someone to share a multitude of daily activities. At this same time, Charles's wife, Joy, joined him at Riyadh Farm; we became a regular threesome.

Rachel, a native of New Mexico, held a master's degree in weed science and had been working full time before coming to Saudi Arabia. An active, busy career woman in the United States, suddenly she found herself an isolated, repressed housewife in Saudi Arabia. When Hafeez, the general manager, offered her the position of landscape planner for the camps, she was absolutely elated. As with many of the hard-to-pin-down promises and agreements that are made and never kept in Saudi Arabia, Rachel's position never materialized. The camps were nothing more than austere living quarters in the desert, surrounded by a fence. Rachel's landscaping was a good idea. It's hard to imagine why the position never came to fruition, but in Saudi tradition, everything is better if it can be done tomorrow or the next day.

During our first years in Saudi Arabia, the road between P1 and P2 was virtually untraveled, so everyday Rachel and I drove a Blazer, available on the farm, to P1 or to Joy's house, which was between our two farms. We always stopped at Joy's for a visit, and if she happened to be gone, we continued on to P1 and visited the cook or checked Terry's office. The trips to P1 gave us a chance to escape the confines of our own camp and to exercise our freedom by driving. Before the year was finished, however, both Terry and Brent became leery of our driving on the main road, and we were stripped of our car privileges. Needless to say, we felt as though some of our independence was taken from us, but we continued to enjoy each other's company on the farm.

Joy was an animal lover, and from the day she stepped onto the sands of Saudi Arabia, she wanted a pet. She finally located in Eura-Marche a small pet shop where she purchased a cat. We made several trips to Riyadh to a vet for Sahara's shots and checkups. The vet was British and had a great underground business in her home. She was forbidden to work in public, because she was allowed into the country only as a spouse and not on a work visa. Nonetheless, she conducted a regular animal hospital in her villa, with a full schedule of patients. Terry and I kept Sahara for Charles and Joy when they went on vacation. When Joy left Saudi Arabia, she took Sahara with her.

Soon after Joy and Rachel arrived, the three of us planned a trip to Riyadh. We had heard about a new, ultra-modern mall that we wanted to visit. Because few streets were named or numbered at the time, we called our office for directions to this new mall. After a lengthy search, we stumbled upon the Al Akaria Shopping Center. Suniel, our Sri Lankan driver, dropped us off at the front entrance and zoomed away, just as we discovered that the stores in Al Akaria were closed from 1:00 to 4:00 P.M. We had three hours with nothing to do. The mall itself was open, so we walked around peering into the windows of the closed stores. To our delight, we located an open Panda supermarket in one end of the mall.

Panda is the Saudi version of a U.S. supermarket chain. As we secured a basket and strolled toward the first aisle, the afternoon prayer time began. In other grocery stores at that time, I had been allowed to stay inside during prayer time, even though the doors were locked and the lights dimmed. In this store, however, we were chased out with the explanation that we had no male escort with us. We learned later of a report that female Filipino nurses had remained in grocery stores during prayer time to converse with male Filipinos. Because no public contact between the sexes was allowed, no unescorted females would be allowed to remain in a store during prayer time. It wasn't long before the government ruled that no one should remain in a store during prayer time.

We were thrust back into the mall area, where we continued to look through closed doors until Suniel returned. Because our return trip to the farm would take two hours, we didn't wait for the shops in the Al Akaria mall to open. Instead, we went to Safeway to buy groceries. We loved Safeway because it was a reminder of home and one of the few stores in the country that stocked a large number of American brands. To our dismay, Safeway pulled out of Riyadh a couple of years later, because the Saudi partners continually demanded a greater percentage of the profits. Recent reports from friends in Riyadh are that Safeway is alive and well again, testimony to consumers's love of the American store.

While Safeway operated in Riyadh, we became acquainted with the American manager. He told us about some interesting problems that were unique to grocery stores in Saudi Arabia. Unflavored gelatin was banned in the country, because most brands contain pork gelatin. For the same reason, most brands of marshmallows could not be sold. Only those made with beef gelatin were allowed.

With each new item that Safeway imported, we felt more at home. We were so excited when the first shipment of chocolate chips arrived, and our husbands were overjoyed when a few Mexican food items became available. The corn tortillas came in a can and tasted almost like cardboard, but we pretended that they were delicious. Although milk was a local item, it sold for SR 3 (86 cents) a quart, the largest quantity marketed. The expense of the milk was partially because there had been no fresh cow's milk in Saudi Arabia until 1979. Startup costs had yet to be fully recovered, and the special handling of the cows necessitated by the intense heat remained expensive.

Soon after Rachel arrived, she and Brent and Terry and I were invited to spend our New Year's Eve with Hafeez. Hafeez took us to a swank Chinese restaurant in Riyadh and ordered numerous entrees, which we all shared. Hafeez insisted that we remain until midnight to ring in the New Year officially. He offered each of us the opportunity to telephone home on his bill, although I'm sure that Al Emar paid. After we made several quick phone calls and the clock struck midnight, we began our two-hour trip home.

We were carefully navigating the almost deserted streets of Riyadh when a police car appeared in the rear view mirror. We were the only car on the road, so we couldn't lose ourselves in the traffic. Terry drove as carefully as possible, but we realized that the police car had its signal turned on for us to pull over. We couldn't imagine what was the problem, but had no choice other than to stop.

Both Brent and Terry emerged from the car and met the two Saudi policemen at the back of the vehicle. Rachel and I could see that they were asking for a driver's license. Terry handed over his United States license, and both the Saudi men studied it. It soon became apparent that neither man read English. After asking repeatedly in Arabic for the Saudi license, and Terry's pointing repeatedly to his U.S. license, the policemen gave up. Rachel must have been really frightened. She had been apart from Brent for more than three months, and I knew that she had no wish to visit him in a Saudi Arabian jail. The Saudi policemen then began questioning Terry and Brent about where they had been and why they were out on the streets of Riyadh so late. Terry explained in Arabic, as best he could. Finally, the two police seemed satisfied and told Terry and Brent to go back to the Al Kharj area where we belonged and to stay there.

After that New Years in Saudi Arabia we were inclined to pass the occasion without celebration. One year, however, we loaded up our bus and with nine other friends, attended a New Year's Eve party at the Khoeler's in Al Kharj. Dave and Deanna Khoeler were from Nebraska and, along with their three children, were in Saudi Arabia working for Arabian Auto Agency. We had many enjoyable times with them, including their

New Year's Eve party. There was an abundance of food and fun, as well as some homemade liquor and a small quantity of commercial spirits. We then returned to Hafeez's spacious and beautifully decorated villa. Up until this time, the only alcohol that we had seen came from homemade stills and was a 185-proof concoction made from water, sugar, and yeast. The bootleggers, mostly Americans and Europeans, called the mixture, *sadiqi*, "my friend," in Arabic. A number of our group partook and as we started home, we realized several of the young men were visibly drunk. We placed those who had drunk the liquor in the middle of our group in the van, hoping to disguise the problem, just in case we were stopped.

When we were about halfway home, Pat, an Irishman who was then employed on our farm, hollered out something that sounded like, "Let me out," just before he vomited, right in the middle of the van. There was nothing to do, of course, but to pursue our course home, hoping that no one else would be ill. We made it back to the farm without further incident.

On another occasion, Pat took the van to the dairy about thirty miles from us and once again indulged heavily in the homemade brew. On the way home, in the wee hours of the morning, he misjudged the distance between the van and the guard railing on the side of the road and smashed the van into it. Although everyone on the farm and in the head office knew the cause of the accident, Pat's only penalty was to pay for the parts needed to repair the van. From that day on, the van's right door never closed properly, reminding us that alcohol really was available in Saudi Arabia.

While Rachel and Brent were with us in Saudi Arabia, we attended one of the most important events in the Kingdom, the King's annual camel race in Riyadh. It was the only year we were able to attend. We were told that the camel races began at 9:00 A.M., and, although we left the farm at 7:30, we didn't find the track until 10:30. The track was almost an hour's drive from Riyadh, out in the desert. Once we were fairly close to the site, we followed other cars to the exact location.

There was a tall barbed wire fence around the track, and to our dismay, only people with written invitations were admitted inside. The national guard stood around the perimeter, making sure those on the outside didn't get in.

Although the temperature wasn't too warm for a March day, the dust blew. We stood around the fence, watching the small jockeys parade their camels for the crowd. Rachel and I were jostled several times by young Saudi males who evidently wanted to brag that they had brushed against an American woman. Quite a few of the males snapped pictures of us, because cameras were allowed in public for the special occasion. It was evident that we were about the only females standing outside the fence. The people with invitations, on the inside of the fence, were representatives of some of the large companies, such as Mobil and Shell, who were working in Saudi Arabia.

Needing to find a rest room, Rachel and I decided finally that we had to get inside the fence. As we approached the opening in the fence, we saw guards turning away others who were trying either to talk their way or slip in. After almost five minutes of discussion with a guard concerning our need, he allowed us to pass through, with a promise that we would return in five minutes. As we walked through the gate, a cry went up from the crowd in protest that we had talked our way in.

Once inside, we decided to walk around and investigate, making a quick stop at the rest room first. Men in uniform were passing out free canned Pepsi, compliments of the King. A Bedouin was selling small plastic bags of various nuts and seeds from a wheelbarrow. Rachel and I kept wishing there were some way that we might sneak Brent and Terry in so we could all watch the races in grand style. We walked about one hundred yards from the fence where they were standing and tried to scan the immense crowd that had now assembled. Then we heard Terry yell and spotted him at the fence. He and Brent had been desperately scanning the crowd for us, because we had been so long in returning.

As we waved and smiled at them, a polite Saudi man touched my elbow and asked if those were our husbands and did they want to come inside. He motioned them to go to a nearby gate that he opened for them to squeeze through. Once again the crowd around Terry and Brent protested loudly. We found our way to some vacant seats and enjoyed a free Pepsi. Rachel had brought chocolate chip cookies, so we had a snack.

When the King arrived, all of the Moslems in the audience, including the soldiers standing around the fence, joined him in the noon prayer. Then a band dressed in typical Saudi garb marched down the track, playing a variety of instruments, including bagpipes. Finally, the race that had been scheduled for 9:00 began at 12:30.

We didn't hear a gun shot to start the race, but within minutes we heard what sounded like distant thunder and realized that the camels were racing toward us from out in the desert. The nineteen-kilometer race was not very exciting until the Saudis began driving their vehicles onto the track in their excitement to get closer to the action.

Once the camels were on the track area, we were able to see them more clearly. We laughed at their awkward gait. Each camel had an Arabic number painted on its neck to distinguish it from the other camels. The jockeys were little boys about nine years old. Some of the camels were outfitted with saddles, and some were not. As the winning camel crossed the finish line, there was no pomp and circumstance and no announcement of the winner's name. The prizes, furnished by the King, were quite expensive items that included a water tanker.

Two problems on the farm that constantly irritated Rachel and me were that both the generator and the water storage tank were incapable of handling the loads they needed to carry. These problems had been my constant companions since my arrival on the farm. As a result, we were frequently without power almost all day because the generator had shut off and the electricians were miles away. Without fail, the generator would shut off when one of us had a cake in the oven or was about to apply makeup by electric light. Sometimes, the freezer compartments in our refrigerators almost defrosted, leaving us drippy messes.

Likewise with the inadequate water tank, we were constantly running out of water at inopportune moments. When Rachel and I were allowed to drive, either of these two inconveniences would cause us to stomp out to our vehicle to go in search of Brent or Terry. If the condition could not be remedied, we drove over to Joy's house to wait out the problem. Both situations were remedied when the farm purchased a larger generator and Terry asked the gatekeeper to fill the water tank every morning, regardless of its level.

Because Charles worked on a much smaller farm with only eight center pivots, he took off more often to go to town. He was usually accompanied not only by his wife, Joy, but also by Rachel and me. Charles enjoyed telling everyone that we were his three wives. I'm sure many of the small-town Al Kharj shop owners believed him. Charles was one of the rare men who enjoyed shopping and prowling through grocery stores and local markets.

Rachel and I felt like real troopers, living in the desert, and we became more adventurous and resourceful. One time we desperately needed to go to Riyadh, but our vehicle just limped to Al Kharj. Unwilling to admit defeat and turn around, we hailed a Saudi taxi and with our driver, now a passenger, continued on to Riyadh. The ride cost us SR 120, ($34.30), but the experience was well worth the money. When we went by our head office, we discovered that Sheikh Latif was headed for the farm, so we hitched a ride back in his Mercedes! I experienced the smoothest ride of my life as his Mercedes clipped along at ninety to one hundred miles per hour.

After Rachel's first year, Al Emar assigned us a twelve passenger van and driver, so that we no longer had to vie for a spare farm vehicle for travel. Even after Rachel and Joy left Saudi Arabia, I continued to travel on my own with my driver. I would pick up a group of women and take them shopping in Riyadh. It was always a fun mixture of personalities. Many times I went to several farms in the country and job sites in Al Kharj, picking up women for a day out in Riyadh. We shopped all morning and ate lunch at Hardees, a hamburger quick stop. To splurge, we sometimes ate lunch in a hotel.

We always drew stares when we entered Hardees, because there were usually ten of us unveiled women, parading into the establishment without a male companion. Our driver never ate with us at Hardees because an average lunch of a sandwich, French fries and drink was approximately SR 14 ($4). The driver always knew cheaper places to eat, where he might order a quarter of a chicken and rice for SR 5 ($1.43). The Filipino men who worked in Hardees got to know us quite well. Many young Saudi entrepreneurs, who chose Hardees for their lunch break, began to recognize us. Some of them made bold advances, enjoying the opportunity to flirt with foreign women.

After lunch we always descended upon a grocery store. As long as Safeway was still in business, we enjoyed going there and usually shopped in the modern facility for at least an hour, savoring the feeling of home. It was always a challenge to find a place for all of our purchases on the two-hour return trip. Many times our laps were piled with sacks from our excursions to Safeway. All in all these excursions were multicultural affairs. Over the years, the women who rode in my van included Americans, British, Germans, Danes, Irish, Filipinos, Indians, and Pakistanis.

Although we enjoyed prowling the new Al Akaria mall after it opened, our favorite places to shop were the older suqs or markets. Deep within these markets were rows and rows of small gold shops, clothing stores for children, carpet stalls, kitchenware, and bulk spices in baskets, along with general Saudi wares. Sitting on the ground outside these shops were Sudanese women selling nuts and seeds and sometimes canned drinks that were not cold but were wet and quenched our thirst in the hot temperatures. We usually traveled as a pack through the suq, with those who liked to bargain for prices bickering with shopkeepers. Soon after we left Saudi Arabia, we were dismayed to learn that the oldest suq area was scheduled to be torn down so that a Grand Mosque could be built alongside the Justice Palace.

One of my most memorable occasions in Saudi Arabia was when Rachel and I attended a Saudi wedding. The only males allowed to see a Saudi female's uncovered face are her husband, father, brother, and son; therefore, weddings follow society mandates and are separate affairs for males and females. Rachel and I were invited to Jewaher's sister's wedding. We had never met this sister, but were still excited about going to a Saudi wedding. The party was held at the grand ballroom of the Inter-Continental Hotel in Riyadh, and we were told to arrive between seven and eight in the evening. Rachel and I were dressed in our nicest, albeit practical, long dresses.

When we arrived, we attracted attention not only because our faces were uncovered, but also because we were the only foreigners present. It was quite evident that we were completely underdressed. The event was a fashion show with dresses ranging from silk and taffeta to velvet. The style of the dresses went from 18th century to high fashion, all in floor-length versions. We took a seat in the middle of the large room to observe the women as they arrived completely covered in black and slowly unveiled their costume for every eye to behold. The room where we were seated contained about six hundred chairs, and by 11:00 P.M. every seat was taken. Seated on one side of the room were a large group of women who remained completely veiled. We learned later that these ladies had not received invitations, but upon hearing of the grand festivities, had chosen to crash the party, remaining veiled to conceal their identities.

As women streamed in, what appeared to be the band congregated on stage and began to play. The band members were large Sudanese women, most with toothless grins, playing bongo-type drums. The music had a calypso beat, and the band members sang in monotone Arabic. Many young guests edged to the center of the room and swayed to the music. Other women soon joined them, but there were never more than eight on the floor at a time. The dancing consisted of feet shuffling back and forth from front to back, and shoulders shimmying. The girls with longer hair lowered their heads and whipped their hair around and around in a circle. The crowd of women clapped their approval the faster the hair whirled.

From eight to eleven, Arabic coffee was served three times, and sweet hot tea, unusual juices, and dates stuffed with almonds and rolled in sesame seeds were served once. Servants floated among the crowd with containers of burning incense, more than likely frankincense for such an elite affair. Women allowed the smoke to permeate their hair and as much of their gowns as possible. Although we were hungry because we hadn't had supper, the various drinks quieted our hunger pangs.

At eleven o'clock, as if on cue, everyone began covering their faces, and the bride and groom entered the room. The bride was dressed in a beautiful white wedding gown, and the groom wore the typical male garb with a long, white flowing robe. They were preceded by three little girls dressed in green and gold sequined suits. They each carried a decorative brass bowl containing incense. Several other girls served as attendants, probably sisters to the groom because their faces remained uncovered.

The bride and groom walked rigidly to the front of the room and up the stairs to a platform readied with two ornate chairs. They took their places in the chairs, and the three little girls knelt at the couple's feet. The bride and groom exchanged no words, but they smiled and nodded as various women approached in their veils and took pictures. Four girls with very long hair then stood in front of the couple and danced, swinging their hair and swaying to the music. After about thirty minutes the couple departed; Jewaher had video taped the entire ceremony. I learned, interestingly enough, that the bride does not attend the men's ceremony, which is not necessarily held the same day as the women's ceremony.

At approximately 11:45 everyone moved hastily toward the exit doors. We were hustled along with the crowd to an adjoining room by one of Jewaher's relatives. The women who crashed the party pushed and shoved to ensure a place at the meal. The room was a maze of tables filled with food and places set for five hundred. Each table, piled with food, seated six people. We were seated quickly, and our hostess departed.

As a courtesy, Rachel and I waited for the other spaces at our table to fill before we began eating; however, we noted women at other tables eating in great haste. There were varieties of Arabic delicacies, including shish kebabs of lamb, beef, chicken, and shrimp on piles of saffron rice; vegetables in *laban;* lamb and rice; chicken and rice; many salads and fruits; stuffed grape leaves; sambosa; stuffed pies of phyllo dough; meat balls; bell peppers stuffed with rice; shrimp cocktails; jello molds; and a coconut-pistachio dessert. Bottles of apple juice and water sat at each place setting.

Rachel and I ate little because we were watching the other women attack their food. Many of them used large soup spoons to ladle food onto their plates; most of them eventually abandoned their spoons to eat directly from the serving platters with their hands. Within minutes, the first group that had been seated had bolted down their food and given their places to someone else. Incredibly, many among the second group didn't wait for clean plates but began eating off their predecessors'.

We lost our appetites and owing to the lateness of the hour, rose to depart. In the center of the room was a huge wedding cake from which women hacked off chunks with table knives and hands. The cake was never formally cut before we departed. Deciding that we should at least taste a Saudi wedding cake, we ventured close enough to grab a piece of the ten-layer cake. It was very dry and heavy, similar to an American fruit cake, with a very hard, white icing.

Because we didn't leave the party until 1:00 A.M., it was nearly 3:00 A.M. when we arrived at the farm. We learned later, from Jewaher, that after we left, there was more dancing and that most of the women left around 2:30 A.M. Many weddings don't conclude until three or four in the morning.

Several days after the wedding, another sister of the bride came to the farm for a visit, and we had an opportunity to ask her about Saudi weddings. She told us that the bride's father pays for the wedding. The wedding dress is made by a tailor, who uses pictures from European magazines. There is no formal ceremony in a Saudi wedding, but in some families, the father of the bride writes a letter explaining that he is giving his daughter to be married, and the groom signs it. Later, the letter is recorded in court. In many families, there is no paper or written agreement, only a verbal agreement. Because most couples who marry are distantly related, the written agreement isn't very common. Even if the written agreement is not used, the couple is legally married. The groom gives a dowry of money and gifts to the bride and her family when the marriage is agreed upon. The average cost of an opulent wedding is equivalent to one year's living expenses for the newlyweds.

A less pleasant memory of Saudi Arabia, from which I bear scars, are sand fly bites. Although I never saw a sand fly, because they are smaller than can be seen by the naked eye, I was bitten three times. The one on the back of my knee and the one on the back of my arm were small and didn't cause any alarm. The bite on my left arm looked so awful I covered it with a patch solely for cosmetic reasons. Terry had a huge one on his neck, that left a scar he still bears today. Brent had a small one under his arm, but Rachel was never bitten.

The sand fly is a flesh-eating parasite that is so tiny it can come through the screen on a door and window. We heard of all kinds of cures for the bites, including assorted types of ointments and creams. Cash, the nickname of a man named Cecil Ash who had joined our farm, lanced Terry's sore with his pocket knife. It became so unsightly that he covered it with a bandage, also.

The sand fly bites were common among the people who lived out in the desert, and we were approached by people on the streets who gave us advice about how to heal them. Finally, we heard of an Egyptian doctor at a small hospital in Riyadh who treated the bites. One day when we were in Riyadh, we stopped by the hospital, only to discover that the doctor was not available. We made an appointment for the next Sunday. I actually believe that the main reason Terry finally decided my bites were serious enough to merit going all the way to Riyadh to see a doctor was the proximity of our impending vacation. It was April, and Terry didn't want to take me back to the States in another month, looking as if I'd contracted leprosy.

We decided Brent should probably go along with us because he also had a bite, and, of course, Rachel went along for the ride. After almost two hours in the waiting room, we were all three admitted into the doctor's office. After a quick examination, the doctor declared that Brent's bite had never become infected because he was actually immune to the bite. He diagnosed Terry's as being almost cured and not requiring treatment. He claimed, however, that all of mine were active and would have to be frozen.

He requested a cylinder of liquid nitrogen, which arrived after another lengthy wait. The doctor struggled for several minutes to extract the gas, only to pronounce that the cylinder must be empty; I would have to return in another week. He charged us each SR 200 ($57) for the visit.

I returned the next week only to discover that the cylinder still had not been filled. When I tried to schedule another appointment, I was told that the doctor was going on vacation to Egypt for three weeks, and I would have to wait. I explained that the doctor had said that it was imperative that I have the bites frozen as soon as possible. The receptionist only shrugged.

After the doctor returned, the cylinder was filled and my bites were frozen. He again charged me SR 200 ($57), and told me that I probably didn't need to return. Initially, the bites looked worse, but gradually began to heal, leaving a scar. To our relief, we were never bothered by sand flies again.

Chapter
Twenty-Seven

After what seemed like interminable lounging in the desert, Rachel and I decided to combine our talents and become desert entrepreneurs. We noticed that the gas stations along the highway sold all kinds of packaged bakery cookies. The cookies looked good, but they were virtually tasteless. Rachel and I decided that we could out-bake our competition with some real American cookies, including our specialty, chocolate chip. We ran a feasibility study and constructed a professional looking package in which to sell them.

We approached the owner of the gas station closest to our farm, calculating that we should start small. He agreed to sell our cookies at his gas station for SR 6 ($1.70) per package, but he wanted SR 2 (57 cents) for himself. We calculated that we could each make about twenty packages a day, and at that rate, accumulate quite a bit of spending money by the time we went on vacation.

On the first day of our baking venture, we could hardly wait until noon for Brent and Terry to come home to tell us how many of our cookies had sold. We were both disappointed to learn that only two packages had sold. Our husbands encouraged us by saying that once word got

around about how good they were, the cookies would be selling like hot-
cakes. As the days passed, however, our sales didn't improve. The gas
station owner decided to drop the price to SR 5 ($1.42), but he still
wanted SR 2. Finally, after several weeks of throwing out cookies that
didn't sell, we decided to abandon our baking business. We were disappointed to discover that not only had sales of the other cookies actually
increased during that time, but most of our cookies had been purchased
by Brent and Terry.

Rachel and I baked cookies constantly, not only for our business, but
also as gifts for the workers. Somehow two years went by before we considered buying our own groceries, so that we could prepare and eat our
meals at home. During those first two years, we were so determined to
save every penny we made that our own enjoyment of food didn't enter
into the picture. Eventually, however, all four of us grew tired of the
canteen food. The monotony of the menu was getting to us. We knew
that the sanitary conditions in the kitchen weren't equal to our own standards of cleanliness. We couldn't blame the lack of sanitation entirely on
the cooks, because the canteen kitchen was desperately in need of repairs. The holes and spaces were wide enough for any bug or rat to enter
into the kitchen. Brent seemed to have a continual case of dysentery,
and the rest of us were plagued with it occasionally.

Finally, the straw that broke the camel's back was when Terry found
a fly in his spaghetti. Our Friday night treat was spaghetti, made from
minced mutton, but that particular night, his portion included a dead
fly. We immediately asked Hafeez, the general manager, for a food al-
lowance so that we might buy our own food to cook at home. Terry began a rigid cleanup campaign in the kitchen to ensure that the workers
would be fed decent, healthy food. Cooking our own meals changed
our outlooks dramatically. Not only did it engage us and occupy our
time, it made shopping for groceries much more fun. No longer were
we limited to buying ingredients for our cookies.

One of the most glamorous discoveries that we made in Saudi Arabia
was that of the Saudi diamonds. We would never have discovered them
except that Rachel and I became good friends with a charming American lady from Alabama. We first met Linda Blackwell at a cooking class
that we attended at Hotel al Khozama in Riyadh. Linda wore a huge
diamond drop that appeared to be more than two carats, and we assumed
that her husband had a highly paid job with a computer consulting firm

called BDM Corp. Linda was very personable, and when she discovered that we lived ninety miles out in the desert, she invited us to her compound for a swim.

We scheduled a date and brought our swimsuits. Although the compound was located in the center of Riyadh, the garden area surrounding the pool was lush and green. We commented on the beauty of Linda's diamond, and she leaned over to whisper, with a smile, that it was a fake diamond, but a real stone. She was amazed that we hadn't heard about Saudi diamonds, because they were the latest craze among Western women in Saudi Arabia.

Saudi *Qaysumah,* or diamonds, are found along the border between Saudi Arabia on the south, and Kuwait and Jordan on the north where the Trans-Arabian Pipeline approaches the village of *Al Qaysumah.* The *Jeddah Journal,* February 10, 1982, told of a time when the Arabian Peninsula enjoyed a wetter climate. Cobbles and pebbles of igneous and metamorphic rock and quartz along with limestone, sand, and silt were washed from the Hijaz mountains toward what is now called the Persian Gulf.

To find these gems, "diamond" hunters scan the surface of the pebbly Qaysumah desert, looking for a telltale warm glow amid the rocks. Because the angle of the sun is all important in producing the glow, the best times to search for the stones are early morning and late afternoon, ideally between May and September. Once found, Qaysumah diamonds are polished and cut in standard diamond, emerald, and amethyst faceted shapes. The clear Qaysumah diamond is from the same family of microcrystalline minerals as the amethyst and smoky topaz. On the Mohs' Scale, used for gauging the hardness of gems, Qaysumah diamonds have a hardness of seven, compared to window glass at five and true diamonds at ten.

Linda sent her Saudi diamonds by a friend to Thailand, where diamond cutters cut and polished the stones, choosing the loveliest stones to be mounted in 14 karat gold. Rachel and I were anxious to return to the farm to search for Saudi diamonds, because we were told that the stones had migrated to our area. Although we eventually found several stones that resembled Saudi diamonds on one of our many treks around the farm, we were never sure if they were the real thing. We each eventually bought a Saudi diamond already cut, polished, and mounted in gold from a man in Riyadh. He had a large collection of the Saudi diamonds and had showings in his home. Before buying from this man's collection, we inquired about Saudi diamonds at a Riyadh jewelry store, called the White Diamond. Although the jewelers there knew exactly what we were describing, they claimed it was not legal to cut and polish the stones within Saudi Arabia.

Although Rachel and I would both become pregnant in Saudi Arabia, our first close friend to become pregnant there was Evelyn, the Filipino wife of Cash, the farm employee who lanced Terry's sand fly bite. Cash was a sixty-year-old Texan hired by Sheikh Latif after we'd been in Saudi Arabia for several years. Cash, well liked by everyone on the farm, told many tall tales and stories. He became engaged to Evelyn, a Filipino girl, through a Filipino pen pal service. He flew to the Philippines to marry a bride who was thirty years his junior and whom he'd never seen.

Rachel and I liked Evelyn and enjoyed learning about Filipino culture through her. She kept her skin as fair as possible by walking outside in the shade of an umbrella. She was a real bargainer and was always convincing Filipino workers in different businesses to give her free gifts. One time we all walked away with a free hamburger from a fast food restaurant in Riyadh, thanks to the Filipino employee's generosity and Evelyn's tenacity.

Evelyn became pregnant soon after she and Cash were married. Rachel and I took her to the free government hospital in Al Kharj, but after waiting interminably in a room packed with women, most of whom had to sit on the floor, we decided it was worth paying to see a doctor. We decided to take Evelyn to the Egyptian doctor whom Terry saw for his allergies. He gave Evelyn medicine for her morning sickness and some prenatal vitamins.

After we left the doctor's office, we went to the fruit market in the center of Al Kharj. While Afzal, our Pakistani driver, purchased the fruits and vegetables for the canteen, Rachel and I walked about a block down an alley to a bakery that sold the extra thick flat bread. Evelyn was tired and decided to wait in the van.

After buying the steaming hot loaves of flatbread, we were returning to the van when a middle-aged Saudi man with glasses jumped in front of us, shouting in Arabic that we needed to wear a veil. I asked him in Arabic if he was a *Mutawwa*, a religious police. At first he claimed that he was but later admitted that he wasn't. While we hurried toward the van, we explained to him as calmly as possible that we weren't Moslem, and it wasn't necessary for us to be covered.

We tried our best to ignore him, but another man farther down the alley heard the commotion and fell in step with the first, also shouting that we needed to be covered. Because we were both dressed modestly in long dresses with long sleeves, we didn't feel culpable; we simply walked faster and faster to the van.

When we got to the van, we told Afzal to drive away quickly before prayer time started. The first Saudi man had followed us all the way to the van, now shouting at Afzal. We urged Afzal to drive on, but by this time a crowd of men had surrounded our van, and one of the men stood directly in front of the van, pretending that he was writing down our license plate number.

Rachel stuck her head out of the window to say that we didn't have to wear a veil, deliberately including Sheikh Latif's full name in the statement. We observed that several of the men registered recognition, when they heard the name. Meanwhile, in the midst of all the confusion, Evelyn sat smiling and drinking her Pepsi, as cool as a cucumber.

The Saudi in the glasses planted himself at Afzal's window, trying to convince him that we needed to cover our faces. Afzal responded that we were Christian and not obligated to cover. The man then asked Afzal for his company papers, and Afzal gave him a phony paper to see if he could read. The man pretended to study the paper, but it soon became evident that he couldn't read. The man returned the paper, along with a tablet, and said that he wanted our names, Afzal's name, and our company name. Afzal diligently pretended to comply, but told us later that he wrote some phony information in his native tongue of Urdu.

With haste, Afzal handed the tablet back to the man and started the engine. The crowd dissipated as quickly as it had formed and allowed the van to creep away, although the man in the glasses continued shouting. As we were almost out of the parking space, Evelyn suddenly came to life. She tapped on the window, waved at the enraged Saudi, and smiling, called, "Bye, Bye!" The man lurched at the van, but we had the doors locked, and Afzal sped out toward the main road.

We found out later that a group of women from the dairy had been in Al Kharj earlier in the day and also had been accosted by the same man for not having their faces covered. Surprisingly, that incident was the only time that a Saudi male suggested that I should cover my face.

While Rachel lived on our farm in Saudi Arabia, perhaps our most unusual relationship was with an American woman married to a Saudi man. Kay had met her husband-to-be when she was only fourteen years old, and he was a twenty-one-year-old student at a junior college in her hometown. She was instantly smitten by his charm and married him early in her seventeenth year. Kay's hometown where she met her husband, was Levelland, Texas, only two hours from my hometown of Crosbyton. She discovered from a hometown newspaper article that we were in Saudi Arabia and made contact with us.

Kay explained that during the early years of their marriage, her husband, Fawaz, adopted American customs, but then suddenly decided it was time to move his bride back to Saudi Arabia. Fawaz changed gradually into a strict, conservative Moslem husband. She explained that her life changed from being treated as an American woman who went unveiled wherever and whenever she desired, accompanied by a driver, to being treated as a Saudi woman, who had to veil and who could make many fewer decisions on her own. Kay bore Fawaz three sons during the first eight years of marriage, so she was doing fine in the baby-making department. Fawaz gradually began to restrict her freedom, and when we came to know her, he had insisted that she cover as a Saudi woman and not to go out with other Western women.

Kay invited Rachel, Joy, and me to spend a few days with her in Riyadh soon after the birth of her fourth child, a girl name Danyt, or little pearl. As Arabic tradition dictated, her middle name was that of her father, Fawaz. The most astounding part of Kay's story was that she discovered that her husband had found another wife in Jeddah. Fawaz was in Jeddah during the birth of their daughter, looking for a second wife. Kay claimed that he had gone through all of the formalities of marriage except the consummation had not occurred, because he discovered that the woman's family had lied about her age, claiming she was twenty-five instead of thirty-one. He backed out on the deal and now, a matchmaker in Riyadh was looking for a younger wife for him.

Kay told us that in the past, she and the children returned home every summer to visit her family. Then Fawaz joined her and they returned to Saudi Arabia together. After she learned of his desire for a second wife, she wanted to remain in the States and not return to Saudi Arabia, but she was afraid that Fawaz might keep the boys. The story sounded like a Middle Eastern soap opera, but it is a common one among such mixed marriages. Our contact with Kay gradually ended, but I learned that eventually she and the four children were successful in leaving Fawaz and returning to the States, permanently.

Female companionship improved my life in the desert dramatically, yet we all felt trapped so far from civilization. During one of the long winters, Terry and I planned a short trip out of the confines of the farm to the neighboring country of Egypt. Charles and Joy agreed to take us to the airport. They arrived to pick us up in time to make the two-hour trek to the airport, with a few minutes to check in. As we were speeding through the desert toward the airport we had to pull over to secure a loose radiator cap. All of the water spewed out of the radiator, leaving us unable to drive the automobile. Tempers and temperatures were hot, because I knew we'd miss our flight. Charles and Terry walked toward the desert where they could see a well. Terry spotted an empty water bottle and, to our great fortune, they were able to fill the radiator with water from the well. What a stroke of luck that our misfortune occurred right next to a well and a container on the lone highway. We arrived at the airport as the last economy seat was assigned and wound up enjoying first class seats, even though our tickets were for economy.

Because we had seen the eastern coast of Saudi Arabia on our trips to visit friends in Aramco, we wanted also to see the western side of the country on the Red Sea. Jeddah is the most prominent city on the west coast and the most modern city in the Kingdom. Jeddah was an important center for the caravan trade between Egypt and the Orient during the sixth century. It was considered to be more liberal than other cities in Saudi Arabia because as a seaport city, it had long been exposed to outside factors. The city boasts a population of two million. The name Jeddah itself means Grand Mother in reference to the Biblical Eve. The Moslems believe that Eve came to this city looking for Adam and then died. While we were there, we viewed what is known as Eve's grave. Another famous guest who passed through the Jeddah area was Lawrence of Arabia. The city was reconstructing the building where he is said to have stayed. Many of the Western workers took extended weekend trips to Jeddah to enjoy the beach. There was an abundance of sand native to the beach area, but to please royal tastes, the sand along the Royal Cornice in Jeddah was imported from Belgium and Sweden.

In March 1986, we planned the trip to Jeddah with a charming couple from England, Jean and Alec Coverly, who were living in Al Kharj and working for the electric company. Jean was a good friend who always went on the van trips to Riyadh. She had once been a hairdresser, so she cut our hair and gave us permanents. Jean and Alec were also members of our square dancing group. The four of us joined a Riyadh scuba diving group that was making the trip to Jeddah. Many people learned to scuba dive in swimming pools in the middle of the desert and then went on real dives in the Red Sea off the coast of Jeddah. Before going, we had heard that Western women were allowed to wear knee-length dresses and that on many of the private beaches, men and women were allowed to swim in the sea together. Despite Jeddah's liberal reputation, Jean and I were disappointed to discover that just as in Riyadh, we were not allowed to use the swimming pool because we were women.

The Red Sea is beautiful, and the coral and fish underwater are fantastic. We were only qualified to snorkel, but we saw jellyfish, puffer fish, rainbow fish, and even an octopus. I could hardly believe that I was in the same Red Sea that had parted for Moses centuries before.

Shopping was fun in Jeddah, although we had a frightening experience in a carpet store in an older shopping district in the heart of the city. We were inside the carpet store when the call for noon prayer time began. This meant that all stores would be closed from noon to four o'clock. We ignored the call, along with Jean and Alec, in an attempt to finalize our purchases. A *Mutawwa* appeared at the door of the shop and shouted accusations. Before we could react, the Afghan shopkeeper, shaking with fright, locked the shop door and ran into a back room where he locked himself in. Meanwhile, the *Mutawwa's* shouting had drawn another *Mutawwa*, a regular policeman, and a large crowd of spectators.

The *Mutawwa*, both older men with gray hair, continued shouting, beating on the door, and walking from window to window, rattling each to see if one was unlocked. Terry, Jean, Alec, and I were all crouched behind large piles of carpets, peeking occasionally at the window. We knew that our efforts were futile, because the *Mutawwa* had clearly seen us and knew that we were hiding. The *Mutawwa* shook the stick he was holding, indicating that he was about to break a window.

We all agreed that we should emerge from hiding at the same time and approach the window. Terry tried to open the door, only to discover that it was locked from the inside with a key, and the shopkeeper had taken the key with him. We gestured to the *Mutawwa* that the door was locked from the inside, but our movement only seemed to enrage them more. Alec and Terry walked to the back of the store to persuade the shopkeeper to come out. Jean and I scurried after them, not wanting to be left vulnerable through the clear glass. After a few moments of persuasion, the shopkeeper emerged from his locked closet and shuffled toward the front door with the key.

As soon as he had unlocked the door, the two *Mutawwa* and the policeman burst into the store. The crowd pressed toward the door as closely as the policeman would allow. The shopkeeper talked excitedly in Arabic, trying to convince the *Mutawwa* that he was in the back praying and didn't realize that we were still in the store. The oldest of the two *Mutawwa* grabbed the owner's collar and whacked him hard across the shoulder with his stick. A cheer went up from the crowd when the blow was delivered. The Afghan winced with pain and cowered from the religious authorities.

The policeman turned on us, almost as if he had forgotten we were present, pushed us out the door of the shop and gestured for us to leave. We fought our way through the crowd, literally running to the hotel bus that had delivered us for our shopping trip. I'm sure that if we had been of a Third World nationality, we would have been dealt with in the same manner as the shopkeeper. The driver of the bus, a Pakistani, was almost beside himself with worry. He had observed the entire incident from inside the bus and figured that if anything happened to us, he would lose his job.

We learned that the normal penalty for not closing a business establishment for prayer time was five days in jail. At the *Mutawwa's* discretion, however, a shop may be closed permanently. We felt guilty because we were at fault for not voluntarily leaving when the call to prayer sounded. We had been too intent on completing our purchases, and I know the shopkeeper wanted to make the sale.

Despite our disquieting incident, we continued to explore Jeddah—one of the few places in Saudi Arabia that is actually preserving and restoring its past. Most historic sites in other parts of the country have been replaced with modern shopping centers or left to decay. In Jeddah, many newly constructed buildings have the same wooden frames around the windows as the architecture in the old buildings. Numerous old dwellings, as old as five hundred years, still stand, and almost all of them are inhabited, even though they were made of coral and limestone and put together with date paste for cement.

Jeddah is an oasis in the desert, but this feat was not achieved without time and money. In 1928, it was said to contain only one tree. Today, there are five million trees in Jeddah. Also, the municipality spends four and one-half million dollars a year for cleaning and maintenance. The streets are swept twice each day.

Before oil was discovered in Saudi Arabia, Jeddah's main and almost only income was revenue from Moslem pilgrims passing through on their way to perform the *Umrah*, the "lesser" pilgrimage to Mecca, often a prelude to the Hajj, but acceptably performed at any time of the year. At the time of our visit, instead of collecting money from pilgrims, the generous citizens of Jeddah were said to give money to their Moslem brothers from poorer countries.

On one of our day outings we passed the entrance to Mecca, noting the many signs and warnings that divided traffic between Moslems and non-Moslems. Failure to follow the directives may result in a person's vehicle being impounded, leaving him stranded in the desert. We also were able to see, from a distance, the newly constructed megatents, a thicket of 210 fiberglass tent modules that shade thousands of Moslem pilgrims on their way to Mecca. The desired tent effect was achieved with a costly substance known as Beta yarn, a Teflon-coated fiberglass, stretched taut by cables, grommets, and tension rings. The airy tent's life span is short, usually twenty to thirty years, and construction costs are often as lofty as the structures themselves. Recently, the International Stadium in Riyadh and the King Abdul Aziz Sport Center in Jeddah also had been constructed of the same material.

Jeddah appeared to have been suffering somewhat from over expansion at the time we were there. Hotels were hurting for business, and many newly constructed complexes stood empty. Construction of the world's largest hotel/shopping center had halted because of the lack of money, owing to the drop in oil prices.

The royalty seemed to be unaware, however, of any financial crunch. They continued to build palace after palace, all heavily guarded. Once a new palace was finished, all existing structures within viewing range were purchased for security reasons. The beautiful Inter-Continental hotel fell to such a fate after the 1985 completion of King Fahad's new Jeddah palace. Also for security reasons, the Sheraton Hotel became occupied by the National Guard.

King Fahad commissioned a yacht to be built in Denmark at a cost of one hundred million dollars. The vessel, which was sometimes docked near Riyadh, could sleep sixty guests, and each cabin was fitted with a marble bathroom with gold-plated fixtures. Two swimming pools, a ballroom, a gym, a sauna, a theater, and a fully equipped hospital with operating rooms and an intensive-care unit were included on the yacht. The 482-foot-long vessel was constructed in secrecy to prevent spies and potential terrorists from obtaining information that could be used in an assassination attempt. The yacht even carried four American-made Stinger missiles, each capable of shooting down an enemy plane.

Chapter Twenty-Eight

Although the Saudis imported Americans to manage their farms, they still enjoyed wielding control. We heard stories of Saudi bosses who got in the way of work, driving exasperated farm managers to resign from their positions. John Zielske reported that his Sheikh reprimanded him for planting wheat on November 15th, a date that the Sheikh declared was too early. John stomped back to his house and returned with his diary of the preceding year, to point out to the Sheikh that he had told John, the year before, that November 14 was too late to start planting.

The Saudis were sometimes fickle and never prompt, but they could be quite generous. After several years, we began farming two pivots for Abdul Rahman, who was married to Jewaher's sister and who had taken us to the John Deere distributor in Riyadh our first year in the Kingdom. On one occasion, he gave Terry a heavy, wool floor length coat like the Saudi men wear in the winter. I'm sure the coat was very expensive.

During one season, Abdul Rahman challenged Terry to produce a total of four hundred tons, or eighty bushels per acre of wheat on his two pivots. Terry accepted the challenge, and Abdul Rahman offered to buy him a Rolex watch if he succeeded. The two pivots actually produced 411 tons of wheat. This was not an extraordinary feat, considering we averaged 100 bushels per acre of wheat on seven thousand acres. We had never seen wheat so lush coming from West Texas where we grew twenty- bushels-per-acre dryland wheat. Because a Rolex watch was an expensive item, we were skeptical whether Abdul Rahman would maintain his end of the bargain. We were elated when he drove up to our house one day, after harvest was completed, to present Terry with a brand new one. The following year the pivots produced yields that were as good as the previous year. After harvest, Abdul Rahman asked us to stop by his office in Riyadh where he presented a Rolex watch to me.

The Rolexes weren't the only gifts we received in Saudi Arabia. During the five years that we lived there, we were given many gifts. After two years of working closely with them, the Sri Lankan workers invited Terry and me to join them in the men's quarters one night, after we ate supper in the canteen. After serving us cookies, canned cheese, and Pepsi that they had purchased from the gas station, they presented us each with a Seiko watch. Someone had written, in calligraphy "Mr. Kirk" and "Mrs. Kirk" on our respective watch boxes.

Kalapuhana, one of the workers who was fairly fluent in English, gave a short speech of appreciation. The gifts meant a great deal to us, because we knew the sacrifice that these men made to buy them for us. Many of the men supported poor families back home in Sri Lanka, which made their sacrifices even more poignant. Kalapuhana became a good friend and a prized employee, who advanced from a common laborer making $125 a month to a management position with a salary of $1,200 plus per month. He was the first Sri Lankan to be promoted to management. Terry recognized Kalapuhana's leadership qualities and initiated the promotion, forever changing the course of his life. Kalapuhana would later become farm manager and move into our house.

The workers continued through the years to present us with gifts. Many times the gifts were unusual souvenirs from their countries. One time a Sri lankan returned from vacation with a cake wrapped in newspaper for me. It was several days old, but had weathered the trip successfully. Proudly, I took several photographs of the cherished cake.

Sheikh Latif gave Terry a really fun gift. After a holiday trip to Greece, Sheikh Latif sent word by one of the workers that he wanted to talk to Terry. He was at the fish ponds when Terry approached. He smiled broadly and presented Terry with a 36-inch-long remote-control electric boat. Sheikh Latif was as excited as a schoolboy when he explained to Terry that he had purchased one for himself, also, so that he and Terry could race against each other on the fish ponds. The boats cost one hundred dollars apiece, and Sheikh Latif insisted that Terry take his boat back to the States for his future sons.

Despite Terry's efforts to produce the best possible yields of wheat, we were at the mercy of unforeseen problems as are farmers everywhere. An unforgettable accident occurred in January at P1 during the wheat season of 1984. Pivot 28 encountered disaster in the middle of the night. Because the pivot was irrigating only half a circle, it was programmed to rotate as a windshield wiper, back and forth rather than in a complete circle. Owing to some failure in the mechanism, the pivot continued traveling in a full circle and hit a neighbor's pivot. The neighbor's pivot was unharmed; however, our pivot was damaged and required several new span pipes. Remarkably, the pivot was repaired without too much difficulty.

We had another problem with our farm workers that caused us constant concern. Although they were willing to labor at any task, they were not trained in farm skills. Many had never been on a farm. For this reason, they often took dangerous risks. One of our favorite workers, a Sri Lankan electrician, Wigatelica, was to check and service a number of the engines on each pivot. One morning he was examining an engine that had a water leak. The area all around the engine was very muddy. In his haste, Wigatelica slipped into the mud and fell onto the spinning drive shaft. He was very fortunate not to have lost a limb, and to have escaped with only a skinned arm. By law, in the States, the drive shaft must be covered, but no such law existed in Saudi Arabia, and most Saudi farmers viewed the covers as unnecessary.

In another incident, disastrous weather struck. While we were still living in the container, we had invited several of the area farmers over for dinner when a foul wind began to blow, and we sensed that the weather was changing. Between 8:30 and 9:00 P.M. hail fell, accompanied by rain and heavy wind. The wind blew such torrents of rain into the generator that it shut off, and we were without electrical power. The generator couldn't be repaired until midafternoon the next day. Everything in the freezer thawed into a dripping mess.

The wind and rain knocked down the wheat, or as the Saudis say, caused the wheat "to sleep." The storm was followed by a night of gentle rain. The tarp that was held down by large rocks on the top of our trailer house blew off, and large puddles of water leaked into the container.

The rain brought the city dwellers out to the country to play in the puddles of water.

One of the more unusual aspects of life in Saudi Arabia was the way the Saudis handle and regard accidents. Moslems believe that if a person is killed in a car accident, it is the will of Allah. They believe that if the person had not died in the accident, he or she would have died at that time in some way.

This attitude was evidenced in an article that we read in *Newsweek* in 1990, after we returned home. During Islam's most important holiday, Feast of Sacrifice, 1,426 pilgrims to Mecca had died. During the rush to perform a final ritual, some fifty thousand people had jammed into a space designed for one thousand. King Fahad, whose titles includes "Custodian of the Two Holy Mosques" responded, "God's will. . . .. Had they not died there, they would have died elsewhere and at the same predestined moment."

Yet this fatalism was not always apparent in the police's handling of tragic accidents. Once a group of John Zielskie's workers had gone into town on a Friday in a farm vehicle with a Sudanese man driving and the two Egyptians riding in the front with him. The pickup had a blowout, and two Egyptians were thrown from the car and killed. The Sudanese man was barely hurt, but was taken to jail because, according to Saudi law, there should have been only two people in the front seat. Although this law was rarely enforced, the police were holding not fate but the Sudanese man responsible for the deaths. Under Saudi law, the families of the two dead men were allowed to demand either blood money from the Sudanese man or his head.

The Sudanese man was given a certain amount of time to raise the necessary sum. He was trying to accomplish this by collecting money from his fellow Sudanese. If the man could not come up with the full amount, he would be beheaded. The situation was even more tragic because one of the dead Egyptians had been scheduled to go on vacation in three days, after having worked in Saudi Arabia for two years. The man had a wife and six children back in Egypt. We never learned what money was actually raised or paid, but we were relieved to know that the Sudanese man did not lose his head.

Terry often came upon accidents that had occurred on the road between P1 and P2. One of the more unusual accidents occurred one morning about six. Terry saw a white Chevrolet Caprice in the ditch, turned on its side. Upon closer examination, he discovered that the driver's head had been crushed by the car. The lone man was dressed in the traditional Saudi garb, and the body was trapped inside. The police soon arrived on the scene, evidently summoned by another motorist. By this time, several cars had stopped, and a small crowd gathered to watch the police. As they carelessly pulled the body from the car, all the observers were shocked to note that the victim was a woman dressed in male clothing. We surmised that she was either fleeing an unhappy marriage or some other desperate problem that had forced her to do something as unthinkable as dressing as a man and driving a car. Evidently, she knew little about driving, as would be the case with most Saudi women, and had lost control of the vehicle.

One of the most incredible accidents occurred early one morning as Terry drove to P₁. A truck had overturned in the ditch, and Terry stopped to make sure that the survivors had been rescued. As he approached, he heard a loud moaning. He crept closer to the truck. Miraculously, the driver, a Pakistani, was still alive, pinned underneath the vehicle. Terry tried unsuccessfully to pull the truck off the man without injuring him further. He raced to the other farm for a tractor and help to assist him in removing the truck. Terry instructed the men to transport the hysterical victim to the hospital in Al Kharj. What was most incredible was that there were two Egyptian farmers on a plot of land within one hundred yards of the accident who didn't come to the aid of the screaming victim. They stood in their field, watching the entire rescue attempt without offering comment or assistance.

On one of our nighttime trips home from Riyadh, we encountered another traffic accident. The other managers had ridden with us in the van to Riyadh for dinner. On our way home, we happened upon a group of vehicles stopped in disarray along the highway. A man had fallen asleep at the wheel, or had been traveling too fast, and had rolled his car. It was now lying upside down about thirty yards off the highway. Terry and the other men left the van to see if they were needed. A number of Saudis were standing around, looking and talking, but no one was offering aid. Terry and the other managers pushed their way through the crowd of spectators to discover that a young boy was trapped beneath the car. Quickly, they lifted the car off the little boy. A woman, probably the mother, who had been thrown several feet from the car, was crying hysterically. Once the car was moved, several papers blew out the window of the car, and the father of the boy scrambled to retrieve them. The Saudis continued to stare and talk. We drove away to alert the police.

It seemed that no trip to Riyadh was without incident. On one particular trip, Joy, Rachel, and I, in the company of our driver, were again headed for Safeway when we came upon a traffic accident. A car in the center lane had stopped in the flow of traffic to make a left hand turn, not an uncommon practice for Saudi drivers, and caused a three-car pileup. Our driver threw on his brakes in time to avoid hitting the car in front of us. We thought we had escaped the accident, but a car from the rear hit us. The bumper on our van was completely destroyed. Someone called the police. Our driver was a shy Sri Lankan who barely spoke English, so we got out of the car and asked the man who had struck our van to give us his name. He refused. The entire entourage of crashed cars created quite a scene in the middle of the highway, with three American women standing in full view.

After we had waited almost an hour for a policeman to arrive, a young Saudi man stopped his Mercedes to help us. He explained in excellent English that he had been in the United States for six months and loved it. When the police arrived, he did all of the talking for us in Arabic. When the police left, the man gave us his name and telephone number and invited us to be his guests for bowling at the health club where he was a member.

Perhaps the most tragic accident that occurred on the farm happened to Jewaher's only brother. Jewaher's father had two wives and, although both wives had produced more than ten daughters, he had only one son. This brother, who was twenty years old, was out at the farm during a family gathering. He and a cousin were hunting in a pickup. The brother drove and the cousin sat on the passenger side with a loaded .22 rifle resting on his lap. The vehicle hit a bump in the sand dunes and the rifle went off, shooting the brother in the temple. He died at the farm. The family, though extremely grieved, held to the traditional philosophy: *insh Allah*, "if God wills."

Chapter
Twenty-Nine

During several wheat seasons, the farm workers, along with Brent and Terry, spent much of their time chasing camels out of the circles of golden wheat, ripe and nearing harvest. Many nights, Rachel and I sat together in camp or rode in the pickups, enjoying the camel chases. Bedouins, whose camels were caught in the pivots, claimed that the camels had wandered away from their camp. Terry posted night guards who discovered that the Bedouins were intentionally herding the camels into the wheat. The Bedouins would appear from nowhere and herd the camels back into the desert.

After many chases, our head office suggested that we confiscate the camels that we chased out of the pivots. Soon we had a large herd of camels penned in our camp. Naturally, we also had angry Bedouins with whom to contend.

Because of the grazing camels, we finally resorted to building a fence around each of the two farms. Workers built fence during the day; Bedouins tore it down at night. The constant bickering between the farmers and the Bedouins began to ease as the combines rolled, harvesting the wheat. The Bedouins were then content to set up residency in the harvested wheat fields, moving in with tents and animals to glean any remaining kernels and have their fill of wheat stubble.

After the farm began to grow forage, we had a problem with Bedouins' stealing the alfalfa bales. Although stealing is strictly forbidden in the Koran, the Bedouins justified taking the alfalfa in the same way they did helping themselves to the watermelon patch—the goods were on what they considered their land. After bales had been stolen on several different occasions, Terry resorted to setting up boards with nails sticking up so that the culprits wouldn't escape without at least a flat tire as a souvenir.

One particular camel chase occurred with Bill Beason, a fellow Texan who had joined our management. He was in his pickup trying to remove camels from a pivot of wheat, when three Bedouins in a pickup began chasing him. In the normal sequence of events, the Bedouin men would herd the camels or sheep onto the pivots early in the morning, leave the women to watch the animals, and then drive away. Terry or Bill could not have forced the Bedoin women away, so they just drove off the animals. The women always raised their hands, hollered, shook their fists, and threw rocks.

Terry drove up, saw what was happening, and began chasing the three Bedouins who were chasing Bill. At about the same time, a man we called the Colonel, another farm worker, of Arab descent, fell in beside Terry in the chase.

The Colonel loved to chase Bedouins from pivots. Now the tables were turned; with two vehicles chasing them, the Bedouins fled. At that instant, Terry and the Colonel spotted the rarely seen ring leader of the Bedouins in another vehicle and took off chasing him.

The chase turned into a mad dash, with Terry's passing the Bedouin ringleader at a speed of 120 kilometers per hour (75 m.p.h.) across virgin sand. Terry drove alongside the Bedouin, trying to force him to stop, so that they might talk. Both vehicles slowed to a speed of about thirty kilometers per hour (18 m.p.h.) and were running neck and neck. The Bedouin stuck a shotgun out the window, and immediately the door unlatched and swung open. He attempted to load the gun as the pickup continued moving.

When Terry saw the gun, he accelerated his pickup and raced ahead. In the excitement, the Bedouin man jumped out of his pickup for a clearer shot. He had forgotten to take his pickup out of gear, so the vehicle kept going.

The sight was hysterically comical as the Bedouin ran alongside his vehicle, trying to climb in, at the same time hanging on to his gun. Unable to look ahead, the Bedouin didn't notice a sand embankment in his path. Both the pickup and the Bedouin ran headlong into the embankment. The farmers surrounded the vehicle, and the Colonel and a companion who had been riding in his pickup hauled the Bedouin off to the desert police station near our farm.

Terry assumed the matter was finished, until he was summoned to the police station. The Bedouin admitted that he had a gun, but he also claimed that Terry had one, as well. It was almost impossible for a foreigner to obtain a gun in the country of Saudi Arabia, a fact of which the Bedouin was probably unaware.

When Terry arrived at the police station, the chief of police on duty was a good friend of Sheikh Latif's, who also liked Terry. Terry joined the group of policemen, squatting outside the precinct, drinking coffee and eating dates. None of the policemen questioned Terry about possessing a gun. The Bedouin was also in the circle and all appeared jovial. Suddenly, the Saudi employee, who had been with the Colonel, and the Bedouin began arguing, shouting accusations at each other. The policemen made no move to halt the loud talk, waiting with interest to learn the outcome.

Finally, in exasperation, Terry took off his farmer's cap and waved it back and forth, saying, STOP, in Arabic. Terry turned to the policemen and suggested that they allow the two men to box to settle the argument. The policemen and the two men who were arguing laughed at the idea of a boxing match and settled down. The Bedouin, flashing a toothless grin, promised to keep his animals from the pivots, and Terry left with everyone smiling. The Colonel was relieved to be able to leave the police station with everyone in a good mood.

The Colonel was a memorable character. He was really a colonel, retired from the Pakistani army. Sheikh Latif had hired him to relieve the management of some of the work load. His job was to manage the camp facility, a duty he took very seriously.

From the moment he stepped on the farm, the Colonel made enemies. He rationed commodities such as bread and ketchup in the canteen, although these items had never been consumed in extravagance. When the Colonel limited quantities of these items, bulk amounts began disappearing from the canteen. He organized monthly meetings of all camp staff, standing in front of the group, lecturing about various topics, including fire safety. To add to his other self-imposed titles, he appointed himself camp fire marshal and security guard.

The Colonel soon became the brunt of many practical jokes, none of which he found humorous. One of the most memorable was played by Joe Kent Keith, a Texan hired to manage the vegetable project.

Joe, six-and-a-half feet tall, from Guthrie, Texas, was as humorous as he was tall. Everyone on the farm liked him, because of his loud and brash way of making everyone around him feel good and enjoy working with him. Joe adopted a dog soon after his arrival and in honor of the Colonel, named the dog General.

Joe's assistant in the vegetable project was a tiny Sri Lankan, called Pee-Bee, who was only five feet tall. Although he was probably forty-five-years-old, his size and demeanor made him seem childlike. Everyone liked PeeBee, even though they teased him constantly. Joe presented him an award that certified him as a Horticultural Vegetable. Although the certificate made PeeBee the brunt of many jokes, he was extremely proud of his certificate and asked Joe to write him a letter of recommendation before he eventually returned to Sri Lanka.

Besides naming his dog General, Joe badgered the Colonel unmercifully, to the delight of the remainder of the camp. After the Colonel's self-appointment as fire marshal, Joe piled a stack of wooden pallets in a deserted area of the camp, ignited them, and shouted, "FIRE." The Colonel rushed to his vehicle, intending to be the first person on the scene of the fire. Joe, however, had placed the Colonel's vehicle on blocks, and when the Colonel jumped in his pickup to race to the fire, it didn't move, despite his diligent efforts. Naturally, a crowd gathered around to watch the prank, much to the Colonel's embarrassment.

The vegetable project was a story in itself. Because some of the surrounding farms were experimenting with vegetables, Sheikh Latif expressed a desire for Terry to incorporate them into the Green Sands plan. Originally, Terry requested specific vegetable drills for planting the tiny seeds. With the arrival of the planting date and no vegetable drills provided, Terry carefully planted the various seeds with a wheat drill, directly under one of the circles that had formerly been the home of wheat.

The seeds thrived under the hot sun and water from a pivot. Soon the circle was a lush green color, sporting such vegetables as corn, squash, carrots, cabbage, okra (called lady finger in Saudi Arabian markets), eggplant, and tomatoes. Sheikh Latif had been in the States during the planting of the vegetables. On his visit to the farm he gazed upon the lush crop and immediately sent a Sri Lankan to fetch Terry. As he surveyed the different hues of green and textures of leaves in a perfect circle, with a broad grin on this face, Sheikh Latif told Terry that he had just returned from Imperial Valley, California, and he felt as if he were still there. The vegetable experiment lasted only a year and a half, even though Joe did a great job with it. The vegetables grown on the farm were of excellent quality and bumper capacity. Yet the marketing of the produce fell flat, leaving the harvested vegetables to rot.

A problem arose on Al Kharayef, a farm comparable in size to ours, when Bedouins settled on the pivots after harvest and their sheep drank contaminated water. The wheat pivots were equipped with fertilizer injector tanks that allowed the farmers to distribute fertilizer directly through the pivots at the same time water was applied. Gordan, an Englishman who worked for Al Kharayef, removed an injector tank from a pivot that had been harvested. He filled the tank with water to rinse out the remaining chemical and emptied the contaminated water next to the pivot.

Within hours, a group of Bedouins set up camp on the pivot and watered their sheep from the puddle of water. Because the water contained some urea, it killed all of the Bedouin's 140 sheep. The Bedouins went to the police, who in turn apprehended Gordan. He spent two days at the jail, including three hours in a jail cell. After much deliberation, it was decided that Al Kharayef must pay SR 500 ($142.85) compensation for each sheep that died. The decision caused much consternation among the farmers in the area. The Bedouin had been trespassing, yet the farm company was held accountable for the death of his sheep.

During the harvest season, we enjoyed watching Sheikh Latif walk across the fields of wheat in his long, white *thobe*. One day he brought his wife, Jewaher, their two sons, and his mother to the farm. The entire group crammed into the cab of the combine as Sheikh Latif demonstrated to them how to drive the equipment. If his mother hadn't been in the cab, I would have dared to take a picture of all the Saudi faces peering through the glass, watching the golden grain as the combine harvested the wheat. I feared that Sheikh Latif's mother would never consent to having her picture taken and would be very angry if I sneaked a picture of her on the combine. Although harvesting was a stressful, busy time, the months of hard work paid off as the seeds of wheat from the combine poured into the grain carts. Rachel and I baked some kind of treat every day for the workers involved in harvest.

Terry came up with an idea at the end of our second season that proved to be beneficial to the company and challenging to the workers. After all the pivots had been harvested, Terry allowed each driver to take a combine onto any of the previously cut pivots to clean up any wheat left in the field. The driver harvesting the most wheat in a three-hour period of time was awarded a bonus of SR 250 ($71.50). Because there were quite a few different drivers, they drew straws to see which three-hour shift they would drive. In the end, two Filipino drivers tied, each cutting

2.5 tons (5000 pounds) apiece. All of the drivers together gathered an extra 13 tons (25,000 pounds) of wheat. That 13 tons of wheat was worth $8,000 and only cost Al Emar SR 500 ($150) in bonuses. The contest became an annual event on both P1 and P2.

When the Saudi government began to subsidize their wheat program in 1980, they probably had no idea how much wheat would be produced. Even though the Saudi government promised to pay a premium price for the wheat, they were slow to pay the Saudi farmers. As the farming industry in Saudi Arabia grew more sophisticated and yields were maximzed, the government enacted several new regulations. For example, at the end of one particular season, immediately before harvest, we had trouble transporting diesel to the tanks to run the Caterpillar engines that pumped our water and provided electricity. The gas station near us delivered diesel to the farms, but on many occasions the diesel trucks were broken, and farms, including ours, were going without diesel. The wheat could not live a day without water during the hot season with temperatures above 110 degrees. To produce water, the pumps had to have diesel, so we sent our own drivers with trucks from the farm to collect the fuel. The government soon declared that drivers who transported gas or diesel must have a heavy equipment driver's license. The driver's license building was overrun for several weeks with drivers applying for the necessary licenses. In the meantime, the wheat suffered.

The government dropped another bomb when it inflated the price of diesel by seven hundred percent from eight cents per gallon to fifty-six cents per gallon. The price of gasoline doubled also, from around twenty-five cents per gallon to fifty cents per gallon. Both price increases were enacted on the same day. Because the irrigation engines were diesel, our farm operation consumed more than twenty million gallons of diesel annually. Despite the increase in fuel prices, the Saudi farmers still made a tremendous profit on wheat that earned thirty dollars per bushel, the government subsidy price. This was a stark contrast to the three dollars that American farmers were receiving.

When the government planned its domestic wheat production program, it neglected one of the most important aspects of the entire farming program—storage for the harvested wheat. The government built grain silos in various locations across the country, intending to store the wheat in these silos. After the first year of subsidy, with many farms making as much as one hundred bushels per acre of wheat, every government silo was full. Because world market price was one tenth the price the Saudi government was paying its farmers for wheat, the Saudis began shipping boat loads of wheat, as gifts, to different Third World countries. The amount of wheat used in Saudi bread production didn't put a dent in the stored wheat. After the first-year glut, farms such as ours spread tarps on the ground and dumped the wheat on them until the government would accept shipment. If the piles of wheat kernels were peaked in tall mounds, rain water could run off the wheat without causing much damage.

The government erected more silos, but dust had blown into the mounds of wheat and had to be removed before it was augured into the silos. This operation was one of Terry's biggest headaches. He rigged up a system of fans and augers to clean the wheat. It was dirty, time-consuming work. Once a pile of wheat was removed, Bedouin women wandered into camp with burlap sacks and begged to clean what was left on the ground. The Bedouins then had the wheat ground into flour.

Our company decided to erect its own silos the following year. Through a company in the United States, Sheikh Latif hired a man named Leon, from Georgia, to erect five silos on the two farms. From the beginning, the silo project was a disaster. Leon and the two men he brought with him were accustomed to working with experienced men who knew what they were doing.

Because they were erecting the silos in the midst of harvesting, the experienced farm workers were already busy. The crew that Leon worked with was composed of men who were dispensable on other jobs or temporary workers that the head office had sent from Riyadh. Most of the workers had never held a wrench or done any kind of work similar to the task of erecting a grain silo. While Leon trained his crew in the basics of construction, Sheikh Latif and Hafeez breathed down his neck, wanting the silos erected as soon as possible. They made surprise trips to the farm and caught Leon not working a few times. He was not motivated to work on the silos with the unskilled labor available to him.

Finally, with work on the silos progressing so slowly, they offered Leon an extra two months' salary as an incentive to finish the job quickly. Evidently Leon burned out and was unwilling to work, no matter what the price. We were surprised to learn that Leon and his two American helpers hid their luggage in a vehicle one Friday and asked Steve, the Englishman and the current workshop manager, to take them to Riyadh to shop. Once they were in Riyadh, they convinced Steve to take them to the airport, and they flew out of the country.

To leave Saudi without Sheikh Latif's help would have been impossible except that the visitors visas that the men had come in on were exit-reentry visas, good for three months, and time had not expired. Therefore, they still had their passports and could leave unquestioned. This type of visa is usually issued for two-week visits for business contacts. Having only completed two silos, Leon left us with the parts for three unassembled silos. Hafeez boiled with indignation, incredulous that someone would pass up an opportunity to make money. After a few days, the head office sent a note to the farm saying it was going to take legal action against Steve for taking the men to the airport. Of course, Steve was very upset, but with little cause because there was nothing the head office could do to him legally. Leon had told Steve that if he didn't take them to the airport, they would take a taxi. Steve decided to quit and left the country before he had completed his contract.

One would think that another contractor would have been hired immediately to finish the silo job. Yet our company waited until the following year, when once again we were in such a bind for the silos that we had to dump wheat on the ground.

Chapter Thirty

The last year that we were in Saudi Arabia, I began to write my thesis for my master's degree in Home Economics, from Texas Tech University, Lubbock, Texas. This was the biggest personal challenge that I faced while I lived in Saudi Arabia. I had worked on my degree before moving to Saudi Arabia and planned to write my thesis on home economics education for women in Saudi Arabia. Because I was totally unfamiliar with the education system in this country, I procrastinated; I did not know how to collect the information that I needed. Finally, I approached Jewaher and asked her to help me get started. I was surprised to learn that she had a sister with a master's degree in home economics from a college in Riyadh.

At Jewaher's suggestion we visited the girls side of the private school that her son Ziad attended and talked to some of the teachers. Jewaher explained that they sent Ziad to private school because the government schools teach very little English. Naturally, we visited only the girls school, because males and females are separated in school from kindergarten through college. It was very evident that schools in Saudi Arabia aren't open for outside inspection. If I hadn't been with Jewaher, an influential parent of a student in the school, I would have never gotten past the front door. With Jewaher, however, I talked to the head mistress and interviewed the home economics teacher. Even though they both spoke limited English, they preferred to speak Arabic and have Jewaher translate. The information that I obtained there about the education system for females was useful, but I learned later that visitation to any school from the elementary to the university level by a foreigner is forbidden in Saudi Arabia.

I discovered my breach accidentally when Jewaher and I visited the college where her sister had studied home economics. Even though I wore a long dress, Jewaher suggested that I also wear an abaya for extra covering. Jewaher's driver let us out in front of the main gate of the college. Because the Saudi girls and women are unveiled within the confines of the school, all facilities are not only surrounded by high walls, but also are carefully guarded at the gates by men.

Jewaher and I fell in line with the young women streaming in through the main gate on their way to the first class of the day. I tried to blend in with the other women, but attracted attention because my face and hair were uncovered. I regretted immediately that I did not cover both my face and hair when the old man standing guard shouted *"Inglizi"* as I entered the gates. Jewaher did her best to outshout the old man by loudly explaining the reason for my presence in the college. He was immovable in his stance not to allow me to pass inside and avoided my gaze, probably because he was embarrassed by my uncovered face.

Jewaher and I returned to her car, where she explained that the guard had said that I would have to obtain permission from The General Presidency of Girls' Education. She assured me that her husband Abdul Latif would be able to get the permission for me without any problem. The General Presidency of Girls' Education is the governing body for female education in Saudi Arabia. Only one branch of this governing body, the General Bureau of Educational Supervision and Guidance, is composed of women. All other branches and departments of the General Presidency for Girls' Education are composed of men.

Little did we realize that day what I was truly up against in my pursuit of academic inquiry. Sheikh Latif was unable to secure permission for me and was told that foreigners don't need to study the Saudi Arabian school system. Another source advised me to obtain a letter of explanation from my thesis committee members on official Texas Tech University letterhead, to prove the legitimacy of my request. Several weeks later, I had obtained such a document from Texas Tech University, yet my request to visit schools was rejected once again.

I had just about given up when I explained my plight to Tariq, our young Saudi friend at Basil-Salmia farm. Tariq's father was Assistant Deputy Governor of Riyadh, and Tariq promised me that his father could obtain permission for me. I doubted the credulity of Tariq's statement, because I had been through months of failed attempts. I had forgotten that not only did Tariq's father hold a very prestigious position, but he was also married to a member of the royal family.

To my delight, in a few weeks, I was presented with written permission to enter the schools. Colleges were under a different jurisdiction, and although I was eventually granted permission to enter them, I was told I would have to wait until the following fall to enter women's schools beyond the high school level. Needing to complete my research well before then, I allowed myself to be smuggled into one of the women's colleges.

My cohort was an Egyptian female college student who was studying journalism. I met Amani when I was working on my literature review at King Saud University, a school for males only. Amani and I were both at the library, because females were allowed to use the brand new library (starting in 1987) on the males' campus from 8:00 A.M. to 2:00 P.M. on Thursdays. Classes were not conducted on Thursday or Friday, so the governing body allowed females to use the multimillion dollar facility on those days when males would not be there.

I was skeptical whether I would even be allowed entrance the first morning that I arrived to use the library. There was a mere skeleton crew of women working early the first Thursday that I arrived, so I managed to slip in with the other college students. I dressed in an abaya and covered my head. Once inside, all the women unveiled, and I felt that I was among friends.

During the six hours that the library was open to women, I collected the books that I needed, planning to do the actual reading at home. There was an extensive collection of Arab and Moslem books that had been translated into English, but I'm sure many would not have been available in the States. As 2:00 P.M. quickly arrived, I stood in line with the students to check out the books. When my turn came, the older librarian gave me a scrutinizing gaze and asked for my student card. When I shook my head that I wasn't a student, she gestured with a wave of her hand, for me to move on. I quickly presented my permission, obtained through Tariq's father, scripted in Arabic. She scanned the document, replying that because I wasn't a student in a Saudi university I could not check out a book. Almost in tears, I stepped out of the line and slumped on a nearby couch. Amani, one of the students who had observed the entire scene, came over and told me that she would check the books out for me with her library card. This offer began a wonderful relationship between this Egyptian student and me.

Not only did Amani continue to check out books that I needed, she also managed to take me inside the college, where I was surprised to see that behind the veils and coverings, the college students looked much like college students anywhere, except they all wore long dresses or skirts. One girl even wore a Mickey Mouse t-shirt over her long, black skirt. Amani introduced me to home economics professors and females majoring in the field. Because of her, I obtained the information I needed to complete my thesis.

Amani also provided me with the opportunity to interview a famous Saudi, Prince Sultan ibn Salman ibn Abdul Aziz al-Saud, who had been the payload specialist on American space shuttle mission 51-G in 1985. Because Amani was a journalism major who also worked as a reporter for a Riyadh newspaper, she had already met and interviewed the Prince and arranged an interview for me. The Prince's male secretary scheduled the appointment for 10:00 P.M., not unusual for Saudis who sometimes don't retire for bed until two or three in the morning. His home was a palace. Terry, Amani, and I sat wide-eyed, while we sipped the carrot juice we were served and gazed around at the elaborate furnishings, while we waited for the prince.

The prince, one of the most eligible bachelors in Saudi Arabia, was gracious, warm, and receptive to every question that I asked. Concerning the future of education for females, he felt the opportunities were unlimited. He did stress, however, that because women and men must always be separated in public, there would continue to be limited job access for women.

When I asked whether his marriage would be arranged, as was the custom, he responded that he would prefer to select his own wife. Two years after the interview, I read in the newspaper that he had married a distant relative, with whom, I surmised, the marriage was arranged.

I continued to use my special pass to visit other school facilities, high school level and below, discovering that although male and female students are segregated, they take the same courses, except the two areas of home economics and physical education. Females are required to study home economics from the fourth through twelfth grades; they are not provided any form of physical education. Boys cannot study home economics, but take physical education classes instead.

In researching my thesis, I had to deal with the language barrier and get all of my documents translated from Arabic to English. I encountered other obstacles as well. Because women were not allowed to drive or enter certain public places unaccompanied, I had to have a driver and many times, a male escort. A written questionnaire would have been impossible to distribute, and few would have been returned to me. Moreover, to minimize the difficulties in communication, I assiduously avoided telephone interviews.

Despite the tremendous oil revenues, progress in early education in Saudi Arabia was impeded by lack of funds, poor transportation, and communication systems. Moreover, much of the country was unmapped and relatively unexplored, and there were great shortages of teachers. The majority of schooling for the masses was conducted strictly in the home. The *kutab*, as this early method of education was called, was religious instruction based almost entirely on the Koran, taught by a woman for girls and a man for boys. It consisted of very elementary tutoring in language, reading, writing, and math. Foreign education, even for males, was regarded with mistrust. In the 1940s, when a few boys were sent abroad to Egypt or to English boarding schools, mothers came to the late King Faisal's wife in tears, begging her to use her influence to prevent their sons from obtaining scholarships to study abroad.

In the early 1960s, the illiteracy rate for the age group of fifteen to twenty-four years was no less than 95 percent in Saudi Arabia. Because of the high rate of illiteracy, a concentrated effort was made to expand primary and intermediate schools. Nonetheless, by the mid-1970s, few pupils who qualified for secondary education were enrolling. Most chose instead to join the armed forces or vocational schools or religious institutions. Recognizing the importance of education the government began encouraging its youth to pursue higher education.

In implementing its educational programs the Saudi government maintained a careful balance between curricula and Islamic directives. All educational framework has always been carefully screened and approved by the Ulama, the religious leaders in Saudi Arabia.

Nonetheless, it was not unusual at first for fundamentalist Moslems to predict that if a girl learned to write, she would soon start writing letters to men or would begin to argue with them. However, starting schools for girls was the special concern of the late King Faisal's wife, Iffat al Thunayan. She faced a great challenge by working for the education of females. At the same time she introduced Western subjects to the curriculum and sent students for education outside Saudi Arabia. Her work was not infrequently a cause for alarm in male educational circles.

The forerunner of formal education for females was the opening in Jeddah of a girls' institution called *Dar al Hanan,* the House of Affection, in 1956. The students were allowed to care for orphaned children, in direct compliance with the Koranic commandment concerning orphans. But even slaves and servants of the royal household were reluctant to allow their young female relatives to enter the House of Affection. Iffat tried to explain the need for such an educational institute with an article entitled, "The mother can be a school in herself, and if you prepare her well, you have created a generation with good roots." She pointed out that the goal was to produce better mothers and homemakers through Islamic instruction based on modern educational theories.

The first formal school for females was opened with the aid of the Saudi National Guard in September 1963, again with the help of Iffat. The National Guard was necessary to protect prospective students from the citizens of the town of Buraydah, who were trying to surround the school building. King Faisal said, "Tradition should be made the ally of development, not its victim." King Faisal sent the National Guard to keep the Buraydah girls' school open; however, no parents were forced to send their daughters to school.

Education for females has progressed and grown tremendously since its true beginning in 1963. Families are very eager to educate their daughters. By 1985, there were nearly 800,000 girls in full time education at the primary and secondary levels. Half of all female pupils who completed the intermediary stage of education in 1985 progressed to secondary school. Despite such progress, the basic value orientation of the society has not been shaken. For example, girls continue to be educated in separate schools by females, from elementary through the university level.

Saudi Arabia lacked a university of its own until 1957, when King Saud University was founded with nine instructors and 21 male students. It offered a program similar to liberal arts in the U.S. Because of the lack of universities and the prestige of studying abroad, Sheikh Latif, Abdul Rahman, and a large number of their peers studied in the United States. These men, educated in the States in the late 1970s, returned with worldly as well as academic knowledge. For this reason in part, the trend reversed, and graduates in the 1980s sought bachelor's degrees within Saudi Arabia at an increasing number of institutes of higher education. As a result, the Saudis who would be running the country in the next century were getting their education at home, instead of living abroad for five to ten years. This new generation of university graduates was much less comfortable with English and did not have the level of understanding of Western ideas as did the previous generation.

In 1987, there were eight universities for males in Saudi Arabia, a ratio of one for each one million in population. Saudi Arabia wanted to create a showcase for education, as evidenced in The King Saud University of Riyadh, which has been described as the largest project of its kind in history. The campus was completed by the fall of 1984, with construction crews from twenty-six countries. The university spread over an area of nine square kilometers, accommodating more than fifteen thousand male students and was built at a cost of four billion dollars. The sixteen academic buildings had 1,492 classrooms and laboratories, an eight hundred-bed teaching hospital, a two million-volume library, a pair of auditoriums, and a magnificent mosque. Buildings were grouped around a large concourse with a ceiling seven stories high and an inlaid marble floor that covered an area approximately the size of two American football fields. The enrollment of central and branch campuses of King Saud's University had grown to nearly 30,000 students, all of them male.

By 1987, however, for the first time graduates of universities in Saudi Arabia were facing a degree of uncertainty in terms of job possibilities. The Saudi economy was suddenly incapable of offering the kind of job opportunities that many young Saudi graduates envisioned when they enrolled.

Unfortunately, the typical graduate, not unlike those in other parts of the world, wanted only a managerial position. At one time, with the shortage of university graduates, a university diploma was a guarantee of a job. The job market was able to absorb the 3,000 students who graduated from King Saud in the spring of 1987 only if the graduates were willing to move to where the jobs were located. However, this situation was not uncommon, reflecting what was happening at many other college graduates in other parts of the world.

Part of the problem was the ratio of majors in nontechnical studies (seventy percent) versus technical studies and the sciences (thirty percent). For example in 1987, there were then 150,000 foreigners holding highly skilled jobs in the government grain silo project; Saudi graduates could fill these positions if they chose to study in the fields of science and engineering. Efforts were being made at that time to channel more students into these fields.

The problem in Saudi Arabia was that too many aspiring Saudis wanted a university degree, when there was a desperate need to fill medium-skilled jobs that required training in one of the country's 27 vocational centers. According to the director of King Saud University the Saudi people wanted a university education primarily for the status it carried, not as training for a job.

The number of females attending Saudi universities increased dramatically in the late 1970s, with the opening of a Teachers' Training College in Riyadh, the forerunner of higher education for females. The first university opened to women was King Abdul Aziz University in Jeddah in 1971. Women were taught by male professors via a closed circuit television system on Thursday evenings on the male campus. Because interaction between female students and male teachers was not allowed, it was soon decided that separate but equal facilities must be provided. The King Abdul Aziz University women's campus was the first in Saudi Arabia to give women facilities that equaled those of men. In most situations, university education for women in the Kingdom is relegated to older campuses formerly used by the males. All departments at the university level except engineering accept women.

The time I spent studying the educational system in Saudi Arabia made me realize the absolute gift that education provides. Education for women in Saudi Arabia created a whole new world for the Saudi female, providing her a chance to leave the home for personal growth not just for visiting or shopping. When I asked where the female college graduates would be employed, I was told somewhat vaguely that positions would be created within the educational system for females.

Chapter
Thirty-One

Perhaps our most enjoyable learning experiences in the desert were our visits with Midwess and his family. One starry night we sat on a blanket, drinking fresh camel's milk, when the discussion turned to camels. We found it strange that Midwess and his family were unaware that there are camels with two humps, because they had never seen one. With a stick, Midwess drew a picture of a two hump camel in the sand throughout the evening. No doubt, he was trying to imagine how one might look.

Even though we ate often with Midwess, and he ate with us occasionally, his family only ate with us once. I told Rashmi that I wanted to cook for her because she always cooked for me. Every time I took cookies out to their tent, she was interested in learning to make them herself. I showed her my oven whenever she came for a visit, but I wanted to demonstrate cooking a complete meal for her. Finally, the entire family agreed to come eat with us.

We had assured them that the women would eat in the kitchen, and the men would eat in the dining room. The entire family arrived exactly as scheduled, and I noticed that they all wore shoes or sandals, which they removed immediately once they stepped inside the house. I could see that they were clad in their best finery and were very nervous.

I served the traditional Arabic coffee and dates while we all sat together in the living room. I had decided that I should serve rice and chicken, because I knew that was accepted fare, but I did show Rashmi how to make chocolate chip cookies while they were there. The meal went very smoothly even though Rashmi refused to remove her veil to eat, as I had expected. She and the children ate very sparingly, probably unaccustomed to different flavorings in the dishes that I prepared. They all took seconds from the platter of cookies.

Rashmi was extremely nervous that the children might make a mess or bother something in my house. I sensed that she wished for a real house, where she would not have to worry about things such as bugs crawling on her baby. Although I killed many camel spiders and scorpions in my house, I felt much safer there than in a tent.

The highlight of the evening was showing a video tape on our television that we had taken with our new video camera. At various times, we had taken videos of us in our swimming hole on the farm and of Midwess and his boys. We played the scenes over and over for them because they were mesmerized by the miracle of the video. I knew that this would be the first and probably the last time that they'd ever see Midwess on television, and I'm sure it was a memorable moment in their lives.

Although the Bedouins live a remote, isolated life, we were surprised by their currency in world news, which stimulated long and impassioned discussions around the campfire. Many nights around the campfire, we discussed American-Israeli policy, Yassar Arafat and the PLO, or even Khadafi or Khomeni. At one time, someone from the United States sent us a cartoon of Khomeni, and Terry posted it in his office at the farm. A Bedouin wandered in, looked at the cartoon and recognized Khomeni. The Bedouin knew Midwess's close relationship with Terry and went straight to Midwess to demand that Terry take down the cartoon. Even after Terry explained the jest of the comic to Midwess, Midwess continued to urge him to take it down, which he did.

Bedouins didn't understand Americans' making fun of their enemies and absolutely couldn't fathom making fun of the president of one's country. The Bedouins spoke of King Fahad with great respect, worshipfully. As soon as Terry took down the cartoon, the Bedouin became a friend again.

This particular Bedouin, whose name was Saeed, wore a wide leather belt around his waist over his *thobe*. Attached to the belt was a long sword. The next time the Bedouin entered the office, Terry ceremoniously took out his pocket knife and opening the blade, hung it from his belt. Terry then put his arm around the Bedouin and stated as the Bedouins do, *"same, same,"* meaning *we are the same.* The man came by the office every day for the next week, insisting that Terry come to drink camel's milk with him.

Most of the encounters with Bedouins were positive and enlighten-
ing, but I had a few less cordial encounters. On one occasion, I was jogging around the farm and a Bedouin in an old, beat up pickup happened
to notice me. His companion had a worn pair of binoculars that he used
to watch me as they drove closer and closer to me. The pickup slowed to a
crawl in order to drive alongside me as I jogged, and both young Bedouins took turns staring at me through the binoculars! Because I was jogging as fast as I could at this point, I endured their stares from three feet
away until they realized I wasn't going to acknowledge them, and they
spun off into the desert, leaving me in a cloud of dust. I had to admit to
myself, of course, that their behavior could have seemed no more brazen
to me than mine surely had to them.

One of our greatest disappointments turned out to have a happy ending. Midwess announced one day that he was moving to Al Flaj, a small
community about 450 kilometers (270 miles) from where we lived. The
company had instructed Terry to encourage Midwess to find another
job, because we had no more bulldozer work to do. The desert terrain
had been cajoled into prime farming land, complete with asphalt roads
to every pivot. Midwess's brother purchased a gas station about twenty
miles out in the desert from Al Flaj, and Midwess decided it was time to
join him as a partner. Our farewells were tearful and sad, because we all
realized that we might never see each other again, even though we promised to visit each other. Midwess knew that life on the farm was continually busy and more than likely, we would never be able to visit him.
Rashmi and I had bumped up against the language barrier continually,
but had communicated miraculously nevertheless, and I knew I would
miss her sorely.

Happily, we did find a good excuse to visit Midwess and his family. Our
problems with Bedouins and their livestock camping and grazing in our
wheat had continued. The head office decided to hire a guard to patrol
the farms at night. The guard needed to be able to converse with the
Bedouins, and Midwess seemed perfect for the job. One of our workers,
a Yemeni named Faisal, volunteered to be our guide and went along
with us because he had relatives in Al Flaj. Faisal was twenty-four and
had been living and working in Saudi Arabia since he was sixteen. At
that time, North and South Yemen were separate, and Faisal was from
democratic South Yemen.

We left early one morning. Wearing my long dress, I climbed into the pickup between Terry and Faisal. It took us a little over five hours to reach Al Flaj, stopping here and there at lone gas stations to stretch and buy canned drinks. We drove through dust storms that were occasionally so severe that we could barely see the road. We passed through several oases in the desert, where there was a water supply and a few trees. After a couple of hours, we entered desolate country, driving for miles and miles without encountering any farms, towns, or cars on the road. When we passed the Layla Lakes, close to Al Flaj, we knew that we were near our destination.

Although we knew that Midwess's gas station was about twenty miles on the other side of Al Flaj, we had no idea of the exact location. When we stopped at a campsite of several tents to ask the location of Midwess Dowas's camp, the Bedouins seemed suspicious of two Americans and a Yemeni asking for Midwess and refused to talk. Terry tried to explain in Arabic that we were friends, coming to visit. The longer he spoke Arabic, the softer their faces became. Soon the older men with their toothless grins began smiling and pointing. I guess they figured that an American who spoke Arabic with a definite Bedouin dialect couldn't be too bad.

They gave us directions to the next gas station, where we hoped to see Midwess, but we were disappointed to find an Indian hired to manage the facility for Midwess. The gas station was connected to a tiny restaurant that sold the Arabic chicken or lamb with rice. The cook inside was also an Indian, who struggled to give us directions to Midwess's camp. He kept pointing and saying that Midwess's camp was back by the mountains.

Fearing that we had come this far only to be unable to find him, we bravely drove off the main highway, across the sand that stretched for miles in all directions. The landmarks the cook had given us were dips in the land and scattered sagebrush trees. After driving across the lake of endless sand for almost fifteen minutes, we were about to give up and return to the gas station, when we spotted a wadi. We drove in that direction where we could see camels and sheep. Long before either Terry or I saw anything, Faisal excitedly exclaimed that he saw a tent. Hoping that we might have discovered Midwess's camp, we drove on. We discovered a commune of tents, and our arrival created quite a commotion.

The men were congregated in a large tent on one side of the camp, and the women were in a tent on the other side. Children chased each other around the tents, sometimes throwing a stick or empty soft drink can at each other. Stray lambs wandered freely around the camp. Then we spotted Midwess.

He told us later that as we approached, one of the Bedouins announced that a white Chevrolet pickup was approaching with an *Inglizi* driving. Without even looking, Midwess boasted that he knew it was us. As we stepped out of the car, we were surrounded by curious men and children who had never been so close to Westerners. The women remained in the background because of modesty and custom, but came as close as they dared in order to get a glimpse of us. Even though it was almost 2:00 P.M. and too early for the Bedouins' main meal, Midwess insisted on sending someone to bring food from his restaurant.

The men drew Terry into their tent, and as I approached the women's tent, Rashmi ran and hugged me. She was so excited that I was going to join the women in their tent. As we sat down together, the women crowded around me, many of them touching my face and hair. I'm sure most of them had never even seen a white-faced woman before. I spoke very little Arabic, so our conversation was limited. Yet because Rashmi felt a kinship to me, the other women extended the same kindness. I had brought a large batch of chocolate chip cookies with me, and the women and children ate them excitedly in less than five minutes. Abdallah grabbed the cookie box, and put it on his head, playing with it until he completely destroyed it.

I was surprised to see one of the women bare her breast to nurse not only a tiny baby, but also a toddler of about three years. The curly haired, dark-skinned boy sat on her knee and jumped around as he nursed. None of the other women took any notice of her, so I tried not to stare. With great concern, the women asked Rashmi where I had left my babies. When Rashmi answered that I didn't have any, even though I had been married several years, I sensed their pity. The oldest of the women commiserated with me, patting my hand and saying something about Allah.

Midwess's brother's wife had a new baby who lay in a contraption that looked somewhat like an American Indian papoose board, but more like a hammock. The hammock, made from sheepskin, was suspended from two leather strips. The temperature was mild, but the sleeping baby was covered with several blankets. I was interested to discover the system for diapering in the desert. The baby didn't wear a diaper, but the bottom of the hammock had a layer of fresh sand. Although the baby wasn't especially clean, he didn't have diaper rash. I assumed this method of nondiapering had been used frequently for centuries among desert dwellers where water was scarce for washing.

Some of the women were sewing when we arrived and resumed their activity. It was amazing to watch the creations they made from the old, hand-cranked sewing machines. They measured with their hands, using different finger lengths as a gauge. Much of the measuring seemed to be guesswork, and I noticed that several times they had to rip out the seam and sew again. With great dexterity, they held the material between their toes when they were measuring.

I wanted to take a picture of the children, so the two oldest boys, Abdallah and Hidi put on little army suits, complete with hats and tiny play swords. The outfits were grimy and had buttons missing, but they were so proud of them and looked so cute. For the picture, two of the girls, who appeared to be about ten years old and whose faces were still unveiled, slipped on unfinished dresses that the women were sewing. Both girls had tiny sticks in their right nostrils, making a hole for a ring they would eventually wear. I had been unaware of this practice, because I had seen very few Bedouin women's faces. I believe they were afraid to remove their veils even if only women and children were present, not only because of modesty but also for fear that a man might well appear in camp unexpectedly. I asked them if they all had rings in their noses, and Midwess's sister lifted her veil to reveal a large, flat stud earring in her nostril. They nodded in agreement that they each wore one. I noticed that the sister's face was light and smooth compared to her skin that had been exposed to the sun.

The food arrived from the gas station's restaurant, and a small portion of the large platter from the men's tent was delivered to our tent by a young Saudi boy. Evidently I was the only one who was going to eat. I motioned that I wanted to share, even though the portion was meager. After several offers to share, Rashmi and her two small boys sat down and ate with me. I was self-conscious of my clumsy attempts to eat the rice and meat with my right hand. I tried to eat very quickly. While we were eating, a tiny lamb wandered into the tent, sniffing the aroma of the food. Only when it was within an arm's length of our food, did Rashmi quit eating and chase it from the tent.

As soon as I finished eating, one of the women brought out the traditional tiny box of Tide and poured water over my hands while I rubbed them together. I explained to her that I needed to go to the bathroom, so Rashmi jumped up and folded back a piece of the tent to reveal a barrel. She left me and returned with water for washing, but I had thought to carry toilet paper in my pocket this time.

I glanced back into the tent to see Rashmi combining our leftovers with the remains from the men's platter. She quickly ate a few more handfuls before summoning the other women to eat. I joined Rashmi as the other women practically attacked the remainder of the food. Terry told me later that the men's large platter had been piled with rice and lamb. This saddened me because the women had never been able to go into the restaurant to eat, I'm sure they'd rarely, if ever, eaten restaurant food.

We sat down together again, and one by one the women returned to our original circle. Several minutes were spent in complete silence as they studied me, and I gazed out the tent flap into the desert. When they became more comfortable with my presence, they began talking to each other. Several times I realized that they were talking about me, but their words seemed positive. As we talked, we shared dates and Arabic coffee.

They opened one of the old trunks and after sifting through several layers of material, one of the women produced some *nougat*, like I had seen Rashmi and Mama making from goat's milk, when they lived on our farm. The taste was bitter and sour, but the women put a piece in their mouths and took a quick drink of hot, sweet tea to wash it down. I did the same and was able to swallow the delicacy.

After a couple of hours, Terry walked about half way between the men's tent and the women's tents and called my name. The women quickly checked their veils, even though Terry didn't come close enough to see anyone. I left the tent and saw Midwess holding Terry's hand. The long trip to Al Flaj had been fruitful; Terry had convinced Midwess to return with his family to be the company's night guard for P1 and P2. Midwess, in turn, was trying to convince Terry that we should spend the night. We didn't even consider it, but have come to agree it would have been an experience to treasure. We looked back, as we sped across the desert, to see the women peering from behind their coverings, and the men gesturing and waving.

On our trek back to the highway, we spotted a well in the desert and a Bedouin filling a water tank in the back of his pickup. We stopped and learned that the Bedouin was Midwess's older brother. He told us that both he and Midwess were born in this area. He begged us to return with him to his tent. We told him we'd return another time, although we knew that we'd never have the opportunity.

Terry told me that while he and the men in Midwess's clan were visiting, a Bedouin parked beside the tent and crawled under his Datsun pickup. Moments later he emerged with the starter in his hand. He reached in the back of the pickup and pulled out a new starter. Returning beneath the pickup, he installed the new starter in a matter of minutes. The Bedouin proudly crawled from underneath the pickup, climbed inside, cranked the engine and roared off into the desert. Midwess explained that the man had been push-starting the vehicle for several days and had just returned from town with the new starter.

We stopped in Al Flaj so Faisal could visit his mother's sister. Terry and I waited in the sitting room while Faisal visited with his aunt in another room. Normally, the woman's husband would have entertained Terry in the sitting room, but he was away. After twenty minutes or so, Faisal brought in coffee and dates, and the three of us sat together on the floor and ate. It felt very awkward—almost unthinkable—to be enjoying the hospitality of this woman whom we hadn't even seen. Yet she wouldn't come in the room because of Terry's presence.

Faisal rose for his evening prayers, and I asked the small children, who had been peeping around the corner, to take me to the bathroom. The conditions in the bathroom were repugnant. There was no light, with only the bare wire hanging from the ceiling. The toilet was a cement tile hole, flush with the ground. I wondered why such a nice house would have a bathroom that was so primitive.

As I was returning to the sitting room, the aunt chanced to see me and became excited. She pulled me into a room that was apparently reserved for women and adjoined the kitchen. She had six children, and her two oldest girls spoke a little English. They ran out of the room, returning with their English books from school, and read to me from the books. The aunt produced a huge platter of fruit and a bowl of dates. I discovered later that she had also sent such a platter into the sitting room for Faisal and Terry. We visited as well as we could, considering the language barrier, and I could see that she really enjoyed the opportunity. I wished that I had been bolder and had gone back to her sooner.

When I insisted that we had to leave, she placed ten pieces of fruit in a sack and insisted that I take it for the *sayarra* (the car), so we could eat while we were traveling. On the way home I asked Faisal at what age the two girls, who were learning English, would marry, and he answered that it was customary for girls to marry at age sixteen. He beamed with pleasure when I told him that I really liked his aunt.

We made good time going home. Terry and I wore our seat belts, but Faisal didn't because he didn't want to soil his white *thobe*. I had never seen a Saudi wearing a seat belt. I assumed that the attitude of *insh Allah* (God's will) prevailed. After I dusted the seat belt with my handkerchief, Faisal consented to wear it. It was a good idea, too, because we were almost run off the road by two young Bedouin boys who appeared to be no more than thirteen years old. They slowed down and sped up, driving parallel to each other while we were caught in the middle, until one of the boys decided to speed off into the desert. The time passed quickly on the way home, with Faisal teaching me to count in Arabic.

We stopped in Al Kharj for a hamburger, the latest novelty to hit the small village. *Hamburger Lathetha* was operated by Egyptians, but it was good to know that we could find a hamburger only thirty-five miles from our farm, instead of the ninety miles to Riyadh. The limited menu offered large hamburgers and small hamburgers, and cheeseburgers, but it sufficed.

I'll never forget Faisal because of his friendliness and ingenuity. Once when I returned from vacation in the States, both Terry and Faisal were there to meet me at the airport in Riyadh. Faisal had come in his own vehicle in case one of the new men hired from the States had traveled with me. Because I arrived alone, Faisal took off in his vehicle. We learned later that he was stopped by the police on his way back to the farm. He and five other men were apprehended and taken to jail for not having driver's licenses. Fortunately when he entered the lobby of the jail, Faisal was able to separate himself from the other men and pretended to be looking around. When another policeman questioned him and Faisal said that he was looking for someone the policeman ordered him to leave.

Within a month, Midwess and his family were back on the farm. Rashmi welcomed the return, and this time they moved their tent only one hundred yards from our house. I'm sure if we'd stayed a few years longer, they would have moved even closer to us. In their new location, they were able to hook up to our camp generator so that they had electricity for their radio and the refrigerator that had been stored in Terry's office.

On one visit to Midwess's tent, we commiserated over the year-long drought in our area. Midwess recalled that fifteen years earlier the area had gone without rain for seven straight years and that wherever people traveled, they saw dead camels and sheep. While Midwess reflected on the past, his thoughts turned to his Mama. He recalled that Mama was only about fifteen when she married, and he wasn't sure how old she was now. For that matter, he laughed, he wasn't sure how old he was either. Older Saudis do little celebrating for birthdays, rarely even marking the date. Families with young children are now beginning to observe birthdays.

Once I asked Rashmi how old she was when she married Midwess. She seemed puzzled by the question and after several minutes of concentration, she replied that she was probably about sixteen. She promised to ask Midwess, and appeared at my doorstep the next morning with the answer. Midwess remembered that he had married her one year after she began covering her face. Traditionally, she would have begun to cover her face at the start of Ramadan during the year she reached puberty; therefore, she hypothesized that she was fourteen when she married. Because Midwess was almost ten years older than Rashmi, he had seen her with her face uncovered, playing around the camp before he married her. He boasted that he knew she was pretty even before he married her. Several weeks later, after a trip home to visit her family, Rashmi said that her mother recalled that she had married Midwess at the age of twelve and had her first baby at thirteen. When the doctor delivered her baby by Caesarean section, he told Midwess that he was bad for making such a young girl pregnant.

Rashmi seemed always to be pregnant or just recovering from childbirth. She had three children and one miscarriage during our five years in Saudi Arabia. Because neither of us knew the correct words in the other's language for such intimate details, she had difficulty explaining to me that she had miscarried. She believed that a terrible storm, with high winds and blowing dust, had caused her misfortune. Although I knew that the storm did not cause it, I didn't contradict her reasoning. As with everything in life, I knew that she accepted the miscarriage as God's will.

Although birth control pills are somewhat controversial in Saudi Arabia, the pharmacies did carry them while we were there. After we left, we heard that the government had taken birth control pills from the shelves of pharmacies, but that it was still possible to obtain them if a woman had at least five children. Although I'm sure that the Bedouin women never took them, they had no trouble understanding what I meant when I told them I wasn't pregnant because I was taking The Pill.

As Rashmi's third baby became more and more aware of his surroundings, he began to cry every time I approached the tent. Rashmi explained that the baby, Abdul Latif, named, of course, for Sheikh Latif, was afraid of me because he wasn't accustomed to seeing women with their faces uncovered. Once he recognized my face, he seemed to smile more at me than at the women whose faces and smiles were covered.

Midwess's children entertained me royally when I visited their tent. When I wore sunglasses and a hat for shade, Abdallah would take them from me, put them on, and dance around the tent. Latifa, the only little girl among three male siblings, sang off-key at the top of her lungs, while Abdallah imitated his Daddy's sword dance with his play sword. I always tried to think of American things to show the children. Once I took a deck of playing cards and tried to teach the children to match the four suits. After a few minutes of diligent concentration on the matching game, I noticed that they had taken Rashmi's rusty sewing scissors and cut the cards into tiny pieces.

At one point in our relationship, Rashmi and I planned a visit to some Bedouins who were camping on our farm on their way to another area. They were taking advantage of the harvested pivots to graze their sheep and camels. I wore one of the dresses that Rashmi had sewn for me and as an afterthought, added the four gold bracelets that Terry had given me over several birthdays.

Mohammed, Midwess's son from his first wife, now thirteen years old, appointed himself as our driver. Including the children, there were seven of us crammed into the cab of the small, beat-up pickup. Although it was only mid-morning, the late May temperature was already well over 100 degrees. As we pulled up to the tent, a swarm of children gathered around the cab of the pickup to watch us peel ourselves out of the vehicle. They didn't seem too surprised at our visit until I emerged from the vehicle. Their faces registered disbelief that they were seeing an American woman with a group of Bedouins.

Their mother, to my surprise, didn't have her face covered when we arrived, nor did she make any move to cover it. I was startled to see that she had a black tattoo on the left side of her face and on the back of her left hand. For some reason, Rashmi speculated later that the woman was probably from Iraq. The woman gazed steadily at me and gestured for us to follow her into the tent.

The women had tied a newborn lamb to one of the tent stakes. The tiny animal's droppings created a strong odor in the tent, but I was the only one who seemed to notice. The older woman with the tattoos immediately asked Rashmi if I had babies. When Rashmi shook her head, the old woman squinted and continued to stare at me. Three small children scurried in and out of the tent. Although it was a very hot mid-July day, one of the little boys wore a tattered warm-up top underneath his dirty *thobe*. Not far from the camp, a girl of about twelve years herded the sheep as they grazed on the wheat stubble covering the harvested pivot circle. Leaving her job, she walked into camp to investigate the visitors. Her face was uncovered, and she wore a poorly fitted bra that was exposed above the edge of her dress.

There was little conversation between Rashmi and the other Bedouin women. While Latifa sat rigidly on Rashmi's lap, her stomach made a loud growl. The noise seemed to break the uncomfortable silence. The women imitated the noise and laughed, embarrassing Latifa to the point that she cried and ran back to the pickup. Our hostesses served us the traditional Arabic coffee in cups that appeared to be dirty. Despite the unclean appearance, I drank what I thought to be the sociable three cups. As if on some secret cue, Mohammed and Rashmi rose and nodded to me that it was time to go. The combination of heat, the blowing sand, and the odor of sheep dung had overpowered me, and I staggered slightly as I rose to my feet, amazed that we had only been there forty minutes. The seven of us piled back into the pickup and returned to camp, Rashmi's sweet spirit and graciousness standing in vivid contrast to our reception at the camp we had just departed.

The closer that Rashmi and I became to each other, the more we shared. During one of my visits to her tent, she pulled me into a corner of the tent and gingerly removed her veil, revealing the perfectly smooth, white skin beneath. She carefully unbraided her long, uncut hair and with smooth strokes, began combing it. After she rebraided her hair, she put on a new dress on top of several layers of clothing. Digging deep into a nearby trunk, she produced a cardboard box and carefully pulled out several pieces of gold jewelry. It was the *'Id al-Fitr* holiday, the Festival of Breaking the Fast that marks the end of Ramadan. Children were dressed in their best clothes. Latifa's dress had been washed for the first time. Her actions conveyed how significant and personal a portion of her life she was choosing to share with me.

As Rashmi arranged her gold finery, I was surprised at the nature of the questions that she asked and the topics she discussed. Because I often told her about our eating adventures in the small town of Al

Kharj, she questioned me about where we ate and what we ordered. She also asked whether I'd ever eaten with Sheikh Latif and his wife. I suspect that to her eating with Sheikh Latif must have been the same as eating with the King. During our conversation, she told me that she never took off her veil in front of Midwess, even in private, because she would feel too embarrassed. Her modesty was intense, even with her husband. I took this confession as the highest expression of friendship Rashmi could bestow upon me, even more touching than when she allowed me to take one picture of her with the children, on the condition that I would show it only to my mother.

Our increased intimacy encouraged Rashmi to confide her worries about Midwess taking another wife. He joked constantly about finding another wife, but I never took him seriously. Evidently, Rashmi did. She said that unless he housed a new wife in a separate tent and gave her some new gold jewelry and the same gifts that he gave the new wife, she would divorce him. With determination, she explained that she would leave the children with him and return to her parents, just as the law prescribed. I knew that she would never carry out such a plan, but simply threatening it, she somehow felt better. I didn't believe that Midwess had the money for a second wife, but I assured Rashmi that he wouldn't really want another wife. The next time we ate at Midwess's tent, he brought up the subject of a second wife. After investigating the price of wives, he said that a virgin from Saudi Arabia cost about SR 120,000 ($34,285), but one from Egypt cost only SR 30,000 ($8,571), plus travel fees.

Within a week of this discussion, a Syrian man visited our farm with his wife. He left his wife at my house while he toured the farm, and because she spoke only Arabic, we soon exhausted our conversation. Feeling helpless, I took her out to Rashmi's tent. Midwess happened by while we were visiting. When he learned that she was from Syria, he asked her about how much a Syrian bride cost. She told him that because their country was relatively poor, a Syrian virgin required just a small amount of gold jewelry. She added that in Syria a second wife is usually taken only if the first wife does not produce children. I sensed that Rashmi seemed encouraged by the comment, because she had already produced three children for Midwess, two of them sons.

Eventually, the two oldest sons, Mohammed and Abdallah, left the family tent to attend a newly opened school for nomadic children in Al Flaj. Midwess donated the use of the building next to his gas station for the school. In school, the boys studied Arabic and the Koran. Moreover, they could look forward to accomplishing a feat that their father never could, learning to read and write. Needless to say, the daughter, Latifa, remained at home to take care of the sheep.

After Midwess, Rashmi, and their children had lived on our farm for several years, a guard was no longer required, so he decided to return to the area where we had visited him, near Al Flaj. During the last few days before his departure, only one tent remained erect; most of his equipment and other tents had been packed. While Terry and I were visiting one evening, Rashmi and I sat a comfortable distance from the men, in the same tent. It was the middle of January, so the desert nights were quite cold. We were lost in thought when we heard a vehicle approaching. Rashmi leaped to her feet, and Midwess peered from the tent. With a nod, he signaled to Rashmi to leave. I waited long enough to see that the visitor was another Bedouin and followed her.

Midwess must have anticipated that he might need an alternate gathering place for the women, in case of male visitors. We retreated, along with the children, to a literal cage. Our shelter was a cubicle framed in wood and covered with wire that sat directly on the ground. Rashmi placed strips of material around the wire to block a bit of the cold night wind. As we huddled together on a blanket on the ground, we still felt the cold. Although I had worn gloves and a cap, the barefoot children had neither. Abdul Latif, the baby, who had a cold, wore a winter *thobe* of wool, but no coat. The other two children had colds, too. Because the other coffee- and teapot had already been packed, we had no warm liquid to drink. Naturally, the men were allowed the only pots. When it came time to eat, she brought our portion into the tiny cage. Latifa jumped from one foot to the other saying, *macarona,* excited to be having macaroni. When Rashmi handed me a spoon for the macaroni, both Abdallah and Latifa clamored for a spoon for themselves. She had only three pieces of chicken left after serving the men and placed two of the pieces next to my bowl, insisting that she and the two children and the baby would share the other piece of chicken. I adamantly refused to take more than one piece, and I could feel a smile beneath her veil when I passed the extra piece back to her.

After the meal, we huddled together in our shelter, laughing occasionally about our predicament. When it was time for Abdallah and Latifa to go to bed, Rashmi spread another blanket on top of the blanket on which we sat and the children lay down on it. She tucked another blanket around the two sleeping children, who huddled together for warmth.

Abdul Latif had a blanket that he dragged around the camp by a torn edge. I was fascinated when she spread out his blanket and placed him on top. Holding a piece of string between her toes, she draped the blanket around him and proceeded to tie him up tightly in it. He stopped whimpering immediately and nestled down next to the other two children. She explained that if she didn't tie him in his blanket, he might kick off the covers and get cold. Evidently, he felt secure in his confinement.

As I studied the tiny sleeping figure, I thought what a wonderful mother Rashmi was in the midst of such difficult circumstances. The fierceness of the desert had created strength in her small frame, and in her commitment to her children. Terry and I had long since given up the notion of waiting until our final return to the States to begin our family. We had been trying for two years to conceive a child, a secret I had not been able to reveal even to Rashmi. Many pregnancy tests were purchased during those two years, but I never lost faith as I read and imagined all the barren women from the Biblical times who eventually bore children. Abraham's wife, Sarah; Isaac's wife, Rebeccah, and Samuel's mother, Hannah, had all lived mere miles from where I was living in the desert.

We discovered that I was pregnant on our eighth wedding anniversary. At 6:00 A.M. on May 20, 1989 the pregnancy test read positive, and Terry bounded out of the house, announcing to everyone who would listen that he was going to be a father. The farm workers drove to our house immediately to congratulate me. Midwess and Arshad, the Pakistani store manager, insisted that I give up my morning walks. A pair of Bedouins, brother and sister, who had settled on our farm after the harvest, brought me a jug of camel's milk every morning to help the baby that grew inside me. Although I had drunk camel's milk at Midwess's tent many times before my pregnancy, impending motherhood made me more cautious about sanitation and what I consumed. I always accepted the gift graciously, but promptly poured it down the drain.

Because this was my first pregnancy, and we lived ninety miles from the hospital in which I would deliver, we concurred that I should return to the States for the birth of our child, despite the numerous invitations we'd had for me to board with friends in Riyadh. We had some knowledge of the maternity ward of one of the most modern hospitals in Riyadh. Kim Cates, our close friend, gave birth to Eric, her second child and the baby we had kept for two weeks, in a brand new hospital in Riyadh. The hospital was modeled after the British system that requires a doctor to be on duty in the maternity ward but assigns the task of delivery to a midwife. When Kim arrived at the hospital, the delivery had been delayed, and the doctor assisted the midwife. During delivery, the doctor and the midwife, neither of whom spoke English, seemed to be in heated disagreement. Kim sensed that the doctor was telling her to push, while the midwife was arguing that she should not! The baby entered the world, perfectly healthy, but Kim felt lonely and insecure without a medical caregiver with whom she might communicate and family and friends to visit her and her new son. She encouraged me to return to the States to have my baby, even though our company would pay my hospital bills in Saudi Arabia.

I made an appointment to see a doctor at a private hospital in Riyadh before I returned to Texas. I was assigned a British female doctor. She didn't examine me, but sent me across town to have a sonogram to determine my due date because I was unsure of the date of conception. She did give me guidelines to follow during my pregnancy, including appropriate weight gain and dietary habits. With typical British reserve, she exhibited no enthusiasm to match the excitement I felt for my first pregnancy.

Terry and I finally located the small clinic, where I was to receive the sonogram, after numerous stops to ask directions. The clinic's sole purpose was to perform sonograms and was manned by a Syrian technician and several Egyptian nurses. The nurse asked me if I had recently emptied my bladder, and because I had done so, I had to drink a quart of water and wait thirty minutes to allow the water to fill my bladder to ensure a more accurate sonogram. While we waited, a steady stream of women, most of them veiled and Saudi, entered the clinic. The Saudi women hid their faces but allowed the Syrian man to place the sonogram equipment on their bare stomachs. After thirty minutes, we were ushered into a waiting room, where the Syrian doctor quickly performed the sonogram, and estimated that I was six weeks pregnant, calculating the due date to be January 16th. When we paid the fee of SR 800 ($222), we were told that this fee included a second sonogram. Because we were to be leaving Saudi Arabia in less than two months, we decided that another sonogram within a six-week period would probably be of little benefit, but decided to have it as a precautionary measure. The medical bills that we incurred in Saudi Arabia were paid by Al Emar.

As it worked out, I was able to return to the States at the time of our regular annual vacation, so Terry could accompany me. As I made preparation for our return to the States, I was unsure whether I'd ever again set foot on the sands of Saudi Arabia. My body, already in hormonal upheaval, rotated between waves of nostalgia and morning sickness as I surveyed the collection of clothes, jewelry, kitchen gadgets, and books I'd collected in the almost five years I'd lived in the desert. We had collected quite an array of other Saudi paraphernalia too, including camel saddles, carpets, and a five-foot *sheesha,* or water pipe. Other than the luggage we were using on our stopover for ten days in Germany, everything else would be sent in crates. Germany was one country we hadn't visited and despite the odors of sauerkraut and sausage that aggravated my uneasy stomach, we had a wonderful time.

With my comparatively large wardrobe laid out, I suddenly felt like a very spoiled American, thinking of the few changes of clothing that the majority of our workers possessed. On the spur of the moment, I called to Terry, who was sorting through his possessions and suggested that we give the bulk of our clothes and other items to the workers. He readily agreed.

I had fun arranging the different items we wanted to give away. The kitchen and dining room tables were piled with folded shirts, skirts, shorts, shoes, and costume jewelry. Chairs were laden with books and souvenirs from the States that I could easily replace, but which our workers could never obtain. I baked several cakes and an assortment of cookies and invited our labor force over the night before our departure. Because we had kept the purpose of the event a secret, the men began arriving with somber faces, expecting Terry to lecture them to work hard while he was on vacation. As the aroma of baked goods greeted the men, the tense atmosphere evaporated, and a discernible camaraderie began to surface. As Terry instructed the men to pass through the house choosing items for themselves or for a girlfriend, mother, or wife, the room erupted into a party, with men holding dresses up to their frames and everyone hugging Terry and shyly shaking my hand. Men who couldn't read English lovingly handled copies of American novels. After the refreshments were devoured, the men took their leave. All of the items had found a home. We saw the gratitude in the men's eyes and felt the friendship in their hearts as they stepped out into the desert, drove past the Bedouin campfire, and slipped back into their own world. We realized that we had experienced much more in this Kingdom than turning the sand to green.

Epilogue

Upon my return to Texas, I enrolled for the fall 1987 semester of classes at Texas Tech. I was able to complete my master's degree using the information I'd gathered in Saudi Arabia for my thesis on home economics instructional programs in Saudi Arabia. Terry traveled back and forth to Saudi Arabia during this time, acting as a consultant for our company and facilitating a smooth transition to another farm manager. He returned from his last trip that winter, just in time to attend three of six required childbirth classes. Abigail Louise was born exactly on her due date, January 16th, 1988.

Despite protests by friends and family, and our earlier decision that I would not travel with the baby, we boarded a plane for Saudi Arabia when Abilou was only seven weeks old. It seemed only right that she and I accompany Terry as he completed his obligation to Al Emar. We had taken Abilou to a photographer for her passport picture when she was three days old, because she needed both her own passport and entry visa to accompany me to Saudi Arabia. Abilou was so tiny that during the flight she slept on the foldout tray-table in front of our seats. We had a six-hour layover in Frankfurt, Germany, where the airport was so crowded that every available seat was taken in our assigned waiting area. Terry finally lifted me onto a vacant desk, where I had to nurse Abilou and discovered that my old aversion to feeling conspicuous died hard.

Arriving in Saudi Arabia, I enjoyed the elevated status I was awarded when I cleared customs with our baby in my arms. In the eyes of the Saudi officials, I was fulfilling my purpose in life. Instead of demanding that I stand at the back of the foreign line, custom officials gestured me and my newborn baby to the front of the line and waved me and my luggage through without inspection. Terry grinned, following behind me for a change.

Once we arrived on the farm with our new addition, we were showered with gifts and visitors. It seemed as though every farm worker and

Bedouin for miles around had heard that Mr. Terry had finally become a father, and wanted to check out his offspring. They bestowed gifts that included baby powder from Lebanon and Johnson baby products inscribed in Arabic. Many of the workers brought toys and dolls (most imported from Korea, China, and Thailand), that I had never seen before. Jamshaid, father of four daughters by this time, brought us his cradle and stroller to use as long as we needed them. Arshaid, the Pakistani store manager, fell in love with Abilou, fondly calling her Babylou and referring to himself as uncle.

Two Sri Lankan workers arrived to visit me as Abilou awoke from a nap, eager to be nursed. I stalled awhile, figuring that they would be embarrassed if I nursed in front of them, even though I would cover myself with a blanket. Finally, sensing that they had no intention of departing, I nursed Abilou hesitantly. Their faces registered no shock or surprise, and I realized that nursing one's baby in public was probably a matter of course in Sri Lanka. Many of the workers told Terry that they had supposed a rich American woman would feed with a bottle instead of nursing. They explained that the women in their countries nurse more out of financial necessity than by choice.

We were delighted to find Midwess back on the farm, but surprised and disappointed to find him living as a bachelor. He had left his family back in Al Flaj, where the boys were enrolled in school. Again, Sheikh Latif had summoned him to be the guard, herding the camels and sheep from the pivots. Midwess claimed that Rashmi had refused to return to the farm with him because I was no longer living there. She chose to stay in Al Flaj until he returned. He was excited that Abilou and I had come back with Terry. He lavished more attention on her than I had ever seen him give any of his own children as babies. I regretted that Rashmi and Mama did not get to see Abilou, but I gave him many photographs to take home with him. Several of the Saudis, including Midwess, presented Abilou with gifts of gold, which is customary for the birth of a daughter.

Jewaher enjoyed Abilou because she had four boys. She wanted to present a gift to her, but we left before she gave us anything. I'm sure she assumed we would be in the Kingdom much longer than we were.

During the seven weeks that we were in Saudi Arabia, Terry took Abilou with him every Friday morning to give me some free time. I took a long bath and read, enjoying the solitude. Our house was exactly as we had left it, including the oversized bathtub. On these mornings, Terry was beset with men who volunteered to hold Abilou while he went about his normal routine. Terry kept Abilou also on three different occasions when I went into Riyadh for the day with Genia, my copper companion from Al Sabbar Farm, and Gladys, the Australian woman who was now living on our farm in the container we had once occupied. When Abilou and I arrived with Terry, Gladys appeared at my door the next morning at 7:00, weeping for joy that we had finally arrived, and she had a woman on the farm with whom to talk. I discovered that the company quit providing a van and driver after I left. Gladys was almost hysterical, because she had been confined to the farm for more than six weeks. It reminded me of my first year in Saudi, five years ago. She was my constant companion during my last sojourn in Saudi Arabia.

Although our Middle Eastern friends were thrilled that we finally had produced an offspring, it was evident that they wanted to commiserate with Terry that his firstborn was not a male. Nevertheless, Abilou was greatly admired for her fair skin and deep blue eyes. The first comment the workers made when they saw her was, "She's so white and so beautiful."

My lone negative encounter with the normally hospitable people came when Tariq extended an invitation to us for *kabsa* at his farm. Several influential Saudis were coming to the farm, and his father planned a party. Tariq thought Terry and I would enjoy joining the group for the traditional Arab meal. He warned us before we accepted the invitation that I would have to retreat with the women, while Terry would stay with the men. (After the years we had lived in Saudi Arabia, I was surprised that Tariq thought he had to tell us.)

Once we arrived at Tariq's farm, I was whisked away by one of Tariq's younger brothers to a room inside the villa, where I was left alone. Terry joined the men in the tent where dates and Arabic coffee were already being served. The room where I was stationed was bare except for several large pillows. I anticipated that one of the women would fetch me, but after several minutes of waiting, no one came, so I hesitantly peeked out of the room. Because the room opened to the outside at the back of the villa, I saw only the palm trees that surrounded the building. The men's tent had been erected in the front of the villa, so I was unable to see Terry. I decided to go in search of the other women and had taken just a few steps, when a younger Saudi woman appeared and ushered me back into the room. I asked her in a few words of Arabic where the other women were. She pointed in another direction, explaining that the women were readying the food for the men in another room. I explained that I wanted to join the other women to watch the preparations. After a moment of hesitation, she nodded and steered me out the door into another room.

There were about eight women of different ages in the room, and although their heads were covered, they remained unveiled. I extended the traditional Arabic greeting, and all responded except for the oldest woman, who scowled at me. I guessed that she disapproved of my uncovered hair, although I had worn a long dress. She approached the woman who had brought me into the room and spoke loudly and sternly in Arabic. I pretended to watch the women as they walked about the room, placing canned drinks and fresh fruit on the long carpet that had been covered with a clear plastic tablecloth. There were places on the floor for about thirty people to sit, and the food was catered from Riyadh, so all the women had to do was distribute the fruit and drinks. I assumed that the women would be eating in another room and would not be eating the men's leftovers.

After the older woman finished her speech, my escort motioned me to follow her out the door and back to the room where I had waited originally. In Arabic she told me to wait, and she quickly left the room. She returned in only a few seconds with another Saudi woman who appeared to be in her early twenties. In halting English, she explained to me that her aunt, the older woman who seemed upset earlier, did not want me watching them. One time before, an American woman had lived on the farm and kept a pad and pen with her, writing down everything she observed. The woman claimed that when the American woman returned to the United States, she wrote a bad book about Saudi Arabia. Apologizing, she told me that I must remain in the room, where my food would be served.

The incident was so totally opposite from the way I had always been treated in Saudi Arabia, that when they brought me a plate piled with food, I shook my head and refused to eat. As soon as I calculated that Terry and the men had finished eating, I hurriedly exited my room of imprisonment, went over to the men's tent, and stepped inside the flap to search the faces for Terry. When he saw me, he jumped to his feet, surprised that I had invaded the men's domain. I whispered, "Let's go," and Terry followed immediately, sensing that something was wrong. We didn't wait to find Tariq to tell him that we were leaving. Later Tariq made a point to question the women as to our hasty departure.

When he discovered the reason, he immediately came to our farm delivering a formal apology. We assured Tariq that we were not angry, and the subject never came up again. I realized the women had possibly experienced only one encounter with a Western woman, and that it had been negative.

After spending nearly two months in the desert with our baby daughter, we departed Saudi Arabia for the last time in May 1988. Little did we realize that in the fall of 1990, U.S. troops would be sent to the Middle East, and the entire world would become better acquainted with Saudi Arabia through Operation Desert Shield and subsequently Operation Desert Storm, in January 1991. None of us could have imagined the invasion of Kuwait by Saddam Hussein and his Iraqi soldiers. During the war, Sheikh Latif turned a profit by supplying the American troops with equipment. He obtained a contract from the United States military to manufacture machine gun stands for the rear section of military jeeps. Using the farm workshop, under the guidance of Peter Menage, the Dutch manager, the workers designed and manufactured fifty-four machine gun stands at the rate of three per day for a SR 500,000 ($142,000) altogether.

In a personal phone call, broadcast to citizens in our hometown of Crosbyton, Texas, Sheikh Latif explained that Saudis had always felt the U.S. was a friend, but in the current situation, they realized the true importance of the relationship between the two countries. In the midst of the daily Scud attacks, Sheikh Latif said that life progressed normally for the men, but that women and children of the Kingdom were frightened by the daily threat of Iraqi Scuds and the ultimate threat of fierce combat in their homeland.

As time passes, our few negative memories of Saudi Arabia fade. Our recollections of homesickness and loneliness, persistent flies, terrific sandstorms, and uncomfortable heat grow dim. The terrain was almost devoid of trees and natural vegetation was desolate, but not so unlike our own West Texas. We had turned our tiny island of farmland in the midst of the desert sand into an oasis of green wheat and Rhodes grass. Just as we missed fast foods when we were there, we now miss such things as the fresh, warm Arab flatbread sold in tiny bakeries; orange juice with pulp from Japan that we bought at the gas station in a small can; chocolate bubble gum that came from Spain; the wonderful cheeses and chocolates from France, and the many Lebanese foods and juices in the various restaurants where we ate. We miss the fierce pride of the people, their stubborn loyalty and genuine hospitality. We miss the exposure to the various nationalities that we encountered during our stay, and the strong friendships that ensued.

Our biggest regret is that we are unable to keep in touch or make contact with Midwess and his family. As far as we know, he remains in Al Flaj, living in the desert, unable to read and write, managing his combination desert gas station/restaurant and sending Mohammed and Abdallah to school. Abdul Latif is no longer a baby, and is probably toddling around the camp, picking up empty cans and scraps of paper, pretending that they are toys. He will look forward to attending the Bedouin school, a luxury that Latifa will likely never have nor other Bedouin girls, unless the government provides the funds to send them to school, and their families decide they can be spared from the duties of tending the sheep.

I'm sure Rashmi has had more children since we saw her last—even though Midwess is probably still teasing her about taking a younger wife. Our wildest dream would be to return to Saudi Arabia to drive up to Midwess's tent in Al Flaj, as we did in what seems like another life, long ago. Someone would probably alert him that an *Inglizi* was coming, and he would respond that it was Terry without a moment's hesitation. Midwess would be ecstatic to learn that Terry finally has not only one son, but two: Jordan Robert, born August 6, 1990, and Taylor Clay, born September 10, 1992. We send photos each year to the head office in Riyadh, as well as to the farm, but I'm sure none of these ever make their way to Midwess.

Midwess had often told us that we might take Latifa back to the States with us to raise until she turned eighteen years old, but then she would have to return to Saudi Arabia. I always answered that I would take her gladly if she could remain in America without that stipulation. His suggestion has remained in the back of my mind since the last time I saw Latifa. I believe Midwess was serious, in that he saw the opportunities we could give Latifa in America, but at the same time, he didn't feel at liberty to release her from the life Bedouin women have known for centuries. Letting his only daughter leave home would have been a sacrifice few fathers could handle emotionally.

Often I recall that whenever I visited Midwess's camp, Latifa would don her best dress and flit in and out of the tent. She always stopped in front of me, waiting for me to plant a kiss on her cheek or forehead. Our ritual made me realize that she was starved for physical attention. I observed that the Bedouins rarely kissed and hugged their children once they were old enough to walk. I wondered whether covering their faces made them feel more detached from the children, and the children more detached from them.

I was worlds apart from Latifa, but she seemed to be reaching out to me constantly. I wonder now whether this wasn't her unconscious way of asking me to take her with me. Today, Latifa is learning the skills necessary to survive as a woman in a Bedouin world. She has learned to milk the sheep expertly, and as she grows taller, will master milking a camel. She is probably driving one of the old broken-down pickups around the desert as she shepherds her flock. In only a year, she will begin covering her face with a veil. Her knowledge of cooking is limited to a few staple recipes, but these she can no doubt prepare flawlessly. As a female child, she has always sat with the women when a male visitor was present, waiting on the other side of the tent flap for the males to finish eating before she may partake. Unlike her brothers, she will never make the giant move and join the men in the circle on the other side of the tent flap. We still dream of bringing Latifa to America and wonder what her life and ours would have been like.

We would welcome Midwess and his entire family into our home. They would nod with approval at the Saudi artifacts scattered throughout our house, a reminder on almost every wall of the time we spent in their desert. Escorting Midwess around our country would be a joy, as we recall the time we took him to the Al Akaria Shopping Center in Riyadh and his numerous trips on the escalator, a wonder he had never beheld. We will probably never have the opportunity to make him a part of our world, as he and his people so graciously made us a part of their Kingdom. As we think of our purpose there and the transformed green sands, the miracle of the whole experience remains forever in our hearts and minds.

We continue to correspond with both Sheikh Latif and Hafeez in Riyadh and occasionally receive letters from Kalapuhana on the farm. Farm news has not been encouraging since the drop in oil prices, with Saudi Arabia reversing its emphasis on wheat production and dropping the price per bushel from thirty to fifteen dollars, in 1985. Moreover, by 1993, the government had basically eliminated its wheat production by imposing severe quotas that put the majority of wheat farms out of business. Sheikh Latif's allotment per year on his 7,000 acres dropped from his original 180,000 metrics tons in 1984 to 200 metric tons.

According to Genia Roberts, the government has stipulated that barley is to be grown and has imposed the same quota for barley, even though its price is half that of wheat. Yet on Al Sabbar farm, where she and her husband continue to work, the farm is registered in three names, affording them three separate quotas. This, along with the Rhodes grass, their small allotment of wheat, and the chicken operation, enables them to keep their boss in the farming business. Mastock, the Irish company where our friend Jack King continues to work, is permitted to grow only a minimal amount of barley and no wheat. Instead, the company, which is changing its name to Al Marai, is producing mostly alfalfa.

Hafeez, who is now remarried and the father of three children, tells us to that there is a surplus of good used farm and irrigation equipment from the many farms that have already been abandoned. He hopes that the forage operation will enable Green Sands to continue to exist. I'm confident that Al Emar will go on with or without the farm, owing to Sheikh Latif's entrepreneurial skills. I cannot imagine him anywhere but at the forefront of Saudi Arabia's economic development.

Terry and I were pleased and honored when Sheikh Latif and Jewaher phoned late last spring to ask whether Ziad, their elder son, could stay with us so that he might perfect his oral and written English in the United States. I was thrilled to arranged for Ziad to attend the fall 1994 semester at Crosbyton High School for five weeks, and to have a private English tutor as well. Their family has increased by two, a boy and a girl, and another baby is soon to arrive.

The world seems smaller after our five years in Saudi Arabia. I have a keener appreciation for the freedoms I enjoy as an American woman. Terry and I find that the "Star Spangled Banner" evokes a much stronger response than it did before we lived eight thousand miles from home.